RESEARCH METHODS IN EDUCATION

Fourth edition

Louis Cohen and *Lawrence Manion*

London and New York

First published 1980 by Croom Helm Ltd
Fourth edition published 1994
by Routledge
11 New Fetter Lane, London EC4P 4EE

Simultaneously published in the USA and Canada
by Routledge
29 West 35th Street, New York, NY 10001

Reprinted 1995

Typeset in Baskerville by
J&L Composition Ltd, Filey, North Yorkshire
Printed and bound in Great Britain by
Biddles Ltd, Guildford and King's Lynn

British Library Cataloguing in Publication Data
A catalogue record for this book is available from the British Library

Library of Congress Cataloguing in Publication Data
A catalogue record for this book is available from the Library of Congress

ISBN 0-415-10235-9

CONTENTS

CONTENTS

BOXES

BOXES

LIST OF JOURNALS
ABBREVIATED IN TEXT

Alberta Journal of Educational Research
American Educational Research Journal
American Journal of Psychology
American Journal of Sociology
American Psychologist
Behaviour Research and Therapy
British Educational Research Journal
British Journal of Educational Psychology
British Journal of In-Service Education
British Journal of Medical Psychology
British Journal of Psychiatry
British Journal of Psychology
British Journal of Social and Clinical Psychology
British Journal of the Sociology of Education
Cambridge Journal of Education
Discourse Processes
Durham Research Review
Education
Education and Psychological Measurement
Education 3–13
Educational Management and Administration
Educational Research
Educational Review
Educational Studies
European Journal of Science Education
History of Education
Human Development
International Journal of Criminology and Penology
International Journal of Educational Research
International Journal of Personal Construct Psychology
Journal of Abnormal and Social Psychology
Journal of Career Development

Journal of Child Psychology and Psychiatry
Journal of Curriculum Studies
Journal of Educational Psychology
Journal of Educational Sociology
Journal of Educational Therapy
Journal of Experimental Education
Journal of Experimental Social Psychology
Journal of Further and Higher Education
Journal of Personality and Social Psychology
Journal of the Royal Statistical Society
Journal for Research in Mathematical Education
Journal for the Theory of Social Behaviour
Perceptual and Motor Skills
Psychological Bulletin
Psychological Review
Qualitative Studies in Education
Research in Education
Sagset Journal
School Organisation
School Science and Mathematics
Simulation/Games For Learning
Social Problems
Sociological Review
Sociology
System
Teaching and Teacher Education
Trends in Education

ACKNOWLEDGEMENTS

Our thanks are due to the following publishers and authors for permission to include materials in the text:

Academic Press Inc. London **Box 14.2** p. 303 from Bannister, D. and Mair, J.M.M., *The Evaluation of Personal Constructs* (1968).

Academic Press, New York, N.Y. **Box 10.9** p. 221 from Forgas, J.P., *Journ. Exp. Social Psychol.*, 14, (1978) 434–48.

Addison-Wesley Publishing Co., Reading, MA Words from Lindzey, G. and Aronson, E. (eds), *The Handbook of Social Psychology, Vol. 2*, (1968); **Box 2.6** p. 58 from Holsti, O.R. in Lindzey and Aronson (1968), 604.

Addison-Wesley Publishing Co., Wokingham Words from Boyd-Barrett, D. and Scanlon, E., *Computers and Learning*, (1991).

Associated Book Publishers Ltd., London **Box 14.3** p. 305 from Fransella, F., *Need to Change?*, (1975).

Association of Lecturers in Further and Higher Education, London, for **Box 14.8** p. 314 from Fisher, B. *et al.*, *Journal of Further and Higher Education*, **15**(1) (1991) 44–57.

British Psychological Society, London, for **Box 3.3** p. 73 from Francis, H. *British Journal of Educational Psychology*, **62** (1992) 225–32, and **Box 7.2** p. 160 from Pierce, C.M.B. and Molloy, G.N., *British Journal of Educational Psychology*, **60** (1990) 37–51.

Brown, R. and Herrnstein, R.J., *Psychology*, (1975) **Box 12.4** p. 257.

Carfax Publishing Co., Abingdon **Box 15.5** p. 332 **Box 15.6** p. 333 **Box 15.7** p. 335 from McCormack, J. and Solman, R., *Educational Studies*, 18,2 (1992) 201–22. **Box 3.4** p. 76 from Munn, P. *et al.*, *British Educational Research Journal*, 16,2 (1990) 191–8. **Box 6.4** p. 141 and **Box 6.5** p. 143 from Halpin, D. *et al.*, *British Educational Research Journal*, 16,2 (1990) 163–77.

Corwin Press, Newbury Park, Calif. Words from Millman, J. and Darling Hammond, L. (eds), *The New Handbook of Teacher Evaluation*, (1991).

Countryside Commission, Cheltenham **Box 4.1** p. 84 from Davidson, J., *Outdoor Recreation Surveys: The Design and Use of Questionnaires for Site Surveys*, (1970).

Deakin University Press, Deakin, Australia Words from Kemmis, S. and McTaggart, R., *The Action Research Planner*, (1981).

Forgas, J.P., *Journ. Pers. and Soc. Psychology*, **34**,(2) (1976) 199–209 **Box 10.8** p. 220.

George Allen and Unwin, London **Box 2.8** p. 61 from Plummer, K., *Documents of Life*, (1983).

Good, C.V., *Essentials of Educational Research*, (1963), **Box 2.1** p. 46.

Harcourt Brace Jovanovich, Inc., New York, N.Y. **Box 6.2** p. 131 and **Box 13.1** p. 272 from Tuckman, B.W., *Conducting Educational Research*, (1969).

Harper and Row Publishers, London **Box 15.1** p. 323, **Box 15.2,** p. 324, **Box 15.3** p. 325.

Heinemann Educational Books Ltd, London p. 111–13 and **Box 4.5** p. 100 from Hoinville, G. and Jowell, R., *Survey Research Practice*, (1978).

Her Majesty's Stationery Office, London **Box 3.5** p. 78 from *Annexe I: D.E.S. A Study of School Buildings*, (1977).

Hodder and Stoughton, Sevenoaks Words from Frankfort-Nachmias, C. and Nachmias, D., *Research Methods in the Social Sciences*, (1992).

Holt, Rinehart & Winston, New York, **Box 4.4** p. 95 from Selltiz, C. *et al., Research Methods in Social Relation*, (1976).

Manchester University Press, Manchester, for **Box 14.7** p. 313 from Kremer-Hayon, L., *Research in Education,* **43** (1991) 15–21.

Methuen & Co., London Words from Shipman, M.D., *Inside a Curriculum Project*, (1974).

NFER-Nelson, Slough, for **Box 5.5** p. 115 from Boulton, M.J., *Educational Research,* **34**(3) (1992) 167–82.

Open Books, London **Box 15.4** p. 326 from Bennett, N., *Teaching Styles and Pupil Progress*, (1975).

Open University Press, Milton Keynes Words from Bell, J., *Doing Your Research Project*, (1991) and *A Teacher's Guide to Classroom Research*, (1985); **Box 9.6** p. 201 from Kelly, A. *Science for Girls?*, (1987); Words from Pilliner, A., *Experiment in Educational Research*, E 341, Block 5, (1973).

Paul Chapman Publishing, London **Box 5.7** p. 118 and **Box 5.8** p. 120 from Blease, D. and Cohen, L., *Coping With Computers: An Ethnographic Study in Primary School Classrooms*, (1990).

Peevers, B.H. and Secord, P.F., *Journ. Pers. and Soc. Psychol.*, **27**, 1 (1973) 120–8 **Box 10.10** p. 222.

Routledge, London **Box 2.7** p. 60 from Hitchcock, G. and Hughes, D., *Research and the Teacher: A Qualitative Introduction to School-based Research*, (1989).

Taylor and Francis, London **Box 7.3** p. 162 from McLaughlin, J.F. *et al., Qualitative Studies in Education*, 5,2, (1992) 147–65.

ACKNOWLEDGEMENTS

University of Chicago Press, Chicago Words from Diener, E. and Crandall R., *Ethics in Social and Behavioral Research*, (1978).

Wadsworth Publishing Co. Inc., Belmont, Calif. for notes in **Box 5.3** p. 112 from Lofland, J. *Analysing Social Settings*, (1971).

AUTHORS' NOTE TO THE FOURTH EDITION

It is five years since the third edition of *Research Methods in Education* was published and we are indebted to Routledge for the opportunity of producing a fourth revision. The book continues to be received favourably both at home and abroad and we should like to thank users and reviewers, respectively, for their encouraging remarks and constructive comments. In response to the latter we now include a chapter on the ethics of research, its earlier omission being a regrettable oversight on our part when we planned the book originally. Chapter 16: The Ethics of Educational and Social Research, provides a window onto a complex and increasingly relevant part of researchers' work. We trust that the issues raised there will provide readers with a basic framework that will meet their initial needs.

Elsewhere, we have incorporated studies, many of which reflect concerns and interests that have surfaced in recent years, and concomitant research techniques developed to examine them. By way of example, we refer briefly to Chapter 3: Developmental Research, which includes a study of reading development in the first school that focuses on patterns of progress over a period of time; Chapter 5: Case Studies, which includes research on information technology and the use of computer programs; Chapter 10, Accounts, which introduces bubble dialogue as a means of exploring classroom discourse; Chapter 12: Role-playing, with an investigation of issues relating to gender-stereotyping; and finally, Chapter 15: Multi-dimensional Measurement, where a study applies the techniques of factor analysis to, *inter alia*, the problem of teacher stress. The overall format of the book however, remains unchanged and we hope, user-friendly.

Against a background of administrative and curricular change and straitened economic circumstances, educational research has in the recent past more than held its own and made significant contributions across the whole spectrum of education. Although we are some way from no longer needing to record the fall of every apple, as Peter Medawar described it when speaking of the need for science to be progressively relieved of the burden of singular instances, and thereby making more general statements of wider explanatory power, this need not discourage us from pursuing the quest with full vigour. Educational research will thus continue to have a central role to play in throwing light on all aspects of the learning process as we move towards the new millennium. We hope that the fourth edition of *Research Methods in Education* will have a small part to play in that endeavour.

1

INTRODUCTION: THE NATURE OF INQUIRY[1]

THE SEARCH FOR TRUTH

Men and women have long been concerned to come to grips with their environment and to understand the nature of the phenomena it presents to their senses. The means by which they set out to achieve these ends may be classified into three broad categories: experience, reasoning and research.[2] Far from being independent and mutually exclusive, however, these categories must be seen as complementary and overlapping, features most readily in evidence where solutions to complex modern problems are sought.

The first of these categories, experience, does itself subsume a number of sources of information that may be called upon in a problem-solving situation. The one most immediately at hand for all people, both children and adults, is personal experience: people may thus draw upon their own individually accumulated body of knowledge and skills derived from encounters and acquaintance with facts and events in their environment – a child repairs a puncture in a bicycle inner tube speedily and efficiently because he has done it several times previously; and an adult anticipates the problems and difficulties of buying a house because she has gone through the procedures before. Where solutions to problems clearly lie beyond this corpus of personal knowledge, people may make use of the wider or different experience of other, often older people in their immediate circle – a child turns to a parent or teacher; an adult consults a friend or colleague; a local manager rings up the regional supervisor. Alternatively, where these sources fail, people may search out sources beyond their immediate circle, ones we may designate as 'authoritative'. Rooted in the past or very much part of the present, these may include recognized experts in particular fields – a Dr Spock on childrearing, for instance; a figurehead or leader, as in a religious community; or an authority source hallowed by tradition and custom – the Bible, for example.

In our endeavours to come to terms with the problems of day-to-day

1

living, we are heavily dependent upon experience and authority and their value in this context should not be under-estimated. Nor should their respective roles be overlooked in the specialist sphere of research where they provide richly fertile sources of hypotheses and questions about the world, though, of course, it must be remembered that as tools for uncovering ultimate truth they have decided limitations. The limitations of personal experience in the form of 'common-sense knowing', for instance, can quickly be exposed when compared with features of the scientific approach to problem-solving. Consider, for example, the striking differences in the way in which theories are used. Laypeople base them on haphazard events and use them in a loose and uncritical manner. When they are required to test them, they do so in a selective fashion, often choosing only that evidence that is consistent with their hunches and ignoring that which is counter to them. Scientists, by contrast, construct their theories carefully and systematically. Whatever hypotheses they formulate have to be tested empirically so that their explanations have a firm basis in fact. And there is the concept of 'control' distinguishing the layperson's and the scientist's attitude to experience. Laypeople generally make no attempt to control any extraneous sources of influence when trying to explain an occurrence. Scientists, on the other hand, only too conscious of the multiplicity of causes for a given occurrence, resort to definite techniques and procedures to isolate and test the effect of one or more of the alleged causes. Finally, there is the difference of attitude to the relationships among phenomena. Laypeople's concerns with such relationships are loose, unsystematic and uncontrolled. The chance occurrence of two events in close proximity is sufficient reason to predicate a causal link between them. Scientists, however, display a much more serious professional concern with relationships and only as a result of rigorous experimentation will they postulate a relationship between two phenomena.

Similar warnings have been made against the unconditional acceptance of pronouncements of authorities:

> Experts are essential, particularly in a complex culture such as ours, where knowledge is expanding so rapidly that no one can be an expert at everything. And obviously certain individuals have such wide experience and deep insight that their advice can be of immense benefit. Yet, it must be remembered that no one is infallible, and even the best and most competent are not exclusive possessors of 'the truth, the whole truth, and nothing but the truth'. It would be highly desirable that an 'authority' be still living; as new evidence accumulates, authorities have been known to change their mind. Thorndike reversed himself concerning the negative components of the law of effect, and Spock has changed

his views concerning permissive upbringing. Ancient authorities, confronted with today's greater enlightenment, would very probably want to change their position. In fact, in many instances their views are of greater *historical* than *substantive* interest. (Italics in original)
(Mouly, 1978)

The second category be means of which people attempt to comprehend the world around them, namely, reasoning, consists of three types: deductive reasoning, inductive reasoning, and the combined inductive–deductive approach. Deductive reasoning is based on the syllogism which was Aristotle's great contribution to formal logic. In its simplest form the syllogism consists of a major premiss based on an a priori or self-evident proposition, a minor premiss providing a particular instance, and a conclusion. Thus:

All planets orbit the sun;
The earth is a planet;
Therefore the earth orbits the sun.

The assumption underlying the syllogism is that through a sequence of formal steps of logic, from the general to the particular, a valid conclusion can be deduced from a valid premiss. Its chief limitation is that it can handle only certain kinds of statement. The syllogism formed the basis of systematic reasoning from the time of its inception until the Renaissance. Thereafter its effectiveness was diminished because it was no longer related to observation and experience and became merely a mental exercise. One of the consequences of this was that empirical evidence as the basis of proof was superseded by authority and the more authorities one could quote, the stronger one's position became. Naturally, with such abuse of its principal tool, science became sterile.

The history of reasoning was to undergo a dramatic change in the 1600s when Francis Bacon began to lay increasing stress on the observational basis of science. Being critical of the model of deductive reasoning on the grounds that its major premisses were often preconceived notions which inevitably bias the conclusions, he proposed in its place the method of inductive reasoning by means of which the study of a number of individual cases would lead to an hypothesis and eventually to a generalization. Mouly (1978) explains it like this: 'His basic premiss was that if one collected enough data without any preconceived notion about their significance and orientation – thus maintaining complete objectivity – inherent relationships pertaining to the general case would emerge to be seen by the alert observer.' Bacon's major contribution to science was thus that he was able to rescue it from the death-grip of the deductive method whose abuse had brought scientific progress to a

3

standstill. He thus directed the attention of scientists to nature for solutions to people's problems, demanding empirical evidence for verification. Logic and authority in themselves were no longer regarded as conclusive means of proof and instead became sources of hypotheses about the world and its phenomena.

Bacon's inductive method was eventually followed by the inductive–deductive approach which combines Aristotelian deduction with Baconian induction. In Mouly's words, this consisted of:

> a back-and-forth movement in which the investigator first operates inductively from observations to hypotheses, and then deductively from these hypotheses to their implications, in order to check their validity from the standpoint of compatibility with accepted knowledge. After revision, where necessary, these hypotheses are submitted to further test through the collection of data specifically designed to test their validity at the empirical level. This dual approach is the essence of the modern scientific method and marks the last stage of man's progress toward empirical science, a path that took him through folklore and mysticism, dogma and tradition, casual observation, and finally to systematic observation.
>
> (Mouly, 1978)

Although both deduction and induction have their weaknesses, their contributions to the development of science are enormous and fall into three categories: (1) the suggestion of hypotheses; (2) the logical development of these hypotheses; and (3) the clarification and interpretation of scientific findings and their synthesis into a conceptual framework.

The third means by which we set out to discover truth is research. This has been defined by Kerlinger[3] as the systematic, controlled, empirical and critical investigation of hypothetical propositions about the presumed relations among natural phenomena. Research has three characteristics in particular which distinguish it from the first means of problem-solving identified earlier, namely, experience. First, whereas experience deals with events occurring in a haphazard manner, research is systematic and controlled, basing its operations on the inductive–deductive model outlined above. Second, research is empirical. The scientist turns to experience for validation. As Kerlinger puts it, 'subjective belief ... must be checked against objective reality. Scientists must always subject their notions to the court of empirical inquiry and test.' And third, research is self-correcting. Not only does the scientific method have built-in mechanisms to protect scientists from error as far as is humanly possible, but also their procedures and results are open to public scrutiny by fellow professionals. As Mouly says, 'This self-corrective function is the most important single aspect of science,

4

guaranteeing that incorrect results will in time be found to be incorrect and duly revised or discarded.' Research is a combination of both experience and reasoning and must be regarded as the most successful approach to the discovery of truth, particularly as far as the natural sciences are concerned.

A characteristic of education in the western world has been its fitful and uneven progress. This has been attributed in the main to too great a dependence on the first of the categories identified above, namely experience, as a means of advancement and a corresponding reluctance to apply the principles of research, our third category, to educational issues. Borg[4] has succinctly highlighted the difficulty:

> Perhaps a major reason for the slow and unsure progress in education has been the inefficient and unscientific methods used by educators in acquiring knowledge and solving their problems. An uncritical acceptance of authority opinion that is not supported by objective evidence and an overdependence upon personal experience have been characteristic of the educator's problem-solving techniques.
>
> (Borg, 1963)

This rather gloomy but none the less accurate assessment of the position as it obtained generally for many years and which still characterizes some areas of education has now, fortunately, to be tempered by the knowledge that in the past few years modest advances have been made as a result of the application of the methods of social science to the study of education and its problems. Interestingly, this development has itself resulted in controversy and debate for, in adopting a social scientific orientation, educational research has at the same time absorbed two competing views of the social sciences – the established, traditional view and a more recently emerging radical view. The former holds that the social sciences are essentially the same as the natural sciences and are therefore concerned with discovering natural and universal laws regulating and determining individual and social behaviour; the latter view, however, while sharing the rigour of the natural sciences and the same concern of traditional social science to describe and explain human behaviour, emphasizes how people differ from inanimate natural phenomena and, indeed, from each other. These contending views – and also their corresponding reflections in educational research – stem in the first instance from different conceptions of social reality and of individual and social behaviour. It will help our understanding of the issues to be developed subsequently if we examine these in a little more detail.

TWO CONCEPTIONS OF SOCIAL REALITY

The two views of social science that we have just identified represent strikingly different ways of looking at social reality and are constructed on correspondingly different ways of interpreting it. We can perhaps most profitably approach these two conceptions of the social world by examining the explicit and implicit assumptions underpinning them. Our analysis is based on the work of Burrell and Morgan[5] who identified four sets of such assumptions.

First, there are assumptions of an ontological kind – assumptions which concern the very nature or essence of the social phenomena being investigated. Thus, the authors ask, is social reality external to individuals – imposing itself on their consciousness from without – or is it the product of individual consciousness? Is reality of an objective nature, or the result of individual cognition? Is it a given 'out there' in the world, or is it created by one's own mind? These questions spring directly from what is known in philosophy as the nominalist–realist debate. The former view holds that objects of thought are merely words and that there is no independently accessible thing constituting the meaning of a word. The realist position, however, contends that objects have an independent existence and are not dependent for it on the knower.

The second set of assumptions identified by Burrell and Morgan are of an epistemological kind. These concern the very bases of knowledge – its nature and forms, how it can be acquired, and how communicated to other human beings. The authors ask whether 'it is possible to identify and communicate the nature of knowledge as being hard, real and capable of being transmitted in tangible form, or whether "knowledge" is of a softer, more subjective, spiritual or even transcendental kind, based on experience and insight of a unique and essentially personal nature. The epistemological assumptions in these instances determine extreme positions on the issues of whether knowledge is something which can be acquired on the one hand, or is something which has to be personally experienced on the other' (Burrell and Morgan, 1979). How one aligns oneself in this particular debate profoundly affects how one will go about uncovering knowledge of social behaviour. The view that knowledge is hard, objective and tangible will demand of researchers an observer role, together with an allegiance to the methods of natural science; to see knowledge as personal, subjective and unique, however, imposes on researchers an involvement with their subjects and a rejection of the ways of the natural scientist. To subscribe to the former is to be positivist; to the latter, anti-positivist.

The third set of assumptions concern human nature and, in particular, the relationship between human beings and their environment. Since

6

the human being is both its subject and object of study, the consequences for social science of assumptions of this kind are indeed far-reaching. Two images of human beings emerge from such assumptions – the one portrays them as responding mechanically to their environment; the other, as initiators of their own actions. Burrell and Morgan write lucidly on the distinction:

> Thus, we can identify perspectives in social science which entail a view of human beings responding in a mechanistic or even deterministic fashion to the situations encountered in their external world. This view tends to be one in which human beings and their experiences are regarded as products of the environment; one in which humans are conditioned by their external circumstances. This extreme perspective can be contrasted with one which attributes to human beings a much more creative role: with a perspective where 'free will' occupies the centre of the stage; where man is regarded as the creator of his environment, the controller as opposed to the controlled, the master rather than the marionette. In these two extreme views of the relationship between human beings and their environment, we are identifying a great philosophical debate between the advocates of *determinism* on the one hand and *voluntarism* on the other. Whilst there are social theories which adhere to each of these extremes, the assumptions of many social scientists are pitched somewhere in the range between.
>
> (Burrell and Morgan, 1979)

It would follow from what we have said so far that the three sets of assumptions identified above have direct implications for the methodological concerns of researchers, since the contrasting ontologies, epistemologies and models of human beings will in turn demand different research methods. Investigators adopting an objectivist (or positivist) approach to the social world and who treat it like the world of natural phenomena as being hard, real and external to the individual will choose from a range of traditional options – surveys, experiments, and the like. Others favouring the more subjectivist (or anti-positivist) approach and who view the social world as being of a much softer, personal and humanly-created kind will select from a comparable range of recent and emerging techniques – accounts, participant observation and personal constructs, for example.

Where one subscribes to the view which treats the social world like the natural world – as if it were a hard, external and objective reality – then scientific investigation will be directed at analysing the relationships and regularities between selected factors in that world. It will be predominantly quantitative. 'The concern', say Burrell and Morgan, 'is with the identification and definition of these elements and with the discovery

7

of ways in which these relationships can be expressed. The methodo-logical issues of importance are thus the concepts themselves, their measurement and the identification of underlying themes. This per-spective expresses itself most forcefully in a search for universal laws which explain and govern the reality which is being observed' (Burrell and Morgan, 1979). An approach characterized by procedures and methods designed to discover general laws may be referred to as 'nomothetic'.

However, if one favours the alternative view of social reality which stresses the importance of the subjective experience of individuals in the creation of the social world, then the search for understanding focuses upon different issues and approaches them in different ways. The principal concern is with an understanding of the way in which the individual creates, modifies and interprets the world in which he or she finds himself or herself. The approach now takes on a qualitative as well as quantitative aspect. As Burrell and Morgan observe,

> The emphasis in extreme cases tends to be placed upon the explana-tion and understanding of what is unique and particular to the indivi-dual rather than of what is general and universal. This approach questions whether there exists an external reality worthy of study. In methodological terms it is an approach which emphasizes the relativistic nature of the social world.
>
> (Burrell and Morgan, 1979)

In its emphasis on the particular and individual this approach to understanding individual behaviour may be termed 'idiographic'.

In this review of Burrell and Morgan's analysis of the ontological, epistemological, human and methodological assumptions underlying two ways of conceiving social reality, we have laid the foundations for a more extended study of the two contrasting perspectives evident in the practices of researchers investigating human behaviour and, by adop-tion, educational problems. Box 1.1 summarizes these assumptions in graphic form along a subjective/objective dimension. It identifies the four sets of assumptions by using terms we have adopted in the text and by which they are known in the literature of social philosophy.

Each of the two perspectives on the study of human behaviour outlined above has profound implications for research in classrooms and schools. The choice of problem, the formulation of questions to be answered, the characterization of pupils and teachers, methodological concerns, the kinds of data sought and their mode of treatment – all will be influenced or determined by the viewpoint held. Some idea of the considerable practical implications of the contrasting views can be gained by examining Box 1.2 which compares them with respect to a number of critical issues within a broadly societal and organizational

Box 1.1 The subjective–objective dimension

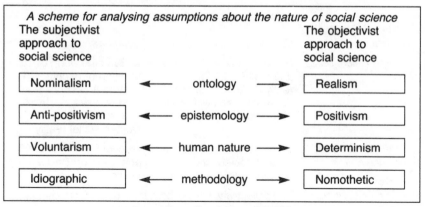

A scheme for analysing assumptions about the nature of social science

The subjectivist approach to social science		The objectivist approach to social science
Nominalism	◄—— ontology ——►	Realism
Anti-positivism	◄—— epistemology ——►	Positivism
Voluntarism	◄—— human nature ——►	Determinism
Idiographic	◄—— methodology ——►	Nomothetic

Source: Burrell and Morgan, 1979

framework. Implications of the two perspectives for research into classrooms and schools will unfold in the course of the text.

Because of its significance to the epistemological basis of social science and its consequences for educational research, we devote much of the rest of this chapter to the positivist and anti-positivist debate.

POSITIVISM

Although positivism has been a recurrent theme in the history of western thought from the Ancient Greeks to the present day, it is historically associated with the nineteenth-century French philosopher, Auguste Comte, who was the first thinker to use the word for a philosophical position.[6] His positivism can be explained in terms of his *Law of Three Stages* according to which the human mind progresses from a theological stage through a metaphysical stage to a final positive stage.[7] At the theological stage, the most primitive attempts are made to explain behaviour in terms of spiritual or supernatural entities. The metaphysical stage is only a modified version of the earlier stage and sets out to explain behaviour in terms of abstractions, essences or forces which Comte regarded as depersonalized beings of the earlier, theological stage. The final, positive stage dispenses with theological and metaphysical concepts and turns to observation and reason as means of understanding behaviour. More simply, explanation now proceeds by way of scientific description.

In his study of the history of the philosophy and methodology of science, Oldroyd says:

Box 1.2 Alternative bases for interpreting social reality

Conceptions of social reality		
Dimensions of comparison	Objectivist	Subjectivist
Philosophical basis	Realism: the world exists and is knowable as it really is. Organizations are real entities with a life of their own.	Idealism: the world exists but different people construe it in very different ways. Organizations are invented social reality.
The role of social science	Discovering the universal laws of society and human conduct within it.	Discovering how different people interpret the world in which they live.
Basic units of social reality	The collectivity: society or organizations.	Individuals acting singly or together.
Methods of understanding	Identifying conditions or relationships which permit the collectivity to exist. Conceiving what these conditions and relationships are.	Interpretation of the subjective meanings which individuals place upon their action. Discovering the subjective rules for such action.
Theory	A rational edifice built by scientists to explain human behaviour.	Sets of meanings which people use to make sense of their world and behaviour within it.
Research	Experimental or quasi-experimental validation of theory.	The search for meaningful relationships and the discovery of their consequences for action.
Methodology	Abstraction of reality, especially through mathematical models and quantitative analysis.	The representation of reality for purposes of comparison. Analysis of language and meaning.
Society	Ordered. Governed by a uniform set of values and made possible only by those values.	Conflicted. Governed by the values of people with access to power.
Organizations	Goal oriented. Independent of people. Instruments of order in society serving both society and the individual.	Dependent upon people and their goals. Instruments of power which some people control and can use to attain ends which seem good to them.

Box 1.2 (cont'd)

	Conceptions of social reality	
Dimensions of comparison	Objectivist	Subjectivist
Organizational pathologies	Organizations get out of kilter with social values and individual needs.	Given diverse human ends, there is always conflict among people acting to pursue them.
Prescription for change	Change the structure of the organization to meet social values and individual needs.	Find out what values are embodied in organizational action and whose they are. Change the people or change their values if you can.

Source: Adapted from Barr Greenfield, 1975[9]

It was Comte who consciously 'invented' the new science of society and gave it the name to which we are accustomed. He thought that it would be possible to establish it on a 'positive' basis, just like the other sciences, which served as necessary preliminaries to it. For social phenomena were to be viewed in the light of physiological (or biological) laws and theories and investigated empirically, just like physical phenomena. Likewise, biological phenomena were to be viewed in the light of chemical laws and theories; and so on down the line.

(Oldroyd, 1986)[8]

Comte's position was to lead to a general doctrine of positivism which held that all genuine knowledge is based on sense experience and can only be advanced by means of observation and experiment. Following in the empiricist tradition, it limited enquiry and belief to what can be firmly established and in thus abandoning metaphysical and speculative attempts to gain knowledge by reason alone, the movement developed what has been described as a 'tough-minded orientation to facts and natural phenomena' (Beck, 1979).

Since Comte, the term 'positivism' has been used in such different ways by philosophers and social scientists that it is difficult to assign it a precise and consistent meaning. Moreover, the term has also been applied to the doctrine of a school of philosophy known as 'logical positivism'.[10] The central belief of the logical positivists is that the meaning of a statement is, or is given by, the method of its verification. It follows from this that unverifiable statements are held to be meaningless, the utterances of traditional metaphysics and theology being included in this class.

However the term 'positivism' is used by philosophers and social scientists, a residual meaning is always present and this derives from an acceptance of natural science as the paradigm of human knowledge.[11] This includes the following connected suppositions which have been identified by Giddens.[12] First, the methodological procedures of natural science may be directly applied to the social sciences. Positivism here implies a particular stance concerning the social scientist as an observer of social reality. Second, the end-product of investigations by social scientists can be formulated in terms parallel to those of natural science. This means that their analyses must be expressed in 'laws' or 'law-like' generalizations of the same kind that have been established in relation to natural phenomena. Positivism here involves a definite view of social scientists as analysts or interpreters of their subject matter.

Positivism may be characterized by its claim that science provides us with the clearest possible ideal of knowledge. As one writer has said,

> Positivism gets much of its strength from the contrast between the continuous and agreed progress which has been achieved in the natural sciences since the time of Galileo, and the situation of dead-lock and disagreement that has at all times obtained in metaphysical philosophy. This seems to suggest that in the special sciences a fruitful method has been employed, whereas metaphysical philosophers have got lost in an intellectual impasse.

> (Acton, 1975)

Where positivism is less successful, however, is in its application to the study of human behaviour where the immense complexity of human nature and the elusive and intangible quality of social phenomena contrast strikingly with the order and regularity of the natural world. This point is nowhere more apparent than in the contexts of classroom and school where the problems of teaching, learning and human interaction present the positivistic researcher with a mammoth challenge.

For further information on positivism within the history of the philosophy and methodology of science, see Oldroyd (1986). We now look more closely at some of the features of this 'fruitful method'.

THE ASSUMPTIONS AND NATURE OF SCIENCE

Since a number of the research methods we describe in this book draw heavily on the scientific method either implicitly or explicitly and can only be fully understood within the total framework of its principles and assumptions, we will here examine some of the characteristics of science a little more closely.

We begin with an examination of the tenets of scientific faith: the kinds of assumptions held by scientists, often implicitly, as they go about their daily work. First, there is the assumption of determinism. This means simply that events have causes, that events are determined by other circumstances; and science proceeds on the belief that these causal links can eventually be uncovered and understood, that the events are explicable in terms of their antecedents. Moreover, not only are events in the natural world determined by other circumstances, but there is regularity about the way they are determined: the universe does not behave capriciously. It is the ultimate aim of scientists to formulate laws to account for the happenings in the world around them, thus giving them a firm basis for prediction and control.

The second assumption is that of empiricism. We have already touched upon this viewpoint, which holds that certain kinds of reliable knowledge can only originate in experience. In practice, therefore, this means scientifically that the tenability of a theory or hypothesis depends on the nature of the empirical evidence for its support. 'Empirical' here means that which is verifiable by observation; and 'evidence', data yielding proof or strong confirmation, in probability terms, of a theory or hypothesis in a research setting. The viewpoint has been summed up by Barratt who writes, 'The decision for empiricism as an act of scientific faith signifies that the best way to acquire reliable knowledge is the way of evidence obtained by direct experience' (Barratt, 1971).[13]

Mouly (1978) has identified five steps in the process of empirical science:

1 *experience* – the starting point of scientific endeavour at the most elementary level
2 *classification* – the formal systematization of otherwise incomprehensible masses of data
3 *quantification* – a more sophisticated stage where precision of measurement allows more adequate analysis of phenomena by mathematical means
4 *discovery of relationships* – the identification and classification of functional relationships among phenomena
5 *approximation to the truth* – science proceeds by gradual approximation to the truth.

The third assumption underlying the work of the scientist is the principle of parsimony. The basic idea is that phenomena should be explained in the most economical way possible. The first historical statement of the principle was by William of Occam when he said that explanatory principles (entities) should not be needlessly multiplied. It may, of course, be interpreted in various ways: that it is preferable to account for a phenomenon by two concepts rather than three; that a simple theory is to be preferred to a complex one; or as Lloyd Morgan did as a guide to the study of animal behaviour: 'In no case may we interpret an action as the outcome of the exercise of a higher psychical faculty, if it can be interpreted as the outcome of the exercise of one which stands lower in the psychological scale'.

The final assumption, that of generality, played an important part in both the deductive and inductive methods of reasoning. Indeed, historically speaking, it was the problematic relationship between the concrete particular and the abstract general that was to result in two competing theories of knowledge – the rational and the empirical. Beginning with observations of the particular, scientists set out to generalize their findings to the world at large. This is so because they are concerned ultimately with explanation. Of course, the concept of generality presents much less of a problem to natural scientists working chiefly with inanimate matter than to human scientists who, of necessity having to deal with samples of larger human populations, have to exercise great caution when generalizing their findings to the particular parent populations.

Having identified the basic assumptions of science, we come now to the core question: What is science? Kerlinger (1970) points out that in the scientific world itself two broad views of science may be found: the static and the dynamic. The static view, which incidentally has particular appeal for laypeople, is that science is an activity that contributes systematized information to the world. The work of the scientist is to uncover new facts and add them to the existing corpus of knowledge. Science is thus seen as an accumulated body of findings, the emphasis being chiefly on the 'present state of knowledge and adding to it'.[14] The dynamic view, by contrast, conceives science more as an activity, as something that scientists *do*. According to this conception it is important to have an accumulated body of knowledge of course, but what really matter most are the discoveries that scientists make. The emphasis here, then, is more on the heuristic nature of science.

Contrasting views exist on the functions of science. We give a composite summary of these in Box 1.3. For the professional scientists however, science is seen as a way of comprehending the world; as a means of explanation and understanding, of prediction and control. For them the ultimate aim of science is theory.

Theory has been defined by Kerlinger as 'a set of interrelated constructs [concepts], definitions, and propositions that presents a systematic view of phenomena by specifying relations among variables, with the purpose of explaining and predicting the phenomena' (Kerlinger, 1970). In a sense, theory gathers together all the isolated bits of empirical data into a coherent conceptual framework of wider applicability. Mouly expresses it thus: 'If nothing else, a theory is a convenience – a necessity, really – organising a whole slough of unassorted facts, laws,

14

Box 1.3 The functions of science

1	Its problem-seeking, question-asking, hunch-encouraging, hypotheses-producing function.
2	Its testing, checking, certifying function; its trying out and testing of hypotheses; its repetition and checking of experiments; its piling up of facts.
3	Its organizing, theorizing, structuring, function; its search for larger and larger generalizations.
4	Its history-collecting, scholarly function.
5	Its technological side; instruments, methods, techniques.
6	Its administrative, executive, and organizational side.
7	Its publicizing and educational functions.
8	Its applications to human use.
9	Its appreciation, enjoyment, celebration, and glorification.

Source: Maslow, 1954[15]

concepts, constructs, principles, into a meaningful and manageable form. It constitutes an attempt to make sense out of what we know concerning a given phenomenon' (Mouly, 1978). More than this, however, theory is itself a potential source of further information and discoveries. It is in this way a source of new hypotheses and hitherto unasked questions; it identifies critical areas for further investigation; it discloses gaps in our knowledge; and enables a researcher to postulate the existence of previously unknown phenomena.

The status of theory varies quite considerably according to the discipline or area of knowledge in question. Some theories, as in the natural sciences, are characterized by a high degree of elegance and sophistication; others, like educational theory, are only at the early stages of formulation and are thus characterized by great unevenness. Mouly (1978) identifies the following characteristics of a good theory which may serve as suitable criteria:

1 A theoretical system must permit deductions that can be tested empirically; that is, it must provide the means for its confirmation or rejection. One can test the validity of a theory only through the validity of the propositions (hypotheses) that can be derived from it. If repeated attempts to disconfirm its various hypotheses fail, then greater confidence can be placed in its validity. This can go on indefinitely, until possibly some hypothesis proves untenable. This would constitute indirect evidence of the inadequacy of the theory and could lead to its rejection (or more commonly to its replacement by a more adequate theory that can incorporate the exception).

2 Theory must be compatible with both observation and previously validated theories. It must be grounded in empirical data that have

15

been verified and must rest on sound postulates and hypotheses. The better the theory, the more adequately it can explain the phenomena under consideration, and the more facts it can incorporate into a meaningful structure of ever-greater generalizability.

3 Theories must be stated in simple terms; that theory is best that explains the most in the simplest way. This is the law of parsimony. A theory must explain the data adequately and yet must not be so comprehensive as to be unwieldy. On the other hand, it must not overlook variables simply because they are difficult to explain.

Sometimes the word 'model' is used instead of, or interchangably with, 'theory'. Both may be seen as explanatory devices or schemes having a broadly conceptual framework, though models are often characterized by the use of analogies to give a more graphic or visual representation of a particular phenomenon. Providing they are accurate and do not misrepresent the facts, models can be of great help in achieving clarity and focusing on key issues in the nature of phenomena.

Scientific theories must, by their very nature, be provisional. A theory can never be complete in the sense that it encompasses all that can be known or understood about the given phenomenon. As Mouly says,

> Invariably, scientific theories are replaced by more sophisticated theories embodying more of the advanced state of the question so that science widens its horizons to include more and more of the facts as they accumulate. No doubt, many of the things about which there is agreement today will be found inadequate by future standards. But we must begin where we are.
>
> (Mouly, 1978)

We have already implied that the quality of a theory is determined by the state of development of the particular discipline. The early stages of a science must be dominated by empirical work, that is, the accumulation and classification of data. This is why, as we shall see, much of educational research is descriptive. Only as a discipline matures can an adequate body of theory be developed. Too premature a formulation of theory before the necessary empirical spadework has been done can lead to a slowing down of progress. Mouly optimistically suggests that some day a single theoretical system, unknown to us at the present time, will be used to explain the behaviour of molecules, animals and people.

In referring to theory and models, we have begun to touch upon the tools used by scientists in their work. We look now in more detail at two such tools which play a crucial role in science – the concept and the hypothesis.

THE TOOLS OF SCIENCE

Concepts express generalizations from particulars – anger, achievement, alienation, velocity, intelligence, democracy. Examining these examples more closely, we see that each is a word representing an idea: more accurately, a concept is the relationship between the word (or symbol) and an idea or conception. Whoever we are and whatever we do, we all make use of concepts. Naturally, some are shared and used by all groups of people within the same culture – child, love, justice, for example; others, however, have a restricted currency and are used only by certain groups, specialists, or members of professions – idioglossia, retroactive inhibition, anticipatory socialization.

Concepts enable us to impose some sort of meaning on the world: through them reality is given sense, order and coherence. They are the means by which we are able to come to terms with our experience. How we perceive the world, then, is highly dependent on the repertoire of concepts we can command. The more we have, the more sense data we can pick up and the surer will be our perceptual (and cognitive) grasp of whatever is 'out there'. If our perceptions of the world are determined by the concepts available to us, it follows that people with differing sets of concepts will tend to view the 'same' objective reality differently – a doctor diagnosing an illness will draw upon a vastly different range of concepts from, say, the restricted and simplistic notions of the layperson in that context; and a visitor to civilization from a distant primitive culture would be as confused by the frenetic bustle of urban life as would the mythical Martian.

So, you may ask, where is all this leading? Simply to this: that social scientists have likewise developed, or appropriated by giving precise meaning to, a set of concepts which enable them to shape their perceptions of the world in a particular way, to represent that slice of reality which is their special study. And collectively, these concepts form part of their wider meaning system which permits them to give accounts of that reality, accounts which are rooted and validated in the direct experience of everyday life. These points may be exemplified by the concept of social class. Hughes says that it offers 'a rule, a grid, even though vague at times, to use in talking about certain sorts of experience that have to do with economic position, life-style, life-chances, and so on. It serves to identify aspects of experience, and by relating the concept to other concepts we are able to construct theories about experience in a particular order or sphere' (Hughes, 1978).[16]

There are two important points to stress when considering scientific concepts. The first is that they do not exist independently of us: they are indeed our inventions enabling us to acquire some understanding at least of the apparent chaos of nature. The second is that they are limited in number and in this way contrast with the infinite number of phenomena they are required to explain.

A second tool of great importance to the scientist is the hypothesis. It is from this that much research proceeds, especially where cause-and-effect or concomitant relationships are being investigated. The hypothesis has been defined by Kerlinger (1970) as a conjectural statement of the relations between two or more variables. More simply, it has been termed 'an educated guess', though it is unlike an educated guess in that it is often the result of considerable study, reflective thinking and observation. Medawar[17] writes incomparably of the hypothesis and its function in the following way:

> All advances of scientific understanding, at every level, begin with a speculative adventure, an imaginative preconception *of what might be true* – a preconception which always, and necessarily, goes a little way (sometimes a long way) beyond anything which we have logical or factual authority to believe in. It is the invention of a possible world, or of a tiny fraction of that world. The conjecture is then exposed to criticism to find out whether or not that imagined world is anything like the real one. Scientific reasoning is therefore at all levels an interaction between two episodes of thought – a dialogue between two voices, the one imaginative and the other critical; a dialogue, if you like, between the possible and the actual, between proposal and disposal, conjecture and criticism, between what might be true and what is in fact the case.
>
> (Medawar, 1972)

Kerlinger (1970) has identified two criteria for 'good' hypotheses. The first is that hypotheses are statements about the relations between variables; and second, that hypotheses carry clear implications for testing the stated relations. To these he adds two ancillary criteria: that hypotheses disclose compatibility with current knowledge; and that they are expressed as economically as possible. Thus if we conjecture that social class background determines academic achievement, we have a relationship between one variable, social class, and another, academic achievement. And since both can be measured, the primary criteria specified by Kerlinger can be met. Neither do they violate the ancillary criteria proposed by Kerlinger (see also Box 1.4).

He further identifies four reasons for the importance of hypotheses as tools of research. First, they organize the efforts of researchers. The relationship expressed in the hypothesis indicates what they should do. They enable them to understand the problem with greater clarity and provide them with a framework for collecting, analysing and interpreting their data. Second, they are, in Kerlinger's words, the working instruments of theory. They can be deduced from theory or from other

Box 1.4 The hypothesis

Once he has a hypothesis to work on, the scientist is in business; the hypothesis will guide him to make some observations rather than others and will suggest experiments that might not otherwise have been performed. Scientists soon pick up by experience the characteristics that make a good hypothesis; . . . almost all laws and hypotheses can be read in such a way as to *prohibit* the occurrence of certain phenomena. . . . Clearly, a hypothesis so permissive as to accommodate *any* phenomenon tells us precisely nothing; the more phenomena it prohibits, the more informative it is.

Again, a good hypothesis must also have the character of *logical immediacy*, by which I mean that it must be rather specially an explanation of whatever it is that needs to be explained and not an explanation of a great many other phenomena besides. . . . The great virtue of logical immediacy in a hypothesis is that it can be tested by comparatively direct and practicable means – that is, without the foundation of a new research institute or by making a journey into outer space. A large part of the *art of the soluble* is the art of divising hypotheses that can be tested by practicable experiments.

Source: Medawar, 1981[18]

hypotheses. Third, they can be tested, empirically or experimentally, thus resulting in confirmation or rejection. And there is always the possibility that a hypothesis, once confirmed and established, may become a law. And fourth, hypotheses are powerful tools for the advancement of knowledge because, as Kerlinger explains, they enable us to get outside ourselves.

Hypotheses and concepts play a crucial part in the scientific method and it is to this that we now turn our attention.

THE SCIENTIFIC METHOD

If the most distinctive feature of science is its empirical nature, the next most important characteristic is its set of procedures which show not only how findings have been arrived at, but are sufficiently clear for fellow-scientists to repeat them, i.e. to check them out with the same or other materials and thereby test the results. As Cuff and his colleagues[19] say: 'A scientific approach necessarily involves standards and procedures for demonstrating the "empirical warrant" of its findings, showing the match or fit between its statements and what is happening or has happened in the world' (Cuff and Payne, 1979). These standards and procedures we will call for convenience 'the scientific method', though this can be somewhat misleading for the following reason: the combination of the definite article, adjective and singular noun conjures up in the minds of some people a single invariant approach to problem-solving,

19

Box 1.5 Stages in the development of a science

---

1 Definition of the science and identification of the phenomena that are to be subsumed under it.
2 Observational stage at which the relevant factors, variables or items are identified and labelled; and at which categories and taxonomies are developed.
3 Correlational research in which variables and parameters are related to one another and information is systematically integrated as theories begin to develop.
4 The systematic and controlled manipulation of variables to see if experiments will produce expected results, thus moving from correlation to causality.
5 The firm establishment of a body of theory as the outcomes of the earlier stages are accumulated. Depending on the nature of the phenomena under scrutiny, laws may be formulated and systematized.
6 The use of the established body of theory in the resolution of problems or as a source of further hypotheses.

---

an approach frequently involving atoms or rats, and taking place within the confines of a laboratory peopled with stereotypical scientists wearing white coats and given to eccentric bouts of behaviour. Yet there is much more to it than this. The term in fact cloaks a number of methods which vary in their degree of sophistication depending on their function and the particular stage of development a science has reached. We refer you at this point to Box 1.5 which sets out the sequence of stages through which a science normally passes in its development or, perhaps more realistically, that are constantly present in its progress and on which scientists may draw depending on the kind of information they seek or the kind of problem confronting them. This latter point would seem to be particularly relevant in the case of an emerging science, such as the scientific study of educational problems, where many workers in different parts of the world are engaged in studying a wide range of problems in an essentially complicated area. Of particular interest to us in our efforts to elucidate the term 'scientific method' are stages 2, 3 and 4. Stage 2 is a relatively uncomplicated point at which the researcher is content to observe and record facts and possibly arrive at some system of classification. Much research in the field of education, especially at classroom and school level, is conducted in this way, e.g. surveys and case studies. Stage 3 introduces a note of added sophistication as attempts are made to establish relationships between variables within a loose framework of inchoate theory. Stage 4 is the most sophisticated stage and often the one that many people equate exclusively with the scientific method. In order to arrive at causality, as distinct from mere measures of association, researchers here design experimental situations

20

in which variables are manipulated to test their chosen hypotheses. Here is how one noted researcher describes the later stages:

> First, there is a doubt, a barrier, an indeterminate situation crying out, so to speak, to be made determinate. The scientist experiences vague doubts, emotional disturbances, inchoate ideas. He struggles to formulate the problem, even if inadequately. He studies the literature, scans his own experience and the experience of others. Often he simply has to wait for an inventive leap of mind. Maybe it will occur; maybe not. With the problem formulated, with the basic question or questions properly asked, the rest is much easier. Then the hypothesis is constructed, after which its implications are deduced, mainly along experimental lines. In this process the original problem, and of course the original hypothesis, may be changed. It may be broadened or narrowed. It may even be abandoned. Lastly, but not finally, the relation expressed by the hypothesis is tested by observation and experimentation. On the basis of the research evidence, the hypothesis is accepted or rejected. This information is then fed back to the original problem and it is kept or altered as dictated by the evidence. Dewey finally pointed out that one phase of the process may be expanded and be of great importance, another may be skimped, and there may be fewer or more steps involved. These things are not important. What is important is the overall fundamental idea of scientific research as a controlled rational process of reflective enquiry, the interdependent nature of the parts of the process, and the paramount importance of the problem and its statement.
>
> (Kerlinger, 1970)

With stages 3 and 4 of Box 1.5 in mind, we may say that the scientific method begins consciously and deliberately by selecting from the total number of elements in a given situation. The elements the researchers fasten on to will naturally be suitable for scientific formulation; this means simply that they will possess quantitative aspects. Their principal working tool will be the hypothesis which, as we have seen, is a statement indicating a relationship (or its absence) between two or more of the chosen elements and stated in such a way as to carry clear implications for testing. Researchers then choose the most appropriate method and put their hypotheses to the test. Box 1.6 exemplifies these points. It is a study concerned to answer the question, 'Does watching aggression on television cause children to become aggressive?' The elements selected for investigation were first, the amount of time children spend watching violence on television; and second, the tendency to choose aggressive solutions to their problems. The hypothesis, that there is a relationship between these two factors, was tested in a simple experimental situation

Box 1.6   Does watching aggression on TV cause kids to become aggressive?

A correlation exists between the amount of time children spend watching violence on TV and their tendency to choose aggressive solutions to their problems. Does this mean that watching aggression on TV causes kids to become aggressive? Not necessarily. It might. But it might also mean that aggressive kids simply like to watch aggression, and that these kids would be just as aggressive if they watched 'Captain Kangaroo' all day long. But then some experimenters came along and proved that watching violence increases violence. How? By randomly assigning some kids to a situation in which they watched an episode of 'The Untouchables' – a TV series in which people beat, kill, rape, bite, and slug each other for fifty minutes per episode. As a control, they randomly assigned some other kids to a situation in which they watched an athletic event for some length of time. The crucial point: each kid stood an *equal chance* of being selected to watch 'The Untouchables'; therefore, any differences in character structure among the kids were neutralized across the two experimental conditions. Thus, when the investigators found that the kids who watched 'The Untouchables' showed more aggressiveness afterwards than those who watched the athletic event, it does suggest quite strongly that watching violence can lead to violence.

Source: Aronson, 1976[20]

using a control group and an experimental group and was found to be upheld. The example is a good illustration of the positivistic approach to the study of social phenomena.

CRITICISMS OF POSITIVISM AND THE SCIENTIFIC METHOD

We have spoken at some length about positivism, the nature of science and the scientific method, yet in spite of the scientific enterprise's proven success – especially in the field of natural science – its ontological and epistemological bases have been the focus of sustained and sometimes vehement criticism from some quarters. Beginning in the second half of the last century, the revolt against positivism occurred on a broad front, attracting some of the best intellectuals in Europe – philosophers, scientists, social critics and creative artists; and even today opponents of positivism are made up of a similar cross-section, including many from within the ranks of social scientists themselves. Essentially, it has been a reaction against the world picture projected by science which, it is contended, denigrates life and mind. The precise target of the anti-positivists' attack has been science's mechanistic and reductionist view of nature which, by definition, excludes notions of choice, freedom, individuality, and moral responsibility.

One of the most sustained and consistent attacks in this respect came from the poet, William Blake, who perceived the universe not as a mechanism, but as a living organism:

> Blake would have us understand that mechanistic science and the philosophy of materialism eliminate the concept of life itself. All they can do is to define life in terms of biochemistry, biophysics, vibrations, wavelengths, and so on; they reduce 'life' to conceivable measurement, but such a conception of life does not embrace the most evident element of all: that life can only be known by a living being, by 'inner' experience. No matter how exact measurement may be, it can never give us an experience of life, for life cannot be weighed and measured on a physical scale.
>
> (Nesfield-Cookson, 1987)[21]

Another challenge to the claims of positivism came from Søren Kierkegaard, the Danish philosopher, from whose work was to originate the movement that became known as Existentialism. Kierkegaard was concerned with individuals and their need to fulfil themselves to the highest level of development. This realization of a person's potential was for him the meaning of existence which he saw as 'concrete and individual, unique and irreducible, not amenable to conceptualization' (Beck, 1979). Characteristic features of the age in which we live – democracy's trust in the crowd mentality, the ascendancy of reason, scientific and technological progress – all militate against the achievement of this end and contribute to the dehumanization of the individual. In his desire to free people from their illusions, the illusion Kierkegaard was most concerned about was that of objectivity. By this he meant the imposition of rules of behaviour and thought, and the making of a person into an observer set on discovering general laws governing human behaviour. The capacity for subjectivity, he argued, should be regained. This he regarded as the ability to consider one's own relationship to whatever constitutes the focus of enquiry. The contrast he made between objectivity and subjectivity is brought out in the following passage:

> When the question of truth is raised in an objective manner, reflection is directed objectively to the truth as an object to which the knower is related. Reflection is not focused on the relationship, however, but upon the question of whether it is the truth to which the knower is related. If only the object to which he is related is the truth, the subject is accounted to be in the truth. When the question of truth is raised subjectively, reflection is directed subjectively to the nature of the individual's relationship; if only the mode of this relationship is in the truth, the individual is in the truth, even if he should happen to be thus related to what is not true.
>
> (Kierkegaard, 1974)[22]

For Kierkegaard, 'subjectivity and concreteness of truth are together the light. Anyone who is committed to science, or to rule-governed morality, is benighted, and needs to be rescued from his state of darkness' (Warnock, 1970).[23]

Also concerned with the dehumanizing effects of the social sciences is Ions. While acknowledging that they can take much credit for throwing light in dark corners, he expresses serious concern at the way in which quantification and computation, assisted by statistical theory and method, are used. On this point, he writes:

> The argument begins when we quantify the process and interpret the human act. In this respect, behavioural science represents a form of collectivism which runs parallel to other developments this century. However high-minded the intention, the result is depersonalization, the effects of which can be felt at the level of the individual human being, not simply at the level of culture.
>
> (Ions, 1977)[24]

His objection is not directed at quantification *per se*, but at quantification when it becomes an end in itself – 'a branch of mathematics rather than a humane study seeking to explore and elucidate the gritty circumstances of the human condition' (Ions, 1977).

Another forceful critic of the objective consciousness has been Roszak. Writing of its alienating effect in contemporary life, he says:

> While the art and literature of our time tell us with ever more desperation that the disease from which our age is dying is that of alienation, the sciences, in their relentless pursuit of objectivity, raise alienation to its apotheosis as our *only* means of achieving a valid relationship to reality. Objective consciousness *is* alienated life promoted to its most honorific status as the scientific method. Under its auspices we subordinate nature to our command only by estranging ourselves from more and more of what we experience, until the reality about which objectivity tells us so much finally becomes a universe of congealed alienation.
>
> (Roszak, 1970)[25]

The justification for any intellectual activity lies in the effect it has on increasing our awareness and degree of consciousness. This increase, some claim, has been retarded in our time by the excessive influence the positivist paradigm has been allowed to exert on areas of our intellectual life. Holbrook, for example, affording consciousness a central position in human existence and deeply concerned with what happens to it, has written:

> (O)ur approaches today to the study of man have yielded little, and are essentially dead, because they cling to positivism – that is, to an

24

approach which demands that nothing must be regarded as real which cannot be found by empirical science and rational methods, by 'objectivity'. Since the whole problem ... belongs to 'psychic reality', to man's 'inner world', to his moral being, and to the subjective life, there can be no debate unless we are prepared to recognize the bankruptcy of positivism, and the failure of 'objectivity' to give an adequate account of existence, and are prepared to find new modes of enquiry.

(Holbrook, 1977)[26]

Other writers question the perspective adopted by positivist social science because it presents a misleading picture of the human being. Hampden-Turner,[27] for example, concludes that the social science view of human beings is biased in that it is conservative and ignores important qualities. This restricted image of humans, he contends, comes about because social scientists concentrate on the repetitive, predictable and invariant aspects of the person; on 'visible externalities' to the exclusion of the subjective world; and – at least as far as psychology is concerned – on the parts of the person in their endeavours to understand the whole.

Two other criticisms are commonly levelled at positivistic social science from within its own ranks. The first is that it fails to take account of our unique ability to interpret our experiences and represent them to ourselves. We can, and do construct theories about ourselves and our world; moreover, we act on these theories. In failing to recognize this, positivistic social science is said to ignore the profound differences between itself and the natural sciences. Social science, unlike natural science, 'stands in a subject–subject relation to its field of study, not a subject–object relation; it deals with a pre-interpreted world in which the meanings developed by active subjects enter the actual constitution or production of the world'.[28]

Second, the findings of positivistic social science are often said to be so banal and trivial that they are of little consequence to those for whom they are intended, namely, teachers, social workers, counsellors, personnel managers, and the like. The more effort, it seems, that researchers put into their scientific experimentation in the laboratory by restricting, simplifying and controlling variables, the more likely they are to end up with a 'pruned, synthetic version of the whole, a constructed play of puppets in a restricted environment.'[29]

These are formidable criticisms; but what alternatives are proposed by the detractors of positivistic social science?

ALTERNATIVES TO POSITIVISTIC SOCIAL SCIENCE

Although the opponents of positivism within social science itself subscribe to a variety of schools of thought each with its own subtly different epistemological viewpoint, they are united by their common rejection of the belief that human behaviour is governed by general laws and characterized by underlying regularities. Moreover, they would agree that the social world can only be understood from the standpoint of the individuals who are part of the ongoing action being investigated; and that their model of a person is an autonomous one, not the plastic version favoured by positivist researchers. In rejecting the viewpoint of the detached, objective observer – a mandatory feature of traditional research – anti-positivists would argue that individuals' behaviour can only be understood by the researcher sharing their frame of reference: understanding of individuals' interpretations of the world around them has to come from the inside, not the outside. Social science is thus seen as a subjective rather than an objective undertaking, as a means of dealing with the direct experience of people in specific contexts. The following extract nicely captures the spirit in which the anti-positivist social scientist would work:

> (T)he purpose of social science is to understand social reality as different people see it and to demonstrate how their views shape the action which they take within that reality. Since the social sciences cannot penetrate to what lies behind social reality, they must work directly with man's definitions of reality and with the rules he devises for coping with it. While the social sciences do not reveal ultimate truth, they do help us to make sense of our world. What the social sciences offer is explanation, clarification and demystification of the social forms which man has created around himself.
>
> (Beck, 1979)

The anti-positivist movement has so influenced those constituent areas of social science of most concern to us, namely, psychology, social psychology and sociology, that in each case a movement reflecting its mood has developed collaterally with mainstream trends. Whether this development is seen in competitive or complementary terms depends to some extent on one's personal viewpoint. It cannot be denied, however, that in some quarters proponents of the contrasting viewpoints have been prepared to lock horns on some of the more contentious issues.

In the case of psychology, for instance, a school of humanistic psychology has emerged alongside the co-existing behaviouristic and psychoanalytic schools. Arising as a response to the challenge to combat the growing feelings of dehumanization which characterize much of the social and cultural milieu of the twentieth century, it sets out to study and understand the person *as a whole*.[30] Humanistic psychologists present a model of people that is positive, active and purposive, and at the same time stresses their own involvement with the life experience itself. They do not stand apart, introspective, hypothesizing. Their interest is directed at the intentional and creative aspects of the human being. The perspective adopted by humanistic psychologists is naturally reflected in their methodology. They are dedicated to studying the individual in preference to the group, and consequently prefer idiographic approaches to nomothetic ones. The implications of the movement's philosophy for the education of the human being have been drawn by Carl Rogers.[31]

Comparable developments within social psychology may be perceived in the emerging 'science of persons' movement. Its proponents contend that because of our self-awareness and powers of language, we must be seen as systems of a different order of complexity from any other existing system whether natural, like an animal, or artificial, a computer, for instance. Because of this, no other system is capable of providing a sufficiently powerful model to advance our understanding of ourselves. It is argued, therefore, that we must use ourselves as a key to our understanding of others and conversely, our understanding of others as a way of finding out about ourselves. What is called for is an anthropomorphic model of man. Since anthropomorphism means, literally, the attribution of human form and personality, the implied criticism is that social psychology as traditionally conceived has singularly failed, so far, to model people as they really are. As one wry commentator has pleaded, 'For scientific purposes, treat people as if they were human beings.'[32]

This approach would entail working from a model of humans that takes account of the following uniquely human attributes:

> We are entities who are capable of monitoring our own performance. Further, because we are aware of this self-monitoring and have the power of speech, we are able to provide commentaries on those performances and to plan ahead of them as well. Such entities it is held, are much inclined to using rules, to devising plans, to developing strategies in getting things done the way they want them doing.
>
> (Harré and Secord, 1972)

Social psychology's task is to understand people in the light of this anthropomorphic model. But what specifically would this involve? Proponents of this 'science of persons' approach place great store on the systematic and painstaking analysis of social episodes. In Box 1.7 we give an example of such an episode taken from a classroom study. Note how the particular incident would appear on an interaction analysis coding sheet of a researcher employing a positivistic approach. Note, too, how this slice of classroom life can only be understood by knowledge of the specific organizational background in which it is embedded.

27

Box 1.7 A classroom episode

Walker and Adelman describe an incident in the following manner:

One lesson the teacher was listening to the boys read through short essays that they had written for homework on the subject of 'Prisons'. After one boy, Wilson, had finished reading out his rather obviously skimped piece of work the teacher sighed and said, rather crossly:

T: Wilson, we'll have to put you away if you don't change your ways, and do your homework. Is that all you've done?
P: Strawberries, strawberries. (Laughter)

Now at first glance this is meaningless. An observer coding with Flanders Interaction Analysis Categories (FIAC) would write down:
'7' (teacher criticises) followed by a,
'4' (teacher asks question) followed by a,
'9' (pupil irritation) and finally a,
'10' (silence or confusion) to describe the laughter

Such a string of codings, however reliable and valid, would not help anyone to *understand* why such an interruption was funny. Human curiosity makes us want to know *why* everyone laughs – and so, I would argue, the social scientist needs to know too. Walker and Adelman asked subsequently why 'strawberries' was a stimulus to laughter and were told that the teacher frequently said the pupils' work was 'like strawberries – good as far as it goes, but it doesn't last nearly long enough'. Here a casual comment made in the past has become an integral part of the shared meaning system of the class. It can only be comprehended by seeing the relationship as developing over time.

Source: Adapted from Delamont, 1976[33]

Box 1.8 An account in episode analysis

Observation:
A boy is seen walking down the road and swiftly using his leg to touch another boy's leg.

Boy's account of the episode:
'He called me names so I kicked him.'
'He is not a good friend.'
'No one was watching.'

Observer elicits boy's detailed definitions of 'names', 'friend', and 'no one' to extrapolate from his account the following understanding of the rules governing the particular episode.

When peers who are not good friends call me names and no salient adults are present, I will (ought, should, am entitled to) 'get even' – physical punishment being one behaviour subsumed under that act.

Source: Adapted from Levine, 1977[35]

The approach to analysing social episodes which we show in Box 1.8 is known as the 'ethogenic method'.[34] Unlike positivistic social psychology which ignores or presumes its subjects' interpretations of situations, ethogenic social psychology concentrates upon the ways in which persons construe their social world. By probing at their accounts of their actions, it endeavours to come up with an understanding of what those persons were doing in the particular episode. The example is purposely simplified and intended only to illustrate the approach rather than the substance in analysing a social episode.

The anti-positivist movement in sociology is represented by three schools of thought – phenomenology, ethnomethodology and symbolic interactionism. A common thread running through the three schools is a concern with phenomena, that is, the things we directly apprehend through our senses as we go about our daily lives, together with a consequent emphasis on qualitative as opposed to quantitative methodology. The differences between them and the significant roles each phenomenon plays in contemporary research in classrooms and schools are such as to warrant a more extended consideration of them in the section which follows.

PHENOMENOLOGY, ETHNOMETHODOLOGY AND SYMBOLIC INTERACTIONISM

In its broadest meaning, phenomenology is a theoretical point of view that advocates the study of direct experience taken at face value; and one which sees behaviour as determined by the phenomena of experience rather than by external, objective and physically described reality.[36] Although phenomenologists differ among themselves on particular issues, there is fairly general agreement on the following points identified by Curtis[37] which can be taken as distinguishing features of their philosophical viewpoint:

1 A belief in the importance, and in a sense the primacy, of subjective consciousness;
2 An understanding of consciousness as active, as meaning bestowing; and
3 A claim that there are certain essential structures to consciousness of which we gain direct knowledge by a certain kind of reflection. Exactly what these structures are is a point about which phenomenologists have differed.

Various strands of development may be traced in the phenomenological movement: we shall briefly examine two of them – the transcendental phenomenology of Husserl; and existential phenomenology, of which Schutz is perhaps the most characteristic representative.

Husserl, regarded by many as the founder of phenomenology, was concerned with investigating the source of the foundation of science and with questioning the commonsense, 'taken-for-granted' assumptions of everyday life (see Burrell and Morgan, 1979). To do this, he set about opening up a new direction in the analysis of consciousness. His catch-phrase was 'back to the things!' which for him meant finding out how things appear directly to us rather than through the media of cultural and symbolic structures. In other words, we are asked to look beyond the details of everyday life to the essences underlying them. To do this, Husserl exhorts us to 'put the world in brackets' or free ourselves from our usual ways of perceiving the world. What is left over from this reduction is our consciousness of which there are three elements – the 'I' who thinks, the mental acts of this thinking subject, and the intentional objects of these mental acts. The aim, then, of this method of *epoché*, as Husserl called it, is the dismembering of the constitution of objects in such a way as to free us from all preconceptions about the world (see Warnock, 1970).

Schutz was concerned with relating Husserl's ideas to the issues of sociology and to the scientific study of social behaviour. Of central concern to him was the problem of understanding the meaning structure of the world of everyday life. The origins of meaning he thus sought in the 'stream of consciousness' – basically an unbroken stream of lived experiences which have no meaning in themselves. One can only impute meaning to them retrospectively, by the process of turning back on oneself and looking at what has been going on. In other words, meaning can be accounted for in this way by the concept of reflexivity. For Schutz, the attribution of meaning reflexively is dependent on the people identifying the purpose or goal they seek (see Burrell and Morgan, 1979).

According to Schutz, the way we understand the behaviour of others is dependent on a process of typification by means of which the observer makes use of concepts resembling 'ideal types' to make sense of what people do. These concepts are derived from our experience of everyday life and it is through them, claims Schutz, that we classify and organize our everyday world. As Burrell and Morgan observe, 'The typifications are learned through our biographical situation. They are handed to us according to our social context. Knowledge of everyday life is thus socially ordered. The notion of typification is thus ... an inherent feature of our everyday world (Burrell and Morgan, 1979).

The fund of everyday knowledge by means of which we are able to typify other people's behaviour and come to terms with social reality varies from situation to situation. We thus live in a world of multiple realities:

30

The social actor shifts between these provinces of meaning in the course of his everyday life. As he shifts from the world of work to that of home and leisure or to the world of religious experience, different ground rules are brought into play. While it is within the normal competence of the acting individual to shift from one sphere to another, to do so calls for a 'leap of consciousness' to overcome the differences between the different worlds.

(Burrell and Morgan, 1979)

Like phenomenology, ethnomethodology is concerned with the world of everyday life. In the words of its proponent, Harold Garfinkel, it sets out 'to treat practical activities, practical circumstances, and practical sociological reasonings as topics of empirical study, and by paying to the most commonplace activities of daily life the attention usually accorded extraordinary events, seeks to learn about them as phenomena in their own right' (Garfinkel, 1968).[38] He maintains that students of the social world must doubt the reality of that world; and that in failing to view human behaviour more sceptically, sociologists have created an ordered social reality that bears little relationship to the real thing. He thereby challenges the basic sociological concept of order.

Ethnomethodology, then, is concerned with how people make sense of their everyday world. More especially, it is directed at the mechanisms by which participants achieve and sustain interaction in a social encounter – the assumptions they make, the conventions they utilize, and the practices they adopt. Ethnomethodology thus seeks to understand social accomplishments in their own terms; it is concerned to understand them from within (see Burrell and Morgan, 1979).

In identifying the 'taken-for-granted' assumptions characterizing any social situation and the ways in which the people involved make their activities rationally accountable, ethnomethodologists use notions like 'indexicality' and 'reflexivity'. Indexicality refers to the ways in which actions and statements are related to the social contexts producing them; and to the way their meanings are shared by the participants but not necessarily stated explicitly. Indexial expressions are thus the designations imputed to a particular social occasion by the participants in order to locate the event in the sphere of reality. Reflexivity, on the other hand, refers to the way in which all accounts of social settings – descriptions, analyses, criticisms, etc. – and the social settings occasioning them are mutually interdependent.

It is convenient to distinguish between two types of ethnomethodologists: linguistic and situational. The linguistic ethnomethodologists focus upon the use of language and the ways in which conversations in everyday life are structured. Their analyses make much use of the unstated 'taken-for-granted' meanings, the use of indexical expressions

31

and the way in which conversations convey much more than is actually said. The situational ethnomethodologists cast their view over a wider range of social activity and seek to understand the ways in which people negotiate the social contexts in which they find themselves. They are concerned to understand how people make sense of and order their environment. As part of their empirical method, ethnomethodologists may consciously and deliberately disrupt or question the ordered 'taken-for-granted' elements in everyday situations in order to reveal the underlying processes at work. An example of such a disruption of the social order from Garfinkel's work is given in Box 1.9.

The substance of ethnomethodology thus largely comprises a set of specific techniques and approaches to be used in the study of what Garfinkel has described as the 'awesome indexicality' of everyday life. It is geared to empirical study, and the stress which its practitioners place upon the uniqueness of the situation encountered, projects its essentially relativist standpoint. A commitment to the development of methodology and field-work has occupied first place in the interests of its adherents, so that related issues of ontology, epistemology and the nature of human beings have received less attention than perhaps they deserve.

Essentially, the notion of symbolic interactionism derives from the work of G.H. Mead.[39] Although subsequently to be associated with such

Box 1.9 Disrupting social order

In order to demonstrate that the 'seen but unnoticed' order of everyday life is an accomplishment, Garfinkel asked some of his students to experiment with disrupting its taken-for-granted routine and familiar nature. The students were asked to see themselves as 'strangers' in their own society, and thereby to suspend their taken-for-granted commonsense understandings. Here is a short extract illustrating the technique:

S. Hi, Ray. How is your girl friend feeling?
E. What do you mean, 'How is she feeling?' Do you mean physical or mental?
S. I mean how is she feeling? What's the matter with you? (He looked peeved).
E. Nothing. Just explain a little clearer what do you mean?
S. Skip it. How are your Med School applications coming?
E. What do you mean? 'How are they?'
S. You know what I mean.

Experiments of this nature, Garfinkel suggests, demonstrate that in their everyday lives members expect others to know what they are really talking about. They also show the moral nature of the familiar social world: upsetting the order, not displaying one's competence, can bring moral sanctions from other members who have been 'troubled'.

Source: Garfinkel, 1968

noted researchers as Blumer, Hughes, Becker and Goffman, the term does not represent a unified perspective in that it does not embrace a common set of assumptions and concepts accepted by all who subscribe to the approach. For our purposes, however, it is possible to identify three basic postulates. These have been set out by Woods as follows.[40] First, human beings act towards things on the basis of the meanings they have for them. Humans inhabit two different worlds: the 'natural' world wherein they are organisms of drives and instincts and where the external world exists independently of them, and the social world where the existence of symbols, like language, enables them to give meaning to objects. This attribution of meanings, this interpreting, is what makes them distinctively human and social. Interactionists therefore focus on the world of subjective meanings and the symbols by which they are produced and represented. This means not making any prior assumptions about what is going on in an institution, and taking seriously, indeed giving priority to, inmates' own accounts. Thus, if pupils appear preoccupied for too much of the time – 'being bored', 'mucking about', 'having a laugh', etc. the interactionist is keen to explore the properties and dimensions of these processes. Second, this attribution of meaning to objects through symbols is a continuous process. Action is not simply a consequence of psychological attributes such as drives, attitudes, or personalities, or determined by external social facts such as social structure or roles, but results from a continuous process of meaning attribution which is always emerging in a state of flux and subject to change. The individual constructs, modifies, pieces together, weighs up the pros and cons and bargains. Third, this process takes place in a social context. Individuals align their actions to those of others. They do this by 'taking the role of the other', by making indications to 'themselves' about 'others' likely responses. They construct how others wish or might act in certain circumstances, and how they themselves might act. They might try to 'manage' the impressions others have of them, put on a 'performance', try to influence others' 'definition of the situation'.

Instead of focusing on the individual, then, and his or her personality characteristics, or on how the social structure or social situation causes individual behaviour, symbolic interactionists direct their attention at the nature of interaction, the dynamic activities taking place between people. In focusing on the interaction itself as a unit of study, the symbolic interactionist creates a more active image of the human being and rejects the image of the passive, determined organism. Individuals interact; societies are made up of interacting individuals. People are constantly undergoing change in interaction and society is changing through interaction. Interaction implies human beings acting in relation to each other, taking each other into account, acting, perceiving, interpreting, acting again. Hence, a more dynamic and active human being emerges rather than an actor merely responding to others.

A characteristic common to the phenomenological, ethnomethodological and symbolic interactionist perspectives – and one which makes them singularly attractive to the would-be educational researcher – is the way they 'fit' naturally to the kind of concentrated action found in classrooms and schools, an action characterized by 'pupils and teachers . . . continually adjusting, reckoning, evaluating, bargaining, acting and changing' (Woods, 1979). Yet another shared characteristic is the manner in which they are able to preserve the 'integrity' of the situation where they are employed. This is to say that the influence of the researcher in structuring, analysing and interpreting the situation is present to a much smaller degree than would be the case with a more traditionally-oriented research approach.

CRITICISMS OF THE NEWER PERSPECTIVES

Critics have wasted little time in pointing out what they regard as weaknesses in these newer qualitative perspectives. They argue that while it is undeniable that our understanding of the actions of our fellow-beings necessarily requires knowledge of their intentions, this, surely, cannot be said to comprise *the* purpose of a social science. As Rex has observed:

> Whilst patterns of social reactions and institutions may be the product of the actors' definitions of the situations there is also the possibility that those actors might be falsely conscious and that sociologists have an obligation to seek an objective perspective which is not necessarily that of any of the participating actors at all. . . . We need not be confined purely and simply to that . . . social reality which is made available to us by participant actors themselves.
>
> (Rex, 1974)[41]

Giddens similarly argues, 'No specific person can possess detailed knowledge of anything more than the particular sector of society in which he participates, so that there still remains the task of making into an explicit and comprehensive body of knowledge that which is only known in a partial way by lay actors themselves' (Giddens, 1976).

While these more recent perspectives have presented models of people that are more in keeping with common experience, their methodologies are by no means above reproof. Some argue that advocates of an anti-positivist stance have gone too far in abandoning scientific procedures of verification and in giving up hope of discovering useful generalizations about behaviour (see Mead, 1934). Are there not dangers, it is suggested, in rejecting the approach of physics in favour of methods more akin to literature, biography and journalism? Some specific criticisms of the methodologies used are well directed:

> If the carefully controlled interviews used in social surveys are inaccurate, how about the uncontrolled interviews favoured by the (newer perspectives)? If sophisticated ethological studies of behaviour are not good enough, are participant observation studies any better?
>
> (Argyle, 1978)[42]

> And what of the insistence of the interpretive methodologies on the use of verbal accounts to get at the meaning of events, rules and intentions? Are there not dangers? Subjective reports are sometimes incomplete and they are sometimes misleading.
>
> (Bernstein, 1974)[43]

Bernstein's criticism is directed at the overriding concern of phenomenologists and ethnomethodologists with the meanings of situations and the ways in which these meanings are 'negotiated' by the actors involved. What is overlooked about such negotiated meanings, observes Bernstein, is that they 'presuppose a structure of meanings (and their history) wider than the area of negotiation. Situated activities presuppose a situation; they presuppose relationships between situations; they presuppose sets of situations' (Bernstein, 1974).

Bernstein's point is that the very process whereby one interprets and defines a situation is itself a product of the circumstances in which one is placed. One important factor in such circumstances that must be considered is the power of others to impose their own definitions of situations upon participants. Doctors' consulting rooms and headteachers' studies are locations in which inequalities in power are regularly imposed upon unequal participants. The ability of certain individuals, groups, classes, and authorities to persuade others to accept their definitions of situations demonstrates that while – as ethnomethodologists insist – social structure is a consequence of the ways in which we perceive social relations, it is clearly more than this. Conceiving of social structure as external to ourselves helps us take its self-evident effects upon our daily lives into our understanding of the social behaviour going on about us.

The task of social science, it is held, is to develop sets of concepts such as norms, expectations, positions and roles in order to formulate a 'generalizing science of behaviour'. Only in this way is it possible to 'move from the interpretation of one specific action or event ... to a theoretical explanation of behaviour' (Dixon, 1973).[44]

A PROBLEM OF TERMINOLOGY: THE NORMATIVE AND INTERPRETIVE PARADIGMS

We are drawing to the close of this chapter and so far have introduced and used a variety of terms to describe the numerous branches and schools of thought embraced by the positivist and anti-positivist viewpoints. As a matter of convenience and as an aid to communication, we introduce at this point two generic terms conventionally used to describe these two perspectives and the categories subsumed under each, particularly as they refer to social psychology and sociology. The terms in question are 'normative' and 'interpretive'. The normative paradigm (or model) contains two major orienting ideas:[45] first, that human behaviour is essentially rule-governed; and second, that it should be investigated by the methods of natural science. The interpretive paradigm, in contrast to its normative counterpart, is characterized by a concern for the individual. Whereas normative studies are positivist, all theories constructed within the context of the interpretive paradigm tend to be anti-positivist.[46] As we have seen, the central endeavour in the context of the interpretive paradigm is to understand the subjective world of human experience. To retain the integrity of the phenomena being investigated, efforts are made to get inside the person and to understand from within. The imposition of external form and structure is resisted, since this reflects the viewpoint of the observer as opposed to that of the actor directly involved.

Two further differences between the two paradigms may be identified at this stage: the first concerns the concepts of 'behaviour' and 'action'; the second, the different conceptions of 'theory'. A key concept within the normative paradigm, behaviour refers to responses either to external environmental stimuli (another person, or the demands of society, for instance) or to internal stimuli (hunger, or the need to achieve, for example). In either case, the cause of the behaviour lies in the past. Interpretive approaches, on the other hand, focus on action. This may be thought of as behaviour-with-meaning; it is intentional behaviour and as such, future oriented. Actions are only meaningful to us in so far as we are able to ascertain the intentions of actors to share their experiences. A large number of our everyday interactions with one another rely on such shared experiences. A child, for example, raises his arm and keeps it above his head. Should he do this at home while watching television, his parents are likely to find his bodily movements curious ('What's the matter with him?' i.e. what immediate, past event caused him to behave like that?). In the setting of the classroom, however, the action is perfectly understandable to all ('What does Billy want now?' i.e. what does he intend? or, alternatively, Billy is letting me know that he is ready to answer my question when I ask him, i.e. future-oriented, intentional behaviour).

As regards theory, normative researchers try to devise general theories of human behaviour and to validate them through the use of increasingly complex research methodologies which, some believe, push them further and further from the experience and understanding of the everyday world and into a world of abstraction. For them, the basic reality is the collectivity; it is external to the actor and manifest in society, its institutions and its organizations. The role of theory is to say how reality hangs together in these forms or how it might be changed so as to be more effective. The researcher's ultimate aim is to establish a comprehensive 'rational edifice', a universal theory, to account for human and social behaviour.

But what of the interpretive researchers? They begin with individuals and set out to understand their interpretations of the world around them. Theory is emergent and must arise from particular situations; it should be 'grounded' on data generated by the research act.[47] Theory should not precede research but follow it.

Investigators work directly with experience and understanding to build their theory on them. The data thus yielded will be glossed with the meanings and purposes of those people who are their source. Further, the theory so generated must make sense to those to whom it applies. The aim of scientific investigation for the interpretive researcher is to understand how this glossing of reality goes on at one time and in one place and compare it with what goes on in different times and places. Thus theory becomes sets of meanings which yield insight and understanding of people's behaviour. These theories are likely to be as diverse as the sets of human meanings and understandings that they are to explain. From an interpretive perspective the hope of a universal theory which characterizes the normative outlook gives way to multifaceted images of human behaviour as varied as the situations and contexts supporting them.

We illustrate the distinction between interpretive and normative approaches with reference to two studies of classrooms. During months of observing and interviewing pupils, Woods and Hammersley[48] explored gender and ethnicity dimensions of children's experiences in school and classroom settings. In actually getting at the realities of the situation, they provide insights of day-to-day discrimination and offer a compelling account of the cultural processes by which pupils' responses to school are mediated. Their approach was interpretive.

In a study of children with special educational needs in mainstream primary schools, Croll and Moses observed randomly-selected children for a few minutes at a time over a total period of two hours, moving from child to child in a predetermined random order.[49] Croll and Moses employed detailed coding schedules and cross-tabulation techniques in teasing out interrelations between categories of behavioural variables. Their purpose was to obtain accurate, objective 'facts' about classroom interaction. The approach was normative.

Some twenty or more years ago, the application of interpretive perspectives to more substantive educational matters characterized the work of Young and his associates.[50] They saw the primary purpose of what was termed, 'a new sociology of education' as being to question much that was taken for granted in the day-to-day life of schools. Why, for example, were certain subjects included in the curriculum and not others? Who was to say what constituted a subject? Who was to define what its knowledge base should consist of? In pointing to such issues, Young 'raised questions about relations between the power structure and curricula; the access to knowledge and the opportunities to legitimate it as "superior"' (Young, 1971). The application of Young's critical perspectives can be illustrated in two classroom studies of that time. In the teaching of English, the Rosens[51] challenged the common emphasis on the study of great literature, arguing that the hidden purpose of this approach was to impose an alien middle-class culture upon working-class pupils, in effect, denying them their sense of identity. A study by Sharp and Green[52] showed how subtle influences of social control intruded upon the child-centred teaching in three infant classrooms to produce similar effects to those readily observable in more formal teaching-centred classes. Studies such as these challenged the assumptions underlying much that took place in educational practice and brought new insights into the complexity of the teaching–learning process. As we shall show in forthcoming chapters, interpretive studies continue to illuminate all aspects of teaching and learning.

We shall review some other distinctions between the normative and interpretive paradigms at the beginning of Chapter 2. For the moment, we refer you to Box 1.10 which summarizes some of the broad differences between the two approaches that we have made so far.

METHODS AND METHODOLOGY

We return to our principal concern, methods and methodology in educational research. By methods, we mean that range of approaches used in educational research to gather data which are to be used as a basis for inference and interpretation, for explanation and prediction. Traditionally, the word refers to those techniques associated with the positivistic model – eliciting responses to predetermined questions, recording measurements, describing phenomena and performing experiments. For our purposes, we will extend the meaning to include not only the methods of normative research but also those associated with the interpretive paradigm – participant observation, role-playing, non-directive interviewing, episodes and accounts. Although methods may

Box 1.10   Differing approaches to the study of behaviour

Normative	Interpretive
Society and the social system	The individual
Medium/large-scale research	Small-scale research
Impersonal, anonymous forces regulating behaviour	Human actions continuously recreating social life
Model of natural sciences	Non-statistical
'Objectivity'	'Subjectivity'
Research conducted 'from the outside'	Personal involvement of the researcher
Generalizing from the specific	Interpreting the specific
Explaining behaviour/seeking causes	Understanding actions/ meanings rather than causes
Assuming the taken-for-granted	Investigating the taken-for-granted
Macro-concepts: society, institutions, norms, positions, roles, expectations	Micro-concepts: individual perspective, personal constructs, negotiated meanings, definitions of situations
Structuralists	Phenomenologists, symbolic interactionists, ethnomethodologists

also be taken to include the more specific features of the scientific enterprise such as forming concepts and hypotheses, building models and theories, and sampling procedures, we will limit ourselves principally to the more general techniques which researchers use.

If methods refer to techniques and procedures used in the process of data-gathering, the aim of methodology then is, in Kaplan's words:

> to describe and analyse these methods, throwing light on their limitations and resources, clarifying their presuppositions and consequences, relating their potentialities to the twilight zone at the frontiers of knowledge. It is to venture generalizations from the success of particular techniques, suggesting new applications, and to unfold the specific bearings of logical and metaphysical principles on concrete problems, suggesting new formulations.
>
> (Kaplan, 1973)[53]

In summary, he suggests, the aim of methodology is to help us to understand, in the broadest possible terms, not the products of scientific enquiry but the process itself.

Our review will begin by examining those techniques associated with normative studies (with the exception of historical research) and will proceed to those used by interpretive researchers. We, for our part, will attempt to present the two perspectives in complementary light and will try to lessen the tension that is sometimes generated between them. Merton and Kendall[54] express the same sentiment when they say, 'Social scientists have come to abandon the spurious choice between qualitative and quantitative data: they are concerned rather with that combination of both which makes use of the most valuable features of each. The problem becomes one of determining *at which points* they should adopt the one, and at which the other, approach' (Merton and Kendall, 1946).

CONCLUSION: THE ROLE OF RESEARCH IN EDUCATION

Our earlier remarks on the nature of research may best be summarized by quoting Mouly's definitive statement on the subject. He writes, 'Research is best conceived as the process of arriving at dependable solutions to problems through the planned and systematic collection, analysis, and interpretation of data. It is a most important tool for advancing knowledge, for promoting progress, and for enabling man to relate more effectively to his environment, to accomplish his purposes, and to resolve his conflicts' (Mouly, 1978).[55]

The term 'research' itself may take on a range of meanings and thereby be legitimately applied to a variety of contexts from, say, an investigation into the techniques of Dutch painters of the seventeenth century to the problem of finding more efficient means of improving traffic flow in major city centres. For our purposes, however, we will restrict its usages to those activities and undertakings aimed at developing a science of behaviour, the word 'science' itself implying both normative and interpretive perspectives. Accordingly, when we speak of social research, we have in mind the systematic and scholarly application of the principles of a science of behaviour to the problems of people within their social contexts and when we use the term educational research, we likewise have in mind the application of these same principles to the problems of teaching and learning within the formal educational framework and to the clarification of issues having direct or indirect bearing on these concepts.

The particular value of scientific research in education is that it will enable educators to develop the kind of sound knowledge base that characterizes other professions and disciplines; and one that will ensure education a maturity and sense of progression it at present lacks.

REFERENCES AND NOTES

1 Parts of this chapter are taken from *Perspectives on Classrooms and Schools* by the present authors with permission from Holt, Rinehart & Winston.
2 Mouly G.J., *Educational Research: the Art and Science of Investigation* (Allyn & Bacon, Boston, 1978).

3 Kerlinger, F.N., *Foundations of Behavioral Research* (Holt, Rinehart & Winston, New York, 1970).

4 Borg, W.R., *Educational Research: An Introduction* (Longman, London, 1963). We are not here recommending, nor would we wish to encourage, exclusive dependence on rationally derived and scientifically provable knowledge for the conduct of education – even if this were possible. There is a rich fund of traditional and cultural wisdom in teaching (as in other spheres of life) which we would ignore to our detriment. What we are suggesting, however, is that total dependence on the latter has tended in the past to lead to an impasse: and that for further development and greater understanding to be achieved education must needs resort to the methods of science.

5 Burrell, G. and Morgan, G., *Sociological Paradigms and Organizational Analysis* (Heinemann Educational Books, London, 1979).

6 Beck, R.N., *Handbook in Social Philosophy* (Macmillan, New York, 1979).

7 Acton, H.B., 'Positivism' in J.O. Urmson (ed.), *The Concise Encyclopedia of Western Philosophy* (Hutchinson, London, 1975).

8 Oldroyd, D., *The Arch of Knowledge: An Introductory Study of the History of the Philosophy and Methodology of Science* (Methuen, New York and London, 1986).

9 Barr Greenfield, T., 'Theory about organisations: a new perspective and its implications for schools' in M.G. Hughes (ed.), *Administering Education: International Challenge* (Athlone Press, London, 1975).

10 Primarily associated with the Vienna Circle of the 1920s whose most famous members included Schlick, Carnap, Neurath and Waisman.

11 Duncan Mitchell, G., *A Dictionary of Sociology* (Routledge & Kegan Paul, London, 1968).

12 Giddens, A., (ed.), *Positivism and Sociology* (Heinemann Educational Books, London, 1975).

13 Barratt, P.E.H., *Bases of Psychological Methods* (Wiley & Sons, Australasia Pty. Ltd., Queensland, Australia, 1971).

14 A classic statement opposing this particular view of science is that of Thomas S. Kuhn in his book *The Structure of Scientific Revolutions* (University of Chicago Press, 1962). Kuhn's book, acknowledged as an intellectual *tour de force*, makes the point that science is not the systematic accumulation of knowledge as presented in text books; that it is a far less rational exercise than generally imagined. In effect, it is 'a series of peaceful interludes punctuated by intellectually violent revolutions . . . in each of which one conceptual world view is replaced by another.' Upholders of Kuhn's view might cite as corroboration a new theory of reality put forward in recent years by scientists such as Karl Pribram and David Bohm which sees the universe as a giant hologram. Described as 'an Occam's razor of incredible sharpness', the theory is impressive in its power and comprehensiveness and offers a putative explanation for a wide range of phenomena in the fields of science, psychology, and religion. For further information, see *The Holographic Paradigm*, Ken Wilbur (ed.), (Shambhala, Boulder, Colo., 1982); *Looking Glass Universe*, John P. Briggs and F. David Peat (Fontana, London, 1984); and *The Holographic Universe*, Michael Talbot (Grafton Books, London, 1991).

15 Maslow, A.H., *Motivation and Personality* (Harper & Row, New York, 1954).

16 Hughes, J.A., *Sociological Analysis: Methods of Discovery* (Nelson & Sons Ltd., Sunbury-on-Thames, 1978).

17 Medawar, P.B., *The Hope of Progress* (Methuen, London, 1972).

18 Medawar, P.B., *Advice to a Young Scientist* (Pan Books, London, 1981).

19 Cuff, E.C. and Payne, G.C.F. (eds), *Perspectives in Sociology* (George Allen & Unwin, London, 1979).
20 Aronson, E., *The Social Animal* (Freeman, San Francisco, 1976).
21 Nesfield-Cookson, B., *William Blake: Prophet of Universal Brotherhood* (Crucible, 1987).
22 Kierkegaard, S., *Concluding Unscientific Postscript* (Princeton University Press, Princeton, 1974).
23 Warnock, M., *Existentialism* (Oxford University Press, London, 1970).
24 Ions, E., *Against Behaviouralism: A Critique of Behavioural Science* (Basil Blackwell, Oxford, 1977).
25 Roszak, T., *The Making of a Counter Culture* (Faber & Faber, London, 1970). For a later study that examines the influence of science and objectivity on the secularization of consciousness, see the same author's *Where the Wasteland Ends* (Faber & Faber, 1972).
26 Holbrook, D., *Education, Nihilism and Survival* (Darton, Longman & Todd, London, 1977).
27 Hampden-Turner, C., *Radical Man* (Schenkman, Cambridge, Mass., 1970).
28 Giddens, A., *New Rules of Sociological Method: A Positive Critique of Interpretative Sociologies* (Hutchinson, London, 1976).
29 Shipman, M.D., *The Limitations of Social Research* (Longman, London, 1972). The formulation of scientific method outlined earlier (pages 19–22) has come in for strong and sustained criticism. Mishler for example, describes it as a 'storybook image of science', out of tune with the actual practices of working scientists who turn out to resemble craftpersons rather than logicians. By craftpersons, Mishler is at pains to stress that competence depends upon 'apprenticeship training, continued practice and experienced-based, contextual knowledge of the specific methods applicable to a phenomenon of interest rather than an abstract "logic of discovery" and application of formal "rules"'. The knowledge base of scientific research, Mishler contends, is largely tacit and unexplicated; moreover, scientists learn it through a process of socialization into a 'particular form of life'. The discovery, testing and validation of findings is embedded in cultural and linguistic practices and experimental scientists proceed in pragmatic ways, learning from their errors and failures, adapting procedures to their local contexts, making decisions on the basis of their accumulated experiences. See for example, Mishler (1990) 'Validation in inquiry-guided research: the role of exemplars in narrative studies' *Harvard Educational Review*, 60 (4): 415–42.
30 Buhler, C. and Allen, M., *Introduction to Humanistic Psychology* (Brooks/Cole, Monterey, California, 1972).
31 See, for example, Rogers, C.R., *Freedom to Learn* (Merrill Pub. Co., Columbus, Ohio, 1969); and also Rogers, C.R. and Stevens, B., *Person to Person: The Problem of Being Human* (Souvenir Press, London, 1967).
32 Harré, R. and Secord, P., *The Explanation of Social Behaviour* (Basil Blackwell, Oxford, 1972).
33 Delamont, S., *Interaction in the Classroom* (Methuen, London, 1976).
34 Investigating social episodes involves analysing the accounts of what is happening from the points of view of the actors and the participant spectator(s)/investigator(s). This is said to yield three main kinds of interlocking material: images of the self and others, definitions of situations, and rules for the proper development of the action. See Harré, R., 'The constructive role of models' in Collins, L. (ed.), *The Use of Models in the Social Sciences* (Tavistock Publications, London, 1976).

35 Levine, R.H., 'Why the ethogenic method and the dramaturgical perspective are incompatible', *Journal of the Theory of Social Behaviour* 7(2) (1977).

36 English, H.B. and English, A.C., *A Comprehensive Dictionary of Psychological and Psychoanalytic Terms* (Longman, London, 1958).

37 Curtis, B., Introduction to Curtis, B. and Mays, W. (eds), *Phenomenology and Education* (Methuen, London, 1978).

38 Garfinkel, H., *Studies in Ethnomethodology* (Prentice-Hall, Englewood Cliffs, N.J., 1968).

39 See Mead, G.H. (ed. Charles Morris), *Mind, Self and Society* (University of Chicago Press, Chicago, 1934).

40 Woods, P., *The Divided School* (Routledge & Kegan Paul, London, 1979).

41 Rex, J. (ed.), *Approaches to Sociology: An Introduction to Major Trends in British Sociology* (Routledge & Kegan Paul, London, 1974).

42 Argyle, M., 'Discussion chapter: an appraisal of the new approach to the study of social behaviour', in M. Brenner, P. Marsh and M. Brenner (eds), *The Social Contexts of Method* (Croom Helm, London, 1978).

43 Bernstein, B., 'Sociology and the sociology of education: a brief account', in J. Rex (ed.), *Approaches to Sociology: An Introduction to Major Trends in British Sociology* (Routledge & Kegan Paul, London, 1974).

44 Dixon, K., *Sociological Theory: Pretence and Possibility* (Routledge & Kegan Paul, London, 1973).

45 Douglas, J.D., *Understanding Everyday Life* (Routledge & Kegan Paul, London, 1973).

46 It may seem paradoxical to some readers that, although we have just described interpretive theories as anti-positivist, they are nevertheless conventionally regarded as 'scientific' (and hence part of 'social science') in that they are concerned ultimately with describing and explaining human behaviour by means of methods that are in their own way every bit as rigorous as the ones used in positivist research (see, for example, Chapter 10).

47 Glaser, B.G. and Strauss, A.L., *The Discovery of Grounded Theory* (Aldine, Chicago, 1967).

48 Woods, P. and Hammersley, M., *Gender and Ethnicity in Schools: Ethnographic Accounts* (Routledge, London, 1993).

49 Croll, P. and Moses, D., *One in Five: The Assessment and Incidence of Special Educational Needs* (Routledge & Kegan Paul, London, 1985).

50 Young, M.F.D. (ed.), *Knowledge and Control: New Directions for the Sociology of Education* (Collier–Macmillan, London, 1971).

51 Rosen, C. and Rosen, H., *The Language of Primary School Children* (Penguin, London, 1973).

52 Sharp, R. and Green, A. (assisted by Lewis, J.), *Education and Social Control: A Study in Progressive Primary Education* (Routledge & Kegan Paul, London, 1975).

53 Kaplan, A., *The Conduct of Inquiry* (Intertext Books, Aylesbury, 1973).

54 Merton, R.K. and Kendall, P.L., 'The focused interview', *American Journal of Sociology* 51 (1946) 541–57.

55 See also Verma, G.K. and Beard, R.M., *What is Educational Research?* (Gower, Aldershot, 1981) for further information on the nature of educational research and also a historical perspective on the subject.

2

HISTORICAL RESEARCH

INTRODUCTION

It must seem strange, on the face of it, that among an assemblage of research methods based on the normative and interpretive paradigms we should include, and even begin with, historical research. A chapter devoted to a method apparently so fundamentally different from methods having a scientific or 'science of persons' basis must at first glance seem out of place. This notwithstanding, we feel it is essential to include it and base our justifications partly on reasons advanced by Travers[1] and partly on our own views. First, a considerable number of education students do pursue historical research into their subject and so the method does have topical relevance. Second, the review of the literature which empirical researchers are required to undertake is in itself a kind of historical study because they are reconstructing what was done in the past in a particular respect; so the principles of historical research have some bearing on part of their work at least. Third, recent years have witnessed a rapprochement between historical research and research into other areas such as sociology and psychology, although until now historians have tended to borrow data and methods from these disciplines and to use them to enhance historical knowledge rather than radically to change its nature. And fourth, historical research does have some features in common with both normative and interpretive approaches to research. In the case of the former, it shares the quest for objectivity and the desire to minimize bias and distortion; and with the latter, it likewise sets out to describe *all* aspects of the particular situation under study, or as many as are accessible, in its search for the *whole* truth. In summary, then, we may agree with Mouly[2] who says that while historical research cannot meet some of the tests of the scientific method interpreted in the specific sense of its use in the physical sciences (it cannot depend, for instance, on direct observation or experimentation, but must make use of reports that cannot be repeated), it qualifies as a scientific endeavour from the standpoint of its subscription to the same principles and the same general scholarship that characterize all scientific research.[3]

Historical research has been defined as the systematic and objective location, evaluation and synthesis of evidence in order to establish facts and draw conclusions about past events.[4] It is an act of reconstruction undertaken in a spirit of critical enquiry designed to achieve a faithful representation of a previous age. In seeking data from the personal experiences and observations of others, from documents and records, researchers often have to contend with inadequate information so that their reconstructions tend to be sketches rather than portraits. Indeed, the difficulty of obtaining adequate data makes historical research one of the most taxing kinds of enquiry to conduct satisfactorily.[5] Reconstruction implies a holistic perspective in that the method of enquiry characterizing historical research attempts to 'encompass and then explain the whole realm of man's past in a perspective that greatly accents his social, cultural, economic, and intellectual development' (Hill and Kerber, 1967).[6] Ultimately, historical research is concerned with a broad view of the conditions and not necessarily the specifics which bring them about, although such a synthesis is rarely achieved without intense debate or controversy, especially on matters of detail. The act of historical research involves the identification and limitation of a problem or an area of study; sometimes the formulation of an hypothesis (or set of questions); the collection, organization, verification, validation, analysis and selection of data; testing the hypothesis (or answering the questions) where appropriate; and writing a research report. This sequence leads to a new understanding of the past and its relevance to the present and future.

The values of historical research have been categorized by Hill and Kerber as follows:

1 it enables solutions to contemporary problems to be sought in the past
2 it throws light on present and future trends
3 it stresses the relative importance and the effects of the various interactions that are to be found within all cultures
4 it allows for the revaluation of data in relation to selected hypotheses, theories and generalizations that are presently held about the past.

As the writers point out, the ability of history to employ the past to predict the future, and to use the present to explain the past, gives it a dual and unique quality which makes it especially useful for all sorts of scholarly study and research.[7]

The particular value of historical research in the field of education is unquestioned. Although one of the most difficult areas in which to undertake research, the outcomes of enquiry into this domain can bring great benefit to educationalists and the community at large. It can, for example, yield insights into some educational problems that could not

45

Box 2.1 Specific competencies to be developed through instruction in the history of education

1 Understanding the dynamics of educational change. 2 Increased understanding of the relationship between education and the culture in which it operates. 3 Increased understanding of contemporary educational problems. 4 Understanding the functions and limitations of historical evidence in analysing educational problems. 5 Development of elementary ability in locating, analysing and appraising historical evidence. 6 Development of a sense of the dignity and responsibility of the teaching profession.

Source: Good, 1963[9]

Box 2.2 Some historical interrelations between men, movements and institutions

Men	Movements	Institutions	
		Type	Specific
Ignatius Loyola	Counter-reformation	Religious teaching order	Society of Jesus, 1534
Benjamin Franklin	Scientific movement; Education for life	Academy	Philadelphia Academy, 1751
John Dewey	Experimentalism Progressive education	Experimental school	University of Chicago Elementary School, 1896

Source: Adapted from Best, 1970

be achieved by any other means. Further, the historical study of an educational idea or institution can do much to help us understand how our present educational system has come about; and this kind of understanding can in turn help to establish a sound basis for further progress. Historical research in education can also show how and why educational theories and practices developed. It enables educationalists to use former practices to evaluate newer, emerging ones. Recurrent trends can be more easily identified and assessed from an historical standpoint – witness, for example, the various guises in which progressivism in education appears. And it can contribute to a fuller understanding of the relationship between politics and education, between school and society, between local and central government, and between teacher and pupil.[8] Specific individual competencies that can be developed

46

through instruction in the history of education have been listed in Box 2.1.

Historical research in education may concern itself with an individual, a group, a movement, an idea or an institution. As Best (1970)[10] points out, however, no one of these objects of historical interest and observation can be considered in isolation. No one person can be subjected to historical investigation without some consideration of his or her contribution to the ideas, movements or institutions of a particular time or place. These elements are always interrelated. The focus merely determines the point of emphasis towards which historical researchers direct their attention. Box 2.2 illustrates some of these relationships from the history of education. For example, no matter whether the historian chooses for study the Jesuit order, religious teaching orders, the Counter-Reformation or Ignatius Loyola, each of the other elements appears as a prominent influence or result, and an indispensable part of the narrative.

CHOICE OF SUBJECT

As with other methods we shall be considering in this book, historical research may be structured by a flexible sequence of stages, beginning with the selection and evaluation of a problem or area of study. Then follows the definition of the problem in more precise terms, the selection of suitable sources of data, collection, classification and processing of the data, and finally, the evaluation and synthesis of the data into a balanced and objective account of the subject under investigation. There are, however, some important differences between the method of historical research and other research methods used in education. The principal difference has been highlighted by Borg:

> In historical research, it is especially important that the student carefully defines his problem and appraises its appropriateness before committing himself too fully. Many problems are not adaptable to historical research methods and cannot be adequately treated using this approach. Other problems have little or no chance of producing significant results either because of the lack of pertinent data or because the problem is a trivial one.

> (Borg, 1963)

One can see from Borg's observations that the choice of a problem can sometimes be a daunting business for the potential researcher. Once a topic has been selected, however, and its potential and significance for historical research evaluated, the next stage is to define it more precisely, or, perhaps more pertinently, delimit it so that a more potent analysis will result. Too broad or too vague a statement can result in the final report lacking direction or impact. Best expresses it like this: 'The experienced historian realises that research must be a penetrating analysis of a limited problem, rather than the superficial examination of a broad area. The weapon of research is the rifle not the shotgun' (Best, 1970). Various prescriptions exist for helping to define historical topics. Gottschalk[11] recommends that four questions should be asked in identifying a topic:

1 Where do the events take place?
2 Who are the people involved?
3 When do the events occur?
4 What kinds of human activity are involved?

As Travers (1969) suggests, the scope of a topic can be modified by adjusting the focus of any one of the four categories; the geographical area involved can be increased or decreased; more or fewer people can be included in the topic; the time span involved can be increased or decreased; and the human activity category can be broadened or narrowed. It sometimes happens that a piece of historical research can only begin with a rough idea of what the topic involves; and that delimitation of it can only take place after the pertinent material has been assembled.

In hand with the careful specification of the problem goes the need, where this is appropriate, for an equally specific and testable hypothesis (sometimes a sequence of questions may be substituted.) As in empirical research, the hypothesis gives direction and focus to data collection and analysis. It imposes a selection, a structure on what would otherwise be an overwhelming mass of information. As Borg (1963) observes:

> Without hypotheses, historical research often becomes little more than an aimless gathering of facts. In searching the materials that make up the sources of historical research data, unless the student's attention is aimed at information relating to specific questions or concerned with specific hypotheses, he has little chance of extracting a body of data from the available documents that can be synthesized to provide new knowledge or new understanding of the topic studied. Even after specific hypotheses have been established, the student must exercise strict self-control in his study of historical documents or he will find himself collecting much information that is interesting but is not related to his area of inquiry. If the student's hypotheses are not sufficiently delimited or specific, it is an easy matter for him to become distracted and led astray by information that is not really related to his field of investigation.

Hill and Kerber (1967) have pointed out that the evaluation and formulation of a problem associated with historical research often involve the personality of the researcher to a greater extent than do other basic types of research. They suggest that personal factors of the investigator such as interest, motivation, historical curiosity, and educational background for the interpretation of historical facts tend to influence the selection of the problem to a great extent.

Although it has been overshadowed to some extent in the past decade by a growing interest in empirical research, historical research has still a significant role to play in education, a role that will enable us to use the past to understand and explain the present more satisfactorily and also enable us to make predictions about educational trends, practices and outcomes with greater confidence. One of the commonest forms of historical research in education is the biography: a study of the life, teachings and subsequent influence of one or other of the great educators. Yet if there are priorities in this area, as determined by current needs, more fruitful problem areas exist. One of these concerns the study of present-day practices in education and how these developed. Studies of this kind often show that current practices were developed in the first place to meet needs that no longer exist. A cognate area is the realm of educational thought and ideas and the way in which they have influenced educational practices. Travers observes, 'So often education has moved through cycles of ideas only to return, ultimately, to the starting point. A better understanding of the history of ideas in education would prevent much activity that has been called "rediscovering the wheel". So often a great new educational program is little more than one that had been in vogue thirty years previously' (Travers, 1969). An investigation, for example, of the factors contributing to the demise of progressive education in the United States some years ago would have striking relevance to the subsequent history of informal and open movements in Great Britain and the United States.

DATA COLLECTION

One of the principal differences between historical research and other forms of research is that historical research must deal with data that already exist. Hockett[12] expresses it thus:

> History is not a science of *direct* observation, like chemistry and physics. The historian like the geologist interprets past events by the traces they have left; he deals with the evidence of man's past acts and thoughts. But the historian, no less than the scientist, must utilize evidence resting on reliable observation. The difference in procedure is due to the fact that the historian usually does not make his own observations, and that those upon whose observations he must depend are, or were, often if not usually untrained

observers. Historical method is, strictly speaking, a process *supplementary* to observations, a process by which the historian attempts to test the truthfulness of the reports of observations made by others. Like the scientist, he examines his data and formulates hypotheses, i.e. tentative conclusions. These conjectures he must test by seeking fresh evidence or re-examining the old, and this process he must continue until, in the light of all available evidence, the hypotheses are abandoned as untenable or modified until they are brought into conformity with the available evidence.

(Hockett, 1955)

Sources of data in historical research may be classified into two main groups: *primary sources*, which are the life-blood of historical research; and *secondary sources*, which may be used in the absence of, or to supplement, primary data.

Primary sources of data have been described as those items that are original to the problem under study and may be thought of as being in two categories, thus:

1 The remains or relics of a given period. Although such remains and artefacts as skeletons, fossils, weapons, tools, utensils, buildings, pictures, furniture, coins and objets d'art were not meant to transmit information to subsequent eras, nevertheless they may be useful sources providing sound evidence about the past.
2 Those items that have had a direct physical relationship with the events being reconstructed. This category would include not only the written and oral testimony provided by actual participants in, or witnesses of, an event, but also the participants themselves. Documents considered as primary sources include manuscripts, charters, laws; archives of official minutes or records, files, letters, memoranda, memoirs, biography, offical publications, wills, newspapers and magazines, maps, diagrams, catalogues, films, paintings, inscriptions, recordings, transcriptions, log books and research reports. All these are, intentionally or unintentionally, capable of transmitting a first-hand account of an event and are therefore considered as sources of primary data. Historical research in education draws chiefly on the kind of sources identified in this second category.

Secondary sources are those that do not bear a direct physical relationship to the event being studied. They are made up of data that cannot be described as original. A secondary source would thus be one in which the person describing the event was not actually present but who obtained descriptions from another person or source. These may or may not have been primary sources. Other instances of secondary sources used in historical research include: quoted material, textbooks, encyclopedias, other reproductions of material or information, prints of paintings or replicas of art objects. Best (1970) points out that secondary sources of data are usually of limited worth because of the errors that result when information is passed on from one person to another.

Various commentators stress the importance of using primary sources of data where possible. Hill and Kerber say in this connection for instance:

> In the process of conducting historical research the investigator should never be satisfied with copies of documents that can be obtained in original form. . . . Relatively insignificant errors in reproduction processes may, through additive or multiplicative effects, produce a resultant error of comparatively great magnitude in the final form of the data. This condition is particularly well illustrated in reporting census data in various forms and indexes, where these final forms are derived through the operations of addition, subtraction, multiplication, and/or division.
>
> (Hill and Kerber, 1967)

The value, too, of secondary sources should not be minimized. There are numerous occasions where a secondary source can contribute significantly to more valid and reliable historical research than would otherwise be the case.

One further point: the review of the literature in other forms of educational research is regarded as a preparatory stage to gathering data and serves to acquaint researchers with previous research on the topics they are studying. It thus enables them to continue in a tradition, to place their work in context, and to learn from earlier endeavours. The function of the review of the literature in historical research, however, is different in that it provides the data for research; the researchers' acceptance or otherwise of their hypotheses will depend on their selection of information from the review and the interpretation they put on it. Borg (1963) has identified other differences: one is that the historical researcher will have to peruse longer documents than the empirical researcher who normally studies articles very much more succinct and precise. Further, documents required in historical research often date back much further than those in empirical research. And one final point: documents in education often consist of unpublished material and are therefore less accessible than reports of empirical studies in professional journals.

For a detailed consideration of the specific problems of documentary research, the reader is referred to the articles by Platt[13] where she considers those of authenticity, availability of documents, sampling problems, inference and interpretation.

EVALUATION

Because workers in the field of historical research gather much of their data and information from records and documents, these must be carefully evaluated so as to attest their worth for the purposes of the particular study. Evaluation of historical data and information is often referred to as historical criticism and the reliable data yielded by the process are known as historical evidence. Historical evidence has thus been described as that body of validated facts and information which can be accepted as trustworthy, as a valid basis for the testing and interpretation of hypotheses. Historical criticism is usually undertaken in two stages: first, the authenticity of the source is appraised; and second, the accuracy or worth of the data is evaluated. The two processes are known as external and internal criticism respectively, and since they each present problems of evaluation they merit further inspection.

External criticism

External criticism is concerned with establishing the authenticity or genuineness of data. It is therefore aimed at the document (or other source) itself rather than the statements it contains; with analytic forms of the data rather than the interpretation or meaning of them in relation to the study. It therefore sets out to uncover frauds, forgeries, hoaxes, inventions or distortions. To this end, the tasks of establishing the age or authorship of a document may involve tests of factors such as signatures, handwriting, script, type, style, spelling and place-names. Further, was the knowledge it purports to transmit available at the time and is it consistent with what is known about the author or period from another source? Increasingly sophisticated analyses of physical factors can also yield clues establishing authenticity or otherwise: physical and chemical tests of ink, paper, parchment, cloth and other materials, for example. Investigations in the field of educational history are less likely to encounter deliberate forgeries than in, say, political or social history, though it is possible to find that official documents, correspondence and autobiographies have been 'ghosted', that is, prepared by a person other than the alleged author or signer.

Internal criticism

Having established the authenticity of the document, the researcher's next task is to evaluate the accuracy and worth of the data contained therein. While they may be genuine, they may not necessarily disclose the most faithful picture. In their concern to establish the meaning and reliability of data, investigators are confronted with a more difficult problem than external criticism because they have to establish the credibility of the author of the documents. Travers (1969) has listed those characteristics commonly considered in making evaluations of writers. Were they trained or untrained observers of the events? In other words, how competent were they? What were their relationships to the events? To what extent were they under pressure, from fear or vanity, say, to distort or omit facts? What were the intents of the writers of the documents? To what extent were they experts at recording those particular events? Were the habits of the authors such that they might interfere with the accuracy of recordings? Were they too antagonistic or too sympathetic to give true pictures? How long after the event did they record their testimonies? And were they able to remember accurately? Finally, are they in agreement with other independent witnesses?

Many documents in the history of education tend to be neutral in character, though it is possible that some may be in error because of these kinds of observer characteristics.

A particular problem arising from the questions posed by Travers is that of bias. This can be particularly acute where life histories are being studied. The chief concern here, as Plummer[14] reminds us, resides in examining possible sources of bias which prevent researchers from finding out what is wanted and using techniques to minimize the possible sources of bias.

Researchers generally recognize three sources of bias: those arising from the subject being interviewed, those arising from themselves as researchers and those arising from the subject–researcher interaction.[12]

WRITING THE RESEARCH REPORT

Once the data have been gathered and subjected to external criticism for authenticity and to internal criticism for accuracy, the researcher is next confronted with the task of piecing together an account of the events embraced by the research problem. This stage is known as the process of synthesis. It is probably the most difficult phase in the project and calls for considerable imagination and resourcefulness. The resulting pattern is then applied to the testing of the hypothesis.

The writing of the final report is equally demanding and calls for creativity and high standards of objective and systematic analysis.

Best (1970) has listed the kinds of problems occurring in the various types of historical research projects submitted by students. These include:

1 Defining the problem too broadly.
2 The tendency to use easy-to-find secondary sources of data rather than sufficient primary sources, which are harder to locate but usually more trustworthy.

3 Inadequate historical criticism of data, due to failure to establish authenticity of sources and trustworthiness of data. For example, there is often a tendency to accept a statement as necessarily true when several observers agree. It is possible that one may have influenced the others, or that all were influenced by the same inaccurate source of information.

4 Poor logical analysis resulting from:
   (a) Oversimplification – failure to recognize the fact that causes of events are more often multiple and complex than single and simple.
   (b) Overgeneralization on the basis of insufficient evidence, and false reasoning by analogy, basing conclusions upon superficial similarities of situations.
   (c) Failure to interpret words and expression in the light of their accepted meaning in an earlier period.
   (d) Failure to distinguish between significant facts in a situation and those that are irrelevant or unimportant.

5 Expression of personal bias, as revealed by statements lifted out of context for purposes of persuasion, assuming too generous or uncritical an attitude towards a person or idea (or being too un-friendly or critical), excessive admiration for the past (sometimes known as the 'old oaken bucket' delusion), or an equally unrealistic admiration for the new or contemporary, assuming that all change represents progress.

6 Poor reporting in a style that is dull and colourless, too flowery or flippant, too persuasive or of the 'soap-box' type, or lacking in proper usage.

In addition to these, Sutherland (1969) has brilliantly illustrated two further common errors among historians of education. These are first, projecting current battles backwards onto an historical background which leads to distortion; and second, 'description in a vacuum' which fails to illustrate the relationship of the educational system to the structure of society.

To conclude on a more positive note, Box 2.3 itemizes five basic criteria for evaluating historical research.

THE USE OF QUANTITATIVE METHODS

By far the greater part of research in historical studies is qualitative in nature. This is so because the proper subject-matter of historical research consists to a great extent of verbal and other symbolic material emanating from a society's or a culture's past. The basic skills required of the researcher to analyse this kind of qualitative or symbolic material

Box 2.3   Criteria for evaluating historical research

1   *Problem*: Has the problem been clearly defined? It is difficult enough to conduct historical research adequately without adding to the confusion by starting out with a nebulous problem. Is the problem capable of solution? Is it within the competence of the investigator?

2   *Data*: Are data of a primary nature available in sufficient completeness to provide a solution, or has there been an overdependence on secondary or unverifiable sources?

3   *Analysis*: Has the dependability of the data been adequately established? Has the relevance of the data been adequately explored?

4   *Interpretation*: Does the author display adequate mastery of his data and insight into the relative significance? Does he display adequate historical perspective? Does he maintain his objectivity or does he allow personal bias to distort the evidence? Are his hypotheses plausible? Have they been adequately tested? Does he take a sufficiently broad view of the total situation? Does he see the relationship between his data and other 'historical facts'?

5   *Presentation*: Does the style of writing attract as well as inform? Does the report make a contribution on the basis of newly discovered data or new interpretation, or is it simply 'uninspired hack-work'? Does it reflect scholarliness?

Source: Mouly, 1978

involve collecting, classifying, ordering, synthesizing, evaluating and interpreting. At the basis of all these acts lies sound personal judgement. In the comparatively recent past, however, attempts have been made to apply the quantitative methods of the scientist to the solution of historical problems.[15] Of these methods, the one having greatest relevance to historical research is that of content analysis, the basic goal of which is to take a verbal, non-quantitative document and transform it into quantitative data.[16]

Content analysis itself has been defined as 'a multipurpose research method developed specifically for investigating a broad spectrum of problems in which the content of communication serves as a basis of inference.[17] The use of content analysis as a technique in social research dates from the early years of this century and since then the method has gone through a number of phases. The earliest attempts at using content analysis involve word counts. As Travers explains,

Writers typically use particular words at their own frequency rates. A word that has a high usage rate by one writer may have a low usage rate by another. The usage rates of different words can be studied to throw light on the authenticity of the source of a document. Word-usage rates can also be used as a basis for inferring inner emotional states, such as anxiety.

(Travers, 1969)

Box 2.4   The purposes of content analysis

1   To describe trends in communication content.
2   To relate known characteristics of sources to messages they produce.
3   To audit communication content against standards.
4   To analyse techniques of persuasion.
5   To analyse style.
6   To relate known attributes of the audience to messages produced for them.
7   To describe patterns of communication.

Source: Holsti, 1968

More sophisticated approaches to content analysis are careful to identify appropriate categories and units of analysis, both of which will reflect the nature of the document being analysed and the purpose of the research. Categories are normally determined after initial inspection of the document and will cover the main areas of content. Categories identifying trends in newspaper content, for example, may include domestic news, foreign affairs, business and financial news, sport, art criticism, television and radio, children's items and cartoons. Units of analysis may include the single word, a theme, a character (of a play or novel), a sentence and a paragraph.

We can readily see how the technique of content analysis may be applied to selected aspects of historical research in education. It could be used, for instance, in the analysis of educational documents. In addition to elucidating the content of the document, the method may throw additional light on the source of the communication, its author, and on its intended recipients, those to whom the message is directed. Further, an analysis of this kind would tell us more about the social context and the kinds of factors stressed or ignored, and of the influence of political factors, for instance. It follows from this that content analysis may form the basis of comparative or cross-cultural studies. Another usage that comes readily to mind would be an examination of the content of textbooks at different points in recent history as a means of indicating, say, cultural differences, cultural censorship or cultural change. Box 2.4 itemizes the seven purposes of content analysis identified by Holsti (1968).

Two very different examples of the use of content analysis in historical contexts are provided by Thomas and Znaniecki[18] and Bradburn and Berlew.[19]

In a classic study, Thomas and Znaniecki (1918) employ content analysis to study 'the role of human attitudes' in the social life of Polish families living 'under strain' at the beginning of the present century as a result of the emigration of family members to the United States of

America. Their data consist of exchange letters between the Old and the New World, letters which reflect the changing relationships within peasant primary groups as communities and families are disrupted by the long absence of an important member as well as by the changing social organization of one rural segment of Eastern Europe. Thomas and Znaniecki introduce each particular volume of letters with interpretations that clarify words or phrases, and explain the attitudes and actions described in the letters. Their introduction to Volume I, for example, runs to some two hundred pages. The amount and the depth of the analyses vary from one series of letters to another. Riley[20] describes them as generally rather 'loose and intuitive'. Often, she observes, the researchers have obtained only one side of the epistolary exchange and, in consequence, are able to cover only part of the interaction. Where however the exchanges represent the entire communication process (that is to say, the letters *are* the interaction), then they provide data that are free from the potential errors that so often beset the observer or the questioner in so far as the preconceptions of the investigator cannot affect what the group members actually write to one another, and there is no opportunity for selective reporting by a researcher. Box 2.5 shows one of the exchange letters that constitute the Thomas and Znaniecki data.

The second example of content analysis in historical settings has to do with McClelland's (1953) study of the relationship between the need to achieve (*n*'ach, for short) among members of a society and the economic

Box 2.5   Jan Kukielka, in America, to his wife in Poland, 30 December 1913

And now, dear wife and daughters, write to me, when do you think it best for me to return home? On Easter or at some other time? And now I greet you, dear wife and daughters, and I greet my dear sisters Katarzyna, Rozalia, Maryanna, with their husbands and children. And now I greet the whole household of father-in-law, father and mother and brothers-in-law. And now, dear wife I inform you [send you this] through the Mrozys [who are returning], and I send you 4 roubles for your expenses. Buy for yourself, Rózia, a white waist and for Nastusia and Jagusia shawls that you may have them for summer when I come home. And now dear wife, tell my sister Rozalia Figlisz not to allow her daughter Marysia to marry Bzdziuch, because no good will come of it. As the father, so is the son, as the tree, so is the wedge. And then it is a near family, and therefore God will not bless such a marriage, because there are enough people in the world. If she does not believe my words let her be persuaded by the example of those who married their relatives. As a good brother, I admonish Sister Rozalia, let her not do it, what she intends to do. [More greetings for the whole family.]

Your husband
Jan Kukielka

Source: Extract adapted from Thomas and Znaniecki, 1918

Box 2.6 English literature *n*'ach levels 1550–1800 compared with coal imports
into London fifty years later

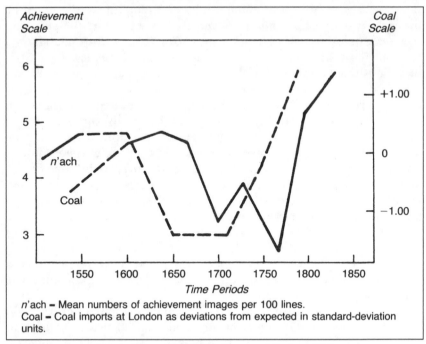

Source: Adapted from Bradburn and Berlew, 1961

growth of the particular society in question.[21] McClelland and his associates develop a measure which they call 'achievement imagery' and seek
to relate the frequency of this factor in the popular literature of a specific period in history to economic indicators of growth and development
in the society under investigation. Box 2.6 shows some of McClelland's
findings as they relate to the close association between achievement
imagery data and the scale of imports of coal into the port of London
over a three hundred year period, after the researchers had allowed for
a time lag of some fifty years between their two sets of figures.

Finally, for a more detailed and technical consideration of the use of
quantitative methods in historical research, a study which looks at the
classifying and arranging of historical data and reviews basic descriptive
statistics, we refer the reader to Floud (1979).[22]

LIFE HISTORIES

Thomas and Znaniecki's monumental study, *The Polish Peasant in Europe
and America* (1918), serves as an appropriate introduction to this section,

for their detailed account of the life and times of Wladek Wisniewski is commonly held to be the first sociological life history.

The life history, according to Plummer (1983), is frequently a full-length book about one person's life in his or her own words. Often, Plummer observes, it is gathered over a number of years, the researcher providing gentle guidance to the subject, encouraging him or her either to write down episodes of life or to tape-record them. And often as not, these materials will be backed up with intensive observations of the subject's life, with interviews of the subject's friends and acquaintances and with close scrutiny of relevant documents such as letters, diaries and photographs. Essentially, the life history is an 'interactive and co-operative technique directly involving the researcher' (Plummer, 1983).

Few contemporary educational researchers engaged in life history studies aim at mammoth books about individual subjects. None the less, recent accounts of the perspectives and interpretations of people in a variety of educational settings are both significant and pertinent,[23] for they provide valuable 'insights into the ways in which educational personnel come to terms with the constraints and conditions in which they work' (Goodson, 1983).[24] Life histories, Goodson argues, 'have the potential to make a far-reaching contribution to the problem of understanding the links between "personal troubles" and "public issues", a task that lies at the very heart of the sociological enterprise'. Their importance, he asserts, 'is best confirmed by the fact that teachers continually, most often unsolicited, import life history data into their accounts of classroom events' (Goodson, 1983).

In exploring the appropriateness of life history techniques to a particular research project, and with ever-present constraints of time, facilities and finance in mind, it is useful to distinguish life histories both by type and mode of presentation, both factors bearing directly upon the scope and feasibility of the research endeavour. Box 2.7 draws on an outline by Hitchcock and Hughes (1989)[25] Readers may wish to refer to the descriptions of types and modes of presentation contained in Box 2.7 in assessing the differing demands that are made on intending researchers as they gather, analyse and present their data. Whether retrospective or contemporaneous, a life history involves five broad research processes. These have been identified and described by Plummer (1983).

Preparation

This involves the researcher both in selecting an appropriate problem and devising relevant research techniques. Questions to be asked at this stage are first, *'Who is to be the object of the study?'* – the great person,

Box 2.7   A typology of life histories and their modes of presentation

---

Types

Retrospective life history
a reconstruction of past events from the present feelings and interpretations of the individual concerned

Contemporaneous life history
a description of an individual's daily life in progress, here and now

Modes of Presentation

Naturalistic
a first-person life history in which the life story is largely in the words of the individual subject, supported by a brief introduction, commentary and conclusion on the part of the researcher.

Thematically-edited
subject's words are retained intact but are presented by the researcher in terms of a series of themes, topics or headings, often in chapter-by-chapter format.

Interpreted and edited
the researcher's influence is most marked in his/her version of a subject's life story which the researcher has sifted, distilled, edited and interpreted.

Source: Adapted from Hitchcock and Hughes, 1989

the common person, the volunteer, the selected, the coerced? Second, *'What makes a good informant?'* Plummer draws attention to key factors such as accessibility of place and availability of time, and the awareness of the potential informant of his/her particular cultural milieu. A good informant is able and willing to establish and maintain a close, intimate relationship with the researcher. It is axiomatic that common sympathies and mutual respect are prerequisities for the sustenance and success of a life history project. Third, *'What needs clarifying in the early stages of the research?'* The motivations of the researcher need to be made explicit to the intended subject. So too, the question of remuneration for the subject's services should be clarified from the outset. The issue of anonymity must also be addressed, for unlike other research methodologies, life histories reveal intimate details (names, places, events) and provide scant cover from prying eyes. The earlier stages of the project also provide opportunities for discussing with the research subject the precise nature of the life history study, the logistics of interview situations and modes of data recording.

Data collection

Central to the success of a life history is the researcher's ability to use a variety of interview techniques (see also Chapter 13). As the occasion demands, these may range from relatively structured interviews that serve as general guides from the outset of the study, to informal, unstructured interviews reminiscent of non-directive counselling approaches espoused by Carl Rogers and his followers.[26] In the case of the latter, Plummer (1983) draws attention to the importance of empathy and 'non-possessive warmth' on the part of the interviewer–researcher. A third interviewing strategy involves a judicious mixture of participant observation (see Chapter 5) and casual chatting, supplemented by note-taking.

Data storage

Typically, life histories generate enormous amounts of data. Intending researchers must make early decisions about the use of tape-recordings, the how, what and when of their transcription and editing, and the development of coding and filing devices if they are to avoid being totally swamped by the materials created. Readers are referred to the discussion in Chapter 5 and to Fiedler's (1978) extensive account of methods appropriate to field studies in natural settings.[27]

Box 2.8 Principal sources of bias in life history research

Source: *Informant*

Is misinformation (unintended) given?
Has there been evasion?
Is there evidence of direct lying and deception?
Is a 'front' being presented?
What may the informant 'take for granted' and hence not reveal?
How far is the informant 'pleasing you'?
How much has been forgotten?
How much may be self-deception?

Source: *Researcher*

Attitudes of researcher: age, gender, class, race, religion, politics etc.
Demeanour of researcher: dress, speech, body language etc.
Personality of researcher: anxiety, need for approval, hostility, warmth etc.
Scientific role of researcher: theory held (etc.), researcher expectancy

Source: *The interaction*

The encounter needs to be examined. Is bias coming from:
The physical setting – 'social space'?
The prior interaction?
Non-verbal communication?
Vocal behaviour?

Source: Adapted from Plummer 1983: Table 5.2, p. 103

Data analysis

Three central issues underpin the quality of data generated by life history methodology. They are to do with representativeness, reliability and validity (see also Chapters 5 and 13).

Plummer draws attention to a frequent criticism of life history research, namely that its cases are atypical rather than representative. To avoid this charge, he urges intending researchers to, 'work out and explicitly state the life history's relationship to a wider population' (Plummer, 1983) by way of appraising the subject on a continuum of representativeness and non-representativeness.

Reliability in life history research hinges upon the identification of sources of bias and the application of techniques to reduce them. Bias arises from the informant, the researcher, and the interactional encounter itself. Box 2.8, adapted from Plummer (1983) provides a checklist of some aspects of bias arising from these principal sources.

Several validity checks are available to intending researchers. Plummer identifies the following:

1 The subject of the life history may present an autocritique of it, having read the entire product.
2 A comparison may be made with similar written sources by way of identifying points of major divergence or similarity.
3 A comparison may be made with official records by way of imposing accuracy checks on the life history.
4 A comparison may be made by interviewing other informants.

Essentially, the validity of any life history lies in its ability to represent the informant's subjective reality, that is to say, his or her definition of the situation.

Data presentation

Plummer provides three points of direction for the researcher intent upon writing a life history. First, have a clear view of who you are writing for and what you wish to accomplish by writing the account. Are you aiming to produce a case history or a case study? Case histories 'tell a good story for its own sake' (Plummer, 1983). Case studies, by contrast, use personal documents for wider theoretical purposes such as the verification and/or the generation of theory. Second, having established the purpose of the life history, decide how far you should intrude upon your assembled data. Intrusion occurs both through editing and interpreting. Editing ('cutting', sequencing, disguising names, places etc.) is almost a *sine qua non* of any life history study. Paraphrasing Plummer, editing involves getting your subject's own words, grasping them from the inside and turning them into a structured and coherent statement that uses the subject's words in places and your own, as researcher, in others, but retains their authentic meaning at all times. Third, as far as the mechanics of writing a life history are concerned, practise writing regularly. Writing, Plummer observes, needs working at, and daily drafting, revising and redrafting is necessary.

Example of life history methodology

We conclude this examination of life history methodology with an example that is representative of a type of study (retrospective) and a mode of presentation (interpreted and edited) familiar in the recent British research literature – J. Evetts's 'The Experience of Secondary headship selection: continuity and change' (1991). Evetts's thesis is that despite changes in the processes of headteacher selection and in the perceptions of the selectors themselves (governors, LEA officers and education committee members) as to which candidates are deemed 'suitable material', there are, nevertheless, salient and unchanging features which continue to be important aspects of the headteacher selection process. Evetts identifies three such elements. Gender differences, she points out, continue to be highly significant in achieving promotions to secondary school principalships. Networking of information about vacancies and likely candidates is a further aspect of the selection process that has remained unchanged over the years. And reputing, that is, the passing on of reputations of individuals, schools and even whole LEAs, features in the sorting and sifting of potential candidates. These fascinating findings emerge from the use of life history interviews with twenty headteachers, ten men and ten women, some long in post, others newly appointed. Evetts's long term aim was 'to explore how individual experiences of career and promotion can alert researchers to institutional constraints and opportunities, to structures and processes, and to continuity and change' (Evetts, 1991). The theoretical purpose identified earlier as distinguishing case study from case history is clearly in evidence in her organization and presentation of data. So too is the editing and interpreting to achieve a judicious balance between the verbatim reports of headteacher respondents and her own analysis of their experiences both during and after the selection process. The result is an account that adds to our understanding of secondary school headteacher selection by letting us see what Dollard describes as 'the pressure of the formal situation and the force of the inner private definition of the situation' (Dollard, 1949).[28]

EXAMPLE OF HISTORICAL RESEARCH IN EDUCATION

We conclude this chapter with reference to an account of the development of teacher training at Birmingham University (Thomas, 1992).[29] This study reveals that both Mason College (the forerunner of the University) and the Birmingham School Board were founded in the same year, 1870. The Birmingham Day Training College established in 1890 was not initially associated with Mason College, although the Birmingham School Board was well aware of the student demand for the successful evening classes held at Mason College for elementary teachers who wished to pursue studies beyond their government examination awards. It was not until 1894 that the Day Training College was transferred as a department of education to Mason College. Mason College itself became the University of Birmingham in 1900.

Early professorial appointments in education at the University appear to have been more concerned with establishing the department in the wider community than with educational scholarship. Organizing the work of the elementary and secondary school student teachers, sitting on numerous Education Committees as far afield as Bridgenorth and Wolverhampton, were intended to 'secure recognition for the University as a natural centre of the educational activity of the Midland district'. In reality, Thomas observes, the education department at Birmingham had a rather anti-intellectual atmosphere.

All of that was to change, however, with the appointment of C.W. Valentine to the Chair of Education in 1919 and his decision to treat education as more of a social science than an arts subject. This move, in Thomas's view, accelerated the development of both higher degrees in education and educational research. Valentine was Head of Department at Birmingham from 1919 to 1949. He established an academic scholarship and a research base in the psychology of education which remains a strength of the University of Birmingham Department of Education in the 1990s.

The advent of Valentine, in Thomas's view, was like the beginning of a Golden Age, that was only brought to an end by the cuts of the early 1980s. There was, however, an obverse side. Those students who did not take degree studies at Birmingham reverted to two-year training courses which were professionally and academically undemanding. The growth and expansion that distinguished the University of Birmingham Department of Education 'was not necessarily of equal value for initial teacher training in either the West Midlands or nationally' (Thomas, 1992).

REFERENCES AND NOTES

1 Travers, R.M.W., *An Introduction to Educational Research* (Collier–Macmillan, London, 1969).

2 Mouly, G.J., *Educational Research: The Art and Science of Investigation* (Allyn & Bacon, Boston, 1978).
3 See also the opening chapters in P. Gardiner, *The Nature of Historical Explanation* (Oxford University Press, Oxford, 1961, reprinted 1978).
4 Borg, W.R., *Educational Research: An Introduction* (Longman, London, 1963).
5 By contrast, the historian of the modern period, i.e. the nineteenth and twentieth centuries, is more often faced in the initial stages with the problem of selecting from too much material, both at the stage of analysis and writing. Here the two most common criteria for such selection are (1) the degree of significance to be attached to data, and (2) the extent to which a specific detail may be considered typical of the whole.
6 Hill, J.E. and Kerber, A., *Models, Methods and Analytical Procedures in Educational Research* (Wayne State University Press, Detroit, 1967).
7 However, historians themselves usually reject such a direct application of their work and rarely indulge in it on the grounds that no two events or contextual circumstances, separated geographically and temporally, can possibly be equated. As the popular sayings go, 'History never repeats itself' and so, 'The only thing we can learn from History is that we can learn nothing from History'.
8 The present status of the history of education as an academic discipline is well summarized and illustrated in G. Sutherland, 'The study of the history of education', *History*, 54(180), February 1969.
9 Good, C.V., *Essentials of Educational Research* (Appleton–Century–Crofts, New York, 1963).
10 Best, J.W., *Research in Education* (Prentice-Hall, Englewood Cliffs, New Jersey, 1970).
11 Gottschalk, L., *Understanding History* (Alfred A. Knopf, New York, 1951).
12 Hockett, H.C., *The Critical Method in Historical Research and Writing* (Macmillan, London, 1955).
13 Platt, J., 'Evidence and proof in documentary research. 1. Some specific problems of documentary research; and 2. Some shared problems of documentary research' *Sociol, Rev.*, 29(1) (1981): 31–52, 53–66.
14 Plummer, K., *Documents of Life: An Introduction to the Problems and Literature of a Humanistic Method* (George Allen & Unwin, London, 1983).
15 Travers (1969), see Note 1. See also the Social Science Research Council's *Research in Economic and Social History* (Heinemann, London, 1971), Chapters 2 and 3.
16 Bailey, K.D., *Methods of Social Research* (Collier–Macmillan, London, 1978).
17 Holsti, O.R., 'Content Analysis', in G. Lindzey and E. Aronson (eds), *The Handbook of Social Psychology. Volume 2: Research Methods* (Addison-Wesley, Reading, Mass. 1968). For a detailed account of the methods and problems involved in establishing the reliability of the content analysis of written data, see: Everett, M., 'The Scottish Comprehensive School: Its function and the roles of its teachers with special reference to the opinions of pupils and student teachers', unpublished Ph.D. dissertation, School of Education, University of Durham, 1984.
18 Thomas, W.I. and Znaniecki, F., *The Polish Peasant in Europe and America* (University of Chicago Press, Chicago, 1918). For a fuller discussion of the monumental work of Thomas and Znaniecki, the reader is referred to Plummer, K., *Documents of Life: An Introduction to the Problems and Literature of a Humanistic Method* (George Allen & Unwin, London 1983), especially Chapter 3, 'The Making of a Method', and to Madge, J., *The Origin of Scientific Sociology* (Tavistock, London, 1963).

19 Bradburn, N.M. and Berlew, D.E., *Economic Development and Cultural Change* (University of Chicago Press, Chicago, 1961).

20 Riley, M.W. *Sociological Research I: A Case Approach* (Harcourt, Brace & World, Inc., New York, 1963).

21 McClelland, D.C., Atkinson, J.W., Clark, R.A. and Lowell, E.L., *The Achievement Motive* (Appleton-Century-Crofts, New York, 1953).

22 Floud, R., *An Introduction to Quantitative Methods for Historians*, 2nd edn (Methuen, London, 1979).

23 Sikes, P., Measor, L. and Woods, P., *Teacher Careers* (Falmer Press, Lewes, 1985). See also: Winkley, D., *Diplomats and Detectives: LEA Advisers and Work* (Robert Royce, London, 1985); Acker, S., *Teachers, Gender and Careers* (Falmer Press, Lewes, 1989); Evetts, J., *Women in Primary Teaching* (Unwin Hyman, London, 1990); Goodson, I., *The Making of Curriculum* (Falmer Press, Lewes, 1988); Smith, L.M., *Kensington Revisited* (Falmer Press, Lewes, 1987); Goodson, I. and Walker, R., 'Putting life into educational research', in R.R. Sherman and R.B. Webb (eds), *Qualitative Research in Education: Focus and Methods* (Falmer Press, Lewes, 1988); Evetts, J., 'The experience of secondary headship selection: continuity and change', *Educational Studies*, 17(3) (1991) 285–94; Blease, D. and Cohen, L., *Coping With Computers: An Ethnographic Study in Primary Classrooms* (Paul Chapman Publishers, London, 1990); Sikes, P. and Troyna, B., 'True stories: a case study in the use of life histories in teacher education', *Educational Review*, 43(1) (1991) 3–16.

24 Goodson, I., 'The use of life histories in the study of teaching', in M. Hammersley (ed.) *The Ethnography of Schooling* (Nafferton Books, Driffield, 1983).

25 Hitchcock, G. and Hughes, D., *Research and the Teacher: A Qualitative Introduction to School-based Research* (Routledge, London, 1989).

26 Rogers, C., 'The non-directive method as a technique for social research', *Amer. J. Sociol.*, 50 (1945) 279–83.

27 Fiedler, J., *Field Research: A Manual For Logistics and Management of Scientific Studies in Natural Settings* (Jossey-Bass, London, 1978).

28 Dollard, J., *Criteria For the Life History* (Yale University Press, New Haven, CT, 1949).

29 Thomas, J.B. 'Birmingham University and teacher training: day training college to department of education', *History of Education*, 21(3) (1992) 307–21.

3

DEVELOPMENTAL RESEARCH

INTRODUCTION

Most educational research methods are descriptive; that is, they set out to describe and to interpret what is. Descriptive research, according to Best, is concerned with

> conditions or relationships that exist; practices that prevail; beliefs, points of views, or attitudes that are held; processes that are going on; effects that are being felt; or trends that are developing. At times, descriptive research is concerned with how *what is* or *what exists* is related to some preceding event that has influenced or affected a present condition or event.
>
> (Best, 1970)

Chapters 2 and 3 and indeed, most of the chapters that follow deal with descriptive research. Chapter 8, 'Experiments, Quasi-experiments and Single-case Research', is a clear exception, descriptive research being fundamentally different from experimental research in that in the former, researchers account for what has already occurred; in the latter, they arrange for events to happen.[1] This overall balance in the text reflects the fact that the majority of education studies that are reported in the literature are descriptive rather than experimental. They look at individuals, groups, institutions, methods and materials in order to describe, compare, contrast, classify, analyse and interpret the entities and the events that constitute their various fields of enquiry.

This chapter deals with three types of descriptive research, which for the present we shall refer to loosely as longitudinal, cross-sectional and trend or prediction studies. Collectively they are termed developmental research because they are concerned both to describe what the present relationships are among variables in a given situation and to account for changes occurring in those relationships as a function of time. The term 'developmental' is primarily biological, having to do with the organization and the life processes of living things. The concept has been appropriated and applied to diverse educational, historical, sociological and psychological phenomena.[2] In education, developmental studies often retain the original biological orientation of the term, having to do with the acquisition of motor and perceptual skills in young children. However, the designation 'developmental' has wider application in education, for example, in connection with Piaget's studies of qualitative changes occurring in children's thinking, and Kohlberg's work on moral development.

Because education is primarily concerned with the individual's physical, social, intellectual and emotional growth, developmental studies continue to occupy a central place in the methodologies used by educational researchers.

THE TERMINOLOGY OF DEVELOPMENTAL RESEARCH

The term 'longitudinal' is used to describe a variety of studies that are conducted over a period of time. Often, as we have seen, the word 'developmental' is employed in connection with longitudinal studies that deal specifically with aspects of human growth.

A clear distinction is drawn between longitudinal and cross-sectional studies. The longitudinal study gathers data over an extended period of time; a short-term investigation may take several weeks or months; a long-term study can extend over many years. Where successive measures are taken at different points in time from the same respondents, the term 'follow-up study' or 'cohort study' is used in the British literature, the equivalent term in the United States being the 'panel study'. Where different respondents are studied at different points in time, the study is called 'cross-sectional'. Where a few selected factors are studied continuously over time, the term 'trend study' is employed.

Cohort studies and trend studies are prospective longitudinal methods, in that they are ongoing in their collection of information about individuals or their monitoring of specific events. Retrospective longitudinal studies, on the other hand, focus upon individuals who have reached some defined end-point or state. For example, a group of young people may be the researcher's particular interest (intending social workers, convicted drug offenders or university dropouts, for example), and the questions to which she will address herself are likely to include ones such as: 'Is there anything about the previous experience of these individuals that can account for their present situation?'[3]

A cross-sectional study is one that produces a 'snapshot' of a population at a particular point in time. The epitome of the cross-sectional study is a national census in which a representative sample of the population consisting of individuals of different ages, different occupations, different educational and income levels, and residing in different parts of the country, is interviewed on the same day.[4] More typically in education, cross-sectional studies involve indirect measures of the nature and rate of changes in the physical and intellectual development of samples of children drawn from representative age levels. The single 'snapshot' of the cross-sectional study provides researchers with data for either a retrospective or a prospective enquiry.

Trend or prediction studies have an obvious importance to educational administrators or planners. Like cohort studies, they may be of relatively short or long duration. Essentially, the trend study examines recorded data to establish patterns of change that have already occurred in order to predict what will be likely to occur in the future. A major difficulty researchers face in conducting trend analyses is the intrusion of unpredictable factors that invalidate forecasts formulated on past data. For this reason, short-term trend studies tend to be more accurate than long-term analyses. The distinctions we have drawn between the various terms used in developmental research are illustrated in Box 3.1.

STRENGTHS AND WEAKNESSES OF COHORT AND CROSS-SECTIONAL STUDIES

Longitudinal studies of the cohort analysis type have an important place in the research armoury of educational investigators. Cohort studies of human growth and development conducted on representative samples of populations are uniquely able to identify typical patterns of development and to reveal factors operating on those samples which elude other research designs. They permit researchers to examine individual variations in characteristics or traits, and to produce individual growth curves. Cohort studies, too, are particularly appropriate when investigators attempt to establish causal relationships, for this task involves identifying changes in certain characteristics that result in changes in others. Cross-sectional designs are inappropriate in causal research. Cohort analysis is especially useful in sociological research because it can show how changing properties of individuals fit together into changing properties of social systems as a whole.[5] For example, the study of staff morale and its association with the emerging organizational climate of a newly-opened school would lend itself to this type of developmental research. A further strength of cohort studies in schools is that they provide longitudinal records whose value derives in part from the known fallibility of any single test or assessment (see Davie, 1972). Finally, time, always a limiting factor in experimental and interview settings, is generally more readily available in cohort studies, allowing the researcher greater opportunity to observe trends and to distinguish 'real' changes from chance occurrences (see Bailey, 1978).

Longitudinal studies suffer several disadvantages (though the gravity

Box 3.1 Types of developmental research

of these weaknesses is challenged by supporters of cohort analysis). The disadvantages are first, that they are time-consuming and expensive, because the researcher is obliged to wait for growth data to accumulate. Second, there is the difficulty of sample mortality. Inevitably during the course of a long-term cohort study, subjects drop out, are lost or refuse further co-operation. Such attrition makes it unlikely that those who remain in the study are as representative of the population as the sample that was originally drawn. Sometimes attempts are made to lessen the effects of sample mortality by introducing aspects of cross-sectional study design, that is, 'topping up' the original cohort sample size at each time of retesting with the same number of respondents drawn from the same population. The problem here is that differences arising in the data from one survey to the next may then be accounted for by differences in the persons surveyed rather than by genuine changes or trends. A third difficulty has been termed 'control effect' (sometimes referred to as measurement effect). Often, repeated interviewing results in an undesired and confusing effect on the actions or attitudes under study, influencing the behaviour of subjects, sensitizing them to matters that have hitherto passed unnoticed, or stimulating them to communication with others on unwanted topics (see Riley, 1963). Finally, cohort studies in education pose considerable problems of organization due to the continuous changes that occur in pupils, staff, teaching methods and the like. Such changes make it highly unlikely that a study will be completed in the way that it was originally planned.

Cohort studies, as we have seen, are particularly appropriate in research on human growth and development. Why then are so many studies in this area cross-sectional in design? The reason is that they have a number of advantages over cohort studies; they are less expensive; they produce findings more quickly; they are less likely to suffer from control effects; and they are more likely to secure the co-operation of respondents on a 'one-off' basis. Generally, cross-sectional designs are able to include more subjects than are cohort designs.

The strengths of cohort analysis are the weaknesses of the cross-sectional design. The cross-sectional study is a less effective method for the researcher who is concerned to identify individual variations in growth or to establish causal relationships between variables. Sampling in the cross-sectional study is complicated because different subjects are involved at each age level and may not be comparable. Further problems arising out of selection effects and the obscuring of irregularities in growth weaken the cross-sectional study so much that one observer[6] dismisses the method as a highly unsatisfactory way of obtaining developmental data except for the crudest purposes.

Douglas,[7] who pioneered the first national cohort study to be undertaken in any country, makes a spirited defence of the method against

Box 3.2   Advantages of cohort over cross-sectional designs

---

1   Some types of information, for example, on attitudes or assessment of potential ability, are only meaningful if collected contemporaneously. Other types are more complete or more accurate if collected during the course of a longitudinal survey, though they are likely to have some value even if collected retrospectively, for example, length of schooling, job history, geographical movement.

2   In cohort studies, no duplication of information occurs, whereas in cross-sectional studies the same type of background information has to be collected on each occasion. This increases the interviewing costs.

3   The omission of even a single variable, later found to be important, from a cross-sectional study is a disaster, whereas it is usually possible in a cohort study to fill the gap, even if only partially, in a subsequent interview.

4   A cohort study allows the accumulation of a much larger number of variables, extending over a much wider area of knowledge than would be possible in a cross-sectional study. This is of course because the collection can be spread over many interviews. Moreover, information may be obtained at the most appropriate time, for example, information on job entry may be obtained when it occurs even if this varies from one member of the sample to another.

5   Starting with a birth cohort removes later problems of sampling and allows the extensive use of subsamples. It also eases problems of estimating bias and reliability.

6   Longitudinal studies are free of one of the major obstacles to causal analysis, namely, the re-interpretation of remembered information so that it conforms with conventional views on causation. It also provides the means to assess the direction of effect.

Source: Adapted from Douglas, 1976

the common criticisms that are levelled against it – that it is expensive and time-consuming. His account of the advantages of cohort analysis over cross-sectional designs is summarized in Box 3.2.

EXAMPLES OF DEVELOPMENTAL RESEARCH

Example 1: a 'true' cohort study: Francis – 'patterns of reading development in the first school'[8]

The title of Francis's study points to her methodology; patterns of development require assessment over time, not simply at one particular point. The research therefore involved testing the reading progress of a cohort of 54 children at six-monthly intervals over a period of approximately two years. Because attempts to predict a child's reading ability at seven years of age from measures taken at the point of school entry are subject to error and lack precision, Francis's approach was to focus attention on patterns of progress during the two-year period of

72

infant schooling. By identifying progress curves and take-off points, the researcher was able to alert teachers to their crucial role in recognizing and acting upon different reading progress patterns in the children in their care.

Reading-age scores on the Shearer and Apps (1975) revision of the Schonell Graded Word Recognition Test were obtained at each of the four testings, together with teachers' assessments of the children's reading, using the McKee *et al. Reading for Meaning* series (1963). The overall measure of agreement between these two forms of assessment (r=0.71 – see page 140) gave the investigator confidence in using the Schonell measures for her analysis of progress curves.

Francis identified children who scored one standard deviation (see page 91) above the sample mean as good readers and those scoring one standard deviation below the sample mean as backward readers. Those scoring within one standard deviation either way were regarded, respectively, as good average and low average. Box 3.3 reports the mean scores for each of these designated groups over the four testings.

The data strongly suggests that the concepts of slow starters and long-term backward readers are applicable to the age range under investigation. Progress patterns are readily identifiable in the Schonell scores by chronological age. Thus:

> *backward readers* made minimal progress over the 18-month period as compared to *low average* readers who made a late start. Some *above average* pupils also were relatively slow starters. Progress curves for the slow starters show a year of comparatively little movement before the take-off in the subsequent six months.
>
> (Francis, 1992)

Box 3.3 Schonell reading ages for groups defined by the extent of their deviation from the sample mean at the final testing – means and standard deviations

Group by Schonell score at chron. age 7·3yrs		Schonell scores by chronological age			
		5·9	6·3	6·9	7·3
>1 SD above mean	(N=10)	6.3	7.6	8.5	9.2
		(1.0)	(1.1)	(0.7)	(0.6)
<1 SD above mean	(N=15)	5.2	5.6	6.4	7.6
		(0.3)	(0.5)	(0.6)	(0.3)
<1 SD below mean	(N=15)	5.0	5.2	5.5	6.4
		(0.1)	(0.2)	(0.4)	(0.4)
>1 SD below mean	(N=10)	5.0	5.1	5.1	5.3
		(0.0)	(0.1)	(0.1)	(0.2)
All scores	(N=50)	5.3	5.8	6.3	7.1
		(0.7)	(1.1)	(1.3)	(1.4)

Source: Francis, 1992

Space precludes an account of the researcher's analyses of development patterns in the Schonell assessments and the relationships between teachers' reading scheme assessments and the Schonell scores. Francis concludes that the close correlation between the Schonell and the reading scheme assessments suggests that teachers can, by their own monitoring, identify each child's reading progress, whatever form it takes, the evidence they need to watch for being the 'take-off' phenomenon. If teachers can alert themselves to the occurrence and significance of 'take-off' for slow starters, they can play a crucial part in promoting it, identifying it, and responding to it. Only a cohort analysis can enable a researcher to make such forthright and unequivocal recommendations as these.

Example 2: a cohort/cross-sectional design: Blatchford – 'Children's attitudes to work at 11 years'[9]

Blatchford interviewed 133 pupils about to leave Infant schools in the then Inner London Education Authority. They were asked about their academic progress and their liking or disliking of individual activities such as maths, reading and writing. In addition, the interviews provided information on a number of other topics – the children's academic self-perceptions, their views on playtime and the games and activities of the playground. Four years later, when they were about to leave Junior school, the same children were interviewed again. The interviews were conducted individually in a private place (generally a spare classroom) by a researcher. Each interview lasted approximately 45 minutes.

The sample of pupils aged seven years was drawn from 33 Infant schools in inner London, predominantly serving multi-racial, working-class neighbourhoods. To be included in the sample, each school was required to enter two children whose parents were white and indigenous, and two whose parents were of Afro-Caribbean origin. For shorthand purposes, the children are henceforth referred to as the 'white' and the 'black' groups. At age eleven years, however, in addition to reinterviewing the original sample of 133, the research team decided to increase the sample size to 175 by taking in all black boys and girls who started school at the same time as the original sample but were not previously interviewed. In addition, they also included one white boy and one white girl, selected at random from each school where there were white children who were not interviewed previously. The final sample at age eleven years consisted of 50 white boys, 38 black boys, 46 white girls and 41 black girls. Why this augmentation of the sample four years on? The researchers' concern to achieve a closer parity of numbers in each of the four pupil groups arose out of their intention to look at interaction effects of sex and ethnicity on pupils' achievements, likes and dislikes at eleven years. Contemporaneous studies had tended to explore main effects (that is sex *or* ethnicity) in relation to younger children's attainment and attitudes. Enlarging the original sample enabled the use of statistical techniques to test the joint effects of sex and ethnicity on pupil attainment.

Blatchford identifies interesting differences in attitudes between younger and older pupils and between subgroups differentiated by ethnicity and sex. Data analyses in the research report, however, do not specifically deal with the views of the original sample of 133 children at ages seven and eleven. Because cross-sectional data take pride of place in the account, the investigator rightly avoids any speculation about causal relationships.

At seven years of age, 42 per cent of the pupils found school 'mostly interesting' while some 26 per cent thought it 'mostly boring'. The same technique used at age seven to elicit children's views of school (a set of five faces ranging from a big smile, saying, 'Great! I love it' to an unhappy face saying, 'Ugh! I hate it') was employed again at age eleven. At that time, 58 per cent of the children chose the smiling face to register their feelings at the end of their Junior school days, only 5 per cent expressing strong distaste.

Children's attitudes towards maths is of particular interest. At seven years of age maths was the most popular subject, 71 per cent choosing one or the other of the smiling faces to express their approval. At eleven years of age, 75 per cent again chose one or other of these affirmative pictograms in their rating of maths. Asked why they felt like that about maths, the most common explanation was that maths was more interesting or more fun, ('gets my brain working', 'enjoy problem solving and finding answers'). The investigators report sex and ethnic differences, the most notable of which, in their view, concerned the popularity of maths among the black boys. Black boys were far more likely to nominate maths as their favourite subject and to say that they loved it; moreover, more said they liked maths because they were better at it. These may seem encouraging findings, observes Blatchford, until one looks at achievement results obtained from the same children at the same time (see Plewis, 1991).[10] The reality of the situation was that this group of black boys had the lowest mean scores of the four groups, and a relative decline over the junior school years relative to black girls, white boys and white girls. For some reason, Blatchford says, the black boys seemed to be out of step with their own achievements. Perhaps not, however, for the author goes on to say that when they were asked to compare themselves with other children in the class, they dropped their self-assessment in maths. A more convincing explanation might be that in general, the black boys' self-perceptions were high but when asked to compare their maths achievement with others whose

Box 3.4 Effectiveness strategies: what do teachers do to get classes to work well?

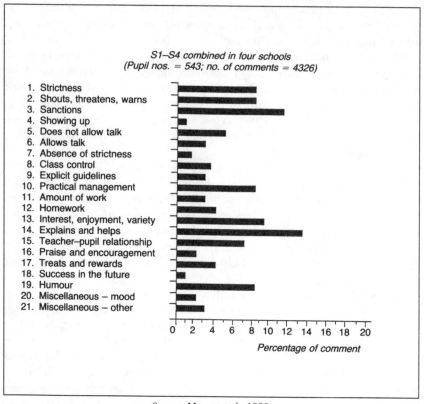

S1–S4 combined in four schools
(Pupil nos. = 543; no. of comments = 4326)

1. Strictness
2. Shouts, threatens, warns
3. Sanctions
4. Showing up
5. Does not allow talk
6. Allows talk
7. Absence of strictness
8. Class control
9. Explicit guidelines
10. Practical management
11. Amount of work
12. Homework
13. Interest, enjoyment, variety
14. Explains and helps
15. Teacher–pupil relationship
16. Praise and encouragement
17. Treats and rewards
18. Success in the future
19. Humour
20. Miscellaneous – mood
21. Miscellaneous – other

Percentage of comment

Source: Munn *et al.*, 1990

performance they were well aware of, they realistically dropped their own self-estimates.

Example 3: A large scale/cross-sectional design: Munn, Johnstone and Holligan – 'Pupils' perceptions of effective disciplinarians'[11]

In the eyes of Munn and her fellow researchers, several previous studies of students' perceptions of teachers are found wanting because of their preoccupations with eliciting descriptions of 'good' and 'ideal' teachers. 'Our work,' the authors assert, 'is . . . based on real teachers . . . we asked the pupils to consider what real teachers did, without setting up ideal traits' (Munn *et al.*, 1990).

From four secondary schools in two Scottish Regions/Divisions, two form classes from each of the years S1, S2, S3, and S4 (12–16 year olds), were selected randomly to constitute the sample of 543 students. Participants were asked to do the following:

Write down the names of three teachers who, in your opinion, are best at getting the class to work well.

On a separate sheet of paper for each named teacher, write about what each teacher does that makes the class work well.

The task given to participants generated some 4300 statements which were laboriously classified, cross-checked and reclassified by members of the research team, to arrive eventually at a 21-category system. That classification is set out in Box 3.4, together with histograms (based upon n=543) denoting the percentage of pupils rating specific strategies as 'effective' in getting classes to work well.

The data in Box 3.4 reveal that:

1 No single strategy constituted more than 14 per cent of the comment, suggesting that teachers rely on a range of strategies in getting classes to work well. Munn and her associates point out that this latter observation held true when histograms for individual year groups in individual schools were examined.

2 'Explains and helps' (Category 14) was the most frequently mentioned category, followed by 'The use of sanctions' (Category 3), suggesting, the authors opine, a carrot-and-stick approach, where explanation and positive relationships are counterbalanced by threats, sanctions and general strictness.

Drawing on data not reported in the published research account, the investigators reveal that while the profile of strategies changes somewhat for particular age groups, certain strategies are least frequently mentioned across all age groups, citing by way of example, 'Showing up' (Category 4), and surprisingly, 'Praise and encouragement' (Category 16). Another trend that was discerned across the age groups was for younger pupils to identify 'Control and rules' strategies more frequently than 'Explains and helps' as ways of getting classes to work well. By sixteen years of age (S4), that pattern was reversed with 'Explains and helps' dominating all other categories. Not unexpectedly, 'Success in the future' (Category 18) was more frequently mentioned by S4 students than by S1. 'Sanctions', (Category 3), constituted 15 per cent of the comments of S1 students as compared with only 6 per cent of the S4 classes.

Par excellence, the cross-sectional design employed by Munn and her colleagues was able to show the pattern of differences existing between the four age-related groups in the sample. In an ideal solution, the S1 cohort of pupils would have been followed throughout its school career

77

Box 3.5 Previous and projected figures of pupil numbers in England and Wales

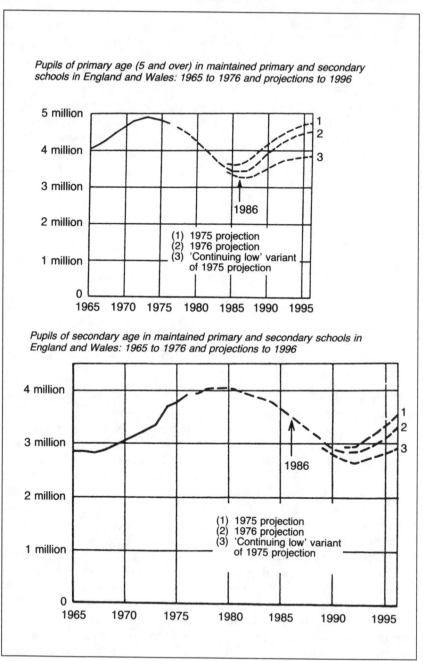

Pupils of primary age (5 and over) in maintained primary and secondary schools in England and Wales: 1965 to 1976 and projections to 1996

(1) 1975 projection
(2) 1976 projection
(3) 'Continuing low' variant of 1975 projection

Pupils of secondary age in maintained primary and secondary schools in England and Wales: 1965 to 1976 and projections to 1996

(1) 1975 projection
(2) 1976 projection
(3) 'Continuing low' variant of 1975 projection

Source: HMSO[12]

78

to allow for observation of the development of 'effective disciplinarian' concepts on the part of the pupils. Because this was a cross-sectional study, conclusions about trends in the development of pupils' views can only be assumptions.

Example 4: a trend or prediction study: Department of Education and Science – a study of school buildings[12]

As an example of a trend or prediction study, we present an outline of the work involved in estimating the overall number of schoolchildren in 1986 who needed to be catered for in school buildings, and the consequent scale of work involved in 'basic need' and 'improvement' building programmes. The phase of the Department of Education and Science study that we describe only partly followed the lines of the trend study set out in Box 3.1 in so far as its primary concern is with predicting future demands.

First, past and projected numbers of births were used to arrive at a projection of the overall school population in 1986. (In practice, a series of projections was made based upon different assumptions about birth trends. The graphs in Box 3.5 show three such projections.) This overall population was then differentiated by regions of England and Wales. Estimates were then made of the number of pupils who would be in school places provided between 1976 and 1986 under basic building programmes. Finally, the number of pupils who needed to be catered for in 1986 in the then existing buildings was arrived at: 3,069,000 primary and 2,871,000 secondary school pupils.

Box 3.5 shows the run of previous and projected figures of the number of pupils of primary and secondary age in maintained schools in England and Wales up to the year 1996. The graphs for primary and secondary projections are similar in shape, though differently sequenced chronologically, each showing an upturn towards the 1990s. The upturns were based on two assumptions. First, one of the reasons for the low numbers of births in the last few years is that many women have postponed, rather than abandoned, starting or adding to their families. The annual number of births is therefore projected to recover quite soon as these women 'catch up'. Second, the average completed family size in the medium-term future will be about 2.1 children. What these projections mean in the actual scale of the decline in school numbers between the years 1976 and 1986 is shown in Box 3.6.

Box 3.6 shows a 28 per cent decline in the primary school population by the year 1986, the corresponding decline in the secondary school age being some 9 per cent. The researchers then went on to estimate the percentage declines in the various regions of England and Wales. These figures are shown in Box 3.7. Estimates were then made of the number

Box 3.6 The decline in the numbers of pupils aged 5 and over in maintained primary and secondary schools, 1976 to 1986: England and Wales

	School population ('000)		Projected decline 1976 to 1986	
	1976	*1986 (projected)*	*Thousands*	*As a percentage of the 1976 population*
Pupils of primary age	4,763	3,429	1,334	28.0
Pupils of secondary age	3,900	3,545	335	9.1

Source: HMSO, 1977

Box 3.7 Projected percentage declines in the numbers of pupils in maintained primary and secondary schools, 1976 to 1986: England and Wales

Area	*Pupils of primary age %*	*Pupils of secondary age %*
Non-Metropolitan Counties		
North	30	15
Yorkshire & Humberside	26	9
North West	24	6
East Midlands	23	6
West Midlands	21	4
East Anglia	18	4
South East	28	5
South West	25	9
Metropolitan Counties		
North	37	22
Yorkshire & Humberside	28	12
North West	33	15
West Midlands	27	5
Greater London	34	14
Wales	27	9
England and Wales	28	9

Source: HMSO, 1977

of places that would be made available through the basic need building programme between 1976 and 1986. Finally, projected needs and estimated availability were brought together to arrive at 'hard' data on which policy decisions could be made for regional planning and expenditure forecasting.

Problems in trend or prediction studies.

We referred earlier to the intrusion of unpredictable factors in trend analyses that make long-term forecasting hazardous. In the present study the researchers identified a number of uncertainties in connection with their predictions.

First, projections of the number of pupils aged under five in 1986 were subject to uncertainty, the number depending upon the number of three- and four-year-olds in the population, the amount of available space, the various admission policies for this age group and the amount of money available. Projections about this age group were therefore excluded from the calculations. As a matter of interest, there were 380,000 under-fives in schools in 1976 and 32,000 in nursery classes. Clearly, these groups would have to figure in long-term estimates of school building needs.

Second, the definition of basic need school building was somewhat ambiguous. Conventionally, say the researchers, school building in a given year comprises basic need building plus improvement building. The basic need part covers places that are built to cater for local increases in the school population. In the past, the demand for basic need building has been thought of as comprising two elements – an overall growth in the school population, and an allowance for pupils shifting from one area of the country to another. In times of growth in pupil numbers the shift allowance hardly figures in estimates when compared with the overall growth aspect. With the decline in school population, the basic need school building becomes simply an estimate of the shift element, a factor that is open to a variety of unknown influences over the projected period of the study.

Third, the estimate of basic need building between 1976 and 1986 was based upon projects actually started, on local authority bids for work from 1976 onwards, and on expectations that the shift-based demand during the 1980s would fall faster than the school population, it being assumed that migration would be proportional to the school population, but that more empty places would be available to accommodate the migrants (Dept of Education and Science, 1977).

It can be seen how difficult the task of the school building planners is, in having to work not only with uncertainties but with imprecise criteria in respect of the very trends that they are trying to predict.

REFERENCES AND NOTES

1 Best, J.W., *Research in Education* (Prentice-Hall, Englewood Cliffs, New Jersey, 1970).
2 Good, C.V., *Introduction to Educational Research* (Appleton-Century-Crofts, New York, 1963).

3 Davie, R., 'The longitudinal approach', *Trends in Education*, 28 (1972) 8–13.
4 Bailey, K.D., *Methods of Social Research* (Collier–Macmillan, London, 1978).
5 Riley, M.W., *Sociological Research 1: A Case Approach* (Harcourt, Brace & World, New York, 1963).
6 Travers, R.M.W., *An Introduction to Educational Research* (Collier–Macmillan, London, 1969).
7 Douglas, J.W.B., 'The use and abuse of national cohorts', in M.D. Shipman (ed.), *The Organization and Impact of Social Research* (Routledge & Kegan Paul, London, 1976). For an account of the National Child Development Study of a cohort of 15,000 children (now adults), see Fogelman, K. (ed.), *Growing Up in Great Britain: Papers from the National Child Development Study* (Macmillan, London, 1983). The third national cohort study (the 1970 cohort) is a detailed account of the health and behaviour of Britain's five-year-olds. See, Butler, N.R. and Golding, J., *From Birth to Five*, (Pergamon Press, Oxford, 1986).
8 Francis, H., 'Patterns of reading development in the first school', *British Journal of Educational Psychology*, 62 (1992) 225–32.
9 Blatchford, P., 'Children's attitudes to work at 11 years', *Educat. Studies*, 18(1) (1992) 107–18.
10 Plewis, I., 'Pupils' progress in reading and maths during primary school: associations with ethnic group and sex', *Educational Research*, 33, (1991) 133–40.
11 Munn, P., Johnstone, M. and Holligan, C., 'Pupils' perceptions of effective disciplinarians', *British Educational Research Journal*, 16(2) (1990) 191–8.
12 Annex 1: Department of Education and Science, *A Study of School Buildings* (HMSO, London, 1977).

4

SURVEYS

INTRODUCTION

In this chapter we discuss what is perhaps the most commonly used descriptive method in educational research – the survey. Typically, surveys gather data at a particular point in time with the intention of describing the nature of existing conditions, or identifying standards against which existing conditions can be compared, or determining the relationships that exist between specific events. Thus, surveys may vary in their levels of complexity from those which provide simple frequency counts to those which present relational analysis.

Surveys may be further differentiated in terms of their scope. A study of contemporary developments in post-secondary education, for example, might encompass the whole of Western Europe; a study of subject choice, on the other hand, might be confined to one secondary school. The complexity and scope of surveys in education can be illustrated by reference to familiar examples. The surveys undertaken for the Plowden Committee on primary school children[1] collected a wealth of information on children, teachers and parents and used sophisticated analytical techniques to predict pupil attainment. By contrast, the small-scale survey of Jackson and Marsden[2] involved a detailed study of the backgrounds and values of 88 working-class adults who had achieved success through selective secondary education.

Whether the survey is large-scale and undertaken by some governmental bureau or small-scale and carried out by the lone researcher, the collection of information typically involves one or more of the following data-gathering techniques: structured or semi-structured interviews, self-completion or postal questionnaires, standardized tests of attainment or performance, and attitude scales. Typically, too, surveys proceed through well-defined stages, though not every stage outlined in Box 4.1 is required for the successful completion of a survey.

We begin with a consideration of some necessary preliminaries to survey planning before going on to outline a variety of sampling

Box 4.1   Stages in the planning of a survey

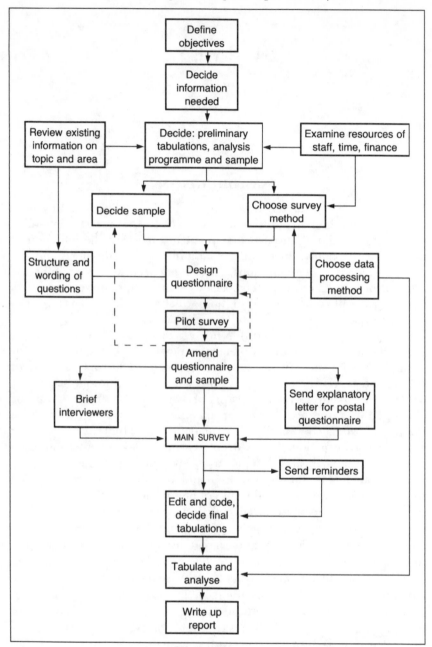

Source: Adapted from Davidson, 1970[3]

strategies that are used in survey research. We then discuss the construction and sequencing of questions in both interviews and questionnaires, prior to a detailed examination of the postal questionnaire as a survey technique. Finally, we identify some of the procedures involved in processing and analysing the results of survey research. Our discussion follows the sequential stages in survey design set out in Box 4.1.

SOME PRELIMINARY CONSIDERATIONS

Three prerequisites to the design of any survey are the specification of the exact purpose of the enquiry; the population on which it is to focus; and the resources that are available. Hoinville and Jowell's[4] consideration of each of these key factors in survey planning can be illustrated in relation to the design of an educational enquiry.

The purpose of the enquiry

First, a survey's general purpose must be translated into a specific central aim. Thus, 'to explore teachers' views about in-service work' is somewhat nebulous, whereas 'to obtain a detailed description of primary and secondary teachers' priorities in the provision of in-service education courses' is reasonably specific.

Having decided upon and specified the primary objective of the survey, the second phase of the planning involves the identification and itemizing of subsidiary topics that relate to its central purpose. In our example, subsidiary issues might well include: the types of courses required; the content of courses; the location of courses; the timing of courses; the design of courses; and the financing of courses.

The third phase follows the identification and itemization of subsidiary topics and involves formulating specific information requirements relating to each of these issues. For example, with respect to the type of courses required, detailed information would be needed about the duration of courses (one meeting, several meetings, a week, a month, a term or a year), the status of courses (non-award bearing, award bearing, with certificate, diploma, degree granted by college or university), the orientation of courses (theoretically-oriented involving lectures, readings, etc., or practically-oriented involving workshops and the production of curriculum materials).

As these details unfold, note Hoinville and Jowell, consideration would have to be given to the most appropriate ways of collecting items of information (interviews with selected teachers, postal questionnaires to selected schools, etc.).

The population upon which the survey is focused

The second prerequisite to survey design, the specification of the population to which the enquiry is addressed, affects decisions that researchers must make both about sampling and resources. In our hypothetical survey of in-service requirements, for example, we might specify the population as 'those primary and secondary teachers employed in schools within a 30-mile radius of Loughborough University of Technology'. In this case, the population is readily identifiable and, given sufficient resources to contact every member of the designated group, sampling decisions do not arise. Things are rarely so straightforward, however. Often the criteria by which populations are specified ('severely handicapped', 'under-achievers', 'intending teachers' or 'highly anxious') are difficult to operationalize. Populations, moreover, vary considerably in their accessibility; pupils and student teachers are relatively easy to survey, gypsy children and headteachers are more elusive. More importantly, in a large survey researchers usually draw a sample from the population to be studied; rarely do they attempt to contact every member. We deal with the question of sampling shortly.

The resources available

The third important factor in designing and planning a survey is the financial cost. Sample surveys are labour-intensive (see Davidson, 1970), the largest single expenditure being the fieldwork where costs arise out of the interviewing time, travel time and transport claims of the interviewers themselves. There are additional demands on the survey budget. Training and supervising the panel of interviewers can often be as expensive as the costs incurred during the time that they actually spend in the field. Questionnaire construction, piloting, printing, posting, coding, together with computer programming – all eat into financial resources.

Proposals from intending education researchers seeking governmental or private funding are often weakest in the amount of time and thought devoted to a detailed planning of the financial implications of the projected enquiries. (In this chapter we confine ourselves from this point to a discussion of surveys based on self-completion questionnaires. A full account of the interview as a research technique is given in Chapter 13.)

SURVEY SAMPLING

Because questions to do with sampling arise directly from the second of our preliminary considerations, that is, defining the population upon which the survey is to focus, researchers must take sampling decisions early in the overall planning of a survey (see Box 4.1). We have already seen that due to factors of expense, time and accessibility, it is not always possible or practical to obtain measures from a population. Researchers endeavour therefore to collect information from a smaller group or subset of the population in such a way that the knowledge gained is representative of the total population under study. This smaller group or subset is a 'sample'. Notice how competent researchers start with the total population and work down to the sample. By contrast, novices work from the bottom up, that is, they determine the minimum number of respondents needed to conduct a successful survey.[5] However, unless they identify the total population in advance, it is virtually impossible for them to assess how representative the sample is that they have drawn. There are two methods of sampling. One yields probability samples in which, as the term implies, the probability of selection of each respondent is known. The other yields non-probability samples, in which the probability of selection is unknown. We deal first with various methods of probability sampling.[6]

Probability samples

Simple random sampling

In simple random sampling, each member of the population under study has an equal chance of being selected. The method involves selecting at random from a list of the population (a sampling frame) the required number of subjects for the sample. Because of probability and chance, the sample should contain subjects with characteristics similar to the population as a whole: some old, some young, some tall, some short, some fit, some unfit, some rich, some poor, etc. One problem associated with this particular sampling method is that a complete list of the population is needed and this is not always readily available.

Systematic sampling

This method is a modified form of simple random sampling. It involves selecting subjects from a population list in a systematic rather than a random fashion. For example, if from a population of, say, 2,000, a sample of 100 is required, then every twentieth person can be selected. The starting point for the selection is chosen at random.

Stratified sampling

Stratified sampling involves dividing the population into homogeneous groups, each group containing subjects with similar characteristics. For example, group *A* might contain males and group *B*, females. In order to obtain a sample representative of the whole population in terms of sex, a random selection of subjects from group *A* and group *B* must be taken. If needed, the exact proportion of males to females in the whole population can be reflected in the sample.

Cluster sampling

When the population is large and widely dispersed, gathering a simple random sample poses administrative problems. Suppose we want to survey children's fitness levels in a particularly large community. It would be quite impractical randomly to select children and spend an inordinate amount of time travelling about in order to test them. By cluster sampling, we can randomly select a specific number of schools and test all the children in those selected schools.

Stage sampling

Stage sampling is an extension of cluster sampling. It involves selecting the sample in stages, that is, taking samples from samples. Using the large community example referred to earlier, one type of stage sampling might be to select a number of schools at random, and from within each of these schools select a number of classes at random, and from within these classes select a number of pupils.

Non-probability samples

Small-scale surveys often resort to the use of non-probability samples because, despite the disadvantages that arise from their non-representativeness, they are far less complicated to set up, are considerably less expensive, and can prove perfectly adequate where researchers do not intend to generalize their findings beyond the sample in question or where they are simply piloting a survey questionnaire as a prelude to their main study. The chief kinds of non-probability sampling are as follows.

Convenience sampling

Convenience sampling – or as it is sometimes called, accidental sampling – involves choosing the nearest individuals to serve as respondents and continuing that process until the required sample size has been obtained. Captive audiences such as pupils or student teachers often serve as respondents in surveys based upon convenience sampling.

Quota sampling

Quota sampling has been described as the non-probability equivalent of stratified sampling (see Bailey, 1978). It attempts to obtain representatives of the various elements of the total population in the proportions in which they occur there. Thus, researchers interested in race relations in a particular community might set a quota for each ethnic group that is proportionate to its representation in the total population in the area under survey.

Purposive sampling

In purposive sampling, researchers handpick the cases to be included in the sample on the basis of their judgement of their typicality. In this way, they build up a sample that is satisfactory to their specific needs.

Dimensional sampling

Dimensional sampling is simply a further refinement of quota sampling. It involves identifying various factors of interest in a population and obtaining at least one respondent of every combination of those factors. Thus, in the study of race relations to which we referred earlier, within each ethnic group, researchers may wish to distinguish between the attitudes of recent immigrants, those who have been in the country for some period of time, and those members of the ethnic group who were born in Great Britain. Their sampling plan might take the form of a multi-dimensional table with 'ethnic group' across the top and 'length of stay' down the side.

Snowball sampling

Researchers identify a small number of individuals who have the characteristics that they require. These people are then used as informants to identify others who qualify for inclusion and these, in turn, identify yet others – hence the term snowball sampling.

SAMPLE SIZE: AN OVERVIEW

A question that often plagues novice researchers is just how large their samples should be in order to conduct an adequate survey. There is, of course, no clear-cut answer, for the correct sample size depends upon the purpose of the study and the nature of the population under scrutiny. However, it is possible to give some advice on this matter. Thus, a sample size of thirty is held by many to be the minimum number of cases if researchers plan to use some form of statistical analysis on their data, though techniques are available for the analysis of samples below thirty. Of more import to researchers is the need to think out in advance of any data collection the sorts of relationships that they wish to explore within subgroups of their eventual sample. The number of variables researchers set out to control in their analyses and the types of statistical tests they wish to make must inform their decisions about sample size prior to the actual research undertaking.

Sample size: some statistical considerations

As well as the requirement of a minimum number of cases in order to examine relationships within subgroups, researchers must obtain the minimum sample size that will accurately represent the population under survey. Where simple random sampling is used, the sample size needed to reflect the population value of a particular variable depends both upon the size of the population and the amount of heterogeneity of the variable in the population (see Bailey, 1978). Generally, for populations of equal heterogeneity, the larger the population, the larger the sample that must be drawn. For populations of equal size, the greater the heterogeneity on a particular variable, the larger the sample that is needed. To the extent that a sample fails to represent accurately the population under survey, there is sampling error.

SAMPLING ERROR

If many samples are taken from the same population, it is unlikely that they will all have characteristics identical either with each other or with the population. In brief, there will be sampling error (see Cohen and Holliday, 1979). Sampling error is not necessarily the result of mistakes made in sampling procedures. Rather, variations may occur due to the chance selection of different individuals. For example, if we take a large number of samples from the population and measure the mean value of each sample, then the sample means will not be identical. Some will be relatively high, some relatively low, and many will cluster around an average or mean value of the samples. Why should this occur? We can explain the phenomenon by reference to the Central Limit Theorem which is derived from the laws of probability. This states that if random, large samples of equal size are repeatedly drawn from any population, then the means of those samples will be approximately normally distributed. Moreover, the average or mean of the sample means will be approximately the same as the population mean. We show this diagrammatically in Box 4.2.

By drawing a large number of samples of equal size from a population,

Box 4.2 Distribution of sample means showing the spread of a selection of sample means around the population mean

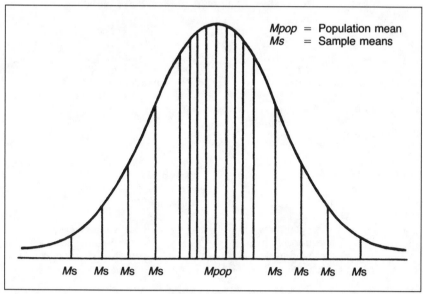

Source: Cohen and Holliday, 1979

we create a sampling distribution. We can calculate the error involved in such sampling. The standard deviation of the theoretical distribution of sample means is a measure of sampling error and is called the standard error of the mean (SE_M). Thus,

$$SE_M = \frac{SD_S}{N}$$

where SD_S = the standard deviation of the sample and
N = the number in the sample

Strictly speaking, the formula for the standard error of the mean is:

$$SE_M = \frac{SD_{pop}}{N}$$

where SD_{pop} = the standard deviation of the population

However, as we are usually unable to ascertain the *SD* of the total population, the standard deviation of the sample is used instead. The

91

Box 4.3   A flow chart technique for question planning

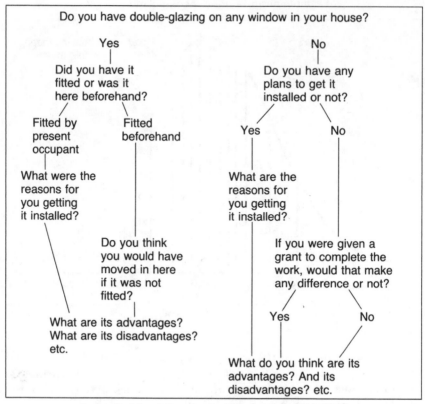

Source: Social and Community Planning Research, 1972[7]

standard error of the mean provides the best estimate of the sampling error. Clearly, the sampling error depends upon the variability (i.e. the heterogeneity) in the population as measured by SD_{pop} as well as the sample size (N). The smaller the SD_{pop}, the smaller the sampling error; the larger the N, the smaller the sampling error. Where the SD_{pop} is very large, then N needs to be very large to counteract it. Where SD_{pop} is very small, then N, too, can be small and still give a reasonably small sampling error.

DESIGNING THE SELF-COMPLETION QUESTIONNAIRE

An ideal questionnaire possesses the same properties as a good law:

It is clear, unambiguous and uniformly workable. Its design must minimize potential errors from respondents . . . and coders. And since people's participation in surveys is voluntary, a question-naire has to help in engaging their interest, encouraging their co-operation, and eliciting answers as close as possible to the truth.

(Davidson, 1970)

With these qualities in mind, we turn to the problem of designing a self-completion questionnaire. Having identified subsidiary topics of interest in their survey and itemized specific information requirements relating to them, the researchers' task now involves the structure of the questionnaire itself.

At this preliminary stage of design, it can sometimes be helpful to use a flow chart technique to plan the sequencing of questions. In this way, researchers are able to anticipate the type and range of responses that their questions are likely to elicit. In Box 4.3, we illustrate a flow chart employed in a commercial survey based upon an interview schedule, though the application of the method to a self-completion questionnaire is self-evident.

Using a flow chart in questionnaire design brings home to researchers the paramount importance of the question in any form of survey work. Whole books have been written on the art of questioning. The brief space we are able to allot to this vital topic in no way reflects the priority that should be given to the framing and testing of questions before any survey is undertaken. We discuss various forms of questions (structured, unstructured and the funnel varieties) in Chapter 13 and illustrate some ways in which respondents may record their answers. For the present, we identify some pitfalls in question construction.

Questions to avoid

Avoid leading questions, that is, questions which are worded (or their response categories presented) in such a way as to suggest to respondents that there is only one acceptable answer. For example:

Do you prefer abstract, academic-type courses, or down-to-earth, practical courses that have some pay-off in your day-to-day teaching?

Avoid highbrow questions even with sophisticated respondents. For example:

What particular aspects of the current positivistic/interpretive debate would you like to see reflected in a course of developmental psychology aimed at a teacher audience?

Where the sample being surveyed is representative of the whole adult population, misunderstandings of what researchers take to be clear, unambiguous language are commonplace.

Avoid complex questions. For example:

Would you prefer a short, non-award bearing course (3,4 or 5 sessions) with part-day release (e.g. Wednesday afternoons) and one evening per week attendance with financial reimbursement for travel, or a longer, non-award bearing course (6, 7 or 8 sessions) with full-day release, or the whole course designed on part-day release without evening attendance?

Avoid irritating questions or instructions. For example:

Have you ever attended an in-service course of any kind during your entire teaching career?

If you are over 40, and have never attended an in-service course, put one tick in the box marked *NEVER* and another in the box marked *OLD*.

Avoid questions that use negatives. For example:

How strongly do you feel that no teacher should enrol on the in-service, award-bearing course who has not completed at least two years full-time teaching?

Avoid open-ended questions on self-completion questionnaires. Because self-completion questionnaires cannot probe respondents to find out just what they mean by particular responses, open-ended questions are a less satisfactory way of eliciting information. (This caution does not hold in the interview situation, however.) Open-ended questions, moreover, are too demanding of most respondents' time. Nothing can be more off-putting than the following format:

Use pages 5, 6 and 7 respectively to respond to each of the questions about your attitudes to in-service courses in general and your beliefs about their value in the professional life of the serving teacher.

On a more positive note, Selltiz and her associates have provided a fairly exhaustive guide to researchers in constructing their questionnaires which we summarize in Box 4.4.

POSTAL QUESTIONNAIRES

Frequently, the postal questionnaire is the best form of survey in an educational enquiry. Take, for example, the researcher intent on investigating the adoption and use made of a new curriculum series in secondary schools in England and Wales. An interview survey based upon some sampling of the population of schools would be both expensive and time-consuming. A postal questionnaire, on the other

Box 4.4 A guide for questionnaire construction

A. *Decisions about question content*
   1. Is the question necessary? Just how will it be useful?
   2. Are several questions needed on the subject matter of this question?
   3. Do respondents have the information necessary to answer the question?
   4. Does the question need to be more concrete, specific and closely related to the respondent's personal experience?
   5. Is the question content sufficiently general and free from spurious concreteness and specificity?
   6. Do the replies express general attitudes and only seem to be as specific as they sound?
   7. Is the question content biased or loaded in one direction, without accompanying questions to balance the emphasis?
   8. Will the respondents give the information that is asked for?
B. *Decisions about question wording*
   1. Can the question be misunderstood? Does it contain difficult or unclear phraseology?
   2. Does the question adequately express the alternative with respect to the point?
   3. Is the question misleading because of unstated assumptions or unseen implications?
   4. Is the wording biased? Is it emotionally loaded or slanted towards a particular kind of answer?
   5. Is the question wording likely to be objectionable to the respondent in any way?
   6. Would a more personalized wording of the question produce better results?
   7. Can the question be better asked in a more direct or a more indirect form?
C. *Decisions about form of response to the question*
   1. Can the question best be asked in a form calling for check answer (or short answer of a word or two, or a number), free answer or check answer with follow-up answer?
   2. If a check answer is used, which is the best type for this question – dichotomous, multiple-choice ('cafeteria' question), or scale?
   3. If a checklist is used, does it cover adequately all the significant alternatives without overlapping and in a defensible order? Is it of reasonable length? Is the wording of items impartial and balanced?
   4. Is the form of response easy, definite, uniform and adequate for the purpose?
D. *Decisions about the place of the question in the sequence*
   1. Is the answer to the question likely to be influenced by the content of preceding questions?
   2. Is the question led up to in a natural way? Is it in correct psychological order?
   3. Does the question come too early or too late from the point of view of arousing interest and receiving sufficient attention, avoiding resistance, and so on?

Source: From Selltiz *et al.*, 1976[8]

hand, would have several distinct advantages. Moreover, given the usual constraints over finance and resources, it might well prove the only viable way of carrying through such an enquiry.

What evidence we have about the advantages and disadvantages of postal surveys derives from settings other than the educational. Many of the findings, however, have relevance to the educational researcher. In Box 13.1 (p. 272), we summarize the relative merits of self-completion questionnaires as compared with interview procedures. Here, we focus upon some of the ways in which educational researchers can maximize the response level that they obtain when using postal surveys.

Research shows that a number of myths about postal questionnaires are not borne out by the evidence (see Hoinville and Jowell, 1978). Response levels to postal surveys are not invariably less than those obtained by interview procedures; frequently they equal, and in some cases surpass, those achieved in interviews. Nor does the questionnaire necessarily have to be short in order to obtain a satisfactory response level. With sophisticated respondents, for example, a short questionnaire might appear to trivialize complex issues with which they are familiar. Hoinville and Jowell identify a number of factors in securing a good response rate to a postal questionnaire.

General

The appearance of the questionnaire is vitally important. It must look easy and attractive. A compressed layout is uninviting; a larger questionnaire with plenty of space for questions and answers is more encouraging to respondents.

Clarity of wording and simplicity of design are essential. Clear instructions should guide respondents – 'Put a tick', for example, invites participation, whereas complicated instructions and complex procedures intimidate respondents.

Arrange the contents of the questionnaire in such a way as to maximize co-operation. For example, include questions that are likely to be of general interest. Make sure that questions which appear early in the format do not suggest to respondents that the enquiry is not intended for them. Intersperse attitude questions throughout the schedule to allow respondents to air their views rather than merely describe their behaviour. Such questions relieve boredom and frustration as well as providing valuable information in the process.

Design and layout

Coloured pages can help to clarify the overall structure of the questionnaire and the use of different colours for instructions can assist respondents.

Putting ticks in boxes by way of answering a questionnaire is familiar to most respondents whereas requests to circle precoded numbers at the right-hand side of the questionnaire can be a source of confusion and error.

The practice of sublettering questions (e.g. Q9 (a) (b) (c) . . .) is a useful technique for grouping together questions to do with a specific issue. It is also a way of making the questionnaire look smaller than it actually is!

Repeating instructions as often as necessary is good practice in a postal questionnaire. Since everything hinges on respondents knowing exactly what is required of them, clear, unambiguous instructions, boldly and attractively displayed, are essential.

Completing a questionnaire can be seen as a learning process in which respondents become more at home with the task as they proceed. Initial questions should therefore be simple, have high interest value, and encourage participation. The middle section of the questionnaire should contain the difficult questions; the last few questions should be of high interest in order to encourage respondents to return the completed schedule.

It bears repeating that the wording of the self-completion questionnaire is of paramount importance and that pretesting is crucial to its success.

Finally, a brief note at the very end of the questionnaire can: ask respondents to check that no answer has been inadvertently missed out; solicit an early return of the completed schedule; thank respondents for their participation, and offer to send a short abstract of the major findings when the analysis is completed.

Initial mailing

Use good-quality envelopes, typed and addressed to a named person wherever possible.

Use first-class postage, stamped rather than franked wherever possible.

Enclose a first-class stamped envelope for the respondent's reply.

In surveys of the general population, Thursday is the best day for mailing out; in surveys of organizations, Monday or Tuesday are recommended.

Avoid at all costs a December survey.

Covering letter

The purpose of the covering letter is to indicate the aim of the survey, to convey to respondents its importance, to assure them of confidentiality, and to encourage their replies. With these intentions in mind, the following practices are to be recommended:

The appeal in the covering letter must be tailored to suit the particular audience. Thus, a survey of teachers might stress the importance of the study to the profession as a whole.

Neither the use of prestigious signatories, nor appeals to altruism, nor the addition of handwritten postcripts affect response levels to postal questionnaires.

The name of the sponsor or the organization conducting the survey should appear on the letterhead as well as in the body of the covering letter.

A direct reference should be made to the confidentiality of respondents' answers and the purposes of any serial numbers and codings should be explained.

A presurvey letter advising respondents of the forthcoming questionnaire has been shown to have substantial effect on response rates.

A short covering letter is most effective; aim at no more than one page.

Follow-up letter

Of the four factors that Hoinville and Jowell discuss in connection with maximizing response levels, the follow-up letter has been shown to be the most productive. The following points should be borne in mind in preparing reminder letters:

All of the rules that apply to the covering letter apply even more strongly to the follow-up letter.

The follow-up should re-emphasize the importance of the study and the value of the respondents' participation.

The use of the second person singular, the conveying of an air of disappointment at non-response and some surprise at non-cooperation have been shown to be effective ploys.

Nowhere should the follow-up give the impression that non-response is normal or that numerous non-responses have occurred in the particular study.

The follow-up letter must be accompanied by a further copy of the questionnaire together with a stamped addressed envelope for its return.

Second and third reminder letters suffer from the law of diminishing returns, so how many follow-ups are recommended and what success rates do they achieve? It is difficult to generalize, but the following points are worth bearing in mind. A well-planned postal survey should obtain at least a 40 per cent response rate and with the judicious use of reminders, a 70 per cent to 80 per cent response level should be possible. A preliminary pilot survey is invaluable in that it can indicate the general level of response to be expected. The main survey should generally achieve at least as high as and normally a higher level of return than the pilot enquiry. The Government Social Survey (now the Office of Population Censuses and Surveys) recommends the use of three reminders which, they say, can increase the original return by as much as 30 per cent in surveys of the general public. A typical pattern of responses to the three follow-ups is as follows:

Original despatch	40 per cent
First follow-up	+20 per cent
Second follow-up	+10 per cent
Third follow-up	+ 5 per cent
Total	75 per cent

Incentives

The fourth and final factor in maximizing response rates is the use of incentives. Although the use of incentives is comparatively rare in British surveys, it can substantially reduce non-response rates particularly when the chosen incentives accompany the initial mailing rather than being mailed subsequently as rewards for the return of completed schedules. The explanation of the effectiveness of this particular ploy appears to lie in the sense of obligation that is created in the recipient. Care is needed in selecting the most appropriate type of incentive. It should clearly be seen as a token rather than a payment for the respondent's efforts and, according to Hoinville and Jowell, should be as neutral as possible. In this respect, they suggest that books of postage stamps or ballpoint pens are cheap, easily packaged in the questionnaire envelopes, and appropriate to the task required of the respondent.

The preparation of a flow chart can help the researcher to plan the timing and the sequencing of the various parts of a postal survey. One such flow chart suggested by Hoinville and Jowell is shown in Box 4.5. The researcher might wish to add a chronological chart alongside it to help plan the exact timing of the events shown here.

Validity

Our discussion, so far, has concentrated on ways of increasing the response rate of postal questionnaires; we have said nothing yet about the validity of this particular survey technique.

Validity of postal questionnaires can be seen from two viewpoints according to Belson (1986).[9] First, whether respondents who complete questionnaires do so accurately and second, whether those who fail to

Box 4.5 A flow chart for the planning of a postal survey

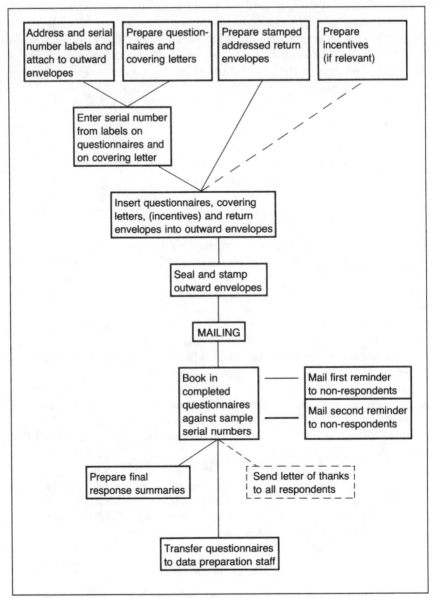

Source: Hoinville and Jowell, 1978

return their questionnaires would have given the same distribution of answers as did the returnees.

The question of accuracy can be checked by means of the intensive interview method, a technique consisting of twelve principal tactics that include

100

familiarization, temporal reconstruction, probing and challenging. The interested reader should consult Belson (1986: pp. 35–8).

The problem of non-response (the issue of 'volunteer bias' as Belson calls it) can, in part, be checked on and controlled for, particularly when the postal questionnaire is sent out on a continuous basis. It involves follow-up contact with non-respondents by means of interviewers trained to secure interviews with such people. A comparison is then made between the replies of respondents and non-respondents.

PROCESSING SURVEY DATA

Let us assume that researchers have followed the advice we have given about the planning of postal questionnaires and have secured a high response rate to their surveys. Their task is now to reduce the mass of data they have obtained to a form suitable for analysis. 'Data reduction', as the process is called, generally consists of coding data in preparation for analysis – by hand in the case of small surveys; by computers when numbers are larger. First, however, prior to coding, the questionnaires have to be checked. This task is referred to as 'editing'.

Editing

Editing interview schedules or self-completion questionnaires is inten-ded to identify and eliminate errors made by interviewers or respon-dents. (In addition to the clerical editing that we discuss in this section, editing checks are also performed by the computer. For an account of computer-run structure checks and valid coding range checks, see Hoinville and Jowell (1978) pp. 150–5. Moser and Kalton[11] point to three central tasks in editing:

1 *Completeness*: a check is made that there is an answer to every question. In most surveys, interviewers are required to record an answer to every question (a 'not applicable' category always being available). Missing answers can sometimes be cross-checked from other sections of the survey. At worst, respondents can be contacted again to supply the missing information.
2 *Accuracy*: as far as is possible a check is made that all questions are answered accurately. Inaccuracies arise out of carelessness on the part of either interviewers or respondents. Sometimes a deliberate attempt is made to mislead. A tick in the wrong box, a ring round the wrong code, an error in simple arithmetic – all can reduce the validity of the data unless they are picked up in the editing process.
3 *Uniformity*: a check is made that interviewers have interpreted instruc-tions and questions uniformly. Sometimes the failure to give explicit

instructions over the interpretation of respondents' replies leads to interviewers recording the same answer in a variety of answer codes instead of one. A check on uniformity can help eradicate this source of error.

Coding

The primary task of data reduction is coding, that is, assigning a code number to each answer to a survey question. Of course, not all answers to survey questions can be reduced to code numbers. Many open-ended questions, for example, are not reducible in this way for computer analysis. Coding can be built into the construction of the questionnaire itself. In this case, we talk of precoded answers. Where coding is developed after the questionnaire has been administered and answered by respondents, we refer to post-coded answers. Precoding is appropriate for closed-ended questions – male 1, female 0, for example; or single 0, married 1, separated 2, divorced 3. For questions such as those whose answer categories are known in advance, a coding frame is generally developed before the interviewing commences so that it can be printed into the questionnaire itself. For open-ended questions (Why did you choose this particular in-service course rather than XYZ?), a coding frame has to be devised after the completion of the questionnaire. This is best done by taking a random sample of the questionnaires (10 per cent or more, time permitting) and generating a frequency tally of the range of responses as a preliminary to coding classification. Having devised the coding frame, the researcher can make a further check on its validity by using it to code up a further sample of the questionnaires. It is vital to get coding frames right from the outset – extending them or making alterations at a later point in the study is both expensive and wearisome.

SURVEY RESEARCH IN EDUCATION: TWO EXAMPLES

We have selected to describe briefly two educational issues in order to illustrate the skill and attention that researchers must give to the preparation and presentation of survey questionnaires.

The first, by Belson and his associates (1975)[10] sought to conceive and construct a measure of theft behaviour for use with a sample of 1425 boys aged between 13 and 16 years. The account of the development of procedures for eliciting information from juveniles about the nature of their thieving warrants close and careful scrutiny. Box 4.6 summarizes the steps taken during the course of the research.

Our second example of a survey involved the total student teacher population of a University Faculty of Education, some 787 men and

Box 4.6   A study of stealing

1. A comprehensive review of the criminological and non-criminological literature was undertaken for leads on technique, format and administration of elicitation procedures.
2. An explanatory study involving intensive interviews with boys was carried out to identify barriers to respondents giving accurate information about their stealing. Findings relating to facilitating and inhibiting factors were then employed in what Belson terms 'a process of progressive modification' to construct a first version of the elicitation procedure.
3. During the first run of the elicitation interview careful attention was paid to factors such as the sample, appointment procedures, location of interviews, selection and training of interviewers, the wording and presentation of the questions etc.
4. Following the first trial form of the elicitation procedure, further progressive modifications were made to the techniques particularly in respect of the form and sequencing of questions and the use of card sort routines and rules for sorting.
5. The modifications of the initial form of the eliciting procedure were then subject to further scrutiny and additions such as, for example, the inclusion of a 'pretending game' (a re-sorting technique) to explore those who selected NEVER cards.
6. All in all, the progressive modification sequence was continued on, to a total of *seven* cycles before the full scale investigation was undertaken.

Source: Belson, 1975

women in all. The research was inspired by some critical remarks by the then Secretary of State for Education concerning teacher training and his intention to increase substantially the amount of time students were to spend in schools rather than in college. Hannan and Newby, the investigators, decided to seek the views of students about these proposed changes.[12]

Of the 787 students contacted, 358 completed the twelve-item questionnaire, a response rate of almost 46 per cent, not atypical for this method of data collection.[13] Both four-year B.Ed and one-year PGCE students were included in the sample. Inter alia, the survey questionnaire put some of the Secretary of State's proposals to the student body. Their views on one of his suggestions are set out in Box 4.7. The data show that a substantial majority of students pursuing both B.Ed. and PGCE routes to teacher status (some 73 per cent overall) were opposed to the Secretary of State's proposal to give schools, rather than higher education institutions, the lead in the teacher training process. Moreover, a close examination of the frequencies of the responses in Box 4.7 suggests differences of perception between PGCE students and B.Ed. students as a whole, and changing weights of rejection within the B.Ed. students when differentiated by year of training. The final question of

103

Box 4.7　An analysis of student teachers' views on proposed changes in their form of training

Item　The Secretary of State's plans seem to favour a form of school-based training in which the school and its teachers are in the lead in the whole of the training process, from the initial design of the course through to the assessment of the performance of the individual student.
What is your view of such an arrangement?

1 = very good idea; *2* = quite a good idea; *3* = don't know; *4* = don't mind; *5* = not a very good idea; *6* = very bad idea; *7* = not answered

Course and year	Responses							
	1	*2*	*3*	*4*	*5*	*6*	*7*	Row Total
PGCE	0	9	3	0	22	7	0	(41)
B Ed Year 1	6	17	9	1	64	15	0	(112)
B Ed Year 2	2	17	7	0	40	10	0	(76)
B Ed Year 3	2	13	3	0	28	16	0	(62)
B Ed Year 4	0	4	2	0	30	29	2	(67)
Totals	10	60	24	1	184	77	2	(358)
(Percentages)	2.8	16.8	6.7	0.3	51.4	21.5	0.6	(100)

Source: Adapted from Hannan and Newby[12]

the survey elicited a wealth of student comment that assisted the researchers in 'fleshing out' the bland statistics of the previous eleven questionnaire items.

CONCLUSION

In conclusion, we suggest that this chapter be studied alongside Chapter 13, which deals with interviews and interviewing.

REFERENCES AND NOTES

1 Central Advisory Council for Education, *Children and their Primary Schools* (HMSO, London, 1967).
2 Jackson, B. and Marsden, D., *Education and the Working Class* (Routledge & Kegan Paul, London, 1962).
3 Davidson, J., *Outdoor Recreation Surveys: The Design and Use of Questionnaires for Site Surveys* (Countryside Commission, London, 1970).
4 Hoinville, G. and Jowell, R., *Survey Research Practice* (Heinemann Educational Books, London, 1978).
5 Bailey, K.D., *Methods of Social Research* (Collier–Macmillan, London, 1978).
6 Cohen, L., and Holliday, M., *Statistics for Education and Physical Education* (Harper & Row, London, 1979).

7 Social and Community Planning Research, *Questionnaire Design Manual No. 5* (London: 16 Duncan Terrace, N1 8BZ, 1972).

8 Selltiz, C., Wrightsman, L.S. and Cook, S.W., *Research Methods in Social Relations* (Holt, Rinehart & Winston, New York, 1976).

9 Belson, W.A., *Validity in Survey Research* (Gower Publishing Co., Aldershot, 1986).

10 Belson, W.A., *Juvenile Theft: Causal Factors* (Harper & Row, London, 1975).

11 Moser, C.A. and Kalton, G., *Survey Methods in Social Investigation* (Heinemann Educational Books, London, 1977).

12 Hannan, A. and Newby, M., 'Student teacher and headteacher views on current provision and proposals for the future of Initial Teacher Education for primary schools', Rolle Faculty of Education, University of Plymouth, July 1992, (mimeo.).

13 The authors are right to be concerned with the fact that over half of the student population failed to take part in the survey. 'It is likely', they observe, 'that those who did respond were those who felt most strongly, one way or the other, with respect to the issues raised and the questions posed.' This may well have been the case. None the less, no attempt was made to follow up non-respondents (see Hannan and Newby, 1992). See p. 98 on non-respondents.

105

5

CASE STUDIES

INTRODUCTION

How can knowledge of the ways in which children learn and the means by which schools achieve their goals be verified, built upon and extended? This is a central question for educational research. The problem of verification and cumulation of educational knowledge is implicit in our discussion of the nature of educational enquiry in the opening chapter of the book. There, we outline two broad approaches to educational research. The first, based on the scientific paradigm, rests upon the creation of theoretical frameworks that can be tested by experimentation, replication and refinement. We illustrate this approach in Chapter 8. Against this scientific, experimental paradigm, we posit an alternative perspective which we describe as interpretive and subjective, a focus we hasten to add that should be seen as complementing rather than competing with the experimental stance.

In this chapter, although our presentation emphasizes the interpretive, subjective dimensions of educational phenomena that are best explored by case study methods, we balance this with examples of quantitative case study research. Our broad treatment of case study techniques follows directly from a typology of observation studies that we develop shortly. We begin with a brief description of the case study itself.

THE CASE STUDY

Unlike the experimenter who manipulates variables to determine their causal significance or the surveyor who asks standardized questions of large, representative samples of individuals, the case study researcher typically observes the characteristics of an individual unit – a child, a clique, a class, a school or a community. The purpose of such observation is to probe deeply and to analyse intensively the multifarious phenomena that constitute the life cycle of the unit with a view to

106

establishing generalizations about the wider population to which that unit belongs.

Present antipathy towards the statistical–experimental paradigm has created something of a boom industry in case study research. Delinquents,[1] dropouts[2] and drug-users[3] to say nothing of studies of all types of schools,[4] attest to the wide use of the case study in contemporary social science and educational research. Such wide use is marked by an equally diverse range of techniques employed in the collection and analysis of both qualitative and quantitative data. Whatever the problem or the approach, at the heart of every case study lies a method of observation.

In this chapter, we discuss six educational case studies. They are chosen to illustrate the use of a particular style of observation within a particular observational setting. In Box 5.1, we set out a typology of observation studies on the basis of which our six examples are selected.

There are two principal types of observation – participant observation and non-participant observation. In the former, observers engage in the very activities they set out to observe. Often, their 'cover' is so complete that as far as the other participants are concerned, they are simply one of the group. In the case of Patrick for example, born and bred in Glasgow, his researcher role remained hidden from the members of the Glasgow gang in whose activities he participated for a period of four months (see Patrick, 1973). Such complete anonymity is not always possible, however. Thus in Parker's study of downtown Liverpool adolescents, it was generally known that the researcher was waiting to take up a post at the university. In the meantime, 'knocking around' during the day with the lads and frequenting their pub at night rapidly established that he was 'OK'.

> I was a drinker, a hanger-arounder, and had been tested in illegal 'business' matters and could be relied on to say nothing since I 'knew the score'.
>
> (Parker, 1974)

Cover is not necessarily a prerequisite of participant observation. In an intensive study of a small group of working-class boys during their last two years at school and their first months in employment, Willis[5] attended all the different subject classes at school – 'not as a teacher, but as a member of the class' – and worked alongside each boy in industry for a short period.

Non-participant observers, on the other hand, stand aloof from the group activities they are investigating and eschew group membership – no great difficulty for King, an adult observer in infant classrooms. Listen to him recounting how he firmly established his non-participant status with young children:

107

Box 5.1 A typology of observation studies

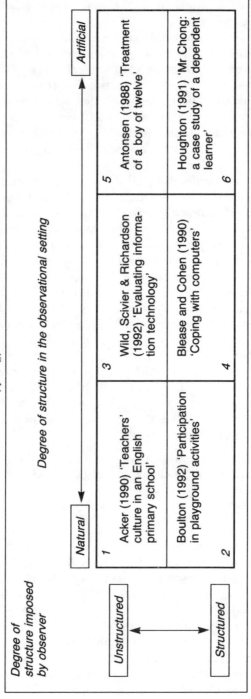

Source: Adapted from Bailey, 1978[6]

I rapidly learnt that children in infants' classrooms define any adult as another teacher or teacher surrogate. To avoid being engaged in conversation, being asked to spell words or admire pictures, I evolved the following technique.

To begin with, I kept standing so that physical height created social distance. . . . Next, I did not show immediate interest in what the children were doing, or talk to them. When I was talked to I smiled politely and if necessary I referred the child asking a question to the teacher. Most importantly, I avoided eye contact: if you do not look you will not be seen.

(King, 1979)

The best illustration of the non-participant observer role is perhaps the case of the researcher sitting at the back of a classroom coding up every three seconds the verbal exchanges between teacher and pupils by means of a structured set of observational categories.

It is frequently the case that the type of observation undertaken by the researcher is associated with the type of setting in which the research takes place. In Box 5.1 we identify a continuum of settings ranging from the 'artificial' environments of the counsellor's and the therapist's clinics (Cell 5 and 6) to the 'natural' environments of school classrooms, staffrooms and playgrounds (Cells 1 and 2). Because our continuum is crude and arbitrary we are at liberty to locate studies of an information technology audit and computer usage (Cells 3 and 4) somewhere between the 'artificial' and the 'natural' poles.

Although in theory each of the six examples of case studies in Box 5.1 could have been undertaken either as a participant or as a non-participant observation study, a number of factors intrude to make one or other of the observational strategies the dominant mode of enquiry in a particular type of setting. Bailey explains as follows:

In a natural setting it is difficult for the researcher who wishes to be covert not to act as a participant. If the researcher does not participate, there is little to explain his presence, as he is very obvious to the actual participants. . . . Most studies in a natural setting are unstructured participant observation studies. . . . Much the opposite is true in an artificial environment. Since there is no natural setting, in a sense none of the persons being studied are really participants of long standing, and thus may accept a non-participant observer more readily. . . . Laboratory settings also enable a non-participant observer to use sophisticated equipment such as videotape and tape recordings. . . . Thus most studies in an artificial laboratory setting will be structured and will be non-participant studies.

(Bailey, 1978)[6]

What we are saying is that the unstructured, ethnographic account of teachers' work (Cell 1) is the most typical method of observation in the natural surroundings of the school in which that study was conducted. Similarly, the structured inventories of study habits and personality employed in the study of Mr Chong (Cell 6) reflect a common approach in the artificial setting of a counsellor's office.

WHY PARTICIPANT OBSERVATION?

The current vogue enjoyed by the case study conducted on participant observation lines is not difficult to account for. This form of research is eminently suitable to many of the problems that the educational investigator faces.

The natural scientist, Schutz points out, explores a field that means nothing to the molecules, atoms and electrons therein.[7] By contrast, the subject matter of the world in which the educational researcher is interested is composed of people and is essentially meaningful. That world is subjectively structured, possessing particular meanings for its inhabitants. The task of the educational investigator is very often to explain the means by which an orderly social world is established and maintained in terms of its shared meanings. How do participant observation techniques assist the researcher in this task? Bailey (1978) identifies some inherent advantages in the participant observation approach:

1 Observation studies are superior to experiments and surveys when data are being collected on non-verbal behaviour.
2 In observation studies, investigators are able to discern ongoing behaviour as it occurs and are able to make appropriate notes about its salient features.
3 Because case study observations take place over an extended period of time, researchers can develop more intimate and informal relationships with those they are observing, generally in more natural environments than those in which experiments and surveys are conducted.
4 Case study observations are less reactive than other types of data-gathering methods. For example, in laboratory-based experiments and in surveys that depend upon verbal responses to structured questions, bias can be introduced in the very data that researchers are attempting to study.

On the other hand, participant observation studies are not without their critics.[8] The accounts that typically emerge from participant observations are often described as subjective, biased, impressionistic, idiosyncratic and lacking in the precise quantifiable measures that are the hallmark of survey research and experimentation. Whilst it is probably true that nothing can give better insight into the life of a gang of juvenile delinquents than going to live with them for an extended period of time, critics of participant observation studies will point to the dangers of 'going native' as a result of playing a role within such a group. How do we know that observers do not lose their perspective and become blind to the peculiarities that they are supposed to be investigating?

These criticisms raise questions about two types of validity in observation-based research. In effect, comments about the subjective and idiosyncratic nature of the participant observation study are to do with its external validity. How do we know that the results of this one piece of research are applicable to other situations? Fears that observers' judgement will be affected by their close involvement in the group relate to the internal validity of the method. How do we know that the results of this one piece of research represent the real thing, the genuine product? In Chapter 4, p. 89 we refer to a number of techniques (quota sampling, snowball sampling, purposive sampling) that researchers employ as a way of checking on the representativeness of the events that they observe and of cross-checking their interpretations of the meanings of those events (see also the discussion in Chapter 10). We can best illustrate the concern of participant observers for the validity of their data by giving a brief outline of a typical strategy in participant observation research. Denzin uses the term 'analytical induction' to describe the broad strategy of participant observation that is set out in Box 5.2.

RECORDING OBSERVATIONS

I filled thirty-two notebooks with about half a million words of notes made during nearly six hundred hours [of observation].

(King, 1979)

Box 5.2   Steps in participant observation

1. A rough definition of the phenomenon is formulated.
2. A hypothetical explanation of that phenomenon is formulated.
3. One case is studied in the light of the hypothesis, with the object of determining whether or not the hypothesis fits the facts in that case.
4. If the hypothesis does not fit the facts, either the hypothesis is reformulated or the phenomenon to be explained is redefined so that the case is excluded.
5. Practical certainty may be attained after a small number of cases has been examined, but the discovery of negative cases disproves the explanation and requires a reformulation.
6. This procedure of examining cases, redefining the phenomenon, and reformulating the hypothesis is continued until a universal relationship is established, each negative case calling for a redefinition of a reformulation.

Source: Denzin, 1970[9]

Box 5.3 Field notes in observation studies

1. Record the notes as quickly as possible after observation, since the quantity of information forgotten is very slight over a short period of time but accelerates quickly as more time passes.
2. Discipline yourself to write notes quickly and reconcile yourself to the fact that although it may seem ironic, recording of field notes can be expected to take as long as is spent in actual observation.
3. Dictating rather than writing is acceptable if one can afford it, but writing has the advantage of stimulating thought.
4. Typing field notes is vastly preferable to handwriting because it is faster and easier to read, especially when making multiple copies.
5. It is advisable to make at least two copies of field notes and preferable to type on a master for reproduction. One original copy is retained for reference and other copies can be used as rough draught to be cut up, reorganized and rewritten.
6. The notes ought to be full enough adequately to summon up for one again, months later, a reasonably vivid picture of any described event. This probably means that one ought to be writing up, at the very minimum, at least a couple of single space typed pages for every hour of observation.

Source: Lofland, 1971

The recording of observations is a frequent source of concern to inexperienced case study researchers. How much ought to be recorded? In what form should the recordings be made? What does one do with the mass of recorded data? Lofland gives a number of useful suggestions about collecting field notes which are summarized in Box 5.3.[10]

The sort of note-taking recommended by Lofland and actually undertaken by King (1979) and Wolcott (1973)[11] in their ethnographic accounts grows out of the nature of the unstructured observation study. Note-taking, confessed Wolcott, helped him fight the acute boredom that he sometimes felt when observing the interminable meetings that are the daily lot of the school principal. Occasionally, however, a series of events would occur so quickly that Wolcott had time only to make cursory notes which he supplemented later with fuller accounts. One useful tip from this experienced ethnographer is worth noting: never resume your observations until the notes from the preceding observation are complete. There is nothing to be gained merely by your presence as an observer. Until your observations and impressions from one visit are a matter of record, there is little point in returning to the classroom or school and reducing the impact of one set of events by superimposing another and more recent set. Indeed, when to record one's data is but one of a number of practical problems identified by Walker, which are listed in Box 5.4.[12]

Box 5.4   The case study and problems of selection

Among the issues confronting the researcher at the outset of his case study
are the problems of selection. The following questions indicate some of the
obstacles in this respect:

1. How do you get from the initial idea to the working design (from the
   idea to a specification, to usable data)?
2. What do you lose in the process?
3. What unwanted concerns do you take on board as a result?
4. How do you find a site which provides the best location for the design?
5. How do you locate, identify and approach key informants?
6. How they see you creates a context within which you see them. How
   can you handle such social complexities?
7. How do you record evidence? When? How much?
8. How do you file and categorize it?
9. How much time do you give to thinking and reflecting about what you
   are doing?
10. At what points do you show your subject what you are doing?
11. At what points do you give them control over who sees what?
12. Who sees the reports first?

Source: Adapted from Walker, 1980

EDUCATIONAL CASE STUDY EXAMPLES

We turn now to a brief exposition of each of the case study examples
identified in our observation typology in Box 5.1.

Cell 1: Acker – 'Teachers' culture in an English primary school'[13]

At the outset of her study of one inner city primary school's responses
to government legislation directed towards its teachers, Acker describes
her orientation as 'a fairly open-ended search for themes of interest
related to teachers' work', a declaration redolent of Wolcott in his
seminal account, *The Man in the Principal's Office* (1973). There, readers
will recall, Wolcott described his participant observer role as, 'a process
of waiting to be impressed by recurrent themes that reappear in various
contexts'.

During the first seventy hours of her ethnographic study, Acker
adopted a 'waiting role'. Later, some 600 hours were spent with four
teachers involved in a school-based innovation. Observing, interviewing,
engaging in informal social contacts, maintaining a written record of
events and happenings, scrutinizing staff-meeting agenda and minutes,
Acker's investigator role is very reminiscent of Wolcott's tactics as he
shadowed Ed Bell, the school principal, both in the school and in the
local community.

'Searching for themes', and 'waiting to be impressed' do not, of course,

113

imply an atheoretical orientation on the part of researchers. King (1979), it will be remembered, in his study of infant school culture, talked of his 'vaguely anthropological model of trying to understand life in classrooms'. Acker is more explicit. How, she asks, shall we 'conceptualise the process by which [a welter of governmental, educational initiatives] is translated into school practice?' Drawing on the literature of educational innovation, she explores three perspectives (House[14]), the technological, the political, and the cultural, opting for the last as her *modus operandi*. Specifically, Acker proposes, implementing the requirements of the 1988 Education Reform Act in an inner-city school is contingent upon the various teacher cultures that predate and mediate any governmental initiatives. Those teacher cultures influence the 'technical process of implementation and the extent to which teachers define innovations as deskilling or professionalizing their work' (Acker, 1990).

From her participant observation of the warp and weft of everyday life at Hillsview Primary School, Acker charts the changes in teachers' perspectives and practices as they react to legislative requirements governing their work in classrooms. A variety of evidence is adduced to support her interpretation of those changes:

1 Staffroom discussions of the National Curriculum and assessment featured more prominently; discussions became more critical, academic, analytical, reflective.
2 Interviews revealed changes over time in the extent to which people were informed and eager to discuss government initiatives.
3 Staff appointments brought a more cosmopolitan view to their teaching.
4 Staff meeting agenda and the time devoted to certain issues revealed changes of focus; quality of interactions and debate suggested 'bounded professionality' (Nias, 1989).[15]
5 Inquiries were made to the researcher about university courses and applications for Advanced Diploma/MA courses.
6 The acting headteacher's liaisons with other schools included piloting records of achievements and assessment innovations.
7 Changes in role orientation and the stress level of the headteacher; the head's emphasis on reassuring her staff.

Acker concludes her research report with the observation that primary school teachers do perceive a threat in the governmental initiatives and are anxious about their ramifications. They are not, however, experiencing these outside pressures as destructive or deskilling. In part, says Acker, this is because for them, education is a child-centred process rather than a product. They are not simply transmitting a cognitive curriculum.

Cell 2: Boulton – 'Participation in playground activities'[16]

Located in the 'natural settings' of school playgrounds, Boulton's research, in contrast to that of Acker, was predominantly a highly-structured, non-participant observation of children's activities, conducted in eight middle schools over a period of five years.

Eschewing previous studies of playground activities that derive from pupils' accounts of what they do, Boulton was determined to use direct observation, employing what he terms, 'focal individual sampling' as his principal technique of data collection. Focal individual sampling involved the researcher in identifying a target child and observing him/her for the whole duration of a playtime session (on average, 35 minutes), recording that individual's behaviour by means of a running commentary spoken into a portable tape recorder. In this way, data were gathered of what the child was doing, the number and relative age (older, younger, the same age) of male and female playmates. Each observation period began when a target child, selected in a predetermined random order, entered the play area, and terminated at the end of the playground session.

From the transcribed tape recordings, each focal child's activities were classified into discrete behavioural categories, using the classificatory system set out in Box 5.5.

Box 5.5   Molar categories of behaviour

Sociable: child, together with at least one other, engaged in one or more of the following actions that are not part of r/t, role play or a rule game: talk with peer, walk with peer, run with peer, sit with peer, stand with peer, groom peer, swop collector cards with peer.

Rule games: child, together with at least one other, engaged in one of the following rule-governed games, or the preliminaries to a rule-governed game, such as picking sides or deciding on the rules: skipping, french skipping (i.e. with elastic), tiggy, delavio (team chase game), other team chase games with rules, hide and seek, clapping songs, chanting, marbles, rounders, football, queenie-o, queenie-o, who's got the ballie-o? (and other ball games with rules), hopscotch, tennis, cricket.

Rough-and-tumble play: child, together with at least one other, engaged in playful fighting and chasing games without explicit rules (playful fighting and chasing distinguished from aggressive fighting and chasing by means of the criteria outlined by Boulton (1992).

Fantasy play: child, together with at least one other, engaged in a fantasy game in which they take on a non-literal role such as 'He man' or 'Mother'.

Solitary: child alone.

Other: any activity that does not fall into one of the above categories such as child with adult, aggression, play with ball, piggyback, dance.

Source: Boulton, 1992

Analysis of variance techniques were used to explore age and sex differences in the proportion of time that pupils spent on rule games, rough-and-tumble play, sociable activities and solitary play. Thus, older children spent significantly more time than younger children in games involving rules, and younger children spent significantly more time alone than older children. Elsewhere in the study, Boulton computed absolute amounts of time spent in particular playground activities (football, tiggy, skipping, rounders, clapping/singing etc.) and these data were subjected to statistical analysis to reveal, not surprisingly, that 'proportionally more boys than girls engage in football, and proportionally more girls than boys engage in skipping' (Boulton, 1992). Where the research report becomes particularly interesting, in our view, is where Boulton conducted *in situ* interviews with target children in order to ascertain their views as to why, for example, girls and younger boys are excluded from the football games of older boys, and why barriers exist to prevent mixed age and mixed sex playground activities.

Readers may well agree that data such as the following put flesh on bare, statistical bones:

Investigator	Do you ever play football with girls?
Errol	Are you joking, they can't play!
Investigator	How do you know if you never play with them?
Errol (laughing)	Watch this. (*Takes football over to group of 11-year-old girls in his class and, as he rolls it at the feet of one of them, shouts, 'Hey, Lola, kick this'. She attempts to do so, but misses the ball, he retrieves it and comes back.*) See what I mean?
Investigator	She wasn't ready for that. That's not fair.
Errol	OK, I'll do it again. (*Rolls ball at Lola's feet. She makes good contact and kicks ball across playground; her friends give loud cheer.*)
Investigator	That's not a bad kick.
Errol	She was lucky, and in a real game nobody gives you the ball like that. Girls are no good. (*Retrieves ball and goes back to friends.*)

(Boulton, 1992)

Cell 3: Wild, Scivier and Richardson – 'Evaluating information technology'[17]

The purpose of the case study was to evaluate a set of audit tools developed at Loughborough University as a way of identifying facilitators and barriers to the acceptance of new information technology systems in schools. Those IT systems were to do with local management and

116

Box 5.6 Acceptability criteria of IT systems

1	*Ease of use*	assessing the effort, difficulty or strain involved in using the system.
2	*Task match*	assessing the degree to which services from the system match the task needs experienced by the user.
3	*User support*	assessing whether help is available when and where it is needed and in the form that is required by the user.
4	*Perceived consequences*	assessing a range of organizational and job-related aspects which are affected by the computer system.

Source: Adapted from Wild *et al.*, 1992

administration. The audit tools, as a whole, focused on users, tasks, context variables and specific technologies. This particular case study, however, dealt solely with users' acceptance of a new information technology system in sixteen larger secondary schools in an East Midlands Local Education Authority.

Participant observers used interviews in their assessments of the efficacy of the IT system. Those interviews were loosely formulated around four criteria of acceptance set out in Box 5.6. Data generated by the interviews were cast into simple counts in reporting users' views on the success or otherwise of the information technology system. No details were included in the case study report of verbatim commentary by participants. Thus, under the first criterion, *Ease of use* (Box 5.6:1) the majority of users (fourteen out of a total of sixteen) affirmed high levels of satisfaction in using the system. *Task match* (Box 5.6:2) elicited only one expression of concern, whereas *User support* (Box 5.6:3) identified five users who found the system difficult and seven who experienced problems in learning to use the new technology. Under criterion 4 (*Perceived consequences*) only three users' overall ratings indicated that perceived 'costs' outweighed 'benefits'. In addition to these rather crude assessments of the efficacy of the IT system, the audit generated specific and detailed information about areas of risk. These potential dangers were prioritized. Thus, by far the most crucial area of risk was *error handling*. This, the case study revealed, had both immediate and long-term consequences, causing increases in work loads for direct users participating in the study, and, in the longer term, potentially serious problems for LEA auditors working, in all likelihood, with inaccurate accounts. The researchers concluded the case study with the observation that the user-acceptance audit tool could form the basis of a vital evaluation process both for schools and LEAs intent on enhancing the success of IT systems in support of local management of schools.

Box 5.7   COMIC classification of the program, 'The Inhabitant'.

	1	2	3	4	5	6	7	8	9	10	11	12	*Total*
1	0	0	0	0	0	0	0	0	0	0	0	4	4
2	0	1003	563	0	29	10	17	85	205	0	5	14	1931
3	0	417	561	0	21	24	6	125	267	0	1	10	1432
4	0	3	7	6	0	0	0	0	3	0	0	0	19
5	0	44	23	3	107	0	1	6	4	0	0	3	191
6	0	25	9	3	0	28	1	10	20	0	1	1	98
7	0	16	8	0	0	0	9	1	5	0	0	2	41
8	0	122	89	4	12	15	1	681	56	1	3	13	997
9	0	292	148	3	13	18	6	80	277	3	5	7	852
10	0	1	3	0	0	0	0	0	0	5	0	0	9
11	0	4	2	0	0	1	0	3	5	0	13	0	28
12	4	8	9	0	6	2	1	12	12	0	0	105	159

Total number of tallies	5761
	%
Steady-state ratio	48.52
Operating hardware	0.07
Operating keyboard	33.52
Reading screen	24.86
Writing or drawing	0.33
Consulting a book or diagram	3.32
Thinking	1.70
Watching another operator	0.71
Talking to teacher on-task	17.31
Talking to a child on-task	14.79
Talking to teacher off-task	0.16
Talking to a child off-task	0.49
Doing something else	2.76
Total off-task	3.40
Total on-task	96.60

Source: Blease and Cohen, 1990[17]

Cell 4: Blease and Cohen – 'Coping with computers' (an evaluation of the drill and practice computer program, 'The Inhabitant')[18]

In contrast to Wild, Scivier and Richardson's approach, (Cell 3) this case study of school technology was highly structured by its non-participant observers in order to obtain precise, quantitative data on the classroom use of a computer program.

As part of a longitudinal study in primary school classrooms, Blease and Cohen conducted a number of small case studies to identify in some detail, the demands of time made by specific computer software on both teachers and pupils, and the typical profiles of individual behaviour and group interaction that those programs demanded of learners.

Categories for Observing Microcomputer use in Classrooms (COMIC) is an observation instrument specifically designed to describe children's behaviour when working at the computer. It was used in the study to obtain a systematic record of the actions of the keyboard operation both in an individual, one-to-one situation and when groups of children were working together. Twelve categories of behaviour are further differentiated depending on whether they relate to on-task or off-task activities, system management, using software, performing computer-related tasks, interaction with others and performing non-computer-related tasks. Data are treated in exactly the same way as those obtained using the Flanders Interaction Analysis Categories (see Flanders, 1970),[19] and are entered on a twelve by twelve grid to reveal an overall profile of the types and frequencies of behaviour. Box 5.7 sets out the complete matrix and results for 'The Inhabitant', a simulation/drill and practice program. The 5761 tallies represent approximately sixteen hours' observation in all.

Similar COMIC profiles to the one shown in Box 5.7 were undertaken for six other computer programs. Pie charts of summary information made visual comparisons easy and provided some surprises for the investigators. Thus, the proportion of time spent operating the keyboard when using 'The Inhabitant' and another drill and practice program called 'The Explorer' was quite different, even though one might have expected these to be similar (see Box 5.8). However, there was a close parallel in respect of talking to child (on-task), where percentaged times were 'The Inhabitant' (15 per cent) and 'The Explorer' (17 per cent), a finding that might have been expected when one considers the way in which teachers encouraged pairs of children to share ideas and discuss their responses to the programs' demands. Box 5.8 presents a visual comparison of the different demands of the two drill and practice programs.

Cell 5: Antonsen – 'Treatment of a boy of twelve'[20]

Unhappiness and failure at school, lack of friends and playmates characterized Jimmy, a 12-year-old who was referred through a Social Welfare Department for psychotherapy at a Child Psychiatric Unit, with a recommendation that he and his younger sister be removed from their home environment and fostered. The family background was one of parental violence, attempted suicides by the mother and a general neglect of the two children. Antonsen took responsibility for Jimmy at the request of the psychiatrist at a team meeting of clinical staff. From the outset of her sessions with Jimmy in a small classroom at the Clinic, the therapist offered no structural set of categories to the boy as a way of helping him with his difficulties. Rather, Jimmy was the one who structured the situations that governed the on-going therapy. Jimmy

Box 5.8   COMIC classification (visual) of two computer programs

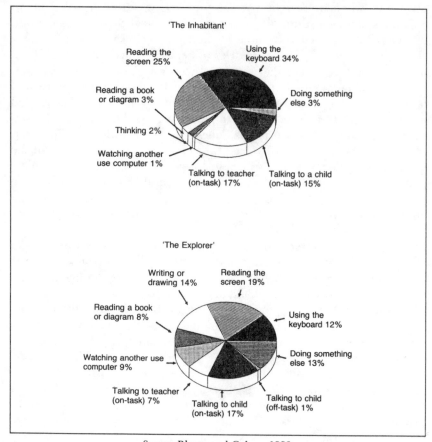

Source: Blease and Cohen, 1990

had expressed great dissatisfaction with his handwriting and had agreed that he would like help to write better. Antonsen's approach was, in her own words, 'to be a mirror' to the boy and thereby to 'make him face the consequences and take responsibility'. The case study is a record of her non-directive approach.

Alongside the work with writing, Antonsen agreed with Jimmy's request to use playroom equipment adjacent to the clinical setting, taking advantage of this opportunity to comment on the boy's activities and to engage with him in some of the play activities. As the therapy continued, Jimmy introduced further opportunities for the therapist to listen to and to react to his concerns. A knife that Jimmy brought to show her had associations with his mother's attempted suicides; problems with his grandmother and aunt about pocket-money and bedtime were explored. At this phase of the therapy treatment, the boy wanted to play card games in which the loser wins. He also wanted to be the teacher, the therapist, and the pupil. In that setting he gave Antonsen very difficult tasks and was quite severe, she reports. This led them to talk about how it felt not to be able to succeed or to influence situations. Jimmy's quarrels and conflicts with other children and his agreeing to talk matters over with the therapist resulted in her drawing the situations involved or writing up a full account of them in the boy's own words which he then corrected until he felt they were an accurate version of events. After a series of such exercises, Antonsen recounts, he began to realize how he could influence social situations.

After a year of therapy, Antonsen believed that the treatment had achieved its goal: 'Jimmy had more self-confidence, self-esteem and self-respect. He was adjusted to his new secondary school, and he could write well.' Sadly, that was not the end of the affair. Interested readers might wish to follow up this case study report, which we have cited as an example of a relatively unstructured encounter in the artificial setting of a psychiatric clinic.

Cell 6: Houghton – 'Mr Chong: a case study of a dependent learner'[21]

Set in a counsellor's office, this case study of an overseas student's dependent approach to learning drew its data from structured sets of test materials and focused interviews with the client, his course tutors and his Director of Studies.

Mr Chong's problems presented themselves in his frequent visits to the English for Academic Purposes tutor (that is, Houghton, the case study researcher) and to individual lecturers in a desperate search for high marks through discovering, in his own words, 'what the lecturers want of us'. To some extent, Houghton opines, this may be particularly problematic for some overseas students like Mr Chong, located in disciplines such as the humanities and social sciences where lecturers emphasize the open-ended nature of many academic issues to the consternation of those students anxious to find one 'correct' answer in order to succeed by 'pleasing the teacher'.

Houghton sees the case study as consisting of four stages:

1 individual sessions in study skills and writing
2 structured explorations of Mr Chong's learning styles, personality and skills in the work environment
3 taped interviews with Mr Chong and interrogation of his responses to the test results obtained in stage 2
4 taped interviews with two of Mr Chong's lecturers and his Director of Studies.

The individual sessions (approximately an hour every two weeks) involved discussions of the client's prepared course texts, help with essay writing, discussions about the minutiae of Mr Chong's courses and discussions about his employment applications. In preparing for stage 3 of the case study, Houghton obtained Mr Chong's responses to three structured inventories, one to do with study habits (Entwistle and Ramsden),[22] one concerned with vocational personality and work environments (Holland)[23] and an identification of team-roles and personality types associated with organizational success (Belbin).[24] On the basis of his responses to these typologies, the researcher explored the implications of the profiles with her client. For example, both agreed that Entwistle and Ramsden's *orientation towards reproduction* best described Mr Chong's ways of learning. On the Holland schedule, Mr Chong saw himself as *intellectual, conventional* and *artistic*, his counsellor agreeing with the first two descriptors. On Belbin's classification of team-roles in an organization, Mr Chong had selected the roles of *company-worker, monitor–evaluator* and *team-worker*, characterized by Belbin as *conservative, dutiful, predictable, hard working* and *self-disciplined*, attributes applicable to Mr Chong, as was that of *monitor–evaluator* – a sober, prudent person, somewhat lacking in inspiration or ability to motivate others.

From her carefully-structured enquiries, Houghton realized that the unique context of Mr Chong's upbringing (not reported here because of pressures of space) helped illuminate his present state of dependency. Interviews with lecturers and the Director of Studies confirmed Mr Chong's difficulties on the management courses for which he was enrolled. We leave interested readers to follow up the full report of Mr Chong and its successful ending. More important are the implications of the study set out by the researcher in her concluding remarks. EAP tutors facing 'dependent' overseas students such as Mr Chong could do well to concentrate on helping them develop group interaction skills. Seminars and group discussions that bring out a variety of viewpoints on a common theme and a variety of solutions to a common problem could be recorded and re-examined to help dependent students see the ways in which successful group interactions in British higher education may differ from those in their home countries. Such an approach would call for close co-operation between academic lecturers and EAP tutors.

CONCLUSION

The different strategies we have illustrated in our six examples of case studies in a variety of educational settings suggest that participant observation is best thought of as a generic term that describes a methodological approach rather than one specific method. What our

Box 5.9   Possible advantages of case study

Case studies have a number of advantages that make them attractive to educational evaluators or researchers. Thus:

1. Case study data, paradoxically, is 'strong in reality' but difficult to organize. In contrast, other research data is often 'weak in reality' but susceptible to ready organization. This strength in reality is because case studies are down-to-earth and attention holding, in harmony with the reader's own experience, and thus provide a 'natural' basis for generalization.
2. Case studies allow generalizations either about an instance or from an instance to a class. Their peculiar strength lies in their attention to the subtlety and complexity of the case in its own right.
3. Case studies recognize the complexity and 'embeddedness' of social truths. By carefully attending to social situations, case studies can represent something of the discrepancies or conflicts between the viewpoints held by participants. The best case studies are capable of offering some support to alternative interpretations.
4. Case studies,[25] considered as products, may form an archive of descriptive material sufficiently rich to admit subsequent reinterpretation. Given the variety and complexity of educational purposes and environments, there is an obvious value in having a data source for researchers and users whose purposes may be different from our own.
5. Case studies are 'a step to action'. They begin in a world of action and contribute to it. Their insights may be directly interpreted and put to use; for staff or individual self-development, for within-institutional feedback; for formative evaluation; and in educational policy making.
6. Case studies present research or evaluation data in a more publicly accessible form than other kinds of research report, although this virtue is to some extent bought at the expense of their length. The language and the form of the presentation is hopefully less esoteric and less dependent on specialized interpretation than conventional research reports. The case study is capable of serving multiple audiences. It reduces the dependence of the reader upon unstated implicit assumptions . . . and makes the research process itself accessible. Case studies, therefore, may contribute towards the 'democratization' of decision-making (and knowledge itself). At its best, they allow readers to judge the implications of a study for themselves.

Source: Adapted from Adelman *et al.*, 1980[26]

examples have shown is that the representativeness of a particular sample often relates to the observational strategy open to the researcher. Generally speaking, the larger the sample, the more representative it is, and the more likely that the observer's role is of a participant nature.

Readers will now have a good idea of the nature and possibilities of case study research and of its particular value to educational researchers. To conclude this chapter, we refer to some of the advantages of this style of research as outlined by Adelman and his colleagues[26] (see Box 5.9).

Indeed, we recommend readers to peruse the whole set of readings from which their paper is drawn.

REFERENCES AND NOTES

1 Patrick, J., *A Glasgow Gang Observed* (Eyre Methuen, London, 1973).
2 Parker, H. J., *View from the Boys* (David & Charles, Newton Abbot, 1974).
3 Young, J., *The Drugtakers* (Paladin, London 1971).
4 King, R. *All Things Bright and Beautiful?* (John Wiley, Chichester, 1979); King's study as a whole is based upon unstructured observations in infant classrooms. For a more structured inquiry into the activities of young children, see Dunn, S., and Morgan, V., 'Nursery and infant school play patterns: sex-related differences,' *British Educational Research Journal*, 13, (3) (1987) 271–81. An earlier study that raised questions about the so-called progressive practices in primary education is provided by Sharp, R., and Green, A., *Education and Social Control: A Study in Progressive Primary Education.* (Routledge & Kegan Paul, London, 1975).
5 Willis, P.E., *Learning to Labour* (Saxon House, London, 1977).
6 Bailey, K.D., *Methods of Social Research* (Collier–Macmillan, London, 1978).
7 Schutz, A., *Collected Papers* (Nijhoff, The Hague, 1962).
8 See for example, Stake, R.E. 'The case study method in social inquiry', *Educational Researcher*, Feb. (1978): 5–8, whose wry comment, 'Our scrap-books are full of enlargements of enlargements,' alludes to the tendency of some case studies to over-emphasize detail to the detriment of seeing the whole picture.
9 Denzin, N.K., *The Research Act in Sociology: A Theoretical Introduction to Sociological Methods* (The Butterworth Group, London, 1970).
10 Lofland, J., *Analysing Social Settings* (Wadsworth, Belmont, Calif., 1971). For a recent text dealing with techniques of observation, see Croll, P., *Systematic Observation* (Falmer Press, Lewes, 1986). For analysing case records (indexing, structuring, restructuring, sequencing, classification and cross-classification, co-ordinating and reducing) see Bromley, D.B., *The Case Study Method in Psychology and Related Disciplines* (John Wiley, Chichester, 1986).
11 Wolcott, H.F., *The Man in the Principal's Office* (Holt, Rinehart & Winston, New York, 1973). For a British study employing ethnographic techniques and looking, *inter alia*, at the leadership of the head teacher, see Burgess, R.G., *Experiencing Comprehensive Education* (Methuen, London 1983). For other case studies of schools the reader is referred to Ball, S.J., *Beachside Comprehensive*, (Cambridge University Press, Cambridge 1981); Ball, S.J., 'School politics, teachers' careers and educational change: a case study of becoming a comprehensive school'; in Barton, L. and Walker, S. (eds), *Education and Social Change*, (Croom Helm, Beckenham 1985); Beynon, J. 'Career histories in a comprehensive school', in Ball, S.J. and Goodson, I.F. (eds), *Teachers' Lives and Careers*, (Falmer Press, Lewes, 1985); Beynon, J., *Initial Encounters in the Secondary School* (Falmer Press, Lewes, 1985); and Davies, L., *Pupil Power: Deviance and Gender in School* (Falmer Press, Lewes, 1984).
12 Walker, R., 'Making sense and losing meaning: Problems of selection in doing Case Study', in Simons, H. (ed.), *Towards a Science of the Singular* (Centre for Applied Research in Education, University of East Anglia, 1980).
13 Acker, S., 'Teachers' culture in an English primary school: continuity and change', *British Journal of Sociology Education*, 11 (3) (1990) 257–73.

14 House, E.R., 'Technology versus craft: a ten-year perspective on innovation,' *Journal of Curriculum Studies*, 11 (1) (1979) 1–15.
15 Nias, J., *Primary Teachers Talking* (Routledge, London, 1989).
16 Boulton, M.J., 'Participation in playground activities at middle school,' *Education Research*, 34 (3) (1992) 167–82.
17 Wild, P., Scivier, J.E. and Richardson, S.J., 'Evaluating information technology-supported local management of schools: the user acceptability audit,' *Education Management and Administration*, 20 (1) (1992) 40–8; see also Mitchell, S. and Wild, P., 'A task analysis of a computerised system to support administration in schools', *Education Management and Administration*, 21 (1) (1993) 53–61.
18 Blease, D. and Cohen, L., *Coping with Computers: An Ethnographic Study In Primary Classrooms* (Paul Chapman Pub., London, 1990).
19 Flanders, N., *Analyzing Teaching Behavior* (Addison-Wesley, Reading, Mass., 1970).
20 Antonsen, E.A., 'Treatment of a boy of twelve: help with handwriting, play therapy and discussion of problems', *Journal of Education Therapy*, 2 (1) (1988) 25–32.
21 Houghton, D., 'Mr Chong: a case study of a dependent learner of English for academic purposes', *System*, 19 (1/2) (1991) 75–90.
22 Entwistle, N.J. and Ramsden, P. *Understanding Student Learning* (Croom Helm, Beckenham, 1983).
23 Holland, J.L., *Making Vocational Choices: A Theory of Vocational Personalities and Work Environments* (Prentice-Hall, Englewood Cliffs, NJ, 1985).
24 Belbin, R.M., *Management Teams: Why they Succeed or Fail* (Heinemann, London, 1981).
25 Case studies of British schools are now sufficiently numerous to provide archival sources for the type of reinterpretation that Adelman refers to. A good example is the work of Stephen Ball, *The Micro-Politics of the School* (Methuen, London 1987) which draws upon a variety of case studies of schools in order to advance a theory of school organization.
26 Adelman, C., Jenkins, D. and Kemmis, S., 'Rethinking case study: Notes from the Second Cambridge Conference', in Simons, H. (ed.), *Towards a Science of the Singular* (Centre for Applied Research in Education, University of East Anglia, 1980).

6

CORRELATIONAL RESEARCH

INTRODUCTION

Human behaviour at both the individual and social level is characterized by great complexity, a complexity about which we understand comparatively little, given the present state of social research. One approach to a fuller understanding of human behaviour is to begin by teasing out simple relationships between those factors and elements deemed to have some bearing on the phenomena in question. The value of correlational research is that it is able to achieve this end.

Before we attempt to describe correlational research as such, it might be useful if we begin by examining 'correlation' and related terms and indicating the purposes they fulfil in statistical analysis. We saw in the introduction that one of the primary purposes of science as it is traditionally conceived is to discover relationships among phenomena with a view ultimately to predicting and, in some situations, controlling their occurrence. As we suggested above, much of social research in general, and educational research more particularly, is concerned at our present stage of development with the first step in this sequence – establishing interrelationships among variables. We may wish to know, for example, how delinquency is related to social class background; or whether an association exists between the number of years spent in full-time education and subsequent annual income; or whether there is a link between personality and achievement. Numerous techniques have been devised to provide us with numerical representations of such relationships and they are known as 'measures of association'. We list the principal ones in Box 6.1.

At this point it is pertinent to say a few words about some of the terms used in Box 6.1 to describe the nature of variables. They enable us to draw a distinction between the concepts of 'association' and 'correlation'. A full treatment of that distinction is inappropriate in an introductory chapter such as this. The interested reader is referred to Cohen and Holliday,[2] a text containing worked examples of the appropriate use

Box 6.1   Common measures of relationship

Measure	Nature of Variables	Comment
Pearson product moment r	Two continuous variables; interval or ratio scale	Relationship linear
Rank order or Kendall's tau	Two continuous variables; ordinal scale	
Correlation ratio, η (eta)	One variable continuous, other either continuous or discrete	Relationship nonlinear
Intraclass	One variable continuous; other discrete; interval or ratio scale	Purpose: to determine within-group similarity
Biserial, r_{bis} Point biserial, $r_{pt\ bis}$	One variable continuous; other (a) continuous but dichotomised. r_{bis}, or (b) true dichotomy, $r_{pt\ bis}$	Index of item discrimination (used in item analysis)
Phi coefficient, φ	Two true dichotomies; nominal or ordinal series	
Partial correlation $r_{12.3}$	Three or more continuous variables	Purpose: to determine relationship between two variables, with effect of third held constant
Multiple correlation $r_{1.234}$	Three or more continuous variables	Purpose: to predict one variable from a linear weighted combination of two or more independent variables
Kendall's coefficient of concordance,[t]	Three or more continuous variables; ordinal series	Purpose: to determine the degree of (say, interrater) agreement

Source: Mouly, 1978[1]

(and limitations) of the correlational techniques outlined in Box 6.1, together with other measures of association such as Kruskal's *gamma*, Somer's *d*, and Guttman's *lambda*.

Look at the words used at the top of the Box to explain the nature of variables in connection with the measure called the Pearson product moment, r. The variables, we learn, are 'continuous' and at the 'interval' or the 'ratio' scale of measurement.

A continuous variable is one that, theoretically at least, can take any value between two points on a scale. Weight, for example, is a continuous variable; so too is time, so also is height. Weight, time and height can take on any number of possible values between nought and infinity, the feasibility of measuring them across such a range being limited only by the variability of suitable measuring instruments.

A ratio scale includes an absolute zero and provides equal intervals. Using weight as our example, we can say that no mass at all is a zero measure and that 1,000 grams is 400 grams heavier than 600 grams and twice as heavy as 500. In our discussion of correlational research that follows, we refer to a relationship as a 'correlation' rather than an 'association' whenever that relationship can be further specified in terms of an increase or a decrease of a certain number of units in the one variable (I.Q. for example) producing an increase or a decrease of a related number of units of the other (e.g. mathematical ability).

Turning again to Box 6.1, we read in connection with the second measure shown there (Rank order or Kendall's tau) that the two continuous variables are at the 'ordinal' scale of measurement. An ordinal scale is used to indicate rank order; that is to say, it arranges individuals or objects in a series ranging from the highest to the lowest according to the particular characteristic being measured. In contrast to the interval scale discussed earlier, ordinal numbers assigned to such a series do not indicate absolute quantities nor can one assume that the intervals between the numbers are equal. For example, in a class of children rated by a teacher on the degree of their co-operativeness and ranged from highest to lowest according to that attribute, it cannot be assumed that the difference in the degree of co-operativeness between subjects ranked 1 and 2 is the same as that obtaining between subjects 9 and 10; nor can it be taken that subject 1 possesses ten times the quantity of co-operativeness of subject 10.

The variables involved in connection with the phi coefficient measure of association (halfway down Box 6.1) are described as 'true dichotomies' and at the 'nominal' scale of measurement. Truly dichotomous variables (such as sex or driving test result) can take only two values (male or female; pass or fail). The nominal scale is the most elementary scale of measurement. It does no more than identify the categories into which individuals, objects or events may be classified. Those categories have to be mutually exclusive of course, and a nominal scale should also be complete; that is to say it should include all possible classifications of a particular type.

The classification of votes in a by-election (Conservative, Labour,

Liberal-Democrat, Communist, Independent, Ecology, etc.) is an example of the use of a complete nominal scale, complete, that is, in the sense that all of the political parties fighting the by-election are represented in the final count of voting preferences.

To conclude our explanation of terminology, readers should note the use of the term 'discrete variable' in the description of the third correlation ratio (eta) in Box 6.1. We said earlier that a continuous variable can take on any value between two points on a scale. A discrete variable, however, can only take on numerals or values that are specific points on a scale. The number of players in a football team is a discrete variable. It is usually eleven; it could be less than eleven, but it could never be $7\frac{1}{4}$!

In our discussion of the principal correlational techniques shown in Box 6.1, three are of special interest to us and these form the basis of much of the rest of the chapter. They are the Pearson product moment correlation coefficient, multiple correlation, and partial correlation.

Correlational techniques are generally intended to answer three questions about two variables or two sets of data. First, 'Is there a relationship between the two variables (or sets of data)?' If the answer to this question is 'yes', then two other questions follow: 'What is the direction of the relationship?' and 'What is the magnitude?'

Relationship in this context refers to any tendency for the two variables (or sets of data) to vary consistently. Pearson's product moment coefficient of correlation, one of the best-known measures of association, is a statistical value ranging from -1.0 to $+1.0$ and expresses this relationship in quantitative form. The coefficient is represented by the symbol r.

Where the two variables (or sets of data) fluctuate in the same direction, i.e. as one increases so does the other, or as one decreases so does the other, a positive relationship is said to exist. Correlations reflecting this pattern are prefaced with a plus sign to indicate the positive nature of the relationship. Thus, $+1.0$ would indicate perfect positive correlation between two factors, as with the radius and diameter of a circle, and $+.80$ a high positive correlation, as between academic achievement and intelligence, for example. Where the sign has been omitted, a plus sign is assumed.

A negative correlation or relationship, on the other hand, is to be found when an increase in one variable is accompanied by a decrease in the other variable. Negative correlations are prefaced with a minus sign. Thus, -1.0 would represent perfect negative correlation, as between the number of errors children make on a spelling test and their score on the test, and -0.30 a low negative correlation, as between absenteeism and intelligence, say. There is no other meaning to the signs used; they indicate nothing more than which pattern holds for any two variables (or sets of data).

Generally speaking, researchers tend to be more interested in the magnitude of an obtained correlation than they are in its direction. Correlational procedures have been developed so that no relationship whatever between two variables is represented by zero (or 0.00), as between body weight and intelligence, possibly. This means that a person's performance on one variable is totally unrelated to her performance on a second variable. If she is high on one, for example, she is just as likely to be high or low on the other. Perfect correlations of $+1.00$ or -1.00 are rarely found and, as we shall see, most coefficients of correlation in social research are around $+0.50$ or less. The correlation coefficient may be seen then as an indication of the predictability of one variable given the other: it is an indication of covariation. The relationship between two variables can be examined visually by plotting the paired measurements on graph paper with each pair of observations being represented by a point. The resulting arrangement of points is known as a 'scatter diagram' and enables us to assess graphically the degree of relationship between the characteristics being measured. Box 6.2 gives some examples of scatter diagrams in the field of educational research.

The coefficient of correlation, then, tells us something about the relations between two variables. Other measures exist, however, which allow us to specify relationships when more than two variables are involved. These are known as measures of 'multiple correlation' and 'partial correlation'.

Multiple correlation measures indicate the degree of association between three or more variables simultaneously. We may want to know, for example, the degree of association between delinquency, social class background and leisure facilities. Or we may be interested in finding out the relationship between academic achievement, intelligence and neuroticism. Multiple correlation, or 'regression' as it is sometimes called, indicates the degree of association between n variables. It is related not only to the correlations of the independent variable with the dependent variables, but also to the intercorrelations between the dependent variables.

Partial correlation aims at establishing the degree of association between two variables after the influence of a third has been controlled or partialled out. Guilford and Fruchter define a partial correlation between two variables as:

one that nullifies the effects of a third variable (or a number of variables) upon both the variables being correlated. The correlation between height and weight of boys in a group where age is

Box 6.2   Correlation scatter diagrams

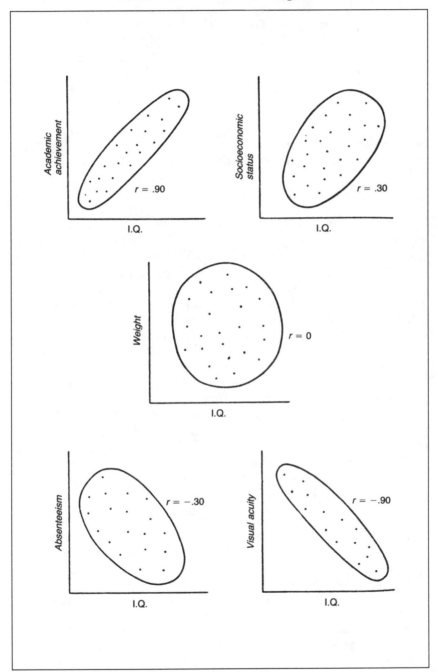

Source: Tuckman, 1972

131

permitted to vary would be higher than the correlation between height and weight in a group at constant age. The reason is obvious. Because certain boys are older, they are both heavier and taller. Age is a factor that enhances the strength of correspondence between height and weight. With age held constant, the correlation would still be positive and significant because at any age, taller boys tend to be heavier.

(Guilford and Fruchter, 1973)[4]

Consider, too, the relationship between success in basketball and previous experience in the game. Suppose, also, that the presence of a third factor, the height of the players, was known to have an important influence on the other two factors. The use of partial correlation techniques would enable a measure of the two primary variables to be achieved, freed from the influence of the secondary variable.

It follows from what we have said so far that correlational research embraces those studies and projects in which attempts are made to discover or clarify relationships through the use of correlation coefficients. Relationships thus disclosed may simply indicate what goes with what in a given context, or else they may provide a basis on which to make predictions about the variables being studied. The basic design of correlational research is simple and involves collecting two or more scores on the same group of subjects and computing correlation coefficients. Many useful studies have been based on this simple design. Those involving more complex relationships, however, utilize multiple and partial correlations in order to provide a clearer picture of the relationships being investigated. One observer[5] points out, however, that the quality of correlation studies is determined not by the complexity of the design or the sophistication of the correlational techniques used but by the level of planning and the depth of the theoretical constructs going into the development of the hypotheses.

One final point: it is important to stress that correlations refer to measures of association and do not necessarily indicate causal relationships between variables. Mouly puts it like this:

> The correlation simply implies concomitance; it is not synonymous with causation. It may suggest causation in the same sense that the variables involved are part of a cause and effect system, but the nature of the system and the direction in which the components operate is not specified in the correlation. The two variables are not necessarily (or perhaps even commonly) the 'cause' and 'effect' of each other. The correlation between X and Y is often nothing more than the reflection of the operation of a third factor.

(Mouly, 1978)

CHARACTERISTICS

We indicated above that correlational studies may be broadly classified as either 'relational studies' or as 'prediction studies'. We now look at each a little more closely.

In the case of the first of these two categories, correlational research is mainly concerned with achieving a fuller understanding of the complexity of phenomena or, in the matter of behavioural and educational research, behavioural patterns, by studying the relationships between the variables which the researcher hypothesizes as being related. As a method, it is particularly useful in exploratory studies into fields where little or no previous research has been undertaken. It is often a shot in the dark aimed at verifying hunches a researcher has about a presumed relationship between characteristics or variables. Take a complex notion like 'teacher effectiveness', for example. This is dependent upon a number of less complex factors operating singly or in combination. Factors such as intelligence, motivation, person perception, verbal skills and empathy come to mind as possibly having an effect on teaching outcomes. A review of the research literature will confirm or reject these possibilities. Once an appropriate number of factors have been identified in this way, suitable measures may then be chosen or developed to assess them. They are then given to a representative sample and the scores obtained are then correlated with a measure of the complex factor being investigated, namely, teacher effectiveness. As it is an exploratory undertaking, the analysis will consist of correlation coefficients only, though if it is designed carefully, we will begin to achieve some understanding of the particular behaviour being studied. The investigation and its outcomes may then be used as a basis for further research or as a source of additional hypotheses.

Exploratory relationship studies may also employ partial correlational techniques. Partial correlation is a particularly suitable approach when a researcher wishes to nullify the influence of one or more important factors upon behaviour in order to bring the effect of less important factors into greater prominence. If, for example, we wanted to understand more fully the determinants of academic achievement in a comprehensive school, we might begin by acknowledging the importance of the factor of intelligence and establishing a relationship between intelligence and academic achievement. The intelligence factor could then be held constant by partial correlation, thus enabling the investigator to clarify other, lesser factors such as motivation, parental encouragement or vocational aspiration. Clearly, motivation is related to academic achievement but if a pupil's motivation score is correlated with academic achievement without controlling the intelligence factor, it will be difficult to assess the true effect of motivation on achievement because the pupil with high intelligence but low motivation may possibly achieve more than pupils with lower intelligence but higher motivation. Once intelligence has been nullified, it is possible to see more clearly the relationship between motivation and achievement. The next stage might be to control the effects of both intelligence and motivation and then to seek a clearer idea of the effects of other selected factors – parental encouragement or vocational aspiration, for instance. Finally, exploratory relationship studies may employ sophisticated, multivariate techniques in teasing out associations between dependent and independent variables (see pages 339–45).

In contrast to exploratory relationship studies, prediction studies are usually undertaken in areas having a firmer and more secure knowledge base. Prediction through the use of correlational techniques is based on the assumption that at least some of the factors that will lead to the behaviour to be predicted are present and measurable at the time the prediction is made (see Borg, 1963).[6] If, for example, we wanted to predict the probable success of a group of salespeople on an intensive training course, we would start with variables that have been found in previous research to be related to later success in saleswork. These might include enterprise, verbal ability, achievement motivation, emotional maturity, sociability and so on. The extent to which these predictors correlate with the particular behaviour we wish to predict, namely, successful selling, will determine the accuracy of our prediction. Clearly, variables crucial to success cannot be predicted if they are not present at the time of making the prediction. A salesperson's ability to fit in with a team of his or her fellows cannot be predicted where these future colleagues are unknown.

In order to be valuable in prediction, the magnitude of association between two variables must be substantial; and the greater the association, the more accurate the prediction it permits. In practice, this means that anything less than perfect correlation will permit errors in predicting one variable from a knowledge of the other. As Mouly explains,

> The correlation must, of course, represent a real relationship rather than simply the operation of chance. Beyond this, what constitutes an adequate correlation between two variables can be appraised only on the basis of what can logically be expected, and, of course, what accuracy of prediction is required to serve the purpose of the study. A coefficient of correlation of $+0.35$ between motivation and grades, for example, is perhaps all that can be expected from our presently crude measures of motivation and of grades.
>
> (Mouly, 1978)

Borg recalls that much prediction research in the United States has been carried out in the field of scholastic success. Some studies in this connection have been aimed at short-term prediction of students' performance in specific courses of study, while other studies have been directed at long-term prediction of general academic success. Sometimes, short-term academic prediction is based upon a single predictor variable. Most efforts to predict future behaviours, however, are based upon scores on a number of predictor variables, each of which is useful in predicting a specific aspect of future behaviour. In the prediction of college success, for example, a single variable such as academic achievement is less effective as a predictor than a combination of variables such as academic achievement together with, say, motivation, intelligence, study habits, etc. More complex studies of this kind, therefore, generally make use of multiple correlation and multiple regression equations.

Predicting behaviours or events likely to occur in the near future is easier and less hazardous than predicting behaviours likely to occur in the more distant future. The reason is that in short-term prediction, more of the factors leading to success in predicted behaviour are likely to be present. In addition, short-term prediction allows less time for important predictor variables to change or for individuals to gain experience that would tend to change their likelihood of success in the predicted behaviour.

One further point: correlation, as Mouly observes, is a group concept, a generalized measure that is useful basically in predicting group performance. Whereas, for instance, it can be predicted that gifted children as a group will succeed at school, it cannot be predicted with certainty that one particular gifted child will excel. As to the relative value of the correlation coefficient he notes:

> Since most correlations between the variables of interest in the social sciences are of the order of 0.50, relatively little confidence can be placed in such prediction in the individual case. It is, therefore, necessary to raise the correlation on the basis of which predictions are made in order to increase their precision. This can be done by refining the instruments used and/or the criterion being predicted, and . . . by combining a number of variables into a composite predictor of the criterion.
>
> (Borg, 1963)

OCCASIONS WHEN APPROPRIATE

From the preceding discussion, we may readily see that the techniques of correlational research are particularly useful in social and educational investigations. Abstracting from the main points of the arguments, then, we may say that correlational research is appropriate in the following two instances. First, it is appropriate when there is a need to discover or clarify relationships and where correlation coefficients will achieve these ends. It is especially useful in this connection in the initial stages of a project where a certain amount of basic groundwork has to be covered to get some idea of the structure of the relationships. In this way it gets at degrees of relationships rather than the all-or-nothing question posed by experimental design – is an effect present or absent? Beyond this stage, relationships may become a source of hypotheses and further research. The correlational approach is also valuable when variables are complex and therefore do not lend themselves to the experimental method and controlled manipulation. It also permits the measurement of several variables and their interrelationships simultaneously in realistic settings. Both of these later instances will be characterized by the use of multiple and partial correlations.

Second, correlational research is appropriate where the objective, or one of a set of objectives, is to achieve some degree of prediction. Correlational techniques make up one of a range of alternative approaches in this regard. We have already identified a number of characteristics of prediction studies and it is sufficient at this point to note them as being occasions when a predictive approach may be fruitful. Thus, prediction studies are appropriate where a firm basis of previous knowledge is present, the assumption being that at least some of the factors will relate to the behaviour to be predicted. There needs, too, to be a reasonable chance of achieving a high or moderately high correlation coefficient. Low coefficients will have little predictive value. Further, for confident results prediction research is more appropriate for events likely to occur in the immediate future than at some point in the distant future. Finally, prediction studies are suitable where a group as opposed to an individual is the focus of a project. Only a high correlation can be regarded as valid for individual prediction.

ADVANTAGES AND DISADVANTAGES

Correlational research possesses a number of advantages and disadvantages which we will here briefly review. As regards its advantages, it is particularly useful in tackling problems in education and the social sciences because it allows for the measurement of a number of variables and their relationships simultaneously. The experimental approach, by contrast, is characterized by the manipulation of a single variable, and is thus appropriate for dealing with problems where simple causal relationships exist. In educational and behavioural research, it is invariably the case that a number of variables contribute to a particular outcome. Experimental research thus introduces a note of unreality into research, whereas correlational approaches, while less rigorous, allow for the study of behaviour in more realistic settings. Where an element of control is required, however, partial correlation achieves this without changing the context in which the study takes place.

A second advantage of correlational research we have already noted: it yields information concerning the degree of relationship between the variables being studied. It thus provides researchers with insights into the way variables operate that cannot be gained by other means. We may itemize the remaining strengths of the method in a few words: as a basis for prediction studies, it enables researchers to make estimates of the probable accuracy of their predictions; it is especially useful for lower-level ground work where it serves as a powerful exploratory tool; and it does not require large samples.

Among its limitations, correlational research only identifies what goes with what – it only implies concomitance and therefore does not necessarily establish cause-and-effect relationships; it is less rigorous than the experimental approach because it exercises less control over the independent variables; it is prone to identify spurious relation patterns; it adopts an atomistic approach; and the correlation index is relatively imprecise, being limited by the unreliability of the measurements of the variables.

INTERPRETING THE CORRELATION COEFFICIENT

Once a correlation coefficient has been computed, there remains the problem of interpreting it. A question often asked in this connection is how large should the coefficient be for it to be meaningful. The question may be approached in three ways: by examining the strength of the relationship; by examining the statistical significance of the relationship; and by examining the square of the correlation coefficient.

Inspection of the numerical value of a correlation coefficient will yield clear indication of the strength of the relationship between the variables in question. Low or near zero values indicate weak relationships, while those nearer to $+1$ or -1 suggest stronger relationships. Imagine, for instance, that a measure of a teacher's success in the classroom after five years in the profession is correlated with her final school experience grade as a student and that it was found that $r = +0.19$. Suppose now that her score on classroom success is correlated with a measure of need for professional achievement and that this yielded a correlation of 0.65. It could be concluded that there is a stronger relationship between success and professional achievement scores than between success and final student grade.

Where a correlation coefficient has been derived from a sample and one wishes to use it as a basis for inference about the parent population, the statistical significance of the obtained correlation must be considered. Statistical significance, when applied to a correlation coefficient, indicates whether or not the correlation is different from zero at a given level of confidence. A statistically significant correlation is indicative of an actual relationship rather than one due entirely to chance. The level of statistical significance of a correlation is determined to a great extent by the number of cases upon which the correlation is based. Thus, the greater the number of cases, the smaller the correlation need be to be significant at a given level of confidence.

Exploratory relationship studies are generally interpreted with reference to their statistical significance, whereas prediction studies depend for their efficacy on the strength of the correlation coefficients. These need to be considerably higher than those found in exploratory relationship studies and for this reason rarely invoke the concept of significance.

The third approach to interpreting a coefficient is provided by examining the square of the coefficient of correlation, r^2. This shows the proportion of variance in one variable that can be attributed to its linear relationship with the second variable. In other words, it indicates the amount the two variables have in common. If, for example, two variables A and B have a correlation of 0.50, then $(0.50)^2$ or 0.25 of the variation shown by the B scores can be attributed to the tendency of B to vary linearly with A. Box 6.3 shows graphically the common variance between reading grade and arithmetic grade having a correlation of 0.65.

Box 6.3   Visualization of correlation of 0.65 between reading grade and arithmetic grade

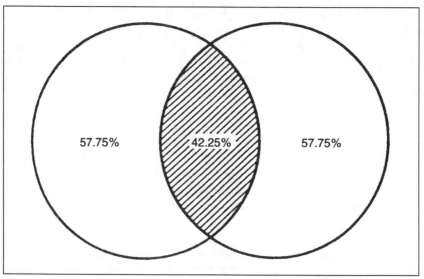

Source: Fox, 1969[6]

There are three cautions to be borne in mind when one is interpreting a correlation coefficient. First, a coefficient is a simple number and must not be interpreted as a percentage. A correlation of 0.50, for instance, does not mean 50 per cent relationship between the variables. Further, a correlation of 0.50 does not indicate twice as much relationship as that shown by a correlation of 0.25. A correlation of 0.50 actually indicates more than twice the relationship shown by a correlation of 0.25. In fact, as coefficients approach $+1$ or -1, a difference in the absolute values of the coefficients becomes more important than the same numerical difference between lower correlations would be.

Second, a correlation does not necessarily imply a cause-and-effect relationship between two factors, as we have previously indicated. It should not therefore be interpreted as meaning that one factor is causing the scores on the other to be as they are. There are invariably other factors influencing both variables under consideration. Suspected cause-and-effect relationships would have to be confirmed by subsequent experimental study.

Third, a correlation coefficient is not to be interpreted in any absolute sense. A correlational value for a given sample of a population may not necessarily be the same as that found in another sample from the same population. Many factors influence the value of a given correlation coefficient and if researchers wish to extrapolate to the populations from which they drew their samples they will then have to test the significance of the correlation.

We now offer some general guidelines for interpreting correlation coefficients. They are based on Borg's (1963) analysis and assume that the correlations relate to a hundred or more subjects.

Correlations ranging from 0.20 to 0.35

Correlations within this range show only very slight relationship between variables although they may be statistically significant. A correlation of 0.20 shows that only 4 per cent of the variance is common to the two measures. Whereas correlations at this level may have limited meaning in exploratory relationship research, they are of no value in either individual or group prediction studies.

Correlations ranging from 0.35 to 0.65

Within this range, correlations are statistically significant beyond the 1 per cent level. When correlations are around 0.40, crude group prediction may be possible. As Borg notes, correlations within this range are useful, however, when combined with other correlations in a multiple regression equation. Combining several correlations in this range can in some cases yield individual predictions that are correct within an acceptable margin of error. Correlations at this level used singly are of little use for individual prediction because they yield only a few more correct predictions than could be accomplished by guessing or by using some chance selection procedure.

Correlations ranging from 0.65 to 0.85

Correlations within this range make possible group predictions that are accurate enough for most purposes. Nearer the top of the range, group predictions can be made very accurately, usually predicting the proportion of successful candidates in selection problems within a very small margin of error. Near the top of this correlation range individual predictions can be made that are considerably more accurate than would occur if no such selection procedures were used.

Correlations over 0.85

Correlations as high as this indicate a close relationship between the two variables correlated. A correlation of 0.85 indicates that the measure used for prediction has about 72 per cent variance in common with the performance being predicted. Prediction studies in education very rarely yield correlations this high. When correlations at this level are obtained, however, they are very useful for either individual or group prediction.

EXAMPLES OF CORRELATIONAL RESEARCH

To conclude this chapter, we illustrate the use of correlation coefficients in a small scale study of young children's attainments and self-images, and, by contrast, we report some of the findings of a very large scale, longitudinal survey of the outcomes of truancy that uses special techniques for controlling intruding variables in looking at the association between truancy and occupational prospects. Finally, we show how partial correlational techniques can clarify the strength and direction of associations between variables.

Small-scale study of attainment and self-image

A study by Crocker and Cheeseman (1988)[7] investigated young children's ability to assess the academic worth of themselves and others. Specifically, the study posed the following three questions:

1 Can children in their first years at school assess their own academic rank relative to their peers?

2 What level of match exists between self-estimate, peer-estimate, teacher-estimate of academic rank?

3 What criteria do these children use when making these judgements?

Using three infant schools in the Midlands the age range of which was from 5 to 7 years, the researchers selected a sample of 141 children from five classes. Observations took place on 20 half-day visits to each class and the observer was able to interact with individual children. Notes on interactions were taken. Subsequently, each child was given pieces of paper with the names of all his or her classmates on them and was then asked to arrange them in two piles – those the child thought were 'better than me' at school work and those the child thought were 'not as good as me'. No child suggested that the task was one which he or she could not do. The relative self rankings were converted to a percentage of children seen to be 'better than me' in each class.

Correspondingly, each teacher was asked to rank all the children in her class without using any standardized test. Spearman's rank order correlations were calculated between self–teacher, self–peer, and peer–teacher rankings. The table below indicates there was a high degree of agreement between self estimates of rank position, peer estimate and teacher estimate. The correlations appeared to confirm earlier researches in which there was broad agreement between self, peer and teacher ratings (see Box 6.4).

Box 6.4   Correlations between the various estimates of academic rank

Class	Self–peer	Self–teacher	Peer–teacher
1	0.68	0.62	0.82
2	0.72	0.74	0.80
3	0.59	0.55	0.86
4	0.83	0.59	0.65
5	0.70	0.68	0.82

Note: All correlations are significant beyond the 0.01 level
Source: Crocker and Cheeseman, 1988[7]

The researchers conclude that the youngest schoolchildren quickly acquire a knowledge of those academic criteria that teachers use to evaluate pupils. The study disclosed a high degree of agreement between self, peers and teacher as to the rank order of children in a particular classroom. It seemed that only the youngest used non-academic measures to any great extent and that this had largely disappeared by the time the children were 6 years old.

Large-scale study of truancy

Drawing on the huge database of the National Child Development Study (a longitudinal survey of all people in Great Britain born in the week 3–9 March, 1958), Hibbett and her associates (1990)[8] were able to explore the association between reported truancy at school, based on information obtained during the school years, and occupational, financial and educational progress, family formation and health, based on interview at the age of 23 years. We report here on some occupational outcomes of truancy.

Whereas initial analyses demonstrated a consistent relationship between truancy and dropping out of secondary education, less skilled employment, increased risk of unemployment and a reduced chance of being in a job involving further training, these associations were derived from comparisons between truants and all other members of the 1958 cohort. In brief, they failed to take account of the fact that truants and non-truants differed in respect of such vital factors as family size, father's occupation, and poorer educational ability and attainment before truancy commenced. Using sophisticated statistical techniques, the investigators went on to control for these initial differences, thus enabling them to test whether or not the outcomes for truants differed once they were being compared with people who were similar in these respects. The multivariate techniques used in the analyses need not concern us here. Suffice it to say that by and large, the differences that were noted before controlling for the intruding variables persisted even when those controls were introduced. That is to say, truancy was found to correlate with:

1 unstable job history
2 a shorter mean length of jobs
3 higher total number of jobs
4 greater frequency of unemployment
5 greater mean length of unemployment spells
6 lower family income.

Thus, by sequentially controlling for such variables as family size, father's occupation, measured ability and attainment at 11 years, etc., the researchers were able to ascertain how much each of these independent variables contributed to the relationship between truancy and the outcome variables that we identify above.

The investigators report their findings in terms such as:

1 truants were 2.4 times more likely than non-truants to be unemployed rather than in work
2 truants were 1.4 times more likely than non-truants to be out of the labour force

3 truants experienced, on average, 4.2 months more unemployment than non-truants
4 truants were considerably less well off than non-truants in net family income per week.

The researchers conclude that their study challenges a commonly-held belief that truants simply outgrow school and are ready for the world of work. On the contrary, truancy is often a sign of more general and long-term difficulties and a predictor of unemployment problems of a more severe kind than will be the experience of others who share the disadvantaged backgrounds and the low attainments that typify truants.

Partial correlation and associations between variables

The ability of partial correlational techniques to clarify the strength and direction of associations between variables is demonstrated in a study by Halpin, Croll and Redman (1990).[9] In an exploration of teachers' perceptions of the effects of in-service education, the authors report correlations between Teaching (T), Organization and Policy (OP), Attitudes and Knowledge (AK) and the dependent variable, Pupil Attainment (PA).

The strength of these associations is shown in Box 6.5, suggesting that there is a strong tendency ($r=0.68$) for teachers who claim a higher level of 'INSET effect' on the Teaching dimension to claim also a higher level of effect on Pupil Attainment and *vice versa*. The correlations between both the dimensions OP and AK and Pupil Attainment, however, are much weaker ($r=0.27$ and $r=0.23$ respectively).

Halpin *et al.* investigate the relationships further by means of partial correlational techniques. Box 6.6 shows the association between various dimensions of effect and pupil attainment. The partial correlation between Teaching and Pupil Attainment is calculated, controlling for

Box 6.5 Correlations between pupil attainment and teaching, organization and policy, and attitudes and knowledge.

	Pupil Attainment (PA)
	r
Teaching (T)	0.68
Organization and Policy (OP)	0.27
Attitudes and Knowledge (AK)	0.23
	n = 196

Source: Halpin *et al.*, 1990

Box 6.6 Partial correlations between pupil attainment and teaching, organization and policy, and attitudes and knowledge.

Correlates	Controlling for	Partial r
PA and T	OP and AK	0.66
PA and OP	T	0.14
PA and AK	T	0.09
		$n = 196$

Source: Halpin *et al.*, 1990

the dimensions OP and AK. Correlations are then calculated between Pupil Attainment and OP and AK, controlling for the effects of Teaching. The results shown in Box 6.6 suggest that the association between Teaching effects and Pupil Attainment effects is unaffected by the introduction of the other dimensions as controls. However, the association between Pupil Attainment and OP and AK is considerably reduced when the association with Teaching is partialled out. The authors conclude that the strong association between Teaching and Pupil Attainment occurs whether or not teachers say that there have been effects on either Organization and Policy or on Attitudes and Knowledge. In other words, improved teaching is seen as improving pupil attainment regardless of any positive effects on organization, policy, attitudes or knowledge. By contrast, 'positive effects on organisation and policy and on attitudes and knowledge, as well as being seen as having a weaker effect on pupil attainment than teaching, have part of their influence on pupil attainment mediated by the teaching variable' (Halpin *et al.* 1990). To some extent, therefore, Organization and Policy, and Attitudes and Knowledge effects influence Pupil Attainment only if improvements in Teaching are reported.

REFERENCES AND NOTES

1 Mouly, G.J., *Educational Research: The Art and Science of Investigation* (Allyn & Bacon, Boston, 1978).
2 Cohen, L. and Holliday, M., *Statistics for Social Scientists* (Harper & Row, London, 1982).
3 Tuckman, B.W., *Conducting Educational Research* (Harcourt Brace Jovanovich, New York, 1972).
4 Guilford, J.P. and Fruchter, B. *Fundamental Statistics in Psychology and Education* (McGraw Hill, New York, 1973).
5 Borg, W.R., *Educational Research: An Introduction* (Longman, London, 1963).
6 Fox, D.J., *The Research Process in Education* (Holt, Rinehart & Winston, New York, 1969).
7 Crocker, A.C. and Cheeseman, R.G., 'The ability of young children to

rank themselves for academic ability', *Educational Studies*, 14, (1) (1988) 105–10.
8 Hibbett, A., Fogelman, K. and Manor, O., 'Occupational outcomes of truancy', *British Journal of Educational Psychology*, 60 (1990) 23–36.
9 Halpin, D., Croll, P. and Redman, K., 'Teachers' perceptions of the effects of inservice education', *British Educational Research Journal*, 16 (2) (1990) 163–77.

7

EX POST FACTO RESEARCH

INTRODUCTION

When translated literally, *ex post facto* means 'from what is done after-wards'. In the context of social and educational research the phrase means 'after the fact' or 'retrospectively' and refers to those studies which investigate possible cause-and-effect relationships by observing an existing condition or state of affairs and searching back in time for plausible causal factors. In effect, researchers ask themselves what factors seem to be associated with certain occurrences, or conditions, or aspects of behaviour. *Ex post facto* research, then, is a method of teasing out possible antecedents of events that have happened and cannot, therefore, be engineered or manipulated by the investigator. The following example will illustrate the basic idea. Imagine a situation in which there has been a dramatic increase in the number of fatal road accidents in a particular locality. An expert is called in to investigate. Naturally, there is no way in which she can study the actual accidents because they have happened; nor can she turn to technology for a video replay of the incidents. What she can do, however, is attempt a reconstruction by studying the statistics, examining the accident spots, and taking note of the statements given by victims and witnesses. In this way the expert will be in a position to identify possible determinants of the accidents. These may include excessive speed, poor road conditions, careless driving, frustration, inefficient vehicles, the effects of drugs or alcohol and so on. On the basis of her examination, she can formulate hypotheses as to the likely causes and submit them to the appropriate authority in the form of recommendations. These may include improving road conditions, or lowering the speed limit, or increasing police surveillance, for instance. The point of interest to us is that in identifying the causes retrospectively, the expert adopts an *ex post facto* perspective.

Kerlinger (1970)[1] has defined *ex post facto* research more formally as that in which the independent variable or variables have already occurred and in which the researcher starts with the observation of a dependent variable or variables. She then studies the independent variable or variables in retrospect for their possible relationship to, and effects on, the dependent variable or variables. The researcher is thus examining retrospectively the effects of a naturally occurring event on a subsequent outcome with a view to establishing a causal link between them. Interestingly, some instances of *ex post facto* designs correspond to experimental research in reverse, for instead of taking groups that are equivalent and subjecting them to different treatments so as to bring about differences in the dependent variables to be measured, an *ex post facto* experiment begins with groups that are already different in some respect and searches in retrospect for the factor that brought about the difference.

Two kinds of design may be identified in *ex post facto* research – the 'co-relational study' and the 'criterion group study'. The former is sometimes termed 'causal research' and the latter, 'causal-comparative research'. A co-relational (or causal) study is concerned with identifying the antecedents of a present condition. As its name suggests, it involves the collection of two sets of data, one of which will be retrospective, with a view to determining the relationship between them. The basic design of such an experiment may be represented thus:[2]

A study by Borkowsky (1970)[3] was based upon this kind of design. He attempted to show a relationship between the quality of a music teacher's undergraduate training (X) and his subsequent effectiveness as a teacher of his subject (O). Measures of the quality of a music teacher's college training can include grades in specific courses, overall grade average and self-ratings, etc. Teacher effectiveness can be assessed by indices of pupil performance, pupil knowledge, pupil attitudes and judgement of experts, etc. Correlations between all measures were obtained to determine the relationship. At most, this study could show that a relationship existed, after the fact, between the quality of teacher preparation and subsequent teacher effectiveness. Where a strong relationship is found between the independent and dependent variables, three possible interpretations are open to the researcher:

1 that the variable X has caused O;
2 that the variable O has caused X; or
3 that some third unidentified, and therefore unmeasured, variable has caused X and O.

It is often the case that a researcher cannot tell which of these is correct.

The value of co-relational or causal studies lies chiefly in their exploratory or suggestive character for, as we have seen, while they are not always adequate in themselves for establishing causal relationships among variables, they are a useful first step in this direction in that they do yield measures of association.

In the criterion-group (or causal-comparative) approach, the investigator sets out to discover possible causes for a phenomenon being studied, by comparing the subjects in which the variable is present with similar subjects in whom it is absent. The basic design in this kind of study may be represented thus:

If, for example, a researcher chose such a design to investigate factors contributing to teacher effectiveness, the criterion group O_1, the effective teachers, and its counterpart O_2, a group *not* showing the characteristics of the criterion group, are identified by measuring the differential effects of the groups on classes of children. The researcher may then examine X, some variable or event, such as the background, training, skills and personality of the groups, to discover what might 'cause' only some teachers to be effective.

Criterion-group or causal-comparative studies may be seen as bridging the gap between descriptive research methods on the one hand and true experimental research on the other.

CHARACTERISTICS OF *EX POST FACTO* RESEARCH

The most distinctive feature of both causal and causal-comparative research we have already established. That they are *ex post facto* indicates that data are collected after the presumed cause or causes have occurred. The researcher takes the effect (or dependent variable) and examines the data retrospectively to establish causes, relationships or associations, and their meanings.

Other characteristics of *ex post facto* research become apparent when it is contrasted with true experimental research. Kerlinger (1970) describes the *modus operandi* of the experimental researcher. ('If *x*, then *y*' in Kerlinger's usage. We have substituted X for *x* and O for *y* to fit in with Campbell and Stanley's conventions throughout the chapter.) Kerlinger hypothesizes: if X, then O; if frustration, then aggression. Depending on circumstances and his own predilections in research design, he uses some method to manipulate X. He then observes O to see if concomitant variation, the variation expected or predicted from the variation in X, occurs. If it does, this is evidence for the validity of the proposition, X–O, meaning 'If X, then O'. Note that the scientist here predicts from a controlled X to O. To help him achieve control, he can use the principle of randomization and active manipulation of X and can assume, other things being equal, that O is varying as a result of the manipulation of X.

In *ex post facto* designs, on the other hand, O is observed. Then a retrospective search for X ensues. An X is found that is plausible and agrees with the hypothesis. Due to lack of control of X and other possible Xs, the truth of the hypothesised relation between X and O cannot be asserted with the confidence of the experimental researcher. Basically, then, *ex post facto* investigations have, so to speak, a built-in weakness: lack of control of the independent variable or variables.

This brief comparison highlights the most important difference between the two designs – control. In the experimental situation, investigators at least have manipulative control; they have as a minimum one active variable. If an experiment is a 'true' experiment, they can also exercise control by randomization. They can assign subjects to groups randomly; or, at the very least, they can assign treatments to groups at random. In the *ex post facto* research situation, this control of the independent variable is not possible, and what is perhaps more important, neither is randomization. Investigators must take things as they are and try to disentangle them, though having said this, we must point out that they can make use of selected procedures that will give them an element of control in this research. These we shall touch upon shortly.

By their very nature, *ex post facto* experiments can provide support for any number of different, perhaps even contradictory, hypotheses; they are so completely flexible that it is largely a matter of postulating hypotheses according to one's personal preference. The investigator begins with certain data and looks for an interpretation consistent with them; often, however, a number of interpretations may be at hand. Consider again the hypothetical increase in road accidents in a given town. A retrospective search for causes will disclose half a dozen plausible ones. Experimental studies, by contrast, begin with a specific interpretation and then determine whether it is congruent with externally derived data. Frequently, causal relationships seem to be established on nothing more substantial than the premiss that any related event occurring prior to the phenomenon under study is assumed to be its cause – the classical *post hoc ergo propter hoc* fallacy. Overlooked is the fact that even when we do find a relationship between two variables, we must recognize the possibility that both are individual results of a common third factor rather than the first being necessarily the cause of the second. And as we have seen earlier, there is also the real possibility of reverse causation, e.g. that a heart condition promotes obesity rather than the other way around, or that they encourage each other. The point is that the evidence simply illustrates the hypothesis; it does not test it, since hypotheses cannot be tested on the same data from which they were derived. The relationship noted may actually exist, but it is not necessarily the only relationship, or perhaps the crucial one. Before we can accept that smoking is the primary cause of lung cancer, we have to rule out alternative hypotheses.

We must not conclude from what has just been said that *ex post facto* studies are of little value; many of our important investigations in education and psychology are *ex post facto* designs. There is often no choice in the matter: an investigator cannot cause one group to become failures, delinquent, suicidal, brain-damaged or dropouts. Research must of necessity rely on existing groups. On the other hand, the inability of *ex post facto* designs to incorporate the basic need for control (e.g. through manipulation or randomization) makes them vulnerable from a scientific point of view and the possibility of their being misleading should be clearly acknowledged. *Ex post facto* designs are probably better conceived more circumspectly, not as experiments with the greater certainty that these denote, but more as surveys, useful as sources of hypotheses to be tested by more conventional experimental means at a later date.

OCCASIONS WHEN APPROPRIATE

It would follow from what we have said in the preceding section that *ex post facto* designs are appropriate in circumstances where the more powerful experimental method is not possible. These would arise when, for example, it is not possible to select, control and manipulate the factors necessary to study cause-and-effect relationships directly; or when the control of all variables except a single independent variable may be unrealistic and artificial, preventing the normal interaction with other influential variables; or when laboratory controls for many research purposes would be impractical, costly or ethically undesirable.

Ex post facto research is particularly suitable in social, educational and – to a lesser extent – psychological contexts where the independent variable or variables lie outside the researcher's control. Examples of the method abound in these areas: the research on cigarette-smoking and lung cancer, for instance; or studies of teacher characteristics; or studies examining the relationship between political and religious affiliation and attitudes; or investigations into the relationship between school achievement and independent variables such as social class, race, sex and intelligence. Many of these may be divided into large-scale or small-scale *ex post facto* studies.

Large-scale study: Stables – 'Differences between pupils from mixed and single-sex schools' (1990)[4]

Research on pupil attainment in mixed and single-sex schools has a venerable history. Whereas earlier studies could find no convincing evidence in favour of single-sex schools in so far as overall academic achievement was concerned, more recent work has argued the case for single-sex schools as preferable for girls' achievement, particularly in certain areas of the secondary curriculum. Stables's interest in the continuing debate focused on the attitudes of boys and girls to school subjects, positive attitudes being associated with perseverance and performance. Specifically, Stables asked, 'Do pupils' perceptions of subject importance differ when those pupils are distinguished by their membership of mixed or single-sex schools?' (Stables, 1990).

The *ex post facto* design used by the researcher separated more than 2300 pupils by type of school (mixed or single-sex), and then compared their perceptions of the importance of all their school subjects by means of a specially designed questionnaire. At the same time, participants were given an 'Attitudes to Physics, Chemistry and Biology' scale consisting of 64 statements to which they responded on a continuum ranging from 'strongly agree' to 'strongly disagree'. Of the thirteen 11–18 comprehensive schools in the study, seven were mixed and six single-sex (three boys' schools and three girls' schools). They drew their students from a mix of rural, suburban, town and inner city locations. On tests of Verbal Reasoning, there were no significant differences between students in mixed and single-sex schools.

Stables's results confirmed earlier studies showing that boys' and girls' attitudes in mixed schools were more strongly polarized than in single-sex schools. The researcher also reported that Drama, Biology and Languages were significantly more highly rated by boys in single-sex schools than by their fellows in mixed establishments. On the other hand, boys in mixed schools recorded greater support for Physics and Physical Sciences than boys in single-sex schools. As far as girls were concerned, Physics was better liked in single-sex schools than in mixed. Physics, incidentally, was the most 'masculine' subject in terms of differences in subject preference between boys and girls. The 'Subject Preference and Perception of Subject Importance Questionnaire' revealed that overall, the effect of being educated in a single-sex or a mixed school seemed to have greater effect on pupils' feelings towards the following subjects: Sciences, Modern Languages, Craft, Drama and Music. The most consistent finding in Stables's investigation was in connection with the 'Attitude to Physics, Chemistry and Biology' scale. Stables reports, 'On every section of the scale the sex difference was greater among co-educated pupils . . . polarisation of feelings tends to occur strongly only in certain areas of the curriculum, but where it does, as in the case of Physics, the results can be quite dramatic.' He concludes, 'The danger is that subject interest and specialisation may be guided to a greater extent by a desire to conform to a received sexual stereotype in mixed schools than in single-sex schools, thus effectively narrowing career choice for co-educated pupils.'

Small-scale study: Arnold and Atkins – 'The social and emotional adjustment of hearing-impaired children' (1991)[5]

Small *ex post facto* studies are commonly reported. In contrast to Stables's 2300 sample, Arnold and Atkins's study consisted of twenty-three hearing-impaired children and twenty-three normally-hearing pupils acting as controls. The causal-comparative design was used to ask the following questions: 'Are hearing-impaired children more mal-adjusted than non hearing-impaired children?, and if so, 'Are they differently maladjusted as revealed by two widely-used measures of maladjustment?'

Arnold and Atkins's research used the 'Bristol Social Adjustment Guide' and 'Rutter's Children's Behaviour Questionnaire' to obtain ratings of their sample. In contrast to other studies, they report that the hearing-impaired were no more maladjusted than the age-matched hearing controls, although there were high levels of maladjustment in both groups. Differences in the scores between the Bristol and the Rutter measures, the researchers opine, might suggest that they measure different behaviours. More importantly, in our view, the authors cite other researchers who question the extent to which existing measures adequately operationalize the complex and multi-faceted concept of maladjustment.

ADVANTAGES AND DISADVANTAGES

We have already touched incidentally on some of the strengths and weaknesses of *ex post facto* research. We will now look at them more systematically. Among the advantages of the approach we may identify the following:

1 *Ex post facto* research meets an important need of the researcher where the more rigorous experimental approach is not possible. In the case of the alleged relationship between smoking and lung cancer, for instance, this cannot be tested experimentally (at least as far as human beings are concerned).
2 The method yields useful information concerning the nature of phenomena – what goes with what and under what conditions. In this way, *ex post facto* research is a valuable exploratory tool.

3 Improvements in statistical techniques and general methodology have made *ex post facto* designs more defensible.

4 In some ways and in certain situations the method is more useful than the experimental method, especially where the setting up of the latter would introduce a note of artificiality into research proceedings.

5 *Ex post facto* research is particularly appropriate when simple cause-and-effect relationships are being explored.

6 The method can give a sense of direction and provide a fruitful source of hypotheses that can subsequently be tested by the more rigorous experimental method.

Among the limitations and weaknesses of *ex post facto* designs the following may be mentioned:

1 There is the problem of lack of control in that the researcher is unable to manipulate the independent variable or to randomize her subjects.

2 One cannot know for certain whether the causative factor has been included or even identified.

3 It may be that no single factor is the cause.

4 A particular outcome may result from different causes on different occasions.

5 When a relationship has been discovered, there is the problem of deciding which is the cause and which the effect; the possibility of reverse causation has to be considered.

6 The relationship of two factors does not establish cause and effect.

7 Classifying into dichotomous groups can be problematic.

8 There is the difficulty of interpretation and the danger of the *post hoc* assumption being made, that is, believing that because X precedes O, X causes O.

9 It often bases its conclusions on too limited a sample or number of occurrences.

10 It frequently fails to single out the really significant factor or factors, and fails to recognize that events have multiple rather than single causes.

11 As a method it is regarded by some as too flexible.

12 It lacks nullifiability and confirmation.

DESIGNING AN *EX POST FACTO* INVESTIGATION

We earlier referred to the two basic designs embraced by *ex post facto* research – the co-relational (or causal) model and the criterion group (or causal-comparative) model. We return to them again here in order to consider designing both types of investigation. As we saw, the causal model attempts to identify the antecedent of a present condition and may be represented thus:

Independent variable   Dependent variable

X	O

Although one variable in an *ex post facto* study cannot be confidently said to depend upon the other as would be the case in a truly experimental investigation, it is nevertheless usual to designate one of the variables as independent (X) and the other as dependent (O). The left to right dimension indicates the temporal order, though having established this, we must not overlook the possibility of reverse causality.

In a typical investigation of this kind, then, two sets of data relating to the independent and dependent variables respectively will be gathered. As indicated earlier in the chapter, the data on the independent variable (X) will be retrospective in character and as such will be prone to the kinds of weakness, limitations and distortions to which all historical evidence is subject. Let us now translate the design into a hypothetical situation. Imagine a secondary school in which it is hypothesized that low staff morale (O) has come about as a direct result of comprehensive reorganization some two years earlier, say. A number of key factors distinguishing the new organization from the previous one can be readily identified. Collectively these could represent or contain the independent variable X and data on them could be accumulated retrospectively. They could include, for example, the introduction of mixed ability and team teaching, curricular innovation, loss of teacher status, decline in pupil motivation, modifications to the school catchment area, or the appointment of a new headteacher. These could then be checked against a measure of prevailing teachers' attitudes (O), thus providing the researcher with some leads at least as to possible causes of current discontent.

The second model, the causal-comparative, may be represented schematically as:

Group   Independent variable   Dependent variable

Group	Independent variable	Dependent variable
E	X	O_1
C		O_2

Using this model, the investigator hypothesizes the independent variable and then compares two groups, an experimental group (E) which has been exposed to the presumed independent variable X and a control group (C) which has not. (The dashed line in the model shows that the comparison groups *E* and *C* are not equated by random assignment, see p. 169.) Alternatively, she may examine two groups that are different in some way or ways and then try to account for the difference or differences by investigating possible antecedents. These two examples reflect two types of approach to causal-comparative research: the 'cause-to-effect' kind and the 'effect-to-cause' kind.[6]

The basic design of causal-comparative investigations is similar to an experimentally designed study. The chief difference resides in the nature of the independent variable, *X*. In a truly experimental situation, this will be under the control of the investigator and may therefore be described as manipulable. In the causal-comparative model (and also the causal model), however, the independent variable is beyond her control, having already occurred. It may therefore be described in this design as non-manipulable.

Two brief examples will underscore these two types of research design: the 'cause-to-effect' kind and the 'effect-to-cause' kind. A researcher may study the influence of school reorganization on low staff morale and then compare staff attitudes with those of teachers in a comparable school that has not undergone reorganization. Or a researcher may investigate the problems of the college dropout by comparing personality characteristics of the dropouts with those of students who stay the course; she may thereby be able to identify the antecedents of failure to stay the course on the part of the dropouts.

PROCEDURES IN *EX POST FACTO* RESEARCH

Ex post facto research is concerned with discovering relationships among variables in one's data; and we have seen how this may be accomplished by using either a causal or causal-comparative model. We now examine the steps involved in implementing a piece of *ex post facto* research. We may begin by identifying the problem area to be investigated. This stage will be followed by a clear and precise statement of the hypothesis to be tested or questions to be answered. The next step will be to make explicit the assumptions on which the hypothesis and subsequent procedures will be based. A review of the research literature will follow. This will enable the investigator to ascertain the kinds of issues, problems, obstacles and findings disclosed by previous studies in the area. There will then follow the planning of the actual investigation and this will consist of three broad stages – identification of the population and samples; the selection and construction of techniques for collecting data; and the establishment of categories for classifying the data. The final stage will involve the description, analysis and interpretation of the findings.

It was noted earlier that the principal weakness of *ex post facto* research

155

is the absence of control over the independent variable influencing the dependent variable in the case of causal designs or affecting observed differences between dependent variables in the case of causal-comparative designs. (We take up the question of control in experimental research in greater detail in the next chapter.) Although the *ex post facto* researcher is denied not only this kind of control but also the principle of randomization, she can nevertheless utilize procedures that will give her some measure of control in her investigation. And it is to some of these that we now turn.

One of the commonest means of introducing control into this type of research is that of matching the subjects in the experimental and control groups where the design is causal-comparative. One group of writers explain it thus:

> The matching is usually done on a subject-to-subject basis to form matched pairs. For example, if one were interested in the relationship between scouting experiences and delinquency, he could locate two groups of boys classified as delinquent and non-delinquent according to specified criteria. It would be wise in such a study to select pairs from these groups matched on the basis of socioeconomic status, family structure, and other variables known to be related to both scouting experience and delinquency. Analysis of the data from the matched samples could be made to determine whether or not scouting characterized the non-delinquent and was absent in the background of the delinquent.
>
> (Ary *et al.*, 1972)[7]

There are difficulties with this procedure, however, for it assumes that the investigator knows what the relevant factors are, that is, the factors that may be related to the dependent variable. Further, there is the possibility of losing those subjects which cannot be matched, thus reducing one's sample.

As an alternative procedure for introducing a degree of control into *ex post facto* research, Ary and his colleagues suggest building the extraneous independent variables into the design and using an analysis of variance technique. They explain:

> Assume that intelligence is a relevant extraneous variable and it is not feasible to control it through matching or other means. In this case, intelligence could be added to the design as another independent variable and the subjects of the study classified in terms of intelligence levels. The dependent variable measures would then be analysed through an analysis of variance and the main and interaction effects of intelligence might be determined. Such a procedure would reveal any significant differences among the

groups on the dependent variable, but no causal relationship between intelligence and the dependent variable could be assumed. Other extraneous variables could be operating to produce both the main effect and any interaction effects.

(Ary *et al.*, 1972)

Yet another procedure which may be adopted for introducing a measure of control into *ex post facto* design is that of selecting samples that are as homogeneous as possible on a given variable. The writers quoted above illustrate the procedure with the following example.

If intelligence were a relevant extraneous variable, its effects could be controlled by using subjects from only one intelligence level. This procedure serves the purpose of disentangling the independent variable in which the investigator may be interested from other variables with which it is commonly associated, so that any effects that are found can justifiably be associated with the independent variable.

(Ary *et al.*, 1972)

Finally, control may be introduced into an *ex post facto* investigation by stating and testing any alternative hypotheses that might be plausible explanations for the empirical outcomes of the study.[7] A researcher has thus to beware of accepting the first likely explanation of relationships in an *ex post facto* study as necessarily the only or final one. A well-known instance is the presumed relationship between cigarette smoking and lung cancer. Government health officials have been quick to seize on the explanation that smoking causes lung cancer. Tobacco firms, however, have put forward an alternative hypothesis – that both smoking and lung cancer are possibly the result of a third, as yet unspecified, factor. In other words, the possibility that both the independent and dependent variables are simply two separate results of a single common cause cannot be ignored.

And, of course, in some situations there is the possibility of reverse causality. Thus, instead of claiming that *A* causes *B*, it might be that *B* is the cause of *A*. A researcher might, for instance, hypothesize that aggressive behaviour is the result of watching violent television programmes. Reverse causality, however, would posit that some people choose to watch violent television programmes because they are aggressive in the first place. Box 7.1 summarizes the procedures just reviewed.

EXAMPLES OF *EX POST FACTO* RESEARCH

We illustrate *ex post facto* research with two studies that employ very different data gathering and analytical techniques. The third example utilizes quantitative and qualitative data in an interesting way.

157

Box 7.1   Some procedures for introducing measures of control into *ex post facto* research designs

---

1. Matching of the subjects in the experimental and control groups where the design of the study is causal-comparative.
2. Building extraneous independent variables into the design and using an analysis of variance technique.
3. Using, where possible, homogeneous samples on a given variable.
4. The testing of rival hypotheses offering alternative explanations.

Example 1: Ben-Peretz and Kremer-Hayon – 'The content and context of professional dilemmas' (1990)[8]

Ben-Peretz and Kremer-Hayon identified novice and senior (i.e. experienced) teachers and then sought to differentiate between them in terms of the content and context of the professional dilemmas they experienced in the course of their professional work, both in and out of school. Three novice teachers selected for interview had been in post for between one and two years; the three senior practitioners chosen had thirty-three years of teaching experience between them. The researchers used in-depth and open-ended interviews, that were transcribed verbatim for analysis.

The analysis revealed several educational contexts that gave rise to dilemmas shared by both groups of teachers. Some, however, were specific to one group or the other. For example, what the investigators termed the 'transition context' caused dilemmas for the novices. These included professional identity, professional competence, group membership, interpersonal relationships and teacher status. 'Teacher planning and curriculum' constituted another set of dilemmas. 'Ethical problems' to do with punishing pupils provided another difficulty for the less experienced teachers.

Summarizing their major findings, Ben-Peretz and Kremer-Hayon discern two explanatory frames for teacher dilemmas. One pertains to the gap between ideology and reality, the other to the multiple obligations that teachers confront. They conclude with the notion of *paradoxical dilemmas*, that is to say, dilemmas that originate in paradoxical views of a situation. By way of example the researchers cite the transcript of one of the novice teachers who was concerned about the issue of appropriate punishment. 'Should I send out a student who disrupts the whole class, or should I try to keep him in the classroom?' The first solution may be easier for the teacher and enable her to continue her teaching for the benefit of the whole group but may be pedagogically wrong for the erring student. After reading her account, the novice commented, 'All this is quite confusing, it reflects how I feel'.

158

Dilemmas, the investigators conclude, present a challenge to deliberate on and think about. As such, they are potential facilitators of
professional development. However, the generally negative tone in
which both groups expressed their dilemmas gave rise for concern, for
viewed as disturbing and unpleasant, dilemmas might lose their power
to promote professional growth.

Example 2: Pierce and Molloy – 'Psychological and biographical differences in teachers experiencing burnout' (1990)[9]

In contrast to Ben Peretz and Kremer Hayon's purely qualitative study,
Pierce and Molloy's research on teacher burnout was founded totally on
quantitative data, no attempt being made to use qualitative techniques
in the collection of psychological and biographical information from the
teachers involved. Rather, long-suffering participants were required to
complete batteries of tests and questionnaires that included the 'Maslach
Burnout Inventory, a Regressive Coping Checklist', which as the name
implies, identified the use of negative coping actions when dealing with
stress; a 'Role Questionnaire' designed to reveal role conflict and
ambiguity; a 'Work Relationship Index' giving a measure of social support; 'The Pupil Control Ideology Form' indicating teachers' attitudes
towards teacher–pupil relationships; a 'Stress Symptoms Scale' listing
twenty-five indicators of high stress; a 'Sources of Stress' measure identifying twenty stressors; 'The Hardiness Inventory' which purports to
measure commitment, control and challenge, and a host of biographical
information, global measures of occupational and non-occupational
stress, career satisfaction, career intention, career importance and self-
confidence, most of these involving some form of rating on ordinal-
measure scales. It is not reported how burnt-out participants were at the
end of this mammoth data collection phase of the study.

Using median scores on three sub-scales (emotional exhaustion, deper-
sonalization and personal accomplishment) of the 'Maslach Burnout
Inventory' as cut-off points, the researchers reduced the original sample
of over 750 teachers to two contrasting groups consisting of 'High
burnouts' ($n = 81$) and 'Low burnouts' ($n = 94$). The ex post facto study
then proceeded to 'look back' at the personality and biographical data,
using a variety of statistical tests to compare High and Low burnout
groups on each of the scales and inventories listed above. Box 7.2 shows
the results of these comparisons. Space precludes an account of the
sophisticated statistical techniques by means of which the researchers
were able to tease out models of burnout from their ample data bank.
Suffice it to say that they were able to ask questions such as, 'To what
extent do lower levels of commitment and control *and* higher levels of
role conflict *and* teaching in socially disadvantaged neighbourhood

Box 7.2 Comparisons between high and low burnout groups

Variable	High Burnout		Low Burnout		df	t
	Mean	N	Mean	N		
Global occupational stress	3.70	81	2.15	94	173	14.16***
Global non-occupational stress	2.05	81	1.92	93	172	1.03
Stress attributed to teaching	3.00	80	1.85	93	171	8.94***
Stress score	1.79	80	0.75	94	172	11.52***
Prof. needs and recognition	1.46	74	0.58	88	160	8.60***
Student concerns	2.22	74	0.95	88	160	12.24***
Time demands	2.07	74	1.28	88	160	7.70***
Commitment	8.07	81	2.68	93	172	9.33***
Control	11.36	80	7.99	92	170	6.36***
Challenge	14.84	81	16.01	93	172	−2.66**
Social Support	14.19	78	21.09	94	170	−7.84***
Role conflict	34.11	81	24.91	94	173	6.01***
Role ambiguity	23.20	81	14.40	94	173	9.80***
Pupil control ideology	60.28	81	52.64	94	173	4.75***
Satisfaction	2.65	81	4.31	94	173	−11.06***
Career intention	3.00	80	2.26	90	168	3.86***
Career likelihood	2.49	81	3.82	92	171	−7.23***
Career importance	4.21	81	5.73	94	173	−8.05***
Self-confidence	3.04	80	3.96	94	172	−9.26***
Physical health	33.63	81	13.77	94	173	11.60***
Short term absences	4.30	79	2.47	94	171	4.64***
Total days absent	11.72	78	4.78	92	168	3.55***
Regressive coping	11.49	80	5.04	94	172	10.45***
Staying at present school	3.00	81	4.29	94	173	−5.91***
Difficulty of school	3.92	79	2.32	92	169	6.23***

$**P<0.01, ***P<0.001$

Source: Pierce and Molloy, 1990

schools contribute to more frequent feelings of emotional exhaustion?'
Acknowledging the 'snap-shot', quantitative design of their study, Pierce
and Molloy conclude with a call for longitudinal designs and qualitative
data to complement their work.

Example 3 McLaughlin *et al.* – 'The schoolchild as health educator' (1992)[10]

McLaughlin *et al.*'s *ex post facto* study of the diffusion of a health
education programme to parents through their children, gathered both
quantitative and qualitative data. The research provides a good illustration of how qualitative data can be used to explain information obtained
quantitatively.

As in the Pierce and Molloy study, 'winnowing' out particular individuals from a large, initial sample was the strategy employed by McLaughlin and her co-workers prior to embarking upon in-depth interviews. A two-week, school-based curriculum project focusing on the control of high blood-pressure consisted of films, slides, group discussions and practical activities that included learning to measure blood-pressure and to practise the use of an aneroid sphygmomanometer. The sixth-grade (12-year-old) pupils were allowed to take aneroid sphygmomanometers home to measure the blood pressure of family members and to engage parents in discussion of what they themselves had learned during the school-based project. Pupils were specifically instructed to discuss life-style and risk factors associated with hypertension. In a word, pupils became teachers.

All 1204 sixth graders and 1446 parents in the study were tested for specific knowledge about high blood-pressure. Pupils were assessed on a scale of self-esteem and parents were tested on a measure of family cohesion. In addition, the researchers devised an information diffusion scale that elicited from parents and children the degree to which they had discussed the heart, blood pressure, diet, regular exercise, smoking and how to take blood pressure.

Two polemically-different groups of parents were selected for interview on the basis of screening the quantitative data gathered during the course of the investigation. They were designated as 'high transfer of information parents' ($n=19$) and 'low transfer of information parents' ($n=14$), hereinafter, 'High Transfers' and 'Low Transfers'. High Transfers had a perfect match between child and parents on the six-item information diffusion measure and had discussed all risk factors in the diffusion questions. Low Transfers, by contrast, had a zero match on the six diffusion questions and had discussed none of the risk factors. Open-ended questions used in the interview guide were intended to answer the investigators' principal aim in conducting the study: 'What was different about those families where high diffusion occurred in contrast to where it did not occur at all?' Audio-taped interviews were conducted at parental homes and lasted, on average, 45 minutes. Transcribed interview data were analysed, using the constant comparative method, a procedure that seeks to generate typologies out of patterns of organization in transcribed texts and repetitions of words and phrases (see Miles and Huberman,[11] Strauss[12]). In this way, the researchers created *substantive codes* that became categories of parent and child. They recorded their emerging ideas on index cards, seeking to ascertain connections between the data. The process has been termed 'memoing' by its leading exponent (Strauss, 1987). By meeting with each other on a regular basis to share on-going analytical frameworks of codings and categories, family typologies and modes of interaction began to

161

Box 7.3   High and low transfer families

High Transfer	regular, frequent and varied interaction among family members	
Low Transfer	less frequent, less varied interaction among family members	
High Transfer	active participation with child in blood-pressure measuring	
Low Transfer	lack of participation, lack of interest and (some) negative reaction to blood-pressure measuring	
Child typologies		
High Transfer	'confident' child	physically, emotionally, academically mature for chronological age
	'nurturing' child	providing social support for mother
	'golden' child	typically last one at home or an only child, strong relational bond
Low Transfer	'shy' child	sensitive, having difficulty interacting with others
	'disengaged' child	heavily involved in extra-curricular activities away from home
	'troublemaker'	lacking in frustration tolerance, difficulty in dealing with authority figures

Source: Adapted from McLaughlin *et al.*, 1992

crystallize. Some of these typologies and ways of interacting are summarized in Box 7.3. The authors concluded that family dynamics could have important effects on the degree to which health information could be diffused within family units. Children's success as message-bearers depended on their roles within families and the quality of intrafamilial relationships and support systems.

REFERENCES AND NOTES

1 Kerlinger, F.N., *Foundations of Behavioral Research* (Holt, Rinehart & Winston, New York, 1970).
2 In Chapters 7 and 8, we adopt the symbols and conventions used in Campbell, D.T. and Stanley, J.C., 'Experimental and quasi-experimental designs for research on teaching', in N.L. Gage (ed.), *Handbook of Research on Teaching* (Rand McNally, Chicago, 1963). These are presented fully on p. 165.
3 Borkowsky, F.T., 'The relationship of work quality in undergraduate music curricula to effectiveness in instrumental music teaching in the public schools', *Journal of Experimental Education* 39 (1970) 14–19.
4 Stables, A., 'Differences between pupils from mixed and single-sex schools in their enjoyment of school subjects and in their attitude to Science in school', *Educational Review* 42 (3) (1990) 221–30.
5 Arnold, P. and Atkins, J., 'The social and emotional adjustment of hearing-impaired children integrated in primary schools', *Educational Researcher* 33(3) (1991) 223–8.

6. Chapin, F.S., *Experimental Designs in Sociological Research* (Harper & Row, New York, 1947).

7 Ary, D., Jacobs, L.C. and Razavieh, A., *Introduction to Research in Education* (Holt, Rinehart & Winston, New York, 1972).

8 Ben-Peretz, M. and Kremer-Hayon, L., 'The content and context of professional dilemmas encountered by novice and senior teachers', *Educational Review* 42 (1) (1990) 31–40.

9 Pierce, C.M.B. and Molloy, G.N., 'Psychological and biographical differences between secondary school teachers experiencing high and low levels of burnout', *British Journal of Educational Psychology* 60 (1990) 37–51.

10 McLaughlin, J.F., Owen, S.L., Fors, S.W. and Levinson, R.M., 'The school-child as health educator: diffusion of hypertension information from sixth-grade children to their parents', *Qual. Studies in Education* 5 (2) (1992) 147–65.

11 Miles, M.B. and Huberman, A.M., *Qualitative Data Analysis* (Sage, Beverly Hills, Calif. 1984).

12 Strauss, A.M., *Qualitative Analysis for Social Scientists* (Cambridge University Press, Cambridge, 1987).

8

EXPERIMENTS, QUASI-EXPERIMENTS AND SINGLE-CASE RESEARCH

INTRODUCTION

In Chapter 7, we described *ex post facto* research as experimentation in reverse in that *ex post facto* studies start with groups that are already different with regard to certain characteristics and then proceed to search, in retrospect, for the factors that brought about those differences. We then went on to cite Kerlinger's description of the experimental researcher's approach:

> If *x*, then *y*; if frustration, then aggression . . . the researcher uses some method to measure *x* and then observes *y* to see if concomitant variation occurs.
>
> (Kerlinger, 1970)[1]

The essential feature of experimental research is that investigators deliberately control and manipulate the conditions which determine the events in which they are interested. At its simplest, an experiment involves making a change in the value of one variable – called the independent variable – and observing the effect of that change on another variable – called the dependent variable. Frequently in learning experiments in classroom settings the independent variable is a stimulus of some kind, a new method in arithmetical computation for example, and the dependent variable is a response, the time taken to do twenty sums using the new method. Most empirical studies in educational settings, however, are quasi-experimental rather than experimental. The single most important difference between the quasi-experiment and the true experiment is that in the former case, the researcher undertakes his study with groups that are intact, that is to say, the groups have been constituted by means other than random selection. We begin by identifying the essential features of pre-experimental, true experimental and quasi-experimental designs, our intention being to introduce the reader to the meaning and purpose of control in educational experimentation.

DESIGNS IN EDUCATIONAL EXPERIMENTATION

In the outline of research designs that follows we use symbols and conventions from Campbell and Stanley:[2]

1 X represents the exposure of a group to an experimental variable or event, the effects of which are to be measured.
2 O refers to the process of observation or measurement.
3 Xs and Os in a given row are applied to the same persons.
4 Left to right order indicates temporal sequence.
5 Xs and Os vertical to one another are simultaneous.
6 R indicates random assignment to separate treatment groups.
7 Parallel rows unseparated by dashes represent comparison groups equated by randomization, while those separated by a dashed line represent groups not equated by random assignment.

A PRE-EXPERIMENTAL DESIGN: THE ONE GROUP PRETEST–POST-TEST

Very often, reports about the value of a new teaching method or interest aroused by some curriculum innovation or other reveal that a researcher has measured a group on a dependent variable (O_1), for example, attitudes towards minority groups, and then introduced an experimental manipulation (X), perhaps a ten-week curriculum project designed to increase tolerance of ethnic minorities. Following the experimental treatment, the researcher has again measured group attitudes (O_2) and proceeded to account for differences between pretest and post-test scores by reference to the effects of X.

The one group pretest–post-test design can be represented as:

Experimental	O_1	X	O_2

Suppose that just such a project has been undertaken and that the researcher finds that O_2 scores indicate greater tolerance of ethnic minorities than O_1 scores. How justified is she in attributing the cause of O_1–O_2 differences to the experimental treatment (X), that is, the term's project work? At first glance the assumption of causality seems reasonable enough. The situation is not that simple, however. Compare for a moment the circumstances represented in our hypothetical educational example with those which typically obtain in experiments in the physical sciences. A physicist who applies heat to a metal bar can confidently attribute the observed expansion to the rise in temperature that she has introduced because within the confines of her laboratory she has excluded (i.e. controlled) all other extraneous sources of variation (this example is suggested by Pilliner (1973)[3]).

The same degree of control can never be attained in educational experimentation. At this point readers may care to reflect upon some possible influences other than the ten-week curriculum project that might account for the O_1–O_2 differences in our hypothetical educational example.

They may conclude that factors to do with the pupils, the teacher, the school, the classroom organization, the curriculum materials and their presentation, the way that the subjects' attitudes were measured, to say nothing of the thousand and one other events that occurred in and about the school during the course of the term's work, might all have exerted some influence upon the observed differences in attitude. These kinds of extraneous variables which are outside the experimenters' control in one-group pretest–post-test designs threaten to invalidate their research efforts. We later identify a number of such threats to the validity of educational experimentation.

The problems arising out of the use of pre-experimental designs are graphically illustrated in the comments of a researcher who employed a pretest–post-test design in six secondary schools in her evaluation of the use of archive materials in the teaching of history.

> The pretests were taken by 158 children in six schools . . . not all the children who had taken the pretests either used the Unit [farming in Leicestershire] or took the post-tests, which were completed by only 72 children. Without the backing of a national body like the Schools Council, one's status and purpose are suspect and offers of assistance are not readily forthcoming. . . . The six schools used were the only ones to offer assistance after a request had been sent to most secondary schools in [the county]. This had two main results. In the first place, the need to work with any school classes whose teachers offered to co-operate in order to obtain a sample of adequate size meant that variables such as age, intelligence, previous learning experiences, etc. could not be controlled. . . . Secondly, although all classes used the same materials, it was impossible to insist on common teaching patterns, equal provision of additional resources, similar periods of time devoted to each section of the materials or the use of control groups. Drop out during the use of the materials due to natural causes such as illness or a teacher's practice of allowing unrestricted choice of work patterns also reduced the size of the sample, resulting in different sample sizes for pre- and post-tests.
>
> (Palmer, 1976)[4]

A 'TRUE' EXPERIMENTAL DESIGN: THE PRETEST–POST-TEST CONTROL GROUP DESIGN

A complete exposition of experimental designs is beyond the scope of this chapter. In the brief outline that follows, we have selected one design from the comprehensive treatment of the subject by Campbell and Stanley (1963) in order to identify the essential features of what they term a 'true experimental' and what Kerlinger (1970) refers to as a 'good' design. Along with its variants, the chosen design is commonly used in educational experimentation.

The pretest–post-test control group design can be represented as:

Experimental	RO_1	X	O_2
Control	RO_3		O_4

It differs from the pre-experimental design that we have just described in that it involves the use of two groups which have been constituted by randomization. As Kerlinger observes, in theory, random assignment to E and C conditions controls all possible independent variables. In practice, of course, it is only when enough subjects are included in the experiment that the principle of randomization has a chance to operate as a powerful control. However, the effects of randomization even with a small number of subjects is well illustrated in Box 8.1.

Box 8.1   The effects of randomization

Select twenty cards from a pack, ten red and ten black. Shuffle and deal into two ten-card piles. Now count the number of red cards and black cards in either pile and record the results. Repeat the whole sequence many times, recording the results each time.

You will soon convince yourself that the most likely distribution of reds and blacks in a pile is five in each: the next most likely, six red (or black) and four black (or red); and so on. You will be lucky (or unlucky for the purposes of the demonstration!) to achieve one pile of red and the other entirely of black cards. The probability of this happening is 1 in 92,378! On the other hand, the probability of obtaining a 'mix' not more than 6 of one colour and 4 of the other is about 82 in 100.

If you now imagine the red cards to stand for the 'better' ten children and the black cards for the 'poorer' ten children in a class of twenty, you will conclude that the operation of the laws of chance alone will almost probably give you close equivalent 'mixes' of 'better' and 'poorer' children in the experimental and control groups.

Source: Adapted from Pilliner, 1973

Randomization, then, ensures the greater likelihood of equivalence, that is, the apportioning[5] out between the experimental and control groups of any other factors or characteristics of the subjects which might conceivably affect the experimental variables in which the researcher is interested. It is, as Kerlinger notes, the addition of the control group in our present example and the random assignment of subjects to E and C groups that radically alters the situation from that which obtains in the pre-experimental design outlined earlier. For if the groups are made equivalent, then any so-called 'clouding' effects should be present in both groups.

> If the mental ages of the children of the experimental group increase, so should the mental ages of the children of the control group. . . . If something happens to affect the experimental subjects between the pretest and the post-test, this something should also affect the subjects of the control groups.
>
> (Kerlinger, 1970)

So strong is this simple and elegant true experimental design, that all the threats to internal validity identified below (pp. 170–1) are, according to Campbell and Stanley (1963), controlled in the pretest–post-test control group design.

One problem that has been identified with this particular experimental design is the interaction effect of testing. Good[6] explains that whereas the various threats to the validity of the experiment listed on pp. 170–1 can be thought of as main effects, manifesting themselves in mean differences independently of the presence of other variables, interaction effects, as their name implies, are joint effects and may occur even when no main effects are present. For example, an interaction effect may occur as a result of the pretest measure sensitizing the subjects to the experimental variable. Interaction effects can be controlled for by adding to the pretest–post-test control group design two more groups that do not experience the pretest measures. The result is a four-group design, as suggested by Solomon.[7] Later in the chapter, we describe an educational study which built into a pretest–post-test group design a further control group to take account of the possibility of pretest sensitization.

A QUASI-EXPERIMENTAL DESIGN: THE NON-EQUIVALENT CONTROL GROUP DESIGN

Often in educational research, it is simply not possible for investigators to undertake true experiments. At best, they may be able to employ something approaching a true experimental design in which they have control over what Campbell and Stanley (1963) refer to as 'the who and to whom of measurement' but lack control over 'the when and to whom of exposure', or the randomization of exposures – essential if true experimentation is to take place. These situations are quasi-experimental and the methodologies employed by researchers are termed quasi-experimental designs. (Kerlinger (1970) refers to quasi-experimental situations as 'compromise designs', an apt description when applied to much educational research where the random selection or random assignment of schools and classrooms is quite impracticable.)

One of the most commonly used quasi-experimental designs in educational research can be represented as:

Experimental	O_1	X	O_2
Control	O_3		O_4

The dashed line separating the parallel rows in the diagram of the non-equivalent control group indicates that the experimental and control groups have not been equated by randomization – hence the term 'non-equivalent'. The addition of a control group makes the present design a decided improvement over the one group pretest–post-test design, for to the degree that experimenters can make E and C groups as equivalent as possible, they can avoid the equivocality of interpretations that plague the pre-experimental design discussed earlier. The equivalence of groups can be strengthened by matching, followed by random assignment to E and C treatments.

Where matching is not possible, the researcher is advised to use samples from the same population or samples that are as alike as possible (Kerlinger, 1970). Where intact groups differ substantially, however, matching is unsatisfactory due to regression effects which lead to different group means on post-test measures. Campbell and Stanley put it this way:

> If [in the non-equivalent control group design] the means of the groups are substantially different, then the process of matching not only fails to provide the intended equation but in addition insures the occurrence of unwanted regression effects. It becomes predictably certain that the two groups will differ on their post-test scores altogether independently of any effects of X, and that this difference will vary directly with the difference between the total populations from which the selection was made and inversely with the test-retest correlation.

> (Campbell and Stanley, 1963)

169

THE VALIDITY OF EXPERIMENTS

As we have seen, the fundamental purpose of experimental design is to impose control over conditions that would otherwise cloud the true effects of the independent variables upon the dependent variables.

Clouding conditions that threaten to jeopardize the validity[8] of experiments have been identified by Campbell and Stanley (1963) and by Bracht and Glass (1968),[9] conditions incidentally that are of greater consequence to the validity of quasi-experiments (more typical in educational research) than to true experiments in which random assignment to treatments occurs and where both treatment and measurement can be more adequately controlled by the researcher. The following summaries adapted from Campbell and Stanley and Bracht and Glass distinguish between 'internal validity' and 'external validity'.

> Internal validity is concerned with the question, do the experimental treatments, in fact, make a difference in the specific experiments under scrutiny?

> External validity, on the other hand, asks the question, given these demonstrable effects, to what populations or settings can they be generalized?

THREATS TO INTERNAL VALIDITY

1 *History* – Frequently in educational research, events other than the experimental treatments occur during the time between pretest and post-test observations. Such events produce effects that can mistakenly be attributed to differences in treatment.

2 *Maturation* – Between any two observations subjects change in a variety of ways. Such changes can produce differences that are independent of the experimental treatments. The problem of maturation is more acute in protracted educational studies than in brief laboratory experiments.

3 *Statistical regression* – Like maturation effects, regression effects increase systematically with the time interval between pretests and post-tests. Statistical regression occurs in educational (and other) research due to the unreliability of measuring instruments and to extraneous factors unique to each experimental group. Regression means, simply, that subjects scoring highest on a pretest are likely to score relatively lower on a post-test; conversely, those scoring lowest on a pretest are likely to score relatively higher on a post-test. In short, in pretest–post-test situations, there is regression to the mean. Regression effects can lead the educational researcher mistakenly to attribute post-test gains and losses to low scoring and high scoring respectively.

4 *Testing* – Pretests at the beginning of experiments can produce effects other than those due to the experimental treatments. Such effects can include sensitizing subjects to the true purposes of the experiment and practice effects which produce higher scores on post-test measures.

5 *Instrumentation* – Unreliable tests or instruments can introduce serious errors into experiments. With human observers or judges, error can result from changes in their skills and levels of concentration over the course of the experiment.

6 *Selection* – Bias may be introduced as a result of differences in the selection of subjects for the comparison groups or when intact classes are employed as experimental or control groups. Selection bias, moreover, may interact with other factors (history, maturation, etc.) to cloud even further the effects of the comparative treatments.

7 *Experimental mortality* – The loss of subjects through dropout often occurs in long-running experiments and may result in confounding the effects of the experimental variables, for whereas initially the groups may have been randomly selected, the residue that stays the course is likely to be different from the unbiased sample that began it.

THREATS TO EXTERNAL VALIDITY

Threats to external validity are likely to limit the degree to which generalizations can be made from the particular experimental conditions to other populations or settings. Below, we summarize a number of factors (adapted from Campbell and Stanley (1963) and Bracht and Glass (1968)) that jeopardize external validity.

1 *Failure to describe independent variables explicitly* – Unless independent variables are adequately described by the researcher, future replications of the experimental conditions are virtually impossible.

2 *Lack of representativeness of available and target populations* – Whilst those participating in the experiment may be representative of an available population, they may not be representative of the population to which the experimenter seeks to generalize her findings.

3 *Hawthorne effect*[10] – Medical research has long recognized the psychological effects that arise out of mere participation in drug experiments, and placebos and double-blind designs are commonly employed to counteract the biasing effects of participation. Similarly, so-called Hawthorne effects threaten to contaminate experimental treatments in educational research when subjects realize their role as guinea pigs.

4 *Inadequate operationalizing of dependent variables* – Dependent variables that the experimenter operationalizes must have validity in the non-experimental setting to which she wishes to generalize her findings. A paper and pencil questionnaire on career choice, for example, may

have little validity in respect of the actual employment decisions made by undergraduates on leaving university.

5 *Sensitization to experimental conditions* – As with threats to internal validity, pretests may cause changes in the subjects' sensitivity to the experimental variables and thus cloud the true effects of the experimental treatment.

6 *Interaction effects of extraneous factors and experimental treatments* – All of the above threats to external validity represent interactions of various clouding factors with treatments. As well as these, interaction effects may also arise as a result of any or all of those factors identified under the section on 'Threats to internal validity' (pp. 170–1).

By way of summary, we have seen that an experiment can be said to be internally valid to the extent that within its own confines, its results are credible (Pilliner, 1973); but for those results to be useful, they must be generalizable beyond the confines of the particular experiment; in a word, they must be externally valid also. Pilliner points to a lopsided relationship between internal and external validity. Without internal validity an experiment cannot possibly be externally valid. But the converse does not necessarily follow; an internally valid experiment may or may not have external validity. Thus, the most carefully designed experiment involving a sample of Welsh-speaking children is not necessarily generalizable to a target population which includes non-Welsh-speaking subjects.

It follows, then, that the way to good experimentation in schools and classrooms lies in maximizing both internal and external validity.

PROCEDURES IN CONDUCTING EXPERIMENTAL RESEARCH

In Chapter 7, we identified a sequence of steps in carrying out an *ex post facto* study. An experimental investigation must also follow a set of logical procedures. Those that we now enumerate, however, should be treated with some circumspection. It is extraordinarily difficult (and indeed, foolhardy) to lay down clear-cut rules as guides to experimental research. At best, we can identify an ideal route to be followed, knowing full well that educational research rarely proceeds in such a systematic fashion. (For a detailed discussion of the practical problems in educational experimentation, see Evans (1978), Chapter 4, 'Planning experimental work'.[11])

First, the researcher must identify and define the research problem as precisely as possible, always supposing that the problem is amenable to experimental methods.

Second, she must formulate hypotheses that she wishes to test. This involves making predictions about relationships between specific variables and at the same time making decisions about other variables that are to be excluded from the experiment by means of controls. Variables, remember, must have two properties.[12] First, they must be measurable. Physical fitness, for example, is not directly measurable until it has been operationally defined. Making the variable 'physical fitness' operational means simply defining it by letting something else that is measurable stand for it – a gymnastics test, perhaps. Second, the proxy variable must be a valid indicator of the hypothetical variable in which one is interested. That is to say, a gymnastics test probably is a reasonable proxy for physical fitness; height on the other hand most certainly is not. Excluding variables from the experiment is inevitable, given constraints of time and money. It follows therefore that one must set up priorities among the variables in which one is interested so that the most important of them can be varied experimentally whilst others are held constant.

Third, the researcher must select appropriate levels at which to test the independent variables. By way of example, suppose an educational psychologist wishes to find out whether longer or shorter periods of reading make for reading attainment in school settings (see Simon, 1978). She will hardly select 5-hour and 5-minute periods as appropriate levels; rather, she is more likely to choose 30-minute and 60-minute levels, in order to compare with the usual timetabled periods of 45 minutes duration. In other words, the experimenter will vary the stimuli at such levels as are of practical interest in the real-life situation. Pursuing the example of reading attainment somewhat further, our hypothetical experimenter will be wise to vary the stimuli in large enough intervals so as to obtain measureable results. Comparing reading periods of 44 minutes, or 46 minutes, with timetabled reading lessons of 45 minutes is scarcely likely to result in observable differences in attainment.

Fourth, in planning the design of the experiment, the researcher must take account of the population to which she wishes to generalize her results. This involves her in decisions over sample sizes and sampling methods. Sampling decisions are bound up with questions of funds, manpower and the amount of time available for experimentation.

Fifth, with problems of validity in mind, the researcher must select instruments, choose tests and decide upon appropriate methods of analysis.

Sixth, before embarking upon the actual experiment, the researcher must pilot test the experimental procedures to identify possible snags in connection with any aspect of the investigation. This is of crucial importance as the following comment from a highly-experienced experimenter makes plain:

Conduct a pretest and then revise your procedure in the light of what you learn from the pretest. Run another pretest. Revise again. And so on until your experimental procedure is pat and airtight.

(Simon, 1978)

Seventh, during the experiment itself, the researcher must endeavour to follow tested and agreed-on procedures to the letter. The standardization of instructions, the exact timing of experimental sequences, the meticulous recording and checking of observations – these are the hallmark of the competent researcher.

With her data collected, the researcher faces the most important part of the whole enterprise. Processing data, analysing results and drafting reports are all extremely demanding activities, both in intellectual effort and time. Often this last part of the experimental research is given too little time in the overall planning of the investigation. Experienced researchers rarely make such a mistake; computer program faults and a dozen more unanticipated disasters teach the hard lesson of leaving ample time for the analysis and interpretation of experimental findings. And on this last point, one final tip from the experienced experimenter we quoted earlier:

This is a particularly good time to discuss your work with your fellow students and staff members. Show them a brief write up of what you are doing and your preliminary results. One of my own major shortcomings as a researcher is that I do too little of this, largely because I hesitate to ask people. I hope that you are less shy about this than I am, but you should at least recognize that someone is doing you one of the greatest favours it is possible for one person to confer on another when she gives you the benefit of her attention, experience and critical imagination.

(Simon, 1978)

EXAMPLES FROM EDUCATIONAL RESEARCH

Example 1: A pre-experimental design

A pre-experimental design was used in a study involving the 1991–1992 Postgraduate Diploma in Education group following a course of training to equip them to teach social studies in senior secondary schools in Botswana. The researcher wished to find out whether the programme of studies he had devised would effect changes in the students' orientations towards social studies teaching.[13] To that end, he employed a research instrument, the Barth/Shermis Studies Preference Scale (BSSPS) which has had wide use in differing cultures including America, Egypt and

174

Nigeria, and whose construction meets commonly-required criteria concerning validity and internal consistency reliability.

The BSSSPS consists of forty-five Likert-type items (see page 280), providing measures of what purport to be three social studies traditions or philosophical orientations, the oldest of which, Citizenship Transmission involves indoctrination of the young in the basic values of a society. The second orientation, called the Social Science is held to relate to the acquisition of knowledge-gathering skills based on the mastery of social science concepts and processes. The third tradition, Reflective Inquiry is said to derive from the philosophy of John Dewey's idea of pragmatism with emphasis on the process of inquiry. Forty-eight Postgraduate Diploma students were administered the BSSSPS during the first session of their one-year course of study. At the end of the programme, the BSSSPS was again completed in order to determine whether changes had occurred in students' philosophical orientations. Briefly, the 'preferred orientation' in the pretest and post-test was the criterion measure, the two orientations least preferred being ignored. Box 8.2 shows the pretest and post-test results. Broadly speaking, students tended to move from a majority holding a Citizenship Transmission orientation at the beginning of the course to a greater affirmation of the Social Science and the Reflective Inquiry traditions. Using the symbols and conventions adopted earlier (see page 165) to represent research designs, we can illustrate the Botswana study as:

Experimental	O_1	X	O_2

The briefest consideration reveals inadequacies in the design. Indeed, Campbell and Stanley describe the one group pretest–post-test design as 'a "bad example" to illustrate several of the confounded extraneous variables that can jeopardize internal validity. These variables offer

Box 8.2 Numbers of students in favour of specific orientations

Social Studies orientations	Before the course	After the course
Citizenship transmission	30	15
Social science	15	21
Reflective inquiry	3	12
	(48)	(48)

Source: Adapted from Adeyemi, 1992

plausible hypotheses explaining an O_1–O_2 difference, rival to the hypothesis that caused the difference' (Campbell and Stanley, 1963). The investigator is rightly cautious in his conclusions: 'it is possible to say that the social studies course *might* be responsible for this phenomenon, although other extraneous variables might be operating' (Adeyemi, 1992, emphasis added). Somewhat ingenuously he puts his finger on one potential explanation, that the changes could have occurred among his intending teachers because the shift from 'inculcation to rational decision-making was in line with the recommendation of the Nine Year Social Studies Syllabus issued by the Botswana Ministry of Education in 1989' (Adeyemi, 1992).

Example 2: A quasi-experimental design

Mason, Mason and Quayle's longitudinal study took place between 1984 and 1992.[14] Its principal aim was to test whether the explicit teaching of linguistic features of GCSE textbooks, coursework and examinations would produce an improvement in performance across the secondary curriculum. The title of their report, 'Illuminating English: how explicit language teaching improved public examination results in a comprehensive school', suggests that the authors are persuaded that they achieved their objective. In light of the experimental design selected for the research, readers may ask themselves whether or not the results are as unequivocal as reported.

The design adopted in the Shevington study (Shevington is the location of the experiment in north-west England) may be represented as:

Experimental	O_1	X	O_2
Control	O_3		O_4

This is, of course, the non-equivalent control group design outlined earlier in this chapter (page 169) in which parallel rows separated by dashed lines represent groups that have not been equated by random assignment.

In brief, the researchers adopted a methodology akin to teaching English as a foreign language and applied this to Years 7–9 in Shevington Comprehensive School and two neighbouring schools, monitoring the pupils at every stage and comparing their performance with control groups drawn both from Shevington and the two other schools. Inevitably, because experimental and control groups were not randomly allocated, there were significant differences in the performance of some groups on pre-treatment measures such as the York Language Aptitude Test. Moreover, because no standardized reading tests of sufficient difficulty were available as post-treatment measures, tests had to be devised by the researchers, who provide no details as to their validity or reliability. These difficulties notwithstanding, pupils in the experimental groups taking public examinations in 1990 and 1991 showed substantial gains in respect of the percentage increases of those obtaining GCSE Grades A–C. The researchers note that during the three years 1989 to 1991, 'no other significant change in the policy, teaching staff or organization of the school took place which could account for this dramatic improvement of 50 per cent' (Mason *et al.*, 1992).

Although the Shevington researchers attempted to exercise control over extraneous variables, readers may well ask whether each of the threats to internal and external validity that we identified earlier (see pages 170–2) was sufficiently met as to allow such a categorical conclusion as, 'the pupils . . . achieved greater success in public examinations as a result of taking part in the project' (Mason *et al.*, 1992).

Example 3: A 'true' experimental design

Another investigation (Bhadwal and Panda, 1991)[15] concerned with effecting improvements in pupils' performance as a consequence of changing teaching strategies used a more robust experimental design. In rural India, the researchers drew a sample of seventy-eight pupils, matched by socio-economic backgrounds and non-verbal IQs, from three primary schools that were themselves matched by location, physical facilities, teachers' qualifications and skills, school evaluation procedures and degree of parental involvement. Twenty-six pupils were randomly selected to comprise the experimental group, the remaining fifty-two being equally divided into two control groups. Before the introduction of the changed teaching strategies to the experimental group, all three groups completed questionnaires on their study habits and attitudes. These instruments were specifically designed for use with younger children and were subjected to the usual item analyses, test–retest and split-half reliability inspections. Bhadwal and Panda's research design can be represented as:

Experimental	RO_1	X	RO_2
First control	RO_3		RO_4
Second control	RO_5		RO_6

Recalling Kerlinger's discussion of a 'good' experimental design, (page 167), the version of the pretest–post-test control design employed here (unlike the design used in Example 2 above) resorted to randomization which, in theory, controls all possible independent variables. Kerlinger adds, however, '*in practice*, it is only when enough subjects are included in the experiment that the principle of randomization has a chance to operate as a powerful control' (Kerlinger, 1970). It is doubtful whether twenty-six pupils in each of the three groups in Bhadwal and Panda's study constituted 'enough subjects'.

In addition to the matching procedures in drawing up the sample, and the random allocation of pupils to experimental and control groups, the researchers also used analysis of covariance[16], as a further means of controlling for initial differences between E and C groups on their pre-test mean scores on the independent variables, study habits and attitudes.

The experimental programme[17] involved improving teaching skills, classroom organization, teaching aids, pupil participation, remedial help, peer-tutoring, and continuous evaluation. In addition, provision was also made in the experimental group for ensuring parental involvement and extra reading materials. It would be startling if such a package of teaching aids and curriculum strategies did not effect significant changes in their recipients and such was the case in the experimental results. The Experimental Group made highly significant gains in respect of its level of study habits as compared with Control Group 2 where students did not show a marked change. What did surprise the investigators, we suspect, was the significant increase in levels of study habits in Control Group 1. Maybe, they opine, this unexpected result occurred because Control Group 1 pupils were tested immediately prior to the beginning of their annual examinations. On the other hand, they concede, some unaccountable variables might have been operating. There is, surely, a lesson here for all researchers!

SINGLE-CASE RESEARCH: ABAB DESIGN

At the beginning of Chapter 5, we described case study researchers as typically engaged in observing the characteristics of an individual unit, be it a child, a classroom, a school, or a whole community. We went on to contrast case study researchers with experimenters whom we described as typically concerned with the manipulation of variables in order to determine their causal significance. That distinction, as we shall see, is only partly true.

Increasingly, in recent years, single-case research as an experimental methodology has extended to such diverse fields as clinical psychology, medicine, education, social work, psychiatry, and counselling. Most of the single-case studies carried out in these (and other) areas share the following characteristics:

178

1 they involve the continuous assessment of some aspect of human behaviour over a period of time, requiring on the part of the researcher the administration of measures on multiple occasions within separate phases of a study.
2 they involve 'intervention effects' which are replicated in the same subject(s) over time.

Continuous assessment measures are used as a basis for drawing inferences about the effectiveness of intervention procedures.

The characteristics of single-case research studies are discussed by Kazdin (1982)[18] in terms of ABAB designs, the basic experimental format in most single-case researches. ABAB designs, Kazdin observes, consist of a family of procedures in which observations of performance are made over time for a given client or group of clients. Over the course of the investigation, changes are made in the experimental conditions to which the client is exposed. The basic rationale of the ABAB design is illustrated in Box 8.3. What it does is this. It examines the effects of an intervention by alternating the baseline condition (the A phase), when no intervention is in effect, with the intervention condition (the B phase). The A and B phases are then repeated to complete the four phases. As Kazdin says, the effects of the intervention are clear if performance improves during the first intervention phase, reverts to or approaches original baseline levels of performance when the treatment is withdrawn, and improves again when treatment is recommenced in the second intervention phase.

Box 8.3 The ABAB design

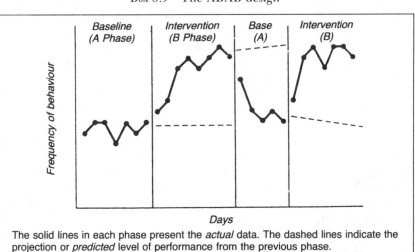

The solid lines in each phase present the *actual* data. The dashed lines indicate the projection or *predicted* level of performance from the previous phase.

Source: Adapted from Kazdin, 1982

Box 8.4:   An ABAB design in an educational setting

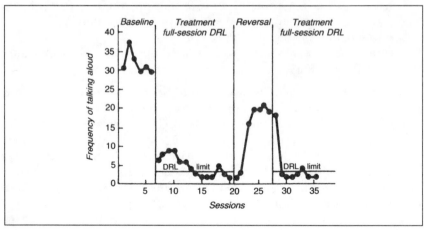

Source: Kazdin, 1982

An example of the application of the ABAB design in an educational setting is provided by Dietz (1977)[19] whose single-case study sought to measure the effect that a teacher could have upon the disruptive behaviour of a mentally-retarded adolescent boy whose persistent talking disturbed his fellow classmates in a special education class.

In order to decrease the unwelcomed behaviour, a reinforcement programme was devised in which the boy could earn extra time with the teacher by decreasing the number of times he called out. The boy was told that when he made three (or fewer) interruptions during any fifty-five-minute class period the teacher would spend extra time working with him. In the technical language of behaviour modification theory, the pupil would receive reinforcing consequences when he was able to show a low rate of disruptive behaviour (in Box 8.4 this is referred to as 'differential reinforcement of low rates' or DRL).

When the retarded child was able to desist from talking aloud on fewer than three occasions during any timetabled period, he was rewarded by the teacher spending fifteen minutes with him helping him with his learning tasks. The pattern of results displayed in Box 8.4 shows the considerable changes that occurred in the boy's behaviour when the intervention procedures were carried out and the substantial increases in disruptions towards baseline levels when the teacher's rewarding strategies were withdrawn. Finally, when the intervention was reinstated, the boy's behaviour is seen to improve again.

By way of conclusion, the single-case research design is uniquely able to provide an experimental technique for evaluating interventions for the individual subject. Moreover, such interventions can be directed towards the particular subject or group and replicated over time or across behaviours, situations, or persons. Single-case research offers an alternative strategy to the more usual methodologies based on between-group designs. There are, however, a number of problems that arise in connection with the use of single-case designs having to do with ambiguities introduced by trends and variations in baseline phase data and with the generality of results from single-case research. The interested reader is directed to Kazdin (1982), Borg (1981)[20] and Vasta (1979)[21].

META-ANALYSIS IN EDUCATIONAL RESEARCH

The study by Bhadwal and Panda (1991)[15] is typical of research undertaken to explore the effectiveness of classroom methods. Often as not, such studies fail to reach the light of day, particularly when they form part of the research requirements for a higher degree. Over the past few years however, a quantitative method for synthesizing research results has been developed by Glass and others.[22] Called 'meta-analysis', it is simple to use and easy to understand, though the statistical treatment that underpins it is somewhat complex. Fitz-Gibbon explains the technique as follows:

> In *meta-analysis* the effects of variables are examined in terms of their *effect size*, that is to say, in terms of *how much* difference they make rather than only in terms of whether or not the effects are statistically significant at some arbitrary level such as 5%. Because, with *effect sizes*, it becomes easier to concentrate on the educational significance of a finding rather than trying to assess its importance by its statistical significance, we may finally see statistical significance kept in its place as just one of many possible threats to internal validity.
>
> (Fitz-Gibbon, 1985)[23]

Among the advantages of using meta-analysis, Fitz-Gibbon cites the following:

> Because educational research will need to proceed with considerable reliance on the use of small experiments, humble, small-scale reports which have simply been gathering dust may now become useful.
>
> Small-scale research conducted by individual students and lecturers will be valuable since meta-analysis provides a way of coordinating results drawn from many studies without having to coordinate the studies themselves.
>
> For historians, a whole new genre of studies is created – the

Box 8.5   Class size and learning in well-controlled and poorly-controlled
studies

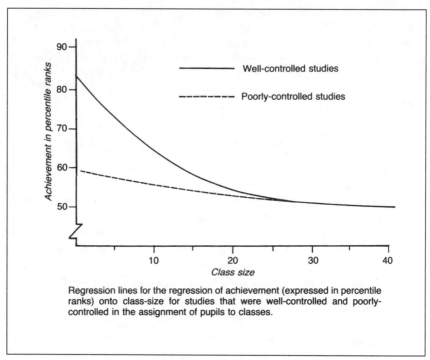

Regression lines for the regression of achievement (expressed in percentile ranks) onto class-size for studies that were well-controlled and poorly-controlled in the assignment of pupils to classes.

Source: Adapted from Glass and Smith, 1978

study of how *effect sizes* vary over time, relating this to historical changes.

(Fitz-Gibbon, 1985)

Meta-analysis is not without its critics. Since so much depends upon the quality of the results that are to be synthesized, there is the danger that adherents may simply multiply the inadequacies of the data base. Because the quantitative mode of (many) studies demands only a few common variables to be measured in each case, argues Tripp,[24] cumulation of the studies tends to increase sample size much more than it increases the complexity of the data in terms of the number of variables. It is the traditional pursuit of generalizations from each quantitative study which has most hampered the development of a data base adequate to reflect the complexity of the social nature of education. The cumulative effects of 'good' and 'bad' experimental studies is graphically illustrated in Box 8.5.

An example of meta-analysis in educational research

Glass and Smith identified seventy-seven empirical studies of the relationship between class size and pupil learning.[25] These studies yielded 725 comparisons of the achievements of smaller and larger classes, the comparisons resting on data accumulated from nearly 900,000 pupils of all ages and aptitudes studying all manner of school subjects. Using regression analysis, the 725 comparisons were integrated into a single curve showing the relationship between class size and achievement in general. This curve revealed a definite inverse relationship between class size and pupil learning. When the researchers derived similar curves for a variety of circumstances that they hypothesized would alter the basic relationship (for example, grade level, subject taught, pupil ability etc.), virtually none of these special circumstances altered the basic relationship. Only one factor substantially affected the curve – whether the original study controlled adequately in the experimental sense for initial differences among pupils and teachers in smaller and larger classes. Adequate and inadequate control curves are set out in Box 8.5.

REFERENCES AND NOTES

1 Kerlinger, F.N., *Foundations of Behavioral Research* (Holt, Rinehart & Winston, New York, 1970).

2 Campbell, D.T. and Stanley, J.C., 'Experimental and quasi-experimental designs for research on teaching', in N.L. Gage (ed.), *Handbook of Research on Teaching* (Rand McNally, Chicago, 1963).

3 Pilliner, A., *Experiment in Education Research*, E341 Block 5 (The Open University Press, Bletchley, 1973).

4 Palmer, M., 'An experimental study of the use of archive materials in the secondary school history curriculum', PhD dissertation (University of Leicester, 1976).

5 Randomization is one way of apportioning out or controlling for extraneous variables. Alternatively, the experimenter may use matched cases, that is, subjects are matched in pairs in terms of some other variable thought likely to affect scores on the dependent variable and pairs are then allocated randomly to E and C conditions in such a way that the means and variances of the two groups are as nearly equal as possible. Finally, analysis of covariance is a powerful statistical procedure which uses pretest mean scores as covariates to control for initial differences between E and C groups on a number of independent variables.

6 Good, C.V., *Introduction to Educational Research* (Appleton-Century-Crofts, New York, 1963).

7 Solomon, R.L., 'An extension of control group design', *Psychological Bulletin*, 46 (1949) 137–50.

8 See also the discussion of validity and reliability in educational research, in Hammersley, M., 'Some notes on the terms 'validity' and 'reliability'', *British Educational Research Journal*, 13(1) (1987) 73–81.

9 Bracht, G.H. and Glass, G.V., 'The external validity of experiments', *American Educational Research Journal*, 4(5) (1968) 437–74.

10 Questions have been raised about the authenticity of both definitions and explanations of the Hawthorne effect. See Diaper, G., 'The Hawthorne Effect: a fresh examination', *Educational Studies*, 16 (3) (1990) 261–7.

11 Evans, K.M., *Planning Small Scale Research* (NFER Publishing Co., Windsor, 1978).

12 Simon, J.L., *Basic Research Methods in Social Science* (Random House, New York, 1978).

13 Adeyemi, M.B., 'The effects of a social studies course on the philosophical orientations of history and geography graduate students in Botswana', *Educational Studies*, 18(2) (1992) 235–44.

14 Mason, M., Mason, B. and Quayle, T., 'Illuminating English: how explicit language teaching improved public examination results in a comprehensive school', *Educational Studies*, 18(3) (1992) 341–54.

15 Bhadwal, S.C. and Panda, P.K., 'The effects of a package of some curricular strategies on the study habits of rural primary school students: a year long study.' *Educational Studies*, 17(3) (1991) 261–72.

16 See Note 5, above.

17 Ethical considerations arising out of such gross differentiation in educational provision to impoverished pupils over a whole year of schooling are taken up in Chapter 16.

18 Kazdin, A.E., *Single-case Research Designs* (Oxford University Press, New York, 1982).

19 Dietz, S.M., 'An analysis of programming DRL schedules in educational settings', *Behaviour Research and Therapy*, 15 (1977) 103–11. The interested reader is referred to the following studies that draw upon single case designs in British schools: Gersch, I., 'Behaviour modification and systems analysis in a secondary school: combining two approaches', *Behavioural Approaches with Children*, 8 (1984) 83–91; Sharpe, P., 'Behaviour modification in the secondary school: a survey of students' attitudes to rewards and praise', *Behavioural Approaches with Children*, 9 (1985) 109–12; McNamara, E., 'The effectiveness of incentive and sanction systems used in secondary schools: a behavioural analysis', *Durham and Newcastle Research Review*, 10 (1986) 285–90; Merrett, F., Wilkins, J., Houghton, S. and Wheldall, K., 'Rules, sanctions and rewards in secondary schools', *Educational Studies*, 14(2) (1988) 139–49; and Wheldall, K. and Panagopoulou-Stamatelatou, A., 'The effects of pupil self-recording of on-task behaviour in primary school children', *British Educational Research Journal* 17(2) (1991) 113–27.

20 Borg, W.R., *Applying Educational Research: A Practical Guide for Teachers* (Longman, New York, 1981), 218–19.

21 Vasta, R., *Studying Children: An Introduction to Research Methods* (W.H. Freeman, San Francisco, 1979).

22 Glass, G.V., McGaw, B. and Smith, M.L., *Meta-Analysis in Social Research* (Sage, Beverly Hills, 1981).

23 Fitz-Gibbon, C.T., 'The implications of meta-analysis for educational research', *British Educational Research Journal*, 11(1) (1985) 45–9.

24 Tripp, D.H., 'Case study generalisation: an agenda for action', *British Educational Research Journal*, 11(1) (1985) 33–43; see also, Hamilton, D., 'Generalisation in the educational sciences: problems and purposes', in T.S. Popkewitz and R.S. Tabachnick (eds) *The Study of Schooling* (Praeger, New York, 1981).

25 Glass, G.V. and Smith, M.L., *Meta-Analysis of Research on the Relationship of Class-size and Achievement* (Farwest Laboratory, San Francisco, 1978); Glass,

G.V., Cahen, L.S., Smith, M.L. and Filby, N.N., *School Class Size: Research and Policy* (Sage, Beverly Hills; London; New Delhi, 1982). Criteria for selecting from a larger pool of studies those deemed to be well-controlled are set out in Cohen, P.A., Kulik, J.A. and Kulik, C.L., 'Educational outcomes of tutoring: a meta-analysis of findings', *American Educational Research Journal*, 19(2) (1982) 237–48. See also Kumar, D.D., 'A meta-analysis of the relationship between science instruction and student engagement', *Educational Review*, 43(1) (1991) 49–56.

9

ACTION RESEARCH

INTRODUCTION

We come now to a style of research that has received rather more publicity over the years than most other methods in the social sciences. This may indeed stem from the implied tension in its name, action research, for *action* and *research* as separate activities in whatever context each have their own ideology and *modus operandi* and when conjoined in this way, lie as uneasy bedfellows. To give a comprehensive definition of the term at this stage is difficult because usage varies with time, place and setting. None the less, we may offer a conventional definition and use this as a starting point: action research is small-scale intervention in the functioning of the real world and a close examination of the effects of such intervention.[1] By looking at a few examples of the use of the method in the research literature, we may further identify other tangible features: action research is situational – it is concerned with diagnosing a problem in a specific context and attempting to solve it in that context; it is usually (though not inevitably) collaborative – teams of researchers and practitioners work together on a project; it is participatory – team members themselves take part directly or indirectly in implementing the research; and it is self-evaluative – modifications are continuously evaluated within the ongoing situation, the ultimate objective being to improve practice in some way or other. According to Blum,[2] the use of action research in the social sciences can be resolved into two stages: a diagnostic stage in which the problems are analysed and the hypotheses developed; and a therapeutic stage in which the hypotheses are tested by a consciously directed change experiment, preferably in a social life situation. As far as educational contexts are concerned, however, Stenhouse[3] is careful to stress that action research should contribute not only to practice but to 'a theory of education and teaching which is accessible to other teachers' (Stenhouse, 1979).

The scope of action research as a method is impressive. Its usage may range at one extreme from a teacher trying out a novel way of teaching social studies with her class to, at another, a sophisticated study of organizational change in industry using a large research team and backed by government sponsors. Whatever the situation, however, the method's evaluative frame of reference remains the same, namely, to add to the practitioner's functional knowledge of the phenomena she deals with. This type of research is therefore usually considered in conjunction with social or educational aims.[4]

It will be useful here if we distinguish action research from applied research, for although they are similar in some ways, there are important differences between them which need to be made explicit, for confusion between the two does sometimes arise. Both utilize the scientific method. Since applied research is concerned mainly with establishing relationships and testing theories, it is quite rigorous in its application of the conditions of this method. To this end, therefore, it insists on: studying a large number of cases; establishing as much control as possible over variables; precise sampling techniques; and a serious concern to generalize its findings to comparable situations. It does not claim to contribute directly to the solution of problems. Action research, by contrast, interprets the scientific method much more loosely, chiefly because its focus is a specific problem in a specific setting. The emphasis is not so much on obtaining generalizable scientific knowledge as on precise knowledge for a particular situation and purpose. The conditions imposed on applied research, therefore, are normally relaxed with action research. Of course, as action research projects become more extensive in their coverage, the boundary between the two methods becomes less easy to define. A curriculum project involving 100 schools, say, or a community action programme embracing a number of major conurbations, will tend to yield rather more generalizable knowledge and information than purely localized undertakings.

Having drawn this distinction between action research and applied research, we are now free to concentrate on the former and ask ourselves the question: what kinds of intervention programme are featured in action research? The following examples, while by no means exhaustive, give some idea of the contexts in which the method may be used. They are not mutually exclusive so there may be considerable overlap between some of them. There is the kind that:

1 acts as a spur to action, its objective being to get something done more expeditiously than would be the case with alternative means;
2 addresses itself to personal functioning, human relations and morale and is thus concerned with people's job efficiency, their motivations, relationships and general well-being;
3 focuses on job analysis and aims at improving professional functioning and efficiency;

4 is concerned with organizational change in so far as it results in improved functioning in business or industry;

5 is concerned with planning and policy-making, generally in the field of social administration;

6 is concerned with innovation and change and the ways in which these may be implemented in ongoing systems;

7 concentrates on problem-solving virtually in any context in which a specific problem needs solving;

8 provides the opportunity to develop theoretical knowledge, the emphasis here being more on the research element of the method.

Equally diverse are the situations in which these different kinds of intervention may be used – almost any setting, in fact, where a problem involving people, tasks and procedures cries out for solution, or where some change of feature results in a more desirable outcome. Notable instances of the use of action research may be found in such starkly contrasting worlds as insurance, prisons, social administration, ships, hospitals, community projects, education, industry, coal-mining and business management. For our own purposes, however, we shall now restrict our discussion chiefly to the use of action research in the field of education.

Although the action research movement in education was initiated in the United States in the 1940s, the scene for its appearance began to be set in that country in the 1920s with the application of the scientific method to the study of educational problems, growing interest in group interaction and group processes, and the emerging progressive movement. Indeed, the last is seen by some as the principal causal agent for subsequent developments in action research. One writer says:

> Action research . . . is a direct and logical outcome of the progressive position. After showing children how to work together to solve their problems, the next step was for teachers to adopt the methods they had been teaching their children, and learn to solve their own problems co-operatively.

> (Hodgkinson, 1957)[5]

Reaching its peak in the 1960s, the movement had multifarious aims of a decidedly practical nature which were often embellished with ideological, even political, counterpoints. Some, for instance, saw it as a necessary corrective to the failure of official bodies to implement traditional research findings; others, as a means of improving the quality of life.

The purposes of action research in school and classroom fall broadly into five categories:

1 it is a means of remedying problems diagnosed in specific situations, or of improving in some way a given set of circumstances;

2 it is a means of in-service training, thereby equipping teachers with new skills and methods, sharpening their analytical powers and heightening their self-awareness;

3 it is a means of injecting additional or innovatory approaches to teaching and learning into an ongoing system which normally inhibits innovation and change;

4 it is a means of improving the normally poor communications between the practising teacher and the academic researcher, and of remedying the failure of traditional research to give clear prescriptions;

5 although lacking the rigour of true scientific research, it is a means of providing a preferable alternative to the more subjective, impressionistic approach to problem-solving in the classroom.

We close our introduction by asking, 'Who actually undertakes action research in schools?' Three possibilities present themselves. First, there is the single teacher operating on her own with her class. She will feel the need for some kind of change or improvement in teaching, learning or organization, for example, and will be in a position to translate her ideas into action in her own classroom. She is, as it were, both practitioner and researcher in one and will integrate the practical and theoretical orientations within herself. Evans's account of her project in mathematics in an infant classroom[6] and Hall's report of the development of a language programme in her primary classroom[7] serve as examples. Second, action research may be pursued by a group of teachers working co-operatively within one school, though of necessity functioning against a bigger backdrop than the teacher working solo. They may or may not be advised by an outside researcher. By way of example, Tanner[8] and Eames,[9] comprehensive school heads of department in, respectively, Mathematics and English, have recorded the action research projects that they and their colleagues instituted in their own schools to effect changes in teaching methods. And third, there is the occasion – perhaps the most characteristic in recent years – where a teacher or teachers work alongside a researcher or researchers in a sustained relationship, possibly with other interested parties like advisers, university departments and sponsors on the periphery as in the GIST project, for example, that we outline later in this chapter.[10] (See Box 9.1.) Carr and Kemmis[11] say of this arrangement:

> In practical action research, participants monitor their own educational practices with the immediate aim of developing their practical judgement as individuals. Thus, the facilitator's role is Socratic: to provide a sounding-board against which practitioners may try out ideas and learn more about the reasons for their own action, as well as learning more about the process of self-reflection. Practical action research may be a stepping-stone to emancipatory

Box 9.1   Aspirations of teacher researchers and non-teacher researchers in action research

1   that the relationship between all collaborative group participants be symmetrical
2   that the practice related to research tasks within the group be owned by the teacher researchers
3   that during the research project's life any of the participants in the group may raise significant questions as to the direction the project may take
4   that the exchange of information between participants is negotiated and controlled by the participants concerned
5   that the roles of teacher, learner and researcher are available to all participants

Source: Holly and Whitehead, 1986

action research in which participants themselves take responsibility for the Socratic role of assisting the group in its collaborative self-reflection.

(Carr and Kemmis, 1986)[12]

This third possibility, though potentially the most promising, may also be the most problematic, at least initially, because of rival characterizations of action and research by the teacher(s) and researcher(s) respectively. We shall return to this point at the end of the chapter. Advocates of action research believe that little can be achieved if only one person is involved in changing her ideas and practices. For this reason, co-operative research tends to be emphasized and encouraged. One commentator notes:

Action research functions best when it is co-operative action research. This method of research incorporates the ideas and expectations of all persons involved in the situation. Co-operative action research has the concomitants of beneficial effects for workers, and the improvement of the services, conditions, and functions of the situation. In education this activity translates into more practice in research and problem-solving by teachers, administrators, pupils, and certain community personnel, while the quality of teaching and learning is in the process of being improved.

(Hill and Kerber, 1967)[13]

We refer the reader at this point to Nixon's book[14] which sets out to offer guidelines to teachers to help them develop an action research style of their own. The first part presents a number of research reports serving as examples of ways of doing research by a teacher in his or her own classroom. The second part places action research in its social context with four studies exploring some of the problems of implementing school-based research. Ways of overcoming problems of organizational

Box 9.2 Action research in classroom and school

---

1 All teachers possess certain skills which can contribute to the research task. The important thing is to clarify and define one's own particular set of skills. Some teachers, for example, are able to collect and interpret statistical data; others to record in retrospective accounts the key moments of a lesson. One teacher may know something about questionnaire design; another have a natural flair for interviewing. It is essential that teachers work from their own particular strengths when developing the research.

2 The situations within which teachers work impose different kinds of constraints. Some schools, for example, are equipped with the most up-to-date audio-visual equipment, others cannot even boast a cassette tape-recorder. Some have spare rooms in which interviews could be carried out, others hardly have enough space to implement the existing time-table. Action research must be designed in such a way as to be easily implemented within the pattern of constraints existing within the school.

3 Any initial definition of the research problem will almost certainly be modified as the research proceeds. Nevertheless, this definition is important because it helps to set limits to the enquiry. If, for example, a teacher sets out to explore through action research the problem of how to start a lesson effectively, the research will tend to focus upon the first few minutes of the lesson. The question of what data to collect is very largely answered by a clear definition of the research problem.

Source: Nixon, 1981

Box 9.3 Teachers as researchers

The teachers as researchers movement entails a radically different role for external change agents; one of facilitation rather than control. Curriculum theorizing and research by external agents is a legitimate part of facilitation, providing it focuses on teachers' conceptions of ends and means and helps them to clarify and extend their ideas through dialogue. Facilitation also involves helping teachers learn techniques for collecting, sharing, and analysing data about their practical problems.

Source: Elliott, 1987

constraint are suggested. The final part of the book is concerned with help from outside agencies. Box 9.2 offers a digest of the rationale behind Nixon's compilation of the classroom and school-based studies used. Box 9.3 contains a brief extract from an article dealing with the subject of teacher as researcher (Elliott, 1987).[15]

CHARACTERISTICS

The principal characteristics of action research are more or less present in all instances of its usage (those having an experimental slant need to be considered in a somewhat different category). We have already referred to its prime feature – that it is essentially an on-the-spot procedure designed to deal with a concrete problem located in an immediate situation. This means that ideally, the step-by-step process is constantly monitored over varying periods of time and by a variety of mechanisms (questionnaires, diaries, interviews and case studies, for example) so that the ensuing feedback may be translated into modifications, adjustments, directional changes, redefinitions, as necessary, so as to bring about lasting benefit to the ongoing process itself rather than to some future occasion, as is the purpose of more traditionally oriented research. Unlike other methods, no attempt is made to identify one particular factor and study it in isolation, divorced from the context giving it meaning. That the findings are applied immediately, then, or in the short term is another important characteristic, although having made this point we need to qualify it to the extent that members of research teams – especially in curriculum projects – frequently have a more long-term perspective.

The principal justification for the use of action research in the context of the school is improvement of practice. This can be achieved only if teachers are able to change their attitudes and behaviour. One of the best means of bringing about these kinds of changes is pressure from the group with which one works. As we have seen, because the problems of teachers are often shared with other teachers in the same school, action research has tended to become co-operative, involving many or all of the teachers in the school. Group interaction is frequently another characteristic, therefore.

A feature which makes action research a very suitable procedure for work in classrooms and schools (as well as other field settings) is its flexibility and adaptability. These qualities are revealed in the changes that may take place during its implementation and in the course of on-the-spot experimentation and innovation characterizing the approach. They come out particularly strongly when set against the usual background of constraints in schools – those to do with organization, resources, timetabling, staff deployment and teachers' attitudes, for example, as well as pressures from other agencies involved and from competing interests (see Nixon, 1981).

Action research relies chiefly on observation and behavioural data. That it is therefore empirical is another distinguishing feature of the method. This implies that over the period of a project information is collected, shared, discussed, recorded in some way, evaluated and acted upon; and that from time to time, this sequence of events forms the basis of reviews of progress (see Box 9.4).[16] In this one respect at least it is superior to the more usual subjective, impressionistic methods we have already alluded to. Where an experimental note is introduced into a

Box 9.4   The ideal teacher for an integrated studies project

The ideal teacher for an Integrated Studies Project would be one willing to maintain his subject discipline within a team and to engage in planning integrated work through discussions with other specialist colleagues. This teacher would be an active producer of new materials, teaching methods and ideas for integrated subject work. He would keep accounts of his innovatory work, fill in the questionnaires sent him by the project team and feed his experience back to them. He would organize his work so that children would not only come to see and use the concepts within separate subject disciplines, but would learn the skills of those subjects through enquiry-based programmes.

Source: Adapted from Shipman, 1974

project, it is generally achieved through the use of control groups with a view to testing specific hypotheses and arriving at more generalizable knowledge.

In our earlier comparison with applied research, we said that action research took a much more relaxed view of the scientific method. We return to this point here because it is a characteristic which forms the basis of persistent criticisms of the method by its opponents. Travers, for example, in reviewing a number of action research projects, writes:

> The writer's evaluation of the last fifty studies which have been undertaken which compare the outcomes of one teaching method-ology with another is that they have contributed almost nothing to our knowledge of the factors that influence the learning process in the classroom. Many of them do not even identify what the experi-mentally controlled variables are and indicate only that the study compares the outcomes of educational practices in the community where the study originates with educational practices elsewhere.
>
> (Travers, 1972)[17]

That the method should be lacking in scientific rigour, however, is not surprising since the very factors which make it distinctively what it is – and therefore of value in certain contexts – are the antithesis of true experimental research. The points usually made are: that its objective is situational and specific (unlike the scientific method which goes beyond the solution of practical problems); its sample is restricted and unrepre-sentative; it has little or no control over independent variables; and its findings are not generalizable but generally restricted to the environ-ment in which the research is carried out. While these criticisms hold in most cases, it is important that we refer again to the qualification made earlier; that as action research programmes become more extensive and use more schools, that is, become more standardized, less personalized and more 'open', some of these strictures at least will become less valid.

193

OCCASIONS WHEN ACTION RESEARCH AS A METHOD IS APPROPRIATE

We come now to a brief consideration of the occasions when the use of action research is fitting and appropriate. The answer in short is this: that action research is appropriate whenever specific knowledge is required for a specific problem in a specific situation; or when a new approach is to be grafted onto an existing system. More than this, however, suitable mechanisms must be available for monitoring progress and for translating feedback into the ongoing system. This means that, other things being equal, the action research method may be applied to any classroom or school situation where these conditions apply. We have already referred to the suitability of the approach to curriculum research and development. Let us now take this further by identifying other areas in school life where action research could be used and illustrating each area with a concrete example:

1 teaching methods – replacing a traditional method by a discovery method
2 learning strategies – adopting an integrated approach to learning in preference to a single-subject style of teaching and learning
3 evaluative procedures – improving one's methods of continuous assessment
4 attitudes and values – encouraging more positive attitudes to work, or modifiying pupils' value systems with regard to some aspect of life
5 in-service development of teachers – improving teaching skills, developing new methods of learning, increasing powers of analysis, of heightening self-awareness
6 management and control – the gradual introduction of the techniques of behaviour modification
7 administration – increasing the efficiency of some aspect of the administrative side of school life.

Of course, it would be naive of us simply to select a problem area *in vacuo*, so to speak. We have also to consider the context in which the project is to be undertaken. More specifically this means bearing in mind factors that will directly affect the outcomes. One of these concerns the teachers themselves and the extent to which they are favourably disposed towards the project, particularly when they are part of a collectivity working with outside agencies for, as we shall see in our final section, this very factor on its own can be a source of intense friction. It is important, therefore, that the teachers taking part in the project are truly involved, that they know what the objectives are, what these imply, and that they are adequately motivated – or at least sufficiently open-minded for motivation to be induced. Another important factor concerns the organizational aspect of the school so that there is a reasonable amount of congruence between the setting and the programme to be initiated. This can be achieved without too much discord when a programme is internally organized by the school itself. When outside parties are involved, however, who themselves are working concurrently in other schools, difficulties may arise over such matters as implementing a new style of teaching, for example, or use of project materials. One further factor concerns resources: are there enough sufficiently competent researchers at hand? And has the school got reasonable access to college and university libraries to consult appropriate professional and research journals should this need arise? Some or all of these factors need to be reviewed as part of the planning stage of an action research programme.

Again we refer the reader to Nixon (1981), especially Part Two which examines, *inter alia*, the problems of school-based research, working with colleagues, and assembling a team. The collection of articles by Holly and Whitehead,[18] Hustler, Cassidy and Cuff,[19] Nias and Groundwater-Smith,[20] and Woods,[21] will give readers some idea of the kinds of topics suitable for action research.

SOME ISSUES

We have already seen that the participants in a change situation may be either a teacher, a group of teachers working internally, or else teachers and researchers working on a collaborative basis. It is this last category, where action research brings together two professional bodies each with its own objectives and values, that we shall consider further at this point because of its inherent problematic nature. Both parties share the same interest in an educational problem, yet their respective orientations to it differ. It has been observed (Halsey 1972, for instance) that research values precision, control, replication and attempts to generalize from specific events. Teaching, on the other hand, is concerned with action, with doing things, and translates generalizations into specific acts. The incompatibility between action and research in these respects, therefore, can be a source of problems. Marris and Rein, for example, on reviewing the relationship between the two in a number of American community action programmes concluded that the principles of action and experienced research are so different and so often mutually exclusive that attempts to link them into a single process are likely to produce internal conflict and the subordination of one element to another. They express it thus:

Research requires a clear and constant purpose, which both defines and precedes the choice of means; that the means be exactly and consistently followed; and that no revision takes place until the sequence of steps is completed. Action is tentative, non-commital and adaptive. It concentrates upon the next step, breaking the sequence into discrete, manageable decisions. It casts events in a fundamentally different perspective, evolving the future out of present opportunities, where research perceives the present in the context of the final outcomes. Research cannot interpret the present until it knows the answers to its ultimate questions. Action cannot foresee what questions to ask until it has interpreted the present. Action attempts to comprehend all the factors relevant to an immediate problem whose nature continually changes as events proceed, where research abstracts one or two factors for attention, and holds to a constant definition of the problem until the experiment is concluded.

(Marris and Rein, 1967)[22]

Those who are not quite as pessimistic about the viability of the action/research coupling would question whether the characterization of action and research as put forward by Marris and Rein necessarily holds in all contexts. They would advocate a more flexible approach to the relationship. Some researchers, for instance, suggest that projects could vary along a number of dimensions such as the degree of control exercised by the action and research components, the amount of knowledge about the means of achieving the desired outcomes, and the level of co-operation between action and research (see Halsey, 1972). Such a classification could be linked to different kinds of action research (see pp. 187–8) and suggest what combinations of action and research were most appropriate for particular conditions. In short, what seems to be needed is a clear unambiguous statement of the project's objectives such that all participants understand them and their implications, and a careful analysis of the context(s) in which the programme is to be mounted to determine the precise, but flexible, relationship between the two components. This would help to ensure that the positive contributions of both are maximized and that the constraints of each on the other are kept to a minimum.

Another issue of some consequence concerns head teachers' and teachers' attitudes to the possibility of change as a result of action research. Hutchinson and Whitehouse, for example, having monitored teachers' efforts to form collaborative groups within their schools, discovered one source of difficulty to be not only resistance from heads but also, and in their view more importantly, from some teachers themselves to the action researcher's efforts to have them scrutinize individual and social practice. As they explain,

This resistance does not just happen incidentally, however. We are going to suggest, on the contrary, that it is an inevitable outcome

Box 9.5 Teachers' reactions to change and improvement

An action researcher has been investigating the possibility of introducing group work in the P4–P7 classes in his school. His principal has encouraged this research in the hope that teachers might be persuaded to adopt the approach as educationally beneficial to the pupils. He had in the past urged teachers to adopt group work making his views known at staff meetings. The researcher had tried to discuss this with his colleagues on staff. He wrote in his case study:

> The principal said, 'As far as I'm concerned the teachers know my attitude to group work, and I think I've made it clear over the years.' Teacher A admits knowing the principal's feelings on group work but goes on to state, 'I don't think he would influence my methods, but as far as I'm aware, he's quite keen on group work'. . . . Another teacher who declined to be interviewed, but did make some statements, was very determined in her attitude towards change. She states, 'I will teach the way which suits me best, after all I've got enough experience and nobody will tell me how or what I should be teaching.'

This example, the authors note, of an entrenched attitude typified teachers' reactions to suggestions for change and improvement.

Source: Hutchinson and Whitehouse, 1986

of the way a school is structured, in short, that the hierarchical order not only differentiates power and responsibility but, in maintaining teacher isolation in the classroom, contributes to the resistance of teachers to criticism, change and improvement.

(Hutchinson and Whitehouse, 1986)[23]

As a result of this, confrontation between action research and the power hierarchy seldom takes place: action research is contained long before it becomes a 'real' threat. The authors conclude,

> Action research is subversive in that it brings into question that which is taken for granted. . . . If action research is to succeed in achieving educational improvement practitioners will need to be able to regard practice and its contexts as cultural constructions rather than as social givens.

(Hutchinson and Whitehouse, 1986)

Finally, Winter draws attention to the problem of interpreting data in action research. He writes:

> The action research/case study tradition does have a methodology for the *creation* of data, but not (as yet) for the interpretation of data. We are shown how the descriptive journal, the observer's field notes, and the open-ended interview are utilized to create accounts of events which will *confront* the practitioner's current pragmatic

197

assumptions and definitions; we are shown the potential value of this process (in terms of increasing teachers' sensitivity) and the problem it poses for individual and collective professional equilibrium. What we are *not* shown is *how* the teacher can or should handle the data thus collected.

(Winter, 1982)[24]

The problem for Winter is how to carry out an interpretive analysis of restricted data, that is, data which can make no claim to be generally representative. In other words, the problem of validity cannot be side-stepped by arguing that the contexts are unique. For further discussion of this issue, we refer you to Winter's paper.

PROCEDURES

We now trace the possible stages and procedures that may be followed in an action research programme, or from which a suitable selection may be made. As we have already seen, projects may vary along a number of dimensions – whether they are to be conducted by teachers only, or by teachers in collaboration with researchers, whether small or large samples of schools are involved, whether they tackle specific problems or more diffuse ones, for example. Given the particular set of circumstances, an appropriate model may be selected to guide procedures, one that will be tailor-made to meet the needs of the change situation in question. As we are here concerned with a review of procedures in general terms, however, and not with a specific instance, we offer a basic, flexible framework by way of illustration: it will need to be interpreted or adjusted in the light of the particular undertaking.

The first stage will involve the identification, evaluation and formulation of the problem perceived as critical in an everyday teaching situation. 'Problem' should be interpreted loosely here so that it could refer to the need to introduce innovation into some aspect of a school's established programme.

The second stage involves preliminary discussion and negotiations among the interested parties – teachers, researchers, advisers, sponsors, possibly – which may culminate in a draft proposal. This may include a statement of the questions to be answered (e.g. 'Under what conditions can curriculum change be best effected?' 'What are the limiting factors in bringing about effective curriculum change?' 'What strong points of action research can be employed to bring about curriculum change?'). The researchers in their capacity as consultants (or sometimes as programme initiators) may draw upon their expertise to bring the problem more into focus, possibly determining causal factors or recommending alternative lines of approach to established ones. This is often the crucial stage for the venture as it is at this point that the seeds of success or failure are planted, for, generally speaking, unless the objectives, purposes and assumptions are made perfectly clear to all concerned, and unless the role of key concepts is stressed (e.g. feedback), the enterprise can easily miscarry.

The third stage may in some circumstances involve a review of the research literature to find out what can be learned from comparable studies, their objectives, procedures and problems encountered.

The fourth stage may involve a modification or redefinition of the initial statement of the problem at stage one. It may now emerge in the form of a testable hypothesis; or as a set of guiding objectives. Sometimes change agents deliberately decide against the use of objectives on the grounds that they have a constraining effect on the process itself. It is also at this stage that assumptions underlying the project are made explicit (e.g. in order to effect curriculum changes, the attitudes, values, skills and objectives of the teachers involved must be changed).

The fifth stage may be concerned with the selection of research procedures – sampling, administration, choice of materials, methods of teaching and learning, allocation of resources and tasks, deployment of staff and so on.

The sixth stage will be concerned with the choice of the evaluation procedures to be used and will need to take into consideration that evaluation in this context will be continuous.

The seventh stage embraces the implementation of the project itself (over varying periods of time). It will include the conditions and methods of data collection (e.g. fortnightly meetings, the keeping of records, interim reports, final reports, the submission of self-evaluation and group-evaluation reports, etc.); the monitoring of tasks and the transmission of feedback to the research team; and the classification and analysis of data.

The eighth and final stage will involve the interpretation of the data; inferences to be drawn; and overall evaluation of the project (see Woods, 1989). Discussions on the findings will take place in the light of previously agreed evaluative criteria. Errors, mistakes and problems will be considered. A general summing-up may follow this in which the outcomes of the project are reviewed, recommendations made, and arrangements for dissemination of results to interested parties decided.

As we stressed, this is a basic framework: much activity of an incidental and possibly *ad hoc* nature will take place in and around it. This may comprise discussions among teachers, researchers and pupils; regular meetings among teachers or schools to discuss progress and problems, and to exchange information; possibly regional conferences; and related activities, all enhanced by the range of current hardware – tapes, video-recordings and transcripts.

CONCLUSION: AN EXAMPLE OF ACTION RESEARCH IN SCHOOLS

Earlier in the chapter (see page 199) we were careful to use the words 'generally speaking' in qualifying our statement about making the objectives of action research perfectly clear to all concerned. The reason for our caution becomes clear in the following account of an action research project in secondary schools. The degree to which the researchers felt unable and unwilling to disclose all of their purposes to teacher collaborators raises ethical issues that we address in detail in Chapter 16.

The Girls Into Science and Technology (GIST) project took place over three years and involved 2000 pupils and their teachers in ten co-educational, comprehensive schools in the Greater Manchester area, eight schools serving as the bases of the 'action', the remaining two acting as 'controls'. Several publications have documented the methodologies and the findings of the GIST study,[25] described by its co-director as 'simultaneous-integrated action research' (Kelly, 1987). This somewhat cumbersome label is intended to convey the distinctive feature of the approach, namely that action and research are integrated and proceed simultaneously.

Kelly is ingenuously open about a fundamental orientation of the GIST project team:

> (We) operated from a feminist standpoint . . . we aimed to change girls' option choices and career aspirations because of our perception that girls were disadvantaged by traditional sex-stereotypes. We saw action in schools as one small part of a mosaic of action to ameliorate women's subordinate position in society as a whole.
>
> (Kelly, 1987)

The research team had reason to believe that the (mainly male) teachers with whom they worked on the project might well have held stereotypic images of feminists and could have felt themselves threatened, and hostile towards many of the ideas of feminism. They therefore took 'a tactical decision to concentrate on the professional aspects of the study and to de-emphasize the more personal ramifications in dealing with teachers' (Kelly, 1987). The project involved dealing with teachers since the interventions that the GIST project envisaged were in the main to be implemented by teachers.[26]

Workshops were designed to sensitize teachers to their own attitudes and expectations in perpetuating sex stereotypes in pupils' subject choice. Teachers were also encouraged to develop their own ideas about ways of intervening with their pupils and to criticize and change the suggestions put forward by the GIST researchers. Among the various interventions that took place, the VISTA programme deserves special

Box 9.6 Girls into science and technology: subject choice – physics

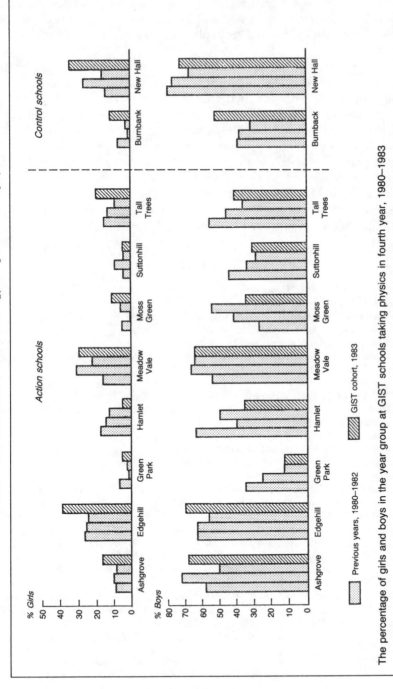

The percentage of girls and boys in the year group at GIST schools taking physics in fourth year, 1980–1983

Source: Kelly, 1987

mention. VISTA consisted of a series of visits to schools by women working in science and technology, the intention being to provide pupils with role models of women successfully engaged in 'masculine' occupations. Visitors included food technologists, trainee plumbers and motor mechanics.

An extensive programme of attitude and achievement testing at the age of 11 years, and then at 14 years when pupils were making their subject option choices for their fourth and fifth years' work provided one assessment of the impact of the intervention programme. Inevitably the results were somewhat ambiguous, the two 'control' schools, for example having a higher proportion of girls taking physics in the GIST cohort than in previous years (see Box 9.6). Interested readers should consult the published reports to see how the researchers accounted for their findings. This observation notwithstanding, there is firm evidence of change following the impact of the GIST project and the wide publicity that it has attracted both nationally and internationally.

REFERENCES AND NOTES

1 Halsey, A.H. (ed.), *Educational Priority: Volume 1: E.P.A. Problems and Policies* (HMSO, London, 1972).
2 National Educational Association of the United States: Association for Supervision and Curriculum Development, *Learning about Learning from Action Research* (Washington, DC, 1959).
3 Stenhouse, L., 'What is action research?' (C.A.R.E., University of East Anglia, Norwich (mimeo. 1979).
4 Corey, S.M., *Action Research to Improve School Practices* (Bureau of Publications, Teachers College, Columbia University, New York, 1953).
5 Hodgkinson, H.L., 'Action research – a critique', *Journal of Educational Sociology*, 31(4) (1957) 137–53.
6 Evans, L., 'Robbing Peter to pay Paul: teaching subtraction through role play', *Education* 3(13) March (1992) 48–53.
7 Hall, K., 'A case study of reading difficulty', *Education* 3(13) October (1992) 47–52.
8 Tanner, H., 'Managing perceptions through action research: introducing investigations and problem-solving – a case study', *School Organisation*, 9(2) (1989) 261–9.
9 Eames, K., 'Growing your own: supporting the development of action researcher within an action-research approach to whole-school development', *British Journal of In-Service Education*, 16(2) (1990) 122–7.
10 Kelly, A. (ed.), *Science for Girls?* (Open University Press, Milton Keynes, 1987).
11 Holly, P. and Whitehead, D., 'Collaborative action research', *Classroom Action Research Network*, Bulletin Vol. 7 (Cambridge Institute of Education, Cambridge, 1986).
12 Carr, W. and Kemmis, S., *Becoming Critical* (The Falmer Press, Lewes, 1986).
13 Hill, J.E. and Kerber, A., *Models, Methods, and Analytical Procedures in Educational Research* (Wayne State University Press, Detroit, 1967).

14 Nixon, J. (ed.), *A Teacher's Guide to Action Research* (Grant McIntyre, London, 1981).

15 Elliott, J., 'Teachers as researchers', in Dunkin, J. (ed.), *The International Encyclopedia of Teaching and Teacher Training* (Pergamon, Sydney, 1987).

16 Shipman, M.D., *Inside a Curriculum Project* (Methuen, London, 1974). Interested readers may wish to compare the quality of the relationships between teachers and researchers reported by Shipman with those said to obtain in the 'Transition to Adult and Working Life Project' (TRAWL 1983/1987) outlined by Peter Daws and Jack Eaton in Osborne, R.D., Cormack, R.J., and Miller, R.L., *Education and Policy in Northern Ireland* (Policy Research Institute, The Queen's University of Belfast and The University of Ulster 1986 pp. 207–17). In this piece of action research the field officers were seconded teachers experienced in curriculum development. From the outset of the study, Daws and Eaton observe, the style was facilitative and non-prescriptive.

17 Travers, R.M.W., extract quoted in Halsey, A.H. (ed.), *Educational Priority: Volume 1: E.P.A. Problems and Policies* (HMSO, London, 1972).

18 Holly, P. and Whitehead, D., 'Action research in schools: Getting it into perspective', Classroom Action Research Network, Bulletin No. 6 (Cambridge Institute of Education, Cambridge, 1984).

19 Hustler, D., Cassidy, A. and Cuff, E.C. (eds), *Action Research in Classrooms and Schools* (Allen & Unwin, London, 1986).

20 Nias, J. and Groundwater-Smith, S., *The Enquiring Teacher: Supporting and Sustaining Teacher Research* (Falmer Press, Lewes, 1988).

21 Woods, P., *Working For Teacher Development* (Peter Francis, Dereham, 1989).

22 Marris, P. and Rein, M., *Dilemmas of Social Reform: Poverty and Community Action in the United States* (Routledge & Kegan Paul, London, 1967).

23 Hutchinson, B. and Whitehouse, P., 'Action research, professional competence and school organization', *British Educational Research Journal*, 12, (1) (1986) 85–94.

24 Winter, R., '"Dilemma Analysis": A contribution to methodology for action research', *Cambridge Journal of Education*, 12(3) (1982) 161–74.

25 Whyte, J. *Girls into Science and Technology: the Story of a Project*, (Routledge & Kegan Paul, London, 1986).
   Kelly, A., 'The development of children's attitudes to science: a longitudinal study', *European Journal of Science Education*, 8 (1986) 399–412.
   Kelly, A. and Smail, B., 'Sex stereotypes and attitudes to science among eleven-year-old children', *British Journal of Educational Psychology*, 56 (1986) 158–68.
   Kelly, A., 'Education or indoctrination? The ethics of school-based action research', in Burgess, R.G. (ed.), *The Ethics of Educational Research* (Falmer Press, Lewes, 1989), pp. 100–13).
   Kelly, A., 'Getting the GIST: A Quantitative Study of the Effects of the Girls Into Science and Technology Project', (Manchester Sociology Occasional Papers, No. 22, 1989).

26 There were other important ethical issues in connection with the GIST project that cannot concern us here. *Inter alia*, the researchers were concerned with the question of their right to 'alter the world in accordance with their values' (Kelly, 1987). The fear that intervention could prove counterproductive and increase sex stereotyping in schools was another matter of concern. Interested readers are referred to Kelly (see Note 10).

10

ACCOUNTS

INTRODUCTION

Although each of us sees the world from our own point of view, we have a way of speaking about our experiences which we share with those around us. Explaining our behaviour towards one another can be thought of as accounting for our actions in order to make them intelligible and justifiable to our fellowmen. Thus, saying 'I'm terribly sorry, I didn't mean to bump into you', is a simple case of the explication of social meaning, for by locating the bump outside any planned sequence and neutralizing it by making it intelligible in such a way that it is not warrantable, it ceases to be offensive in that situation.[1]

Accounting for actions in those larger slices of life called social episodes is the central concern of a participatory psychology which focuses upon actors' intentions, their beliefs about what sorts of behaviour will enable them to reach their goals, and their awareness of the rules that govern those behaviours. Studies carried out within this framework have been termed 'ethogenic', an adjective which expresses a view of the human being as a person, that is, a plan-making, self-monitoring agent, aware of goals and deliberately considering the best ways to achieve them.[2] Ethogenic studies represent another approach to the study of social behaviour and their methods stand in bold contrast to those commonly employed in much of the educational research which we describe in Chapter 8. Before discussing the elicitation and analysis of accounts we need to outline the ethogenic approach in more detail. This we do by reference to the work of one of its foremost British exponents.

THE ETHOGENIC APPROACH

Harré identifies five main principles in the ethogenic approach. They are set out in Box 10.1.[3]

Box 10.1   Principles in the ethogenic approach

1   An explicit distinction is drawn between *synchronic analysis*, that is, the analysis of social practices and institutions as they exist at any one time, and *diachronic analysis*, the study of the stages and the processes by which social practices and institutions are created and abandoned, change and are changed. Neither type of analysis can be expected to lead directly to the discovery of universal social psychological principles or laws.

2   In social interactions, it is assumed that action takes place through endowing intersubjective entities with meaning; the ethogenic approach therefore concentrates upon the *meaning system*, that is, the whole sequence by which a social act is achieved in an episode. Consider, for example, the action of a kiss in the particular episodes of (a) leaving a friend's house; (b) the passing-out parade at St Cyr; and (c) the meeting in the garden of Gethsemane.

3   The ethogenic approach is concerned with speech which accompanies action. That speech is intended to make the action intelligible and justifiable in occurring at the time and the place it did in the whole sequence of unfolding and co-ordinated action. Such speech is *accounting*. In so far as accounts are socially meaningful, it is possible to derive *accounts of accounts*.

4   The ethogenic approach is founded upon the belief that a human being tends to be the kind of person his language, his traditions, his tacit and explicit knowledge tell him he is.

5   The skills that are employed in ethogenic studies therefore make use of commonsense understandings of the social world. As such the activities of the poet and the playwright offer the ethogenic researcher a better model than those of the physical scientist.

Source: Adapted from Harré, 1978

CHARACTERISTICS OF ACCOUNTS AND EPISODES

The discussion of accounts and episodes that now follows develops some of the ideas contained in the principles of the ethogenic approach outlined above.

We have already noted that accounts must be seen within the context of social episodes. The idea of an episode is a fairly general one. The concept itself may be defined as any coherent fragment of social life. Being a natural division of life, an episode will often have a recognizable beginning and end, and the sequence of actions that constitute it will have some meaning for the participants. Episodes may thus vary in duration and reflect innumerable aspects of life. A pupil entering primary school at seven and leaving at eleven would be an extended episode. A two-minute television interview with a political celebrity would be another. And, as we shall shortly illustrate, prospective house buyers recounting their experiences of negotiating a purchase, yet another. The contents of an episode which interest the ethogenic researcher include not only the perceived behaviour such as gesture and speech, but also the thoughts, the feelings and the intentions of those taking part. And the 'speech' that accounts for those thoughts, feelings and intentions must be conceived of in the widest connotation of the word. Thus, accounts may be personal records of the events we experience in our day-to-day lives, our conversations with neighbours, our letters to friends, our entries in diaries. Accounts serve to explain our past, present and future oriented actions.

Providing that accounts are authentic, it is argued, there is no reason why they should not be used as scientific tools in explaining people's actions. Just how accounts can be authenticated will become clear in the following example of how an account may be elicited and analysed (see pp. 235–8 for a discussion of triangulation methods in analysing accounts). The study is to do with an experience familiar to many readers – the processes involved in buying a house.[4]

PROCEDURES IN ELICITING, ANALYSING AND AUTHENTICATING ACCOUNTS: AN EXAMPLE

From the outset of this research project, prime importance was placed upon the authority of each informant to account for his/her own actions. This meant that leading questions and excessive guidance were avoided by the research team although they established the format of the interview in pilot work before the main research endeavour. Care was taken to select informants who were representative of various house buyer needs (newly-weds, large families, divorcees, etc.) and of a range of house styles and prices. The researchers were concerned with the degree to which respondents were actually involved in the house purchase, the recency of the experience, their reasons for participating in the study, and their articulateness and competence in providing information.

These early stages of the research, involving selection and collection activities, served as checks on the authenticity of the accounts provided by those from whom it was possible to obtain adequate information. Further ways of establishing authenticity involved: first, checking with respondents through a process of negotiation during the account-gathering stage, about their perceptions of the events they described; second, using secondary evidence such as expert corroboration from solicitors and estate agents, that is, comparing objective and subjective realities; and third, comparing the separate accounts of other participants in the same event, that is, looking at various subjective realities. We illustrate this last aspect in Box 10.2.[4]

Once accounts had been gathered from informants, the researchers' task was to transform them into working documents which could be

Box 10.2   Accounts of a social episode: house purchase

Mrs Y:	'Agents put us in touch with three people who were interested. Couple X seemed to be the absolutely perfect customer. They gave us the offer we wanted, bought some brand new carpets over and above the asking price. Some problems followed and things were delayed. 'I don't think the X's were quite aware of the urgency. We got the impression from the agents that they were cash buyers. But it turned out they weren't and it was a bit naughty to give us this impression. 'We didn't get on so well with Mr X and Mrs X was a bit of a tough cookie. My husband had words with her and he got a bit ruffled.'
Mrs X:	'It started off a very amicable relationship. We came over here and agreed to buy carpets and curtains. But the whole situation deteriorated which made the whole thing unpleasant. Mr Y would call every night sometimes he would call twice and harangue and harangue. They seemed to think we were cash buyers, the agents having told them so. So I said we are cash buyers only in the sense that we don't have anything to sell. 'It all became more and more abusive, finally I got so upset that I refused any more calls and anything that had to be said should go via a solicitor. Every time the 'phone goes I would just cringe'.

Source: Adapted from Brown and Sime, 1977

coded and analysed. Checks on the authenticity of the accounts were again incorporated at this stage of the research as well as standard checks on the intercoder reliability of those engaged in the transformation of the materials. Depending on the nature of the research problem and the objectives of the enquiry, the analyses that then followed could either be qualitative or quantitative. The final stage in the research was the production of an 'account of the accounts'. Here, the researchers made explicit the controls that they had applied in eliciting accounts from informants and in the transformation process itself. Having satisfied the demands of authenticity in respect of their own account, the final product was then ready to be evaluated. Only when accounts were subjected to these periodic stringent checks for authenticity were they considered as scientific data. The account-gathering method proposed by Brown and Sime is summarized in Box 10.3.[5]

Problems of eliciting, analysing and authenticating accounts are further illustrated in the following outlines of two educational studies. The first is concerned with valuing among older boys and girls; the second is to do with the activities of pupils and teachers in using computers in primary classrooms.

Box 10.3   Account gathering

Research strategy	Control procedure
1 INFORMANTS	
Definition of episode and role groups representing domain of interest	rationale for choice of episode and role groups
Identification of exemplars	degree of involvement of potential informants
Selection of individual informants	contact with individuals to establish motive for participation, competence and performance
2 ACCOUNT GATHERING SITUATION	
Establishing venue	contextual effects of venue
Recording the account	appropriateness and accuracy in documenting account
Controlling relevance of account	accounts agenda
Authenticating account	negotiation and internal consistency
Establishing role of interviewer and interviewee	degree of direction
Post account authentication	corroboration
3 TRANSFORMATION OF ACCOUNTS	
Provision of working documents	transcription reliability; coder reliability
Data reduction techniques	appropriateness of statistical and content analyses
4 RESEARCHERS' ACCOUNTS	
Account of the account – summary, overview, interpretation	description of research operations, explanatory scheme and theoretical background

Source: Brown and Sime, 1981

QUALITATIVE ANALYSIS OF ACCOUNTS OF SOCIAL EPISODES: FURTHER EXAMPLES

In a study of adolescent values, Kitwood[6] developed an experience-sampling method, that is, a qualitative technique for gathering and analysing accounts based upon tape-recorded interviews that were themselves prompted by the fifteen situations listed in Box 10.4.

Because the experience-sampling method avoids interrogation, the material which emerges is less organized than that obtained from a tightly structured interview. Successful handling of individual accounts therefore requires the researcher to know the interview content extremely well and to work toward the gradual emergence of tentative interpretive schemata which he then modifies, confirms or falsifies as the research

Box 10.4 Experience sampling method

Below are listed fifteen types of situation which most people have been in at some time. Try to think of something that has happened in your life in the last year or so, or perhaps something that keeps on happening, which fits into each of the descriptions. Then choose the ten of them which deal with the things that seem to you to be most important, which cover your main interests and concerns, and the different parts of your life. When we meet we will talk together about the situations you have chosen. Try beforehand to remember as clearly as you can what happened, what you and others did, and how you yourself felt and thought. Be as definite as you can. If you like, write a few notes to help you keep the situation in mind.

1 When there was a misunderstanding between you and someone else (or several others) . . .
2 When you got on really well with people . . .
3 When you had to make an important decision . . .
4 When you discovered something new about yourself . . .
5 When you felt angry, annoyed or resentful . . .
6 When you did what was expected of you . . .
7 When your life changed direction in some way . . .
8 When you felt you had done something well . . .
9 When you were right on your own, with hardly anyone taking your side . . .
10 When you 'got away with it', or were not found out . . .
11 When you made a serious mistake . . .
12 When you felt afterwards that you had done right . . .
13 When you were disappointed with yourself . . .
14 When you had a serious clash or disagreement with another person . . .
15 When you began to take seriously something that had not mattered much to you before . . .

Source: Adapted from Kitwood, 1977

continues. Kitwood identifies eight methods for dealing with the tape-recorded accounts. Methods 1–4 are fairly close to the approach adopted in handling questionnaires; and Methods 5–8 are more in tune with the ethogenic principles that we identified earlier:

1 *The total pattern of choice* The frequency of choice of various items permits some surface generalizations about the participants, taken as a group. The most revealing analyses may be those of the least and most popular items.
2 *Similarities and differences* Using the same technique as in Method 1, it is possible to investigate similarities and differences within the total sample of accounts according to some characteristic(s) of the participants such as age, sex, level of educational attainment, etc.
3 *Grouping items together* It may be convenient for some purposes to fuse together categories that cover similar subject matter. For

example, items 1, 5 and 14 in Box 10.3 relate to conflict; items 4, 7 and 15, to personal growth and change.

4 *Categorization of content*   The content of a particular item is inspected for the total sample and an attempt is then made to develop some categories into which all the material will fit. The analysis is most effective when two or more researchers work in collaboration, each initially proposing a category system independently and then exchanging views to negotiate a final category system.

5 *Tracing a theme*   This type of analysis transcends the rather artificial boundaries which the items themselves imply. It aims to collect as much data as possible relevant to a particular topic regardless of where it occurs in the interview material. The method is exacting because it requires very detailed knowledge of content and may entail going through taped interviews several times. Data so collected may be further analysed along the lines suggested in Method 4 above.

6 *The study of omissions*   The researcher may well have expectations about the kind of issues likely to occur in the interviews. When some of these are absent, that fact may be highly significant. The absence of an anticipated topic should be explored to discover the correct explanation of its omission.

7 *Reconstruction of a social life-world*   This method can be applied to the accounts of a number of people who have part of their lives in common, for example, a group of friends who go around together. The aim is to attempt some kind of reconstruction of the world which the participants share in analysing the fragmentary material obtained in an interview. The researcher seeks to understand the dominant modes of orienting to reality, the conceptions of purpose and the limits to what is perceived.

8 *Generating and testing hypotheses*   New hypotheses may occur to the researcher during the analysis of the tape-recordings. It is possible to do more than simply advance these as a result of tentative impressions; one can loosely apply the hypothetico-deductive method to the data. This involves putting the hypothesis forward as clearly as possible, working out what the verifiable inferences from it would logically be, and testing these against the account data. Where these data are too fragmentary, the researcher may then consider what kind of evidence and method of obtaining it would be necessary for more thorough hypothesis testing. Subsequent sets of interviews forming part of the same piece of research might then be used to obtain relevant data.

The experience-sampling method used by Kitwood led him to identify three key second-order concepts by which to explore the nature of adolescent values. The first he called 'conflict in personal relationships', having found a general theme of interpersonal conflict running strongly through the interviews. The second, he identified as 'decision-making' on the evidence of a deep concern and realism among the adolescents interviewed about what might lie ahead of them. The third he termed 'standing alone', a major preoccupation among his subjects and a second-order concept of some complexity which was further broken down into five subcategories for more detailed analysis.

In the light of the weaknesses in account gathering and analysis (see pp. 228–9), Kitwood's suggestions of safeguards are worth mentioning. First he calls for cross-checking between researchers as a precaution against consistent but unrecognized bias in the interviews themselves. Second he recommends member tests, that is, taking hypotheses and unresolved problems back to the participants themselves or to people in similar situations to them for their comments. Only in this way can researchers be sure that they understand the participants' own grounds for action. Since there is always the possibility that an obliging participant will readily confirm the researcher's own speculations, every effort should be made to convey to the participant that one wants to know the truth as he or she sees it, and that one is as glad to be proved wrong as right.

A study by Blease and Cohen (1990)[7] used cross-checking as a way of validating the classroom observation records of co-researchers, and member tests to authenticate both quantitative and qualitative data derived from teacher and pupil informants. Thus, in the case of cross-checking, the classroom observation schedules of research assistants and researchers were compared and discussed, to arrive at definitive accounts of the range and duration of specific computer activities occurring within observation sessions. Member tests arose when interpretations of interview data were taken back to participating teachers for their comments. Similarly, pupils' scores on certain self-concept scales were discussed individually with respondents in order to ascertain why children awarded themselves high or low marks in respect of a range of skills in using computer programs.

NETWORK ANALYSES OF QUALITATIVE DATA

Another technique that has been successfully employed in the analysis of qualitative data is described by its originators as 'systematic network analysis' (Bliss, Monk, and Ogborn, 1983).[8] Drawing upon developments in artificial intelligence, Bliss and her colleagues employed the concept of 'relational network' to represent the content and structuring of a person's knowledge of a particular domain.

Essentially, network analysis involves the development of an elaborate system of categories by way of classifying qualitative data and preserving

211

Box 10.5   Network analysis: pupils' views of their teachers

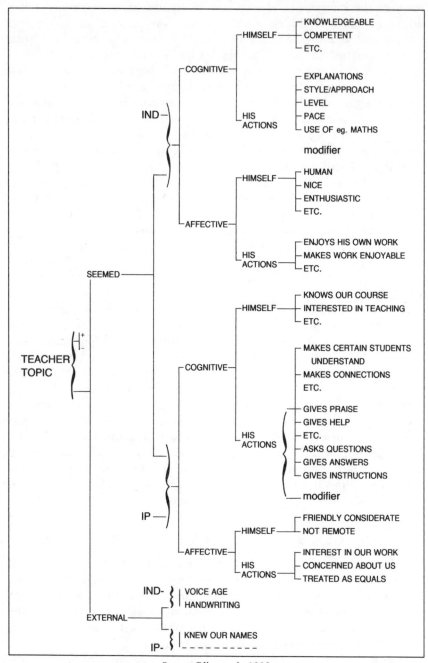

Source: Bliss *et al.*, 1983

212

the essential complexity and subtlety of the materials under investigation. A notational technique is employed to generate network-like structures that show the interdependencies of the categories as they are developed. An example from the work of Bliss and her associates is set out in Box. 10.5 to illustrate the network analysis technique. It is concerned with the classification of children's stories about their teachers. Notice how the very first distinction that the researchers introduce has to do with the difference between things that seemed to the pupil to be the case, and things that could be observed and, in principle, objectively agreed upon. This was found necessary because some of the statements about teachers referred to their age, colour of hair, etc., while others were more a matter of the children's personal judgements, such as their views on a teacher's enthusiasm or competence. A second major classificatory system that the researchers then introduced had to do with the fact that a teacher could seem different when he was on his own (IND = individual) or when he was dealing with a number of pupils (IP = interpersonal). The rest of the teacher network shown in Box 10.5 is self-explanatory.

WHAT MAKES A GOOD NETWORK?

Bliss *et al.* point out that there cannot be one overall account of criteria for judging the merits of a particular network. They do, however, attempt to identify a number of factors that ought to feature in any discussion of the standards by which a network might fairly be judged as adequate.

First, any system of description needs to be valid and reliable: valid in the sense that it is appropriate in kind and, within that kind, sufficiently complete and faithful, reliable in the sense that there exists an acceptable level of agreement between people as to how to use the network system to describe data.

Second, there are properties that a network description should possess such as clarity, completeness and self-consistency. These relate to a further criterion of 'network utility', the sufficiency of detail contained in a particular network. A third property that a network should possess is termed 'learnability'. Communicating the terms of the analysis to others, say the authors, is of central importance. It follows therefore that much hinges on whether networks are relatively easy or hard to teach to others. A fourth aspect of network acceptability has to do with its 'testability'. Bliss *et al.* identify two forms of testability, the first having to do with testing a network as a 'theory' against data, the second with testing data against a 'theory' or expectation via a network.

Finally, the terms 'expressiveness' and 'persuasiveness' refer to qualities of language used in developing the network structure. And here, the authors proffer the following advice. 'Helpful as the choice of an expressive coding mood or neat use of indentation or brackets may be, *the code actually says no more than the network distinguishes*' (our italics).

To conclude, network analysis would seem to have a useful role to play in educational research by providing a technique for dealing with the bulk and the complexity of the accounts that are typically generated in qualitative studies.

DISCOURSE ANALYSIS

Discourse researchers explore the organization of ordinary talk and everyday explanations and the social actions performed in them. Collecting, transcribing and analysing discourse data constitutes a kind of psychological 'natural history' of the phenomena in which discourse analysts are interested.[9]

Recent developments in discourse analysis have made important contributions to our understanding of children's thinking, challenging views (still common in educational circles) of 'the child as a lone organism, constructing a succession of general models of the world as each new stage is mastered'.[10] Rather than treating children's language as representative of an inner cognitive world to be explored experimentally by controlling for a host of intruding variables, discourse analysts treat that language as action, as 'situated discursive practice'.[11]

By way of example, Edwards (1993) explores discourse data emanating from a visit to a greenhouse by 5-year-old pupils and their teacher, to see plants being propagated and grown. His analysis shows how children take understandings of adults' meanings from the words they hear and the situations in which those words are used. And in turn, adults (in this case, the teacher) take from pupils' talk, not only what they might mean but also what they could and should mean. What Edwards describes as 'the discursive appropriation of ideas' (Edwards 1991) is illustrated in Box 10.6.

The application of discourse analysis to our understanding of classroom learning processes is well exampled in a study by Edwards and Mercer (1987).[12] Rather than taking the classroom talk as evidence of children's thought processes, the researchers explore it as 'contextualised dialogue with the teacher. The discourse itself is the educational reality and the issue becomes that of examining how teacher and children construct a shared account, a common interpretative framework for curriculum knowledge and for what happens in the classroom' (Edwards, 1991).

In another detailed examination of teacher–pupil dialogue, this time involving 9-year-olds in a lesson on computer graphics, Edwards asks the telling question, 'When teachers seem so much at pains to display

Box 10.6 Concepts in children's talk

81	Sally	Cuttings can grow to plants.
82	Teacher	[*writing*] 'Cuttings can grow –,' instead of saying 'to
83		plants' you can say 'grow, = ⌈ *in:* ⌉ to plants.'
84	Sally	= You wrote Chris ⌊ tina.⌋
85	Teacher	Oops. Thank you. I'll do this again. 'Cuttings can
86		grow into plants'. That's also good. What is a cutting,
87		Christina?
88	Christina	A cutting is, umm, I don't know.
89	Teacher	Who knows what a cutting is besides Sally? Sam.
90	Sam	It's when you cut off a –, it's when you cut off a piece
91		of a plant.
92	Teacher	Exactly, and when you cut off a piece of a plant, what do
93		you then do with it to make it grow? If you leave
94		⌈it –, ⌉
95	X	⌊Put it in soil.⌋
96	Teacher	Well, sometimes you can put it in soil.
97	Y	And ⌈plant it, ⌉
98	Teacher	⌊But what –,⌋ wait, what else could you put it in?
99	Sam	Put it in a pot?
100	Teacher	Pot, with soil, or . . . ? There's another way.
101	Sally	I know another way. =
102	Teacher	= Wait. Sam, do you know? No? =
103	Sam	= Dirt.
104	Teacher	No, it doesn't have to do with s –, it's not a solid, it's
105		a liquid. What ⌈liquid –, ⌉
106	Meredith	⌊Water. ⌋
107	Teacher	Right. [. . .]

Source: Edwards, 1993

education as drawing out or eliciting from pupils latent thoughts and ideas, why do they overtly elicit everything from the children while simultaneously gesturing, hinting at, implying and cueing the required answers?' (Edwards, 1991). Overriding asymmetries between teachers and pupils, Edwards concludes, both cognitive (in terms of knowledge) and interactive (in terms of power), impose different discursive patterns and functions.

BUBBLE DIALOGUE[13]

Edwards and Westgate (1987)[14] show what substantial strides have been made in recent years in the development of approaches to the investigation of classroom dialogue. Some methods encourage participants to talk; others wait for talk to emerge and sophisticated audio/video techniques record the result by whatever method it is achieved. Thus captured, dialogue is reviewed, discussed and reflected upon; moreover, that reviewing, discussing and reflecting is usually undertaken by researchers. It is they, generally, who read 'between the lines' and 'within the gaps' of classroom talk by way of interpreting the intentionality of the participating discussants.

We have purposely qualified our thumbnail reference to these developments with the words 'generally' and 'usually' in order to describe the emergence of a novel technique for capturing dialogue which involves placing participants in a role play situation, 'allowing them to have their characters create a dialogue and eliciting from them, as they recapture the meaning of dialogue, *their own reflections*', (O'Neill and McMahon, 1990, emphasis added). Bubble dialogue is the name given to this new tool by its creators at the University of Ulster (Coleraine).

The elements of bubble dialogue

Bubble dialogue was born out of children's comic strips. There, according to its creators, three key elements are juxtaposed: graphics, which so stylize characters in a story that often they become cultural icons; narrative text, which conveys the story line; and most importantly, dialogue, which by a well-established graphic convention, is readily identified as either each character's individual speech or thought. Cunningham *et al.* (1991)[15] have extended and powerfully transformed the comic strip in their computer-based application. Four icons, representing a speech bubble and a thought bubble per character are presented alongside two characters on the screen. Clicking on an icon brings up an empty 'say' or 'think' bubble for the chosen character. The comic genre is so well established, the authors opine, that even very young children when presented with empty bubbles, feel compelled to speak for the characters, playing out their roles. Sometimes the authors write in a first speech or thought (an 'opener' as they call it) to get a dialogue started. When pupils are more familiar with the tool, they readily create their own scenes and openers. Box 10.7 shows typical icons used in an opening speech instigated by the bubble dialogue creators.

In bubble dialogue, *characters* are set against a *backdrop*, the presence of which is considered crucial.[16] A *prologue* helps set the *scene* in which the *dialogue* takes place. 'Say' bubbles engage the participant in expressing or exploring the public domain which the characters share. 'Think' bubbles permit participants to relate to the private worlds of the characters. The dialogue grows as 'say' and 'think' bubbles are filled. Users can *review* the dialogue at any point by stepping backwards and forwards through the sequence of completed bubbles, keeping the characters and backdrop in view, or by choosing to look at a *dialogue script* presented as in the script for a play.

Box 10.7   Bubble dialogue showing an opening speech

Source: Cunningham *et al.*, 1991

From the researcher's vantage point, bubble dialogue permits perceived relationships to be varied (by backdrop, prologue, openers). Emerging scripted dialogues reveal the contexts that participants bring to the interaction, that is to say, 'what they think has been said, what they think was meant, what they perceive to be relevant' (O'Neill and McMahon, 1990). Bubble dialogue, its creators conclude, 'is a powerful methodology for users to make public those perceptions of context, content and interaction which might otherwise remain unformed and unsaid as well as unwritten' (O'Neill and McMahon, 1990).

A bubble dialogue application to educational research

Bubble dialogue (in comic script format rather than computer-based application) has been used by Cohen (1993)[17] to explore perceptions and interpretations of racist behaviour in secondary school classrooms. Some 200 student teachers in British universities, polytechnics and colleges of higher education were shown one of four 5-minute videos, each containing enactments of teacher racism. The films were devised, scripted and role-played by twenty-one 14- and 15-year-old pupils in an East Midlands comprehensive school. Each video focuses on a white,

217

female teacher's behaviour towards pupils on the basis of their ethnicity. A gifted teacher of drama skilfully elicited performances from participants and faithfully interpreted their directions in her portrayal of their devised teachers' roles.

Student teacher groups of ten to fifteen people watched a video presentation on two successive occasions without comment before completing first, answers to four open-ended questions about the build-up, the trigger event, the escalation and the finale of the particular classroom episode; and second, a research instrument consisting of some eight or nine still frames from the video, the build-up, trigger event, escalation and finale being illustrated by two frames each in bubble dialogue format. Anonymous responses to the research instruments were analysed and collated, independently, by two judges, before broad accounts of participants' interpretations of the video materials were returned to student groups for comment. The intensity of subsequent discussions and the ratings awarded in evaluative sessions suggest the utility of bubble dialogue as an approach to the exploration of salient and sensitive issues in teacher education.

QUANTITATIVE ANALYSIS OF JUDGEMENTAL RATINGS OF SOCIAL EPISODES

A major problem in the investigation of that natural unit of social behaviour, the 'social episode', has been the ambiguity that surrounds the concept itself and the lack of an acceptable taxonomy by which to classify an interaction sequence on the basis of empirically quantifiable characteristics.[18] In this section we describe a number of quantitative approaches to the study of social episodes in educational settings.

Examples of studies using factor analysis and linkage analysis

The use of factor analysis and linkage analysis in studies of children's judgements of educational situations is illustrated in the work of Magnusson[19] and Ekehammar and Magnusson[20] (see pp. 324–38). In the latter study, pupils were required to rate descriptions of various educational episodes on a scale of perceived similarity ranging from '0 = not at all similar' to '4 = identical'. Twenty different situations were presented, two at a time, in the same randomized order for all subjects. For example, 'listening to a lecture but do not understand a thing' would be judged against 'sitting at home writing an essay'. Product moment correlation coefficients between pairs of similarity matrices calculated for all subjects varied between 0.57 and 0.79, with a median value of 0.71. No individual matrix deviated markedly from any of the others. A factor analysis of the total correlation matrix showed that the descriptions of situations had very clear structures for the children involved. Moreover, judgements of perceived similarity between situations had a considerable degree of consistency over time. Ekehammar and Magnusson compared their dimensional analysis with a categorical approach to the data using elementary linkage (McQuitty, 1957).[21] They reported that this latter approach gave a result which was entirely in agreement with the result of the dimensional analysis. Five categories of situations were obtained with the same situations distributed in categories in the same way as they were distributed in factors in the dimensional analysis.

Examples of studies using multidimensional scaling and cluster analysis

Forgas (1976) studied housewives' and students' perceptions of typical social episodes in their lives, the episodes having been elicited from the respective groups by means of a diary technique. Subjects were required to supply two adjectives to describe each of the social episodes they had recorded as having occurred during the previous 24 hours. From a pool of some 146 adjectives thus generated, ten (together with their antonyms) were selected on the basis of their salience, their diversity of usage and their independence of one another. Two more scales from speculative taxonomies were added to give twelve undimensional scales purporting to describe the underlying episode structures. These scales were used in the second part of the study to rate twenty-five social episodes in each group, the episodes being chosen as follows. An 'index of relatedness' was computed on the basis of the number of times a pair of episodes was placed in the same category by respective housewife and student judges. Data were aggregated over the total number of subjects in each of the two groups. The twenty-five 'top' social episodes in each group were retained. Forgas's analysis is based upon the ratings of twenty-six housewives and twenty-five students of their respective twenty-five episodes on each of the twelve undimensional scales. Box 10.8 shows a three-dimensional configuration of twenty-five social episodes rated by the student group on three of the scales. For illustrative purposes some of the social episodes numbered in Box 10.8 are identified by specific content.

In another study, Forgas examined the social environment of a university department consisting of tutors, students and secretarial staff, all of whom had interacted both inside and outside the department for at least six months prior to the research and thought of themselves as an intensive and cohesive social unit.[22] Forgas's interest was in the relationship between two aspects of the social environment of the department – the perceived structure of the group and the perceptions that were

Box 10.8 Students' perceptions of social episodes

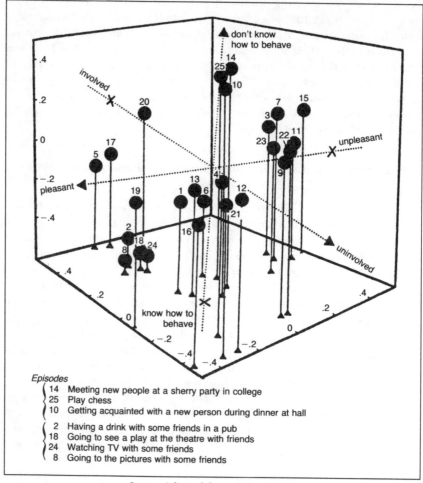

Source: Adapted from Forgas, 1976

held of specific social episodes. Participants were required to rate the similarity between each possible pairing of group members on a scale ranging from '1 = extremely similar' to '9 = extremely dissimilar'. An individual differences multi-dimensional scaling procedure (INDSCAL) produced an optimal three-dimensional configuration of group structure accounting for 68 per cent of the variance, group members being differentiated along the dimensions of sociability, creativity and competence.

A semi-structured procedure requiring participants to list typical and characteristic interaction situations was used to identify a number of

Box 10.9 Perception of social episodes

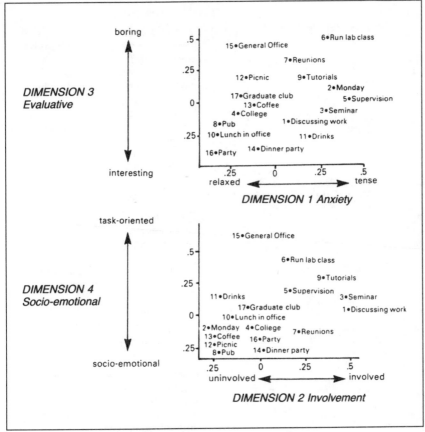

Source: Adapted from Forgas, 1978

social episodes. These in turn were validated by participant observation of the ongoing activities of the department. The most commonly occurring social episodes (those mentioned by nine or more members) served as the stimuli in the second stage of the study. Bipolar scales similar to those reported by Forgas (1976) and elicited in like manner were used to obtain group members' judgements of social episodes.

An interesting finding reported by Forgas was that formal status differences exercised no significant effect upon the perception of the group by its members, the absence of differences being attributed to the strength of the department's cohesiveness and intimacy. In Forgas's analysis of the group's perceptions of social episodes, the INDSCAL scaling procedure produced an optimal four-dimensional solution accounting for 62 per cent of the variance, group members perceiving

Box 10.10 Person concept coding system

Dimension	Levels of descriptiveness
DESCRIPTIVENESS	1 *Undifferentiating* . . . (person not differentiated from his environment) 2 *Simple differentiating* . . . (person differentiated in simple global terms) 3 *Differentiating* . . . (person differentiated in specific characteristics) 4 *Dispositional* . . . (person differentiated in terms of traits)
PERSONAL INVOLVEMENT	*Degrees of involvement* 1 *Egocentric* . . . (other person described in self-oriented terms) 2 *Mutual* . . . (other person described in terms of his relationship to perceiver) 3 *Other oriented* . . . (no personal involvement expressed by perceiver)
EVALUATIVE CONSISTENCY	*Amount of consistency* 1 *Consistent* . . . (nothing favourable about 'disliked', nothing unfavourable about 'liked') 2 *Inconsistent* . . . (some mixture of favourableness and unfavourableness)
DEPTH	*Levels of depth* *Level 1* (includes all undifferentiated and simple differentiated descriptions) *Level 2* (includes differentiated and some dispositional descriptions) *Level 3* (includes explanation-type differentiated and dispositional descriptions)

Source: Adapted from Peevers and Secord, 1973

social episodes in terms of anxiety, involvement, evaluation and socio-emotional versus task orientation. Box 10.9 illustrates how an average group member would see the characteristics of various social episodes in terms of the dimensions by which the group commonly judged them.

Finally we outline a classificatory system that has been developed to process materials elicited in a rather structured form of account gathering. Peevers and Secord's study of developmental changes in children's use of descriptive concepts of persons, illustrates the application of quantitative techniques to the analysis of one form of account.[23]

In individual interviews, children of varying ages were asked to describe three friends and one person whom they disliked, all four people being of the same sex as the interviewee. Interviews were tape-recorded and transcribed. A person-concept coding system was developed, the categories of which are illustrated in Box 10.10. Each person-description was divided into items, each item consisting of one discrete piece of information. Each item was then coded on each of four major dimensions. Detailed coding procedures are set out in Peevers and Secord (1973).

Tests of interjudge agreement on descriptiveness, personal involvement and evaluative consistency in which two judges worked independently on the interview transcripts of twenty-one boys and girls aged between 5 and 16 years resulted in interjudge agreement on those three dimensions of 87 per cent, 79 per cent and 97 per cent respectively.

Peevers and Secord also obtained evidence of the degree to which the participants themselves were consistent from one session to another in their use of concepts to describe other people. Children were re-interviewed between one week and one month after the first session on the pretext of problems with the original recordings. Indices of test–retest reliability were computed for each of the major coding dimensions. Separate correlation coefficients (eta) were obtained for younger and older children in respect of their descriptive concepts of liked and disliked peers. Reliability coefficients are as set out in Box 10.11. Secord and Peevers (1974)[24] conclude that their approach offers the possibility of an exciting line of enquiry into the depth of insight that individuals have into the personalities of their acquaintances. Their 'free commentary' method is a modification of the more structured interview, requiring the interviewer to probe for explanations of why a person behaves the way he or she does or why a person is the kind of person

Box 10.11 Reliability coefficients for peer descriptions

Dimension	Liked peers		Disliked peers	
	Younger subjects	Older subjects	Younger subjects	Older subjects
Descriptiveness	0.83	0.91	0.80	0.84
Personal involvement	0.76	0.80	0.84	0.77
Depth	0.65	0.71	0.65	0.75
Evaluative consistency	0.69	0.92	0.76	0.69

Source: Peevers and Secord, 1973

he or she is. Peevers and Secord found that older children in their sample readily volunteered this sort of information. Harré (1977)[25] observes that this approach could also be extended to elicit commentary upon children's friends and enemies and the ritual actions associated with the creation and maintenance of these categories.

ACCOUNT GATHERING IN EDUCATIONAL RESEARCH: TWO EXAMPLES

The 'free commentary' method that Secord and Peevers recommend as a way of probing for explanations of people's behaviour lies at the very heart of the ethnographer's skills. In the two examples of ethnographic research that now follow, what is common to both is the attempt of the researchers to get below the surface data and to search for the deeper, hidden patterns that are only revealed when attention is directed to the ways that group members interpret the flow of events in their lives.

Heath – 'Questioning at home and at school' (1982)

Heath's study of misunderstandings existing between black children and their white teachers in classrooms in the south of the United States brought to light teachers' assumptions that pupils would respond to language routines and the uses of language in building knowledge and skills just as other children (including their own) did (Heath, 1982).[26] Specifically, she sought to understand why these particular children did *not* respond just as others did. Her research involved eliciting explanations from both the children's parents and teachers. 'We don't talk to our children like you folks do', the parents observed when questioned about their children's behaviour. Those children, it seemed to Heath, were not regarded as information givers or as appropriate conversational partners for adults. That is not to say that the children were excluded from language participation. They did, in fact, participate in a language that Heath describes as rich in styles, speakers and topics. Rather, it seemed to the researcher that the teachers' characteristic mode of questioning was 'to pull attributes of things out of context, particularly out of the context of books and name them – queens, elves, police, red apples' (Heath, 1982). The parents did *not* ask these kinds of questions of their children, and the children themselves had their own ways of deflecting such questions, as the example in Box 10.12 well illustrates.

Heath elicited both parents' and teachers' accounts of the children's behaviour and their apparent communication 'problems' (see Box 10.13). Her account of accounts arose out of periods of participation and observation in classrooms and in some of the teachers' homes. In

Box 10.12 'Ain't nobody can talk about things being about theirselves'

This comment by a 9-year-old boy was directed to his teacher when she persisted in interrogating him about the story he had just completed in his reading group.

Teacher: What is the story about?
Children: (*silence*)
Teacher: Uh . . . Let's see . . . Who is it the story talks about?
Children: (*silence*)
Teacher: Who is the main character? . . . Um . . . What kind of story is it?
Child: Ain't nobody can talk about things being about theirselves.

The boy was saying 'There's no way anybody can talk (and ask) about things being about themselves'.

Source: Adapted from Spindler, 1982[27]

particular, she focused upon the ways in which 'the children learned to use language to satisfy their needs, ask questions, transmit information, and convince those around them that they were competent communicators' (Heath, 1982). This involved her in a much wider and more intensive study of the total fabric of life in Trackton, the southern community in which the research was located.

> Over five years . . . I was able to collect data across a wide range of situations and to follow some children longitudinally as they acquired communicative competence in Trackton. Likewise, at various periods during these years, I observed Trackton adults in public service encounters and on their jobs. . . . The context of language use, including setting, topic, and participants (both those directly involved in the talk and those who only listened) determined in large part how community members, teachers, public service personnel, and fellow workers judged the communicative competence of Trackton residents.
>
> (Heath, 1982)

Riseborough – 'The cream team' (1992)

A second example of the use of accounts in educational research is given in Riseborough's study of vocational students in a tertiary college in Northern England.[28] They were following BTEC National Diploma Courses in Catering and Hotel Management with the intention of entering service industries. The students, Riseborough observes, were outwardly highly conformist, with upward mobility aspirations. The majority were from working class backgrounds. They were 'labour market-wise' and knew the importance of educational qualifications. Riseborough's participant observation study involved him in following

Box 10.13   Parents and teachers: divergent viewpoints on children's communicative competence

Parents	Teachers
The teachers won't listen. My kid, he too scared to talk, 'cause nobody play by the rules he know. At home, I can't shut 'im up.	They don't seem to be able to answer even the simplest questions.
Miss Davis, she complain 'bout Ned not answerin' back. He say she asks dumb questions she already know 'bout.	I would almost think some of them have a hearing problem; it is as though they don't hear me ask a question. I get blank stares to my questions. Yet when I am making statements or telling stories which interest them, they always seem to hear me.
	The simplest questions are the ones they can't answer in the classroom; yet on the playground, they can explain a rule for a ballgame or describe a particular kind of bait with no problem. Therefore, I know they can't be as dumb as they seem in my class.
	I sometimes feel that when I look at them and ask a question I'm staring at a wall I can't break through. There's something there; yet in spite of all the questions I ask, I'm never sure I've gotten through to what's inside that wall.

Source: Adapted from Spindler, 1982

twenty students throughout their time in college. His data are derived from recorded individual and group interviews, or, as he prefers to call them, 'conversations with a purpose' (Burgess, 1985).[29] Those conversations revealed that the students were highly instrumental, wanting their Diplomas without 'the education':

Ben   I knew I wanted to go into catering, anyway. I knew what I wanted to do, to be a chef. I've been wanting to do it since the third year in the senior school.

Eddie   I want to get on the boats. . . . Go round the world on cruise liners. I'm hoping to get a job on the QE2, it's the Ferrari of cruise liners isn't it?

(Riseborough, 1992)

Thus, whilst they were strongly committed to the course and obsessed with getting good grades and passing their examinations, the students were also very critical of the college, finding it 'boring' and 'a waste of time':

Jemma Mr Pastry, Mr Pastry! (*She is tearful and distraught*) I put a right load into that, and John got 85. (*Mr Pastry ignores her and carries on with his clip board assessing work*). MR PASTRY!! (*She is even more distraught*) I put a right load of work into that and I get 60. Look, he won't even look at you will he? (*Addressing other students*) The plonker! It's pointless, a waste of time . . .

Stan It's really boring. You've got to do it to pass. You've got to pass everything. If you fail one paper or test you have to resit. . . . You just go on, and on and on with these bloody boring tests.

The quality of the teaching leaves much to be desired:

Harry Mrs Hygiene, it's the overhead projector! Here's a transparency, copy it down, here's another one, copy it down, here's another one, copy it down, here is another one, copy it. You are there for an hour and a half and you come out like 'Uuuarrr!' (*Zombie-like imitation*). You get totally pissed off, week in week out. Just building up a set of notes and revising those for the test and that's it.

(Riseborough, 1992)

From his analysis of the data, Riseborough concludes that the student subculture at Gastronomic College, characterized by strategic compliance, impression management, a sublimation of overt conflict (and) the exercise of covert manipulation, forms a cultural circle with the occupational culture the students are about to enter. Drawing on Goffman (1969),[30] Riseborough opines that Gastronomic College provides the students with a 'dramaturgical discipline'. When they leave, he observes, they have all the cultural competencies to handle both clients and superordinates:

Jenny There was a woman last Saturday, she sat down and said, 'Can you change this table cloth?' 'Can you do this and I want that'. I could have bloody hit her. 'Can I have some vinegar?' Went and fetched it. 'Can I have some salt as well please?' Went and fetched it, brought it back. She says, 'Have you any pepper as well, please?' Go back and fetch it. I was that close (*finger and thumb gesture*). Oh, I was nearly . . . that close (*gesture*). It's not what you want, there are ways of asking.

GFR   But did you do or say anything?

Jenny No. You have got to get used to it working in a public service
industry, to deal with the public sort of thing . . .

(Riseborough, 1992)

PROBLEMS IN GATHERING AND ANALYSING ACCOUNTS

The importance of the meaning of events and actions to those who are
involved is now generally recognized in social research. The implications
of the ethogenic stance in terms of actual research techniques, however,
remain problematic. Menzel (1978)[31] discusses a number of ambiguities
and shortcomings in the ethogenic approach, arising out of the multiplicity of meanings that may be held for the same behaviour. Most
behaviour, Menzel observes, can be assigned meanings and more than
one of these may very well be valid simultaneously. It is fallacious
therefore, he argues, to insist upon determining 'the' meaning of an act.
Nor can it be said that the task of interpreting an act is done when one
has identified one meaning of it, or the one meaning that the researcher
is pleased to designate as the true one.

A second problem that Menzel raises is to do with actors' meanings as
sources of bias. How central a place, he asks, ought to be given to actors'
meanings in formulating explanations of events? Should the researcher
exclusively and invariably be guided by these considerations? To do so
would be to ignore a whole range of potential explanations which few
researchers would wish to see excluded from consideration.

These are far-reaching, difficult issues though by no means intract-
able. What solutions does Menzel propose? First we must specify 'to
whom' when asking what acts and situations mean. Second, researchers
must make choices and take responsibility in the assignment of meanings
to acts; moreover, problem formulations must respect the meaning of
the act to us, the researchers. And third, explanations should respect
the meanings of acts to the actors themselves but need not invariably be
centred around these meanings.

Menzel's plea is for the usefulness of an outside observer's account of
a social episode alongside the explanations that participants themselves
may give of that event. A similar argument is implicit in McIntyre and
McLeod's (1978)[32] justification of objective, systematic observation in
classroom settings. Their case is set out in Box 10.14.[33]

STRENGTHS OF THE ETHOGENIC APPROACH

The advantages of the ethogenic approach to the educational researcher
lie in the distinctive insights that are made available to her through the

228

Box 10.14 Justification of objective systematic observation in classroom settings

When Smith looks at Jones and says, 'Jones, why does the blue substance spread through the liquid?' (probably with a particular kind of voice inflection), and then silently looks at Jones (probably with a particular kind of facial expression), the observer can unambiguously categorize the event as 'Smith asks Jones a question seeking an explanation of diffusion in a liquid.' Now Smith might describe the event as 'giving Jones a chance to show he knows something', and Jones might describe the event as 'Smith trying to get at me'; but if either of them denied the validity of the observer's description, they would be simply wrong, because the observer would be describing at least part of what the behaviour which occurred means in English in Britain. No assumptions are made here about the effectiveness of classroom communication; but the assumption is made that . . . communication is dependent on the system of conventional meanings available within the wider culture. More fundamentally, this interpretation implies that the systematic observer is concerned with an objective reality (or, if one prefers, a shared intersubjective reality) of classroom events. This is not to suggest that the subjective meanings of events to participants are not important, but only that these are not accessible to the observer and that *there is an objective reality to classroom activity which does not depend on these meanings* [our emphasis].

Source: McIntyre and McLeod, in McAleese and Hamilton, 1978

analysis of accounts of social episodes. The benefits to be derived from the exploration of accounts are best seen by contrasting[33] the ethogenic approach with a more traditional educational technique such as the survey which we discussed in Chapter 4.

There is a good deal of truth in the assertion of the ethogenically-oriented researcher that approaches which employ survey techniques such as the questionnaire take for granted the very things that should be treated as problematic in an educational study. Too often, the phenomena that ought to be the focus of attention are taken as given, that is, they are treated as the starting point of the research rather than becoming the centre of the researcher's interest and effort to discover how the phenomena arose or came to be important in the first place. Numerous educational studies, for example, have identified the incidence and the duration of disciplinary infractions in school; only relatively recently, however, has the meaning of classroom disorder, as opposed to its frequency and type, been subjected to intensive investigation.[34] Unlike the survey, which is a cross-sectional technique that takes its data at a single point in time, the ethogenic study employs an ongoing observational approach that focuses upon processes rather than products. Thus it is the process of becoming deviant in school which would capture the attention of the ethogenic researcher rather than the frequency and type of misbehaviour among k types of ability in children located in n kinds of school.

REFERENCES AND NOTES

1 Harré, R., 'The ethogenic approach: theory and practice', in L. Berkowitz (ed.), *Advances in Experimental Social Psychology*, vol. 10 (Academic Press, New York, 1977).

2 Harré, R., 'Some remarks on "rule" as a scientific concept', in T. Mischel (ed.), *On Understanding Persons* (Basil Blackwell, Oxford, 1974).

3 Harré, R., 'Accounts, actions and meanings – the practice of participatory psychology', in M. Brenner, P. Marsh and M. Brenner (eds), *The Social Context of Method* (Croom Helm, London, 1978).

4 Brown, J. and Sime, J.D., 'Accounts as general methodology', paper presented to the British Psychological Society Conference (University of Exeter, 1977).

5 Brown, J. and Sime, J.D., 'A methodology of accounts', in M. Brenner (ed.), *Social Method and Social Life* (Academic Press, London, 1981).

6 Kitwood, T.M., 'Values in adolescent life: towards a critical description', unpublished PhD dissertation, School of Research in Education (University of Bradford, 1977).

7 Blease, D. and Cohen, L., *Coping with Computers: An Ethnographic Study in Primary Classrooms* (Paul Chapman, London, 1990).

8 Bliss, J., Monk, M. and Ogborn, J., *Qualitative Data Analysis for Educational Research* (Croom Helm, London, 1983).

9 Edwards, D. and Potter, J., 'Language and causation: a discursive action model of description and attribution', *Psychological Review*, 100(1) (1993) 23–41.

10 Edwards, D., 'Discourse and the development of understanding in the classroom', in Boyd-Barrett, O. and Scanlon, E. (eds), *Computers and Learning*, (Addison-Wesley Publishing Co., Wokingham, 1991 186–204).

11 Edwards, D., 'Concepts, memory and the organisation of pedagogic discourse: a case study', *International Journal of Educational Research*, 19(3) (1993) 205–25. See also: Potter, J. and Wetherall, M., *Discourse and Social Psychology: Beyond Attitudes and Behaviour* (Sage, London, 1987); Walkerdine, V., *The Mastery of Reason: Cognitive Development and the Production of Rationality* (Routledge, London, 1988); Edwards, D. and Mercer, N.M. 'Reconstructing context: the conventionalization of classroom knowledge', *Discourse Processes*, 12 (1989) 91–104.

12 Edwards, D. and Mercer, N.M., *Common Knowledge: The Development of Understanding in the Classroom* (Routledge & Kegan Paul, London, 1987).

13 Our account draws on the outline contained in O'Neill, B., and McMahon, H., *Opening New Windows with Bubble Dialogue* (Language Development and Hypermedia Research Group, Faculty of Education, University of Ulster at Coleraine, 1990). See also the taxonomies for the analysis of social episodes by Windisch, V., *Speech and Reasoning in Everyday Life* (Cambridge University Press, Cambridge, 1990); Schonbach, P., *Account Episodes: The Management or Escalation of Conflict* (Cambridge University Press, Cambridge, 1990); Semin, G.R. and Manstead, A.S.R., *The Accountability of Conduct: A Social Psychological Analysis* (Academic Press, London, 1983).

14 Edwards, A.D. and Westgate, D.P.G., *Investigating Classroom Talk* (Falmer Press, Lewes, 1987).

15 Cunningham, D., McMahon, H. and O'Neill, B., *Bubble Dialogue: A New Tool for Instruction and Assessment* (Language Development and Hypermedia Research Group, Faculty of Education, University of Ulster at Coleraine, 1991).

16 An example of the iconic power of a 'backdrop' is graphically illustrated by O'Neill and McMahon (1990) in their work with 13-year-old pupils in a Londonderry school. There, the backdrop to the dialogue is a Janus-like statue, the work of a contemporary sculptor, depicting two figures, fused together, arms outstretched as in a crucifix, one looking out over the Catholic Bogside, the other into the (Protestant) walled city.

17 Cohen, L., *Racism Awareness Materials in Initial Teacher Training* (Report to the Leverhulme Trust, 15–19 New Fetter Lane, London, EC4A 1NR. 1993). The video scenarios are part of an enquiry into pupils' perceptions of the behaviour of white teachers towards minority pupils in school. (See Naylor, P., 'Pupils' perceptions of teacher racism', PhD dissertation, Loughborough University of Technology, 1995.)

18 Forgas, J.P., 'The perception of social episodes: categoric and dimensional representations in two different social milieux', *Journal of Personality and Social Psychology*, 34(2) (1976) 199–209.

19 Magnusson, D., 'An analysis of situational dimensions', *Perceptual and Motor Skills*, 32 (1971) 851–67.

20 Ekehammar, B. and Magnusson, D., 'A method to study stressful situations', *Journal of Personality and Social Psychology*, 27(2) (1973) 176–9.

21 McQuitty, L.L., 'Elementary linkage analysis for isolating orthogonal and oblique types and relevancies', *Education & Psychology Measures*, 17 (1957) 207–29.

22 Forgas, J.P., 'Social episodes and social structure in an academic setting: the social environment of an intact group', *Journal of Experimental Social Psychology*, 14 (1978) 434–48. For a fuller account of Forgas' work on the study of social episodes see Forgas, J.P., *Social Episodes: The study of Interaction Routines* (Academic Press, London, 1981).

23 Peevers, B.H. and Secord, P.F., 'Developmental changes in attribution of descriptive concepts to persons', *Journal of Personality and Social Psychology*, 27(1) (1973) 120–8.

24 Secord, P.F. and Peevers, B.H., 'The development and attribution of person concepts', in T. Mischel (ed.), *On Understanding Persons* (Basil Blackwell, Oxford, 1974).

25 Harré, R., 'Friendship as an accomplishment', in S. Duck (ed.), *Theory and Practice in Interpersonal Attraction* (Academic Press, London, 1977).

26 Heath, S.B., 'Questioning at home and at school: a comparative study', in G. Spindler (ed.), *Doing the Ethnography of Schooling* (Holt, Rinehart & Winston, New York, 1982). Interesting ethnographic studies of children in classrooms and playgrounds appear in the Routledge & Kegan Paul series, 'Social Worlds of Childhood': Davies, B., *Life in the Classroom and Playground: The Accounts of Primary School Children* (Routledge & Kegan Paul, London, 1982), and: Sluckin, A., *Growing up in the Playground: The Social Development of Children* (Routledge & Kegan Paul, London, 1981). See also Woods, P. and Hammersley, M., *Gender and Ethnicity in Schools: Ethnographic Accounts* (Routledge, London, 1993); Troyna, B. and Hatcher, R., *Racism in Children's Lives: A Study in Mainly-White Primary Schools* (Routledge, London, 1992).

27 Spindler, G. (ed.), *Doing the Ethnography of Schooling* (Holt, Rinehart & Winston, New York, 1982).

28 Riseborough, G.F., 'The Cream Team: An ethnography of BTEC National Diploma (Catering and Hotel Management) students in a tertiary college', *British Journal of Sociology and Education*, 13(2) (1992) 215–45.

29 Burgess, R., 'Conversations with a purpose? The ethnographic interview in educational research', paper presented at the British Educational Research Association Annual Conference (Sheffield, 1985).

30 Goffman, E., *The Presentation of Self in Everyday Life* (Penguin, London, 1969).
31 Menzel, H., 'Meaning – who needs it?' in Brenner, M., Marsh, P. and Brenner, M. (eds), *The Social Context of Method* (Croom Helm, London, 1978). For a further discussion of the problem, see Gilbert, G.N., 'Accounts and those accounts called actions', in Gilbert, G.N. and Abell, P., *Accounts and Action* (Gower, Aldershot, 1983).
32 McIntyre, D. and MacLeod, G., 'The characteristics and uses of systematic classroom observation', in McAleese, R. and Hamilton, D. (eds), *Understanding Classroom Life* (NFER, Windsor, 1978) 102–31.
33 The discussion at this point draws on that in Bailey, K.D., *Methods of Social Research* (Collier-Macmillan, London, 1978) 261.
34 See, for example: Hargreaves, D.H., Hester, S.K. and Mellor, F.J., *Deviance in Classrooms* (Routledge & Kegan Paul, London, 1975); Marsh, P., Rosser, E. and Harré, R., *The Rules of Disorder* (Routledge & Kegan Paul, London, 1978).

11

TRIANGULATION

INTRODUCTION

Triangulation may be defined as the use of two or more methods of data collection in the study of some aspect of human behaviour. It is a technique of research to which many subscribe in principle, but which only a minority use in practice. The use of multiple methods, or the multi-method approach as it is sometimes called, contrasts with the ubiquitous but generally more vulnerable single-method approach that characterizes so much of research in the social sciences. In its original and literal sense, triangulation is a technique of physical measurement: maritime navigators, military strategists and surveyors, for example, use (or used to use) several locational markers in their endeavours to pinpoint a single spot or objective. By analogy, triangular techniques in the social sciences attempt to map out, or explain more fully, the richness and complexity of human behaviour by studying it from more than one standpoint and, in so doing, by making use of both quantitative and qualitative data.

The advantages of the multimethod approach in social research are manifold and we examine two of them. First, whereas the single observation in fields such as medicine, chemistry and physics normally yields sufficient and unambiguous information on selected phenomena, it provides only a limited view of the complexity of human behaviour and of situations in which human beings interact. It has been observed that as research methods act as filters through which the environment is selectively experienced, they are never atheoretical or neutral in representing the world of experience (Smith, 1975).[1] Exclusive reliance on one method, therefore, may bias or distort the researcher's picture of the particular slice of reality she is investigating. She needs to be confident that the data generated are not simply artefacts of one specific method of collection (Lin, 1976).[2] And this confidence can only be achieved as far as normative research is concerned when different methods of data collection yield substantially the same results. (Where triangulation is used in interpretive research to investigate different actors' viewpoints, the same method, e.g. accounts, will naturally produce different sets of data.) Further, the more the methods contrast with each other, the greater the researcher's confidence. If, for example, the outcomes of a questionnaire survey correspond to those of an observational study of the same phenomena, the more the researcher will be confident about the findings. Or, more extreme, where the results of a rigorous experimental investigation are replicated in, say, a role-playing exercise, the researcher will experience even greater assurance. If findings are artefacts of method, then the use of contrasting methods considerably reduces the chances that any consistent findings are attributable to similarities of method (Lin, 1976).

We come now to a second advantage: some theorists have been sharply critical of the limited use to which existing methods of enquiry in the social sciences have been put. One writer, for example, comments, 'Much research has employed particular methods or techniques out of methodological parochialism or ethnocentrism. Methodologists often push particular pet methods either because those are the only ones they have familiarity with, or because they believe their method is superior to all others' (Smith, 1975). The use of triangular techniques, it is argued, will help to overcome the problem of 'method-boundedness', as it has been termed. One of the earliest scientists to predict such a condition was Boring, who wrote:

> as long as a new construct has only the single operational definition that it received at birth, it is just a construct. When it gets two alternative operational definitions, it is beginning to be validated. When the defining operations, because of proven correlations, are many, then it becomes reified.
>
> (Boring, 1953)[3]

The following typify the kinds of current problems that critics point to: attitude scales are often selected for their convenience and accessibility rather than for their psychological criteria; many studies are culture-bound, that is, they are limited to one country; the vast majority are also time-bound, that is, they are limited to one point in time and do not take into consideration the fact of social change; sociological studies, which by definition imply a macro level of analysis, make excessive use of individuals; and rarely are studies replicated (Denzin, 1970).[4] Criticisms of this sort can be met by taking a more extended view of triangulation which we will consider shortly.

The principle of triangulation is illustrated at its most simple in a typical attitude scale. If you examine the example in Box 11.1, you will find ten items making up an attitude scale measuring a teacher's view of his role. One item, or 'locational marker', by itself will tell us very little

234

Box 11.1 A teacher's attitude to his role

The scale below measures the extent to which a teacher interprets his role in either 'educational' or 'academic' terms. In using different 'locational markers', it gives a more representative picture of the respondent's orientation to his role and in so doing illustrates the principle of triangulation in simple form.

1 A teacher should teach informally most of the time.
2 A teacher should be emotionally involved with his pupils.
3 A teacher should use many and varied materials.
4 He should regard scholarly attitudes to be of primary importance for his pupils.
5 He should develop most of the work done in class from the children's own interests.
6 A teacher should get to know children as individuals.
7 A teacher should use corporal punishment.
8 A teacher should look out for children with serious personal problems.
9 A teacher should maintain discipline at all times.
10 A teacher should get his chief satisfaction from interest in his subject or from administrative work in the school, rather than from classroom teaching.

Source: Constructed by David Marsland

about a teacher's attitude in this respect. But ten such related items, or 'locational markers', will give a much fuller picture. Imagine now a detailed study of a class of pupils in a secondary school which involves teachers' ratings of pupils, school records, psychometric data, sociometric data, case studies, questionnaires and observation. Add to this the findings of investigations of similar classes in ten other secondary schools and we then have an illustration of the principle of triangulation at a more complex level.

In its use of multiple methods, triangulation may utilize either normative or interpretive techniques; or it may draw on methods from both these approaches and use them in combination.

TYPES OF TRIANGULATION AND THEIR CHARACTERISTICS

We have just seen how triangulation is characterized by a multi-method approach to a problem in contrast to a single-method approach. Denzin (1970) has, however, extended this view of triangulation to take in several other types as well as the multi-method kind which he terms 'methodological triangulation'. These he designates time triangulation, space triangulation, combined levels of triangulation, theoretical triangulation, investigator triangulation and – as already noted – methodological triangulation. The use of these several types of triangulation goes

Box 11.2 The principal types of triangulation used in research

1 *Time triangulation*: this type attempts to take into consideration the factors of change and process by utilizing cross-sectional and longitudinal designs.
2 *Space triangulation*: this type attempts to overcome the parochialism of studies conducted in the same country or within the same subculture by making use of cross-cultural techniques.
3 *Combined levels of triangulation*: this type uses more than one level of analysis from the three principal levels used in the social sciences, namely, the individual level, the interactive level (groups), and the level of collectivities (organizational, cultural or societal).
4 *Theoretical triangulation*: this type draws upon alternative or competing theories in preference to utilizing one viewpoint only.
5 *Investigator triangulation*: this type engages more than one observer.
6 *Methodological triangulation*: this type uses either (a) the same method on different occasions, or (b) different methods on the same object of study.

Source: Based on Denzin's typology[4]

some way to meet the kinds of methodological criticisms we have already referred to. We now briefly identify the characteristics of each type and refer you to Box 11.2 for a summary of their purpose.

The vast majority of studies in the social sciences are conducted at one point only in time, thereby ignoring the effects of social change and process. Time triangulation goes some way to rectifying these omissions by making use of cross-sectional and longitudinal approaches. Cross-sectional studies collect data concerned with time-related processes from different groups at one point in time; longitudinal studies collect data from the same group at different points in the time sequence. The use of panel studies and trend studies may also be mentioned in this connection. The former compare the same measurements for the same individuals in a sample at several different points in time; and the latter examine selected processes continually over time. The weaknesses of each of these methods can be strengthened by using a combined approach to a given problem (see p. 69).

Space triangulation attempts to overcome the limitations of studies conducted within one culture or subculture. As one writer says, 'Not only are the behavioural sciences culture-bound, they are sub-culture-bound. Yet many such scholarly works are written as if basic principles have been discovered which would hold true as tendencies in any society, anywhere, anytime' (Smith, 1975). Cross-cultural studies may involve the testing of theories among different people, as in Piagetian and Freudian psychology; or they may measure differences between populations by using several different measuring instruments. Levine describes how he used this strategy of convergent validation in his comparative studies:

I have studied differences of achievement motivation among three Nigerian ethnic groups by the analysis of dream reports, written expressions of values, and public opinion survey data. The convergence of findings from the diverse set of data (and samples) strengthens my conviction ... that the differences among the groups are not artifacts produced by measuring instruments.

(Levine, 1966)[5]

Social scientists are concerned in their research with the individual, the group and society. These reflect the three levels of analysis adopted by researchers in their work. Those who are critical of much present-day research argue that some of it uses the wrong level of analysis – individual when it should be societal, for instance – or limits itself to one level only when a more meaningful picture would emerge by using more than one level. Smith extends this analysis and identifies seven possible levels: the aggregate or individual level, and six levels that are more global in that 'they characterize the collective as a whole, and do not derive from an accumulation of individual characteristics' (Smith, 1975).

The six include: group analysis (the interaction patterns of individuals and groups); organizational units of analysis (units which have qualities not possessed by the individuals making them up); institutional analysis (relationships within and across the legal, political, economic and familial institutions of society); ecological analysis (concerned with spatial explanation); cultural analysis (concerned with the norms, values, practices, traditions and ideologies of a culture); and societal analysis (concerned with gross factors such as urbanization, industrialization, education, wealth, etc.) Where possible, studies combining several levels of analysis are to be preferred.

Researchers are sometimes taken to task for their rigid adherence to one particular theory or theoretical orientation to the exclusion of competing theories. Thus, advocates of Piaget's developmental theory of cognition rarely take into consideration Freud's psychoanalytic theory of development in their work; and Gestaltists work without reference to S–R theorists. Few published works, as Smith points out, even go as far as to discuss alternative theories after a study in the light of methods used, much less consider alternatives prior to the research. As he recommends:

The investigator should be more active in designing his research so that competing theories can be tested. Research which tests competing theories will normally call for a wider range of research techniques than has historically been the case; this virtually assures more confidence in the data analysis since it is more oriented towards the testing of rival hypotheses.

(Smith, 1975)

Investigator triangulation refers to the use of more than one observer (or participant) in a research setting. Observers and participants working on their own each have their own observational styles and this is reflected in the resulting data. The careful use of two or more observers or participants independently, therefore, can lead to more valid and reliable data. Smith comments:

> Perhaps the greatest use of investigator triangulation centres around validity rather than reliability checks. More to the point, investigators with differing perspectives or paradigmatic biases may be used to check out the extent of divergence in the data each collects. Under such conditions if data divergence is minimal then one may feel more confident in the data's validity. On the other hand, if their data is significantly different, then one has an idea as to possible sources of biased measurement which should be further investigated.

(Smith, 1975)

We have already considered methodological triangulation in our introduction. Denzin identifies two categories in his typology: 'within methods' triangulation and 'between methods' triangulation. Triangulation within methods concerns the replication of a study as a check on reliability and theory confirmation (see Smith, 1975). Triangulation between methods, as we have seen, involves the use of more than one method in the pursuit of a given objective. As a check on validity, the between methods approach embraces the notion of convergence between independent measures of the same objective as has been defined by Campbell and Fiske (1959).[6]

OCCASIONS WHEN TRIANGULATION IS PARTICULARLY APPROPRIATE

Having outlined the principle of triangulation and described the types and their characteristics, we now consider the occasions when the technique is particularly appropriate and in so doing will be mainly concerned with the field of education. So complex and involved is the teaching–learning process in the context of the school that the single-method approach yields only limited and sometimes misleading data. Yet, ironically, this is the method that figures most in educational research. It is only comparatively recently that the utility of the multiple-method approach has come to be appreciated. Of the six categories of triangulation in Denzin's typology, something like four have been used in education. These are: time triangulation with its longitudinal and cross-sectional studies; space triangulation as on the occasions when a number of schools in an area or across the country are investigated in some way; investigator triangulation as when two observers independently rate the same classroom phenomena; and methodological triangulation. Of these four, methodological triangulation is the one used most frequently and the one that possibly has the most to offer. All four approaches, however, present practical and financial obstacles to researchers and sponsors.

Educational outcomes

Triangular techniques are suitable when a more holistic view of educational outcomes is sought. Mortimore's (1988) search for school effectiveness is an apt example.[7] This large-scale study of fifty inner-city schools over a period of four years employed a wide variety of measures and assessments in teasing out complex relationships between, on the one hand, classroom and school variables, and on the other, cognitive and non-cognitive pupil outcomes. The study is a veritable feast of triangulations! By way of example, in assessing teacher strategies, two systematic observation schedules were used, supplemented by case studies, observation notes and verbatim descriptions provided by the fieldworkers.

Complex phenomena

Triangulation has special relevance where a complex phenomenon requires elucidation. Imagine a comparative study of a formal and an informal classroom. Because of the contrasting philosophies, objectives and practices in the two classes, a single-method approach – say a measure of achievement in basic skills – would provide data of very limited value in that it would in no way reflect the more subtle, intangible features and the non-academic factors distinguishing the two classrooms. The adoption of the multi-method approach would give a very different picture. Box 11.3 gives some suggested methods for tackling this kind of problem. The combination of academic criteria (achievement tests, record cards, assessment of class work) and non-academic factors (attitudes of children and teachers, relationships, interview data and observation by a researcher) will generate a fuller and more realistic view of the respective classes and thus enable the investigators to talk about them on a comparative basis.

Evaluation of teaching methods

Triangulation is also appropriate when different methods of teaching are to be evaluated. Mevarech and her associates (1992)[8] studied the combined and separate effects of teaching methods involving computers

Box 11.3   A multi-method approach to the study of two top-junior classes: one taught formally; the other, informally

---

Objective: To investigate the practices, interactions, climates and outcomes of a formal and an informal classroom in two junior schools over the period of one term.

Methods:
1 Measures of achievement in reading, written language and maths.
2 Analysis and classification of children's written and practical work.
3 Classroom observation.
4 Examination of records.
5 Tests of attitudes of children to school and school work.
6 Tests of attitudes of teachers to respective teaching methods.
7 Interviews with samples of children.
8 Interviews with teachers.

---

and video programmes on students' achievement in geometry. A total of 268 12-year-olds studied the same content, for the same amount of time, under different instructional technologies. Results suggested that more media do not necessarily lead to better mathematics learning. The combination of computer and video programme yielded similar low learning outcomes as when no media were employed. By contrast, when each of the instructional aids was used by itself, significant gains in pupil achievement were recorded. Had the researchers not explored four teaching method conditions (computer group, video group, computer plus video group, and no media group), this interesting finding would not have been disclosed.

Controversial studies

Multiple methods are suitable where a controversial aspect of education needs to be evaluated more fully. The issue of comprehensive schools, for example, has been hotly debated since their inception; yet even at this point there has been little serious research investigating these institutions as totalities. It is not sufficient to judge these schools solely on the grounds of academic achievement with 'league tables' based on O and A level results, important as these are. A much more rounded portrayal of these institutions is required and here is a clear case for the advocacy of multiple methods. These could measure and investigate factors such as academic achievement, teaching methods, practical skills, cultural interests, social skills, interpersonal relationships, community spirit and so on. Validity could then be greatly increased by researching a large sample of schools (space triangulation) once a year say, over a period of five years (time triangulation).

Broader perspectives

Triangulation is useful when an established approach yields a limited and frequently distorted picture. We are reminded here of the traditional dichotomies – normative versus interpretive, nomothetic versus idiographic, statistical versus clinical. The first of each pairing is associated with groups and more objective scientific data; the second, with individuals and subjective data. Again, by using, or drawing from, each of these usually mutually exclusive categories, contrasting perspectives are disclosed.

Case studies

Finally, triangulation can be a useful technique where a researcher is engaged in case study, a particular example of 'complex phenomena'. In this connection, Adelman *et al.* write:

> The advantages of a particular technique for collecting witnesses' accounts of an event – *triangulation* – should be stressed. This is at the heart of the intention of the case study worker to respond to the multiplicity of perspectives present in a social situation. All accounts are considered in part to be expressive of the social position of each informant. Case study needs to represent, and represent fairly, these differing and sometimes conflicting viewpoints.
>
> (Adelman *et al.*, 1980)[9]

SOME ISSUES AND PROBLEMS

The chief problem confronting researchers using triangulation is that of validity. This is particularly the case where researchers use only qualitative techniques as, for example, in ethnographic research to collect data on a particular or single event. McCormick and James write,

> there is no absolute guarantee that a number of data sources that purport to provide evidence concerning the same construct in fact do so. . . . In view of the apparently subjective nature of much qualitative interpretation, validation is achieved when others, particularly the subjects of the research, recognise its authenticity. One way of doing this is for the researcher to write out his/her analysis for the subjects of the research in terms that they will understand, and then record their reactions to it. This is known as respondent validation.
>
> (McCormick and James, 1983)[10]

Having given primacy to a consideration of validity, the researchers are then confronted with three broad questions when contemplating a multi-method approach to a problem: 'Which methods are to be selected?' 'How are they to be combined?' 'How are the data to be used?'

As far as the first question is concerned – which methods are to be selected – we take it as axiomatic that any one method can be efficient, less efficient or inefficient depending on the kind of information desired and the context of the research. Where a researcher seeks information from which her inferences can be generalized to wider populations, methods yielding statistical data will be most efficient. Where she looks for information representing a personal or phenomenological perspective, or process rather than product, accounts or interviews will meet her need more successfully. If she wants to integrate objective and subjective perspectives, she will use contrasting methods. The first task, therefore, will be to decide what kinds of information the researcher wants and, further, what she is to do with it. Perhaps she might want to raise educational standards, introduce correctives, make modifications, or merely acquire a fuller understanding of some situation. The next stage is to decide the most appropriate methods (or sources) for providing this information. To make all this more comprehensible, we have given a hypothetical example in Box 11.4. Imagine a researcher wanting to compare a formal and an informal classroom in two junior schools with particular reference to academic and non-academic factors, children's personality characteristics, social behaviour and classroom climates. The left-hand vertical column itemizes the kinds of information she wants from each classroom – knowledge of the class's academic skills, children's personality characteristics and so on. The top horizontal row identifies the total number of methods (or sources) in respect of the information sought. Broadly speaking, the first four methods itemized yield quanti-fiable data (1–4); and the remaining four, non-quantifiable data (5–8). The system of double and single crosses illustrates the methods most efficient and the methods most supportive of these respectively so that, for example, the perspective of the individual pupil will best be expressed through an attitude questionnaire, a taped account of his or her view of classroom life, and an interview. So to return to our original question, the researcher will combine those methods (or sources) that will, in complementing each other, build up as full a picture of the areas she is investigating as time and facilities permit. You will notice that the combined methods approach may break down the traditional barriers between the normative and the interpretive approaches, the idiographic and the nomothetic, and the statistical and clinical.

No simple directive can be given for the question, how are the methods to be combined, for the answer will depend to a great extent on the objectives of the study, the particular situation, and the relative weightings which the researcher considers desirable to assign to the methods providing her with data. To take the issue of weightings

Box 11.4 Kinds of information sought and methods for obtaining them

Kinds of information	Methods used	1 Achievement tests	2 Personality tests	3 Attitude tests	4 Sociometric tests	5 Participant observation	6 Interviewing	7 Accounts	8 Teachers' assessments
1 Academic skills		xx					x		xx
2 Personality characteristics			xx			x	x		xx
3 Social skills				x		xx	x		xx
4 Social relationships				x	xx	xx	x		xx
5 Individual pupil viewpoint				xx			x	xx	
6 Classroom climate						xx			x

xx = most efficient means
x = supportive means

further, in some schools, for example, teachers' assessments of pupil achievement (Box. 11.4, column 8) will serve merely as glosses on formal examinations of academic achievement. In others, by contrast, teachers' opinions may play a much more decisive part in such assessments. These are the kinds of factors affecting a researcher's weightings. The crucial factor when it comes to integrating or contrasting the data and drawing inferences from them is the researcher's own judgement.

The third question, how are the data to be used, will depend on the researcher's original objectives in undertaking the study, her choice of methods and the kinds of data she accumulates. She will attempt, for instance, to impose some kind of meaning on normative or quantifiable data, possibly in line with a favoured theory or hypothesis. With interpretive or qualitative data, however, she will endeavour to draw meanings or explanations from the data themselves or, where appropriate, negotiate meanings with the subjects who are their source. Two kinds of problems face her here: first, those stemming from inconsistencies between quantified measures because of weaknesses in available measuring instruments; and second, differences between quantifiable and qualitative data, or between different sets of qualitative data. The first calls for more refined and valid instrumentation; the second, an imaginative leap. The lurking danger in the case of the second problem is that of presenting discrepant sets of data in the form of a collage. Naturally enough, it is not to be expected that complete consensus among data can or should be achieved. Indeed, the very burden of the interpretive approach is that different actors in a situation will have different meanings and that each meaning is equally valid. What is required, however, is that some attempt be made to relate incongruent sets of data in some way or other. Accounting for differences would be one way; using them as a basis for further hypotheses, another.

PROCEDURES

We now outline a possible sequence of procedures for implementing a multi-method approach to a chosen problem. The first stage is to select an area of interest and then to formulate a specific research problem or a set of research objectives within this general framework so as to reduce the scope of the project to manageable proportions. The second stage will be concerned with the more practical aspects of the research – choosing a school or setting, administrative or organizational factors, financial requirements and procedural problems. The third stage will involve decisions concerning the extent and range of information required so as to meet the research objectives or to solve the problems stated. The aim here will be to provide a balanced framework within which to operate. The fourth stage will be concerned with the choice of methods or sources necessary to provide the information desired. This will involve listing the possibilities and setting them against the kinds of information required so as to get a total picture of which ones will be efficient, which supportive and which unsuitable. It is at this point that the researcher will need to decide the extent to which she will seek quantifiable and/or non-quantifiable data, or use individual and/or group responses, for example. This stage will also be a suitable point in the sequence of procedures to consider the respective weightings that are to be given to the chosen methods. The fifth stage will involve implementing the research, and this will include collecting and analysing the data. The sixth and final stage will be the point where the data are interpreted and inferences drawn.

EXAMPLES OF THE USE OF TRIANGULAR TECHNIQUES IN EDUCATIONAL RESEARCH

In conclusion, we refer to three instances of the use of triangulation in educational research.

Blease and Lever – 'What do primary headteachers do?' (1992)[11]

In describing respondent validation (page 241) as a means of checking the authenticity of ethnographic material, we noted that this procedure involves recording the reactions of respondents to data that they have provided. Our first example of triangulation illustrates the use made of respondent validation in a study that asked, 'What do headteachers actually do in their schools?'

Box 11.5 sets out a summary of headteachers' activities based on a notional 35-hour working week. As part of the inquiry, heads were asked to estimate how much time they actually spent on each of the nine areas of activity and how much time, ideally, they would like to spend. At the same time, the participants were requested to keep a diary for one week of everything that they actually did during the course of a school day. The analyses of both sets of data (estimates of real and ideal time apportionment, and the diary records) were returned to the heads for their scrutiny and comments. By and large, headteachers acknowledged and confirmed the accuracy of the evidence presented to them. For many, the data came as no surprise:

'You've confirmed my worst fears!'

For a few, however, there was shock and disbelief:

'That's not typical.'
'I don't conform to that.'
'Why, *I* teach more than your whole total!'

Box 11.5   Summary of headteachers' activities

1 Dealing directly with children (including planned teaching, assemblies, one-to-one contacts) 2 Dealing directly with teaching staff (including in-room support, staff meetings, one-to-one contacts) 3 Dealing directly with non-teaching staff 4 Dealing with parents 5 Dealing with officers of the Authority 6 Dealing with other visitors 7 Dealing with administrative matters/duties 8 Having time to themselves (including break-times, lunch-times, periods set aside for planning) 9 Engaging in miscellaneous, mundane matters not covered by 1 to 8

Source: Blease and Lever, 1992

Box 11.6   Some aspects of the role of the primary headteacher

1 Headteachers have to respond to situations as they arise. One aspect of the headteacher's skill and expertise is the ability to cope with the unexpected, to react instantly and decisively in a crisis, to manage situations not created by themselves. 2 Many low-value tasks must be carried out and often, the head is the only person 'free' and available to perform them. 3 Schools face and must deal with an increasing administrative burden. New initiatives are being produced at an alarming rate, and merely keeping pace with them is difficult. 4 The headteacher's day is not synonymous with the school day. As one participant put it, 'The length of my day is the length of time it takes me to be no further behind at the end than I was at the beginning.' 5 Whilst all heads thought they were fulfilling their role to the best of their ability, no-one ever confirmed this for them, nor did they ever really get to know what others expected of them. 6 Heads felt a certain unease about their inability to fulfil the ideal role of the headteacher. Several believed themselves to be failing yet no one had indicated this to be the case.

Source: Adapted from Blease and Lever, 1992

Now confident of the broad authenticity of their data, the researchers went on to draw out some major areas of potential conflict in the role of the contemporary primary head. Their findings are illustrated in Box 11.6.

Blease and Cohen – 'Coping with computers' (1990)[12]

Our second example is drawn from a study of the introduction of computers into primary school classrooms. Blease and Cohen's account contains examples of investigator triangulation, methodological triangulation and time triangulation.

Box 11.7   Data on 'target' pupil, Robert

A   *Self concept of ability as a computer user* (7 items)
   (e.g.)   Pressing the right keys most of the time.
   Knowing all about how to use the computer.
   Getting the right answers to the computer's questions.

B   *Researcher's interview of Robert* about his self-awarded scores on A
   (above).
   (e.g.)   'I don't really think I can beat my friends.' (hence $^5/_{10}$)

C   *Out-of-school computer access and use* (score 0 to 8)

D   *Teacher's rating* of Robert on (a) self-image as a computer user,
   (b) determination to succeed (c) popularity as a work partner.

E   *COMIC record profiles* illuminated by research assistants' verbatim
   commentaries on interesting and/or noteworthy events occurring during
   observation periods.
   (e.g.)   17.6.87. (10 a.m.) Robert is paired with a fourth year girl,
   Melanie, an able and helpful computer operator. Robert and
   Melanie worked well together, Robert listening attentively to
   instructions.
   17.6.87. (10.30 a.m.) Robert and Erica act as checkers to
   Stephen. They explain what is required clearly and Stephen
   finishes quickly. Robert is now in the teacher role. He enjoys his
   new responsibilities.

F   *Robert's logbook of computer use*
   (e.g.)   Sept. 9th.   AMX ART   60 minutes
   Sept. 16th.   PROMPT WRITER   60 minutes
   Sept. 24th.   FRONT PAGE   90 minutes

G   *School record on Robert*
   (e.g.)   Robert is a bilingual child, mother North-European, father a
   teacher.
   9 to 10 years old (Robert had left the school for a year in
   Scandinavia.)
   Robert returned to Mrs Brown's class. Handwriting has become
   extremely small. Always appears tense. Represents the school
   at football, swimming and athletics. Good at all games. Very
   competitive. Able and intelligent boy . . .

H   *Research Assistant's diary* (Program: 'Inhabitants').
   (e.g.)   Gregory and Robert were observed for half an hour before
   break. They appeared shy and hesitant. They were, in fact, quite
   capable. Their responses were not very adventurous. They
   chose to go to the Arctic, saw polar bears and whales and heard
   ice cracking. (The class topic had recently been on Eskimos).
   . . . Whenever the computer summarised their choices they
   copied the summaries meticulously into their notebooks. When
   asked whether their notes were going to be useful later on (for
   writing an account or story), they didn't know.

Source: Blease and Cohen, 1990

Investigator triangulation

COMIC (Categories for Observing Microcomputer Use in Classrooms) is an observation instrument specifically designed to describe children's behaviour when working at the computer. It is used to obtain a systematic record of the actions of a keyboard operator both in an individual, one-to-one situation and when groups of children are working together. Derived from the Flanders Inter Action Categories,[13] COMIC consists of twelve observation categories subdivided into two groups, one for 'on-task' behaviour, the other for 'off-task' behaviour. Blease and Cohen employed two research assistants using COMIC to record the behaviour of pupils working on a variety of computer programs. Investigator triangulation involved them in making independent observations of the same events and reaching stringent levels of intercoder reliability.

Methodological triangulation

Blease and Cohen used interaction coding schedules, questionnaires, diaries, self-concept scales, sociometric measures, interviews, school records, teachers' ratings and research assistants' observations in helping to build up a valid assessment of changes occurring in specially selected 'target' pupils over the period of the study. For example, they drew on several sources of data such as those shown in Box 11.7 to describe the changes that took place in 'target' pupils such as Robert.

Time triangulation

Two major objectives of Blease and Cohen's ethnographic study were to understand the ways in which pupils and teachers came to grips with the computers introduced into their classrooms and to identify ways of maintaining the momentum of innovation once external support was withdrawn. Time triangulation enabled an assessment of the relative success of the second objective to be made by Blease in a 'three years on' follow up study. Extracts from his account are shown in Box 11.8.[14]

Quicke – 'Personal and social education' (1986)[15]

Finally, Quicke's study set out to evaluate a Personal and Social education (PSE) curriculum innovation in a comprehensive school using a triangulated approach. This comprised the use of participant observation along with formal and informal interviews of both pupils and teachers. The principal question guiding the research was the extent to which the innovative programme was successful in establishing practices derived from a 'respect for persons'. As the author explains, 'A concern

Box 11.8   Broadwood School update January 1991. The integration of IT into
the curriculum: three years on

Three years after completing our project, the school roll is still around the
250 mark. There have been a few staff changes during this time, principally
due to the loss of Pat and Janet. Pat has become a deputy headteacher and
Janet an IT co-ordinator. It seems that both appointments were considerably
influenced by their experience gained participating in our project.

In view of this it was all the more interesting to note the extent to which
the school had managed to develop its IT profile in their absence. In
particular, we were interested to see the extent to which they had achieved
their target of one computer for every classroom and our target of integration
of IT into the school curriculum, using parent-helpers. Had our policy of
permeation worked? Would they all be using their computers or would it still
be left to a few enthusiasts?

First of all, what about hardware? When we began the project the school
had just one computer and no printer. This meant that the pupil/computer
ratio stood at about 250:1. By the end of the project they had three
computers with disc drives and one printer, so the ratio had reduced to about
80:1. Three years on they have nine computers with printers including one
colour printer for ten classes, a ratio of roughly 28:1. They have adopted a
deliberate policy of providing the children with experience of a variety of
models, some BBCs, some Nimbus and some Archimedes. They also have
two concept keyboards for use with Year 1 and with those having special
needs throughout the school.

What about the teachers? Certainly a higher level of funding and
resourcing is not enough to ensure that IT becomes integrated into the
curriculum. As we discovered in our project, teachers must be able to identify
a definite advantage of IT both for themselves and for their pupils before
they will give it serious consideration. To what extent did Pat and Janet's
example have a lasting effect on their colleagues? Nine out of ten classes
now have a permanent computer. Two adjacent infant classes share one
computer. On some days it is possible to walk through the school at any
time to find all the computers switched on and in use. All of the teachers in
the school have become involved in their use and regularly take part in the
evaluation of new software packages. This is not a task left to the IT
co-ordinator. Our emphasis upon content-free programs such as data
bases, word processors and design packages has been maintained,
something that is in evidence on the walls throughout the school.

What about parents? During the project we tried unsuccessfully to
encourage some parents to act as helpers. They now have six or more
parents who take on this supporting role on a regular basis, all of them
trained to use the computers by the teachers themselves. Ancillary helpers
are also computer literate and assist the children in running the school bank
which is fully computerised.

Source: Blease, 1991

for pupils' dignity leads to the development of curricula premised on a
respect for pupils' ability to think, participate in the learning process
and make a positive contribution to school life.'

One class was observed for a whole term, the researcher acting as an

Box 11.9 Sample interview from triangulated study

Int.	What's been a good PSE (personal and social education) lesson?
V	When you have to get into groups . . .
Int.	What's the idea of getting into groups?
V	To get to know each other and to work together.
Int.	Some people haven't been too happy about the way the groups have been arranged . . .
U	I don't like it and when I get split up from H or someone like that and go with someone I barely ever knew, I don't like that when we split up.
Int.	What's wrong with that then?
U	Getting to know people's not wrong it's just that you don't know what they're like and that and how to talk to them . . . just don't know how you talk.
Int.	But how are you going to get to know them if you don't work with them in a group?
U	If you just like say I go with H and put two other friends together with us, we'll start to know them and they'll start to know us . . . so then we'll keep swopping round.
Int.	Oh, I see, so that as long as you're in a pair . . .
U	As long as I'm with someone I know.

Source: Quicke, 1986

assistant to the teacher. Group interviews with the pupils were tape-recorded (see Box 11.9 for an extract), while the teachers were interviewed individually and notes made of their responses. As the author explains, the function of the interview was partly to check categories drawn from the observational data.

The researcher's findings suggest that the programme had some positive aspects: thus he perceived 'an attempt to change classroom rules to facilitate a more flexible, friendly form of teacher–pupil relationship and a more humanistic socio-emotional climate in the classroom' (Quicke, 1986). Pupils were also encouraged to get to know each other and to work co-operatively in a more informed way. However, these successes were offset by an enduring tendency for pupils 'to be differentiated according to academic criteria, to be underestimated with respect to their social awareness and to be regarded as of low status in the institution' (Quicke, 1986).

The researcher suggests that the way forward is for the teacher to recognize a more favourable and positive view of the pupils and to operate from this perspective.

REFERENCES AND NOTES

1 Smith, H.W., *Strategies of Social Research: The Methodological Imagination* (Prentice-Hall, London, 1975).

2 Lin, N. *Foundations of Social Research* (McGraw-Hill, New York, 1976).

3 Boring, E.G., 'The role of theory in experimental psychology', *American Journal of Psychology*, 66 (1953) 169–84.
4 Denzin, N.K., *The Research Act in Sociology: A Theoretical Introduction to Sociological Method* (The Butterworth Group, London, 1970).
5 Levine, R.A., 'Towards a psychology of populations: the cross-cultural study of personality', *Human Development*, 3 (1966) 30–46.
6 Campbell, D.T. and Fiske, D., 'Convergent and discriminant validation by the multi-trait multimethod matrix', *Psychological Bulletin*, 56 (1959) 81–105.
7 Mortimore, P., Sammons, P., Stoll, L., Lewis, D. and Ecob, R., *School Matters: The Junior Years* (Open Books, London, 1988).
8 Mevarech, Z., Shir, N. and Movshovitz-Hadar, N., 'Is more always better? The separate and combined effects of computer and video programme on mathematics learning', *British Journal of Educational Psychology*, 62 (1992) 106–16.
9 Adelman, C., Jenkins, D. and Kemmis, S., 'Rethinking case study: notes from the Second Cambridge Conference', in H. Simons (ed.), *Towards a Science of the Singular* (Centre for Applied Research in Education, University of East Anglia, 1980).
10 McCormick, R. and James, M., *Curriculum Evaluation in Schools* (Croom Helm, Beckenham, 1983).
11 Blease, D. and Lever, D., 'What do primary headteachers do?', *Educational Studies*, 18(2) (1992) 185–99.
12 Blease, D. and Cohen, L., *Coping with Computers: An Ethnographic Study in Primary Classrooms* (Paul Chapman, London, 1990).
13 Flanders, N., *Analyzing Teacher Behaviour* (Addison-Wesley, Reading, Mass., 1970).
14 Blease, D., 'Broadwood School Update, 1991: Integration of I.T. into the Curriculum Three Years On', Unpublished document, Department of Education, Loughborough University of Technology.
15 Quicke, J.C., 'Personal and Social Education: a triangulated evaluation of an innovation', *Educational Review*, 38(3) (1986) 217–28.

12

ROLE-PLAYING

INTRODUCTION

Much current discussion of role-playing occurs within the context of a
protracted and continuing debate over the use of deception in experimental social psychology. Inevitably therefore, the following account of
role-playing as a research tool involves some detailed comment on the
'deception' versus 'honesty' controversy. But role-playing has a much
longer history of use in the social sciences than as a substitute for deceit.
It has been employed for decades in assessing personality, in business
training and in psychotherapy.[1] In this latter connection, role-playing
was introduced to the United States as a therapeutic procedure by
Moreno in the 1930s. His group therapy sessions were called 'psychodrama', and in various forms they spread to the group dynamics movement which was developing in America in the 1950s. Current interest
in encounter sessions and sensitivity training can be traced back to the
impact of the originator of studies in role-taking and role-enactment,
J.L. Moreno.

The focus of this chapter is on the use of role-playing as a technique of
educational research. Role-playing is defined as participation in simulated
social situations that are intended to throw light upon the role/rule contexts governing 'real' life social episodes. The present discussion aims to
extend some of the ideas set out in Chapter 10 which dealt with account
gathering and analysis. We begin by itemizing a number of role-playing
methods that have been reported in the literature.

Various role-play methods have been identified by Hamilton[2] and
differentiated in terms of a passive–active distinction. Thus, an individual may role-play merely by reading a description of a social episode
and filling in a questionnaire about it; on the other hand, a person may
role-play by being required to improvise a characterization and perform
it in front of an audience. This passive–active continuum, Hamilton
notes, glosses over three important analytical distinctions.

First, the individual may be asked simply to imagine a situation or actually to perform it. Hamilton terms this an 'imaginary–performed' situation. Second, in connection with performed role-play, he distinguishes between structured and unstructured activities, the difference depending upon whether the individual is restricted by the experimenter to present forms or lines. This Hamilton calls a 'scripted–improvised' distinction. And third, the participant's activities may be verbal responses, usually of the paper and pencil variety, or behavioural, involving something much more akin to acting. This distinction is termed 'verbal–behavioural'. Turning next to the content of role-play, Hamilton distinguishes between relatively involving or uninvolving contents, that is, where a subject is required to act or to imagine herself in a situation or, alternatively, to react as she believes another person would in those circumstances, the basic issue here being what person the subject is supposed to portray. Furthermore, in connection with the role in which the person is placed, Hamilton differentiates between studies that assign the individual to the role of laboratory subject and those that place her in any other role. Finally, the content of the role-play is seen to include the context of the acted or the imagined performance, that is, the elaborateness of the scenario, the involvement of other actors, and the presence or absence of an audience. The various dimensions of role-play methods identified by Hamilton are set out in Box 12.1.

To illustrate the extremes of the range in the role-playing methods identified in Box 12.1 we have selected two studies, the first of which is passive, imaginary and verbal, typical of the way in which role-playing is often introduced to pupils; the second is active, performed and behavioural, involving an elaborate scenario and the participation of numerous other actors.

In a lesson designed to develop empathizing skills,[3] a number of magazine pictures were selected. The pictures included easily observed

Box 12.1   Dimensions of role-play methods

	FORM	CONTENT
Set:	imaginary v performed	*Person*: self v another
Action:	scripted v improvised	*Role*: subject role v another role
Dependent variables:	verbal v behavioural	*Context*: scenario other actors audience

Source: Adapted from Hamilton, 1976

253

Box 12.2   Developing empathizing skills

1   How do you think the individual(s) is (are) feeling?
2   Why do you think this is? (Encourage students to be specific about observations from which they infer emotions. Distinguish between observations and inferences.)
3   Might the person(s) be feeling a different emotion than the one you inferred? Give an example.
4   Have you ever felt this way? Why?
5   What do you think might happen next to this person?
6   If you inferred an unpleasant emotion, what possible action might the person(s) take in order to feel better?

Source: Rogers and Atwood, 1974

clues that served as the basis for inferring an emotion or a situation. Some pictures showed only the face of an individual, others depicted one or more persons in a particular social setting. The pictures exhibited a variety of emotions such as anger, fear, compassion, anxiety and joy. Pupils were asked to look carefully at a particular picture and then to respond to questions that included or were similar to those in Box 12.2.

The second example of a role-playing study is the well-known Stanford Prison experiment carried out by Zimbardo and his associates,[4] a brief overview of which is given in Box 12.3.

Enthusiasts of role-playing as a research methodology cite experiments such as the Stanford Prison study to support their claim that where realism and spontaneity can be introduced into role-play, then such experimental conditions do, in fact, simulate both symbolically and phenomenologically, the real-life analogues that they purport to represent. Advocates of role-play would concur with the conclusions of Zimbardo and his associates that the simulated prison developed into a psychologically compelling prison environment and they, too, would infer that the dramatic differences in the behaviour of prisoners and guards arose out of their location in different positions within the institutional structure of the prison and the social psychological conditions that prevailed there, rather than from personality differences between the two groups of subjects (see Banuazizi and Movahedi).[5]

On the other hand, the passive, imaginary role-play required of subjects taking part in the lesson cited in the first example has been the focus of much of the criticism levelled at role-playing as a research technique. Ginsburg (1978) summarizes the argument against role-playing as a device for generating scientific knowledge:

1   Role-playing is unreal with respect to the variables under study in that the subject reports what she *would do*, and that is taken as though she did do it.[6]

Box 12.3   The Stanford Prison experiment

The study was conducted in the summer of 1971 in a mock prison constructed in the basement of the psychology building at Stanford University. The subjects were selected from a pool of 75 respondents to a newspaper advertisement asking for paid volunteers to participate in a psychological study of prison life. On a random basis half of the subjects were assigned to the role of guard and half to the role of prisoner. Prior to the experiment subjects were asked to sign a form, agreeing to play either the prisoner or the guard role for a maximum of two weeks. Those assigned to the prisoner role should expect to be under surveillance, to be harassed, but not to be physically abused. In return, subjects would be adequately fed, clothed and housed and would receive 15 dollars per day for the duration of the experiment.

The outcome of the study was quite dramatic. In less than two days after the initiation of the experiment, violence and rebellion broke out. The prisoners ripped off their clothing and their identification numbers and barricaded themselves inside the cells while shouting and cursing at the guards. The guards, in turn, began to harass, humiliate and intimidate the prisoners. They used sophisticated psychological techniques to break the solidarity among the inmates and to create a sense of distrust among them. In less than 36 hours one of the prisoners showed severe symptoms of emotional disturbance, uncontrollable crying and screaming and was released. On the third day, a rumour developed about a mass escape plot. The guards increased their harassment, intimidation and brutality towards the prisoners. On the fourth day, two prisoners showed symptoms of severe emotional disturbance and were released. On the fifth day, the prisoners showed symptoms of individual and group disintegration. They had become mostly passive and docile, suffering from an acute loss of contact with reality. The guards on the other hand, had kept up their harassment, some behaving sadistically. Because of the unexpectedly intense reactions generated by the mock prison experience, the experimenters terminated the study at the end of the sixth day.

Source: Adapted from Banuazizi and Movahedi, 1975

2 The behaviour displayed is not spontaneous even in the more active forms of role-playing.
3 The verbal reports in role-playing are very susceptible to artefactual influence such as social desirability.
4 Role-playing procedures are not sensitive to complex interactions whereas deception designs are.

In general, Ginsburg concludes, critics of role-playing view science as involving the discovery of natural truths and they contend that role-playing simply cannot substitute for deception – a sad but unavoidable state of affairs.

ROLE-PLAYING VERSUS DECEPTION: THE ARGUMENT

As we shall shortly see, those who support role-playing as a legitimate scientific technique for systematic research into human social behaviour reject such criticisms by offering role-playing alternatives to deception studies of phenomena such as destructive obedience to authority and to conventional research in, for example, the area of attitude formation and change.

The objections to the current widespread use of deception in experimental research are articulated as follows:

1 Lying, cheating and deceiving contradict the norms that we typically try to apply in our everyday social interactions. The use of deception in the study of interpersonal relations is equally reprehensible. In a word, deception is unethical.

2 The use of deception is epistemologically unsound because it rests upon the acceptance of a less than adequate model of the subject as a person. Deception studies generally try to exclude the human capacities of the subject for choice and self-presentation. They tend therefore to focus upon 'incidental' social behaviour, that is, behaviours that are outside of the subject's field of choice, intention and self-presentation that typically constitute the main focus of social activity among human actors (see Forward et al., 1976).[7]

3 The use of deception is methodologically unsound. Deception research depends upon a continuing supply of subjects who are naive to the intentions of the researchers. But word soon gets round and potential subjects come to expect that they will be deceived. It is a fair guess that most subjects are suspicious and distrustful of psychological research despite the best intentions of deception researchers.

Finally, advocates of role-playing methods deplore the common practice of comparing the outcomes of role-playing replications against the standard of their deception study equivalents as a means of evaluating the relative validity of the two methods. The results of role-playing and deception, it is argued, are not directly comparable since role-playing introduces a far wider range of human behaviour into experiments (see Forward et al., 1976). If comparisons are to be made, then role-playing results should provide the yardstick against which deception study data are measured and not the other way round as is generally the case. We invite readers to follow this last piece of advice and to judge the well-known experiments of Milgram (1974)[8] on destructive obedience to authority against their role-playing replications by Mixon.[9,10] A more sustained discussion of ethical problems involved in deception is reserved for Chapter 16.

ROLE-PLAYING VERSUS DECEPTION: THE EVIDENCE

Milgram's obedience-to-authority experiments

In a series of studies from 1963 to 1974, Milgram carried out numerous variations on a basic obedience experiment which involved individuals acting, one at a time, as 'teachers' of another subject (who was, in reality, a confederate of the experimenter). Teachers were required to administer electric shocks of increasing severity every time the learner failed to make a correct response to a verbal learning task. Over the years, Milgram involved over 1,000 subjects in the experiment – subjects, incidentally, who were drawn from all walks of life rather than from undergraduate psychology classes. Summarizing his findings, Milgram (1974) reported that typically some 67 per cent of his teachers delivered the maximum electric shock to the learner despite the fact that such a degree of severity was clearly labelled as highly dangerous to the physical well-being of the person on the receiving end.

Milgram's explanation of destructive obedience to authority is summarized in Box 12.4.[11]

Mixon's role-playing replications of the Milgram experiment

Mixon's starting point was a disaffection for the deceit that played such an important part in generating emotional stress in Milgram's subjects, and a desire to explore alternative approaches to the study of destructive obedience to authority. Since Milgram's dependent variable was a rule-governed action, Mixon reasoned (Mixon, 1974) the rule-governed behaviour of Milgram's subjects could have been uniform or predictable.

Box 12.4 Obedience to authority: an explanation

Milgram believes that an orientation to obedience to authority essentially follows from the hierarchical organization of all sorts of social systems. Social hierarchy, he argues, is a form of organization that has repeatedly evolved in animal species because it promotes the survival of the species. For human beings, too, various forms of social hierarchy have survival value. When the individual operates in a hierarchy, he cedes control to superior persons who co-ordinate the system. Since system coherence must be the most important consideration in a hierarchy, the individual in the hierarchy must be able to operate in what Milgram calls the *agentic mode*. 'The person entering into an authority system', Milgram explains, 'no longer views himself as acting out of his own purposes but rather comes to see himself as an agent for executing the wishes of another person.' Milgram's experiments on obedience are said to reveal some of the factors that trigger the agentic frame of mind.

Source: Adapted from Brown and Herrnstein, 1975

But it was not. Why, then, did some of Milgram's subjects obey and some defy the experimenter's instructions? The situation, Mixon notes, seemed perfectly clear to most commentators; the command to administer an electric shock appeared to be obviously immoral and all subjects should therefore have disobeyed the experimenter. If defiance was so obviously called for when looking at the experiment from the outside, why, asks Mixon, was it not obvious to those taking part on the inside? Mixon found a complete script of Milgram's experiment and proceeded to transform it into an active role-playing exercise.

> One of the first things I did was to take the role of the naive subject in order to look at the scene through his eyes. Later I took the roles of both experimenter and victim and repeated the scene over and over again using a different person each time in the role of naive subject. The repetition allowed me to become thoroughly familiar with each detail of the scene and by changing actors I was able to question many people about what was going on.
>
> (Mixon, 1974)

Mixon's role-playing replication of the Milgram experiment involved an exploratory method that he calls the 'all-or-none' technique, an account of which is given in Box 12.5.

But let Mixon speak for himself:

> Previous interpretations [of the Milgram data] have rested on the assumption that obedient subjects helplessly performed an obviously immoral act. From the outside the situation seemed clear. It was otherwise to the actors. The actors in my role playing version could not understand why the experimenter behaved as if feedback from the 'victim' was unimportant. The feedback suggested that something serious had occurred, that something had gone badly wrong with the experiment. The experimenter behaved as if nothing

Box 12.5 Milgram's experiment: an alternative explanation

The 'all-or-none' method utilized continuous interaction and feedback from participants in the role-playing replication. Mixon succeeded in constructing several versions of the Milgram 'script' and produced the full range of possible obedience responses ranging from 0 per cent to 100 per cent. By exploring and specifying the particular meanings attributed to variations in the role/rule context of 'legitimate authority in experiments', and by being able to produce and observe the whole range of possible obedience responses, Mixon was better able to claim that he had an adequate conceptualization and description of obedience in this particular social context.

Source: Adapted from Forward *et al.*, 1976

serious had or could happen. The experimenter in effect contra-
dicted the evidence that otherwise seemed so clearly to suggest that
the 'victim' was in serious trouble. ... Using the 'all-or-none'
method I found that when it became perfectly clear that the
experimenter believed the 'victim' was being seriously harmed all
actors indicated defiance to experimental commands. Briefly summarised, the 'all-or-none' analysis suggests that people will obey
seemingly inhumane experimental commands so long as there is
no good reason to think experimental safeguards have broken
down; people will defy seemingly inhumane experimental commands when it becomes clear that safeguards have broken down –
when consequences may indeed be what they appear to be. *When
the experimental situation is confusing and mystifying as in Milgram's
study, some people will obey and some will defy experimental commands.*

(Mixon, 1974, emphasis added)

We leave readers to compare Mixon's explanations with Milgram's
account set out in Box 12.4.

In summary, sophisticated role-playing methods such as those used
by Mixon offer exciting possibilities to the educational researcher. They
avoid the disadvantages of deception designs yet are able to incorporate
many of the standard features of experiments such as constructing
experimental conditions across factors of interest (in the Mixon studies
for example, using scripts that vary the states of given role/rule contexts), randomly assigning actors to conditions as a way of randomizing
out individual differences, using repeated-measures designs, and stan-
dardizing scripts and procedures to allow for replication of studies
(Forward *et al.*, 1976).

Despite what has just been said about the possibilities of incorporating
experimental role-playing methodologies in exploratory rather than
experimental settings, Harré and Secord distinguish between 'exploration' and 'experiment' as follows. Whereas the experiment is employed
to test the authenticity of what is known, exploration serves quite a
different purpose:

> In exploratory studies, a scientist has no very clear idea of what
> will happen, and aims to find out. He has a feeling for the direction
> in which to go ... but no clear expectations of what to expect. He
> is not confirming or refuting hypotheses.

(Harré and Secord, 1972)[12]

Increasingly, exploratory (as opposed to experimental) research into
human social behaviour is turning to role-playing methodologies. The
reason is plain enough. Where the primary objective of such research is
the identification and elucidation of the role/rule frameworks governing

social interaction, informed rather than deceived subjects are essential if the necessary data on how they genuinely think and feel are to be made available to the researcher. Contrast the position of the fully participating, informed subject in such research with that of the deceived subject under the more usual experimental conditions. Argyris's experimenter speaks to her subject thus:

> I want to design the environment in such a way that when you enter it, I will have done my best to have induced you to behave as I predicted you would. However, I must be certain that if you behaved in the way I predicted you would, it was because you wanted to, because it made sense to you to do so, because the choice was genuinely yours. In order to maximise this possibility, I must design the entire experiment rigorously and keep all of the key elements of the design secret from you until you have finished participating in it. Also I cannot permit or encourage you to learn (ahead of time or during the experiment) anything about the experiment. I cannot encourage you to confront it, or to alter it. The only learning that I permit is learning that remains within the purposes of the experiment.
>
> (Argyris, 1975)[13]

It can be argued that many of the more pressing social problems that society faces today arise out of our current ignorance of the role/rule frameworks governing human interactions in diverse social settings. If this is the case, then role-playing techniques could offer the possibility of a greater insight into the natural episodes of human behaviour that they seek to elucidate than the burgeoning amount of experimental data already at hand. The danger may lie in too much being expected of role-playing as a key to such knowledge. Ginsburg (1978) offers a timely warning. Role-playing, he urges, should be seen as a complement to conventional experiments, survey research and field observations. That is, it is an important addition to our investigative armamentarium, not a replacement.

ROLE-PLAYING IN EDUCATIONAL SETTINGS

Role-playing, gaming and machine or computer simulation are three strands of development in simulation studies that have found their way into British classrooms.[14] Their discovery and introduction into primary and secondary schools as late as the 1960s is somewhat surprising in view of the unqualified support that distinguished educational theorists from Plato onwards have accorded to the value of play and games in education.[15]

The distinction between these three types of simulation – role-playing, games and machines/computers – is by no means clear-cut; for example, simulation games often contain role-playing activities and may be designed with computer back-up services to expedite their procedures (see Taylor and Walford, 1972).

In this section we focus particularly upon role-playing aspects of simulation, beginning with some brief observations on the purposes of role-playing in classroom settings and some practical suggestions directed towards the less experienced practitioners of role-playing methods.

THE USES OF ROLE-PLAYING

The uses of role-playing are classified by van Ments[16] as:

1 *Developing sensitivity and awareness.* The definitions of positions such as mother, teacher, policeman and priest, for example, explicitly or implicitly incorporate various role characteristics which often lead to the stereotyping of position occupants. Role-playing provides a means of exploring such stereotypes and developing a deeper understanding of the point of view and feelings of someone who finds herself in a particular role.

2 *Experiencing the pressures which create roles.* Role-playing provides study material for group members on the ways in which roles are created in, for example, a committee. It enables subjects to explore the interactions of formal structure and individual personalities in role taking.

3 *Testing out for oneself possible modes of behaviour.* In effect, this is rehearsal; trying out in one's mind in advance of some new situation that one has to face. Role-playing can be used for a wide variety of situations where the subject, for one reason or another, needs to learn to cope with the rituals and conventions of social intercourse and to practise them so that they can be repeated under stress.

4 *Simulating a situation for others (and possibly oneself) to learn from.* Here, the role-player provides materials for others to use and work upon. In the simplest situation, there is just one role-player acting out a specific role. In more complex situations such as the Stanford Prison study discussed in Box 12.3, role-playing is used to provide an environment structured on the interactions of numerous role incumbents. Suggestions for running role-play sessions are set out in Box 12.6.[17] They are particularly appropriate to teachers intent upon using role-play in classroom settings.

Setting objectives

The first observation made by van Ments is that teachers must begin by asking themselves what exactly their intentions are in teaching by means

Box 12.6 A flow chart for using role-play

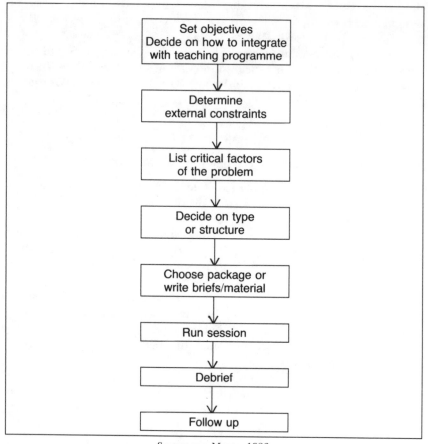

Source: van Ments, 1983

of role-play. Is it, for example, to teach facts, or concepts, or skills, or awareness, or sensitivity? Depending on the specific nature of the teacher's objective, role-play can be fitted into the timetable in several ways. van Ments identifies the following:

1 as an introduction to the subject
2 as a means of supplementing or following on from a point that is being explored
3 as the focal point of a course or a unit of work
4 as a break from the routine of the classroom or the workshop
5 as a way of summarizing or integrating diverse subject matter
6 as a way of reviewing or revising a topic
7 as a means of assessing work.

Box 12.7 Critical factors in a role-play: smoking and young people

---

Roles involved: young people, parents, teachers, doctors, youth leaders, shopkeeper, cigarette manufacturer.

Critical issues: responsibility for health, cost of illness, freedom of action, taxation revenue, advertising, effects on others.

Key communication channels: advertisements, school contacts, family, friends.

Source: Adapted from van Ments, 1983

Determining external constraints

Role-play can be extremely time consuming. It is vital therefore that from the outset, teachers should be aware of factors that may inhibit or even preclude the running of a role-play (see van Ments):

1 suitable room or space (size, layout, furniture, etc.)
2 sufficient time for warm up, running the actual role-play and debriefing
3 availability of assistance to help run the session.

Critical factors

The teacher, van Ments advises, must look at the critical issues involved in the problem area encompassed by the role-play and decide who has the power to influence those issues as well as who is affected by the decisions to be taken. By way of example, Box 12.7 identifies some of the principal protagonists in a role-play session to do with young people smoking.

Choosing or writing the role-play

The choice lies with teachers either to buy or borrow a ready-made role-play or to write their own. In practice, van Ments observes, most role-plays are written for specific needs and with the intention of fitting into a particular course programme. Existing role-plays can, of course, be adapted by teachers to their own particular circumstances and needs. On balance it's probably better to write the role-play in order to ensure that the background is familiar to the intended participants and they can see its relevance to the specific problem that concerns them.

Running the role-play

The counsel of perfection, van Ments reminds us, is always to pilot test the role-play material that one is going to use, preferably with a similar audience. In reality, pilot testing can be as time consuming as the play itself and may therefore be totally impracticable given timetable pressures. But however difficult the circumstances, any form of piloting, says van Ments, is better than none at all, even if it is simply a matter of talking procedures through with one or two colleagues.

Once the materials are prepared, then the role-play follows its own sequence: introduction, warm up, running, and ending. One final word of caution. It's particularly important to time the ending of the role-play in such a way as to fit into the whole programme. One method of ensuring this is to write the mechanism for ending into the role-play itself. Thus: 'You must have reached agreement on all five points before 11.30 a.m. when you have to attend a meeting of the board of directors.'

Debriefing

Debriefing is more than simply checking that the right lesson has been learnt and feeding this information back to the teacher. Rather, van Ments reminds us, it is a two-way process, during which the consequences of actions arising in the role-play can be analysed and conclusions drawn. It is at that point in the role-play sequence when mistakes and misunderstandings can be rectified. Most important of all, it is from well-conducted debriefing sessions that the teacher can draw out the implications of what the pupils have been experiencing and can then plan the continuation of their learning about the topic at hand.

Follow-up

To conclude, van Ments notes the importance of the follow-up session in the teacher's planning of the ways in which the role-play exercise will lead naturally into the next learning activity. Thus, when the role-play session has attempted to teach a skill or rehearse a novel situation, then it may be logical to repeat it until the requisite degree of competence has been reached. Conversely, if the purpose of the exercise has been to raise questions, then a follow-up session should be arranged to answer them. 'Whatever the objectives of using role play', van Ments advises, 'one must always consider the connection between it and the next learning activity' (van Ments, 1983). Above all else, avoid leaving the role-play activity in a vacuum.

STRENGTHS AND WEAKNESSES OF ROLE-PLAYING AND OTHER SIMULATION EXERCISES

Taylor and Walford (1972) identify two prominent themes in their discussion of some of the possible advantages and disadvantages in the use of classroom simulation exercises. They are, first, the claimed enhancement of pupil motivation and second, the role of simulation in the provision of relevant learning materials. The motivational advantages of simulation are said to include:

1 a heightened interest and excitement in learning
2 a sustained level of freshness and novelty arising out of the dynamic nature of simulation tasks
3 a transformation in the traditional pupil–teacher subordinate–superordinate relationship
4 the fact that simulation is a universal behavioural mode.

As to the learning gains arising out of the use of simulation, the authors identify:

1 the learning that is afforded at diverse levels (cognitive, social and emotional)
2 the decision-making experiences that participants acquire
3 an increased role awareness
4 the ability of simulation to provide a vehicle for free interdisciplinary communication
5 the success with which the concrete approach afforded by simulation exercises bridges the gap between 'schoolwork' and 'the real world'.

What reservations are there in connection with simulation exercises? Taylor and Walford (1972) identify the following:

1 Simulations, however interesting and attractive, are time-demanding activities and ought therefore to justify fully the restricted time-tabling allotted to competing educational approaches.
2 Many simulation exercises are in the form of game kits and these can be quite expensive.
3 Simulation materials may pose problems of logistics, operation and general acceptance as legitimate educational techniques particularly by parent associations.

Our discussion of the strengths and weaknesses of role-playing has focused upon its application in pupil groups. To illustrate Taylor and Walford's point that simulation is a universal behavioural mode, the detailed example of a role-play exercise that now follows is to do with students in further education.

ROLE-PLAYING IN AN EDUCATIONAL SETTING: AN EXAMPLE

Robinson and Collier's 'Sugar 'n' Spice' is a simulation intended for use with adults on professional training courses.[18] It focuses on issues relating to gender stereotyping. The authors' account highlights the typical needs for change both in the structure and content of simulations arising from participants' responses to trialling materials and methods. The aim of 'Sugar 'n' Spice' is to explore the issue of sexism in what the authors describe as a 'safe environment' where it is possible to develop an enjoyable and participatory form of consciousness-raising as a prelude to a full discussion of gender stereotyping. To that end, Robson and Collier were concerned that the simulation activities should be non-competitive. It seemed self-evident to them that if they were to engender a critique of stereotyping and power relationships between the sexes in society, that every effort should be made to locate that debate within a co-operative context and to ensure, through the design of group work and presentations, that ample opportunities be created for sharing ideas and for a positive collective experience to be enjoyed by all.

A second and no less important aim was that the simulation should be constructive. By this, the authors meant that participants should be afforded opportunities to create anti-sexist materials rather than simply review critiques of existing ones. An underlying assumption of the simulation was that much of what is produced by the media is sexist in orientation and that the challenge to participants was to create an alternative that was not. Those engaged in the exercise were to be left to arrive at their own understanding of the term 'anti-sexist' as a result of their deliberations and interactions.

Three years of trialling and modifications resulted in the format of 'Sugar 'n' Spice' set out below:

1 The simulation lasts approximately two hours and, ideally, involves nine participants though it can be run with 6–12 people.
2 Participants are allocated to three groups identified as writers, designers and promoters, each group having its own equipment and documentation.
3 The task is to produce a new magazine called *Changes* which is to replace a run-of-the-mill journal called *Woman's Way*. Participants are members of a Co-operative, sharing equally in the new enterprise.
4 Specifically, the writers group has to produce an outline of a sample story, the designers, a new cover design and the promoters, an audio-tape to present the new magazine on local radio.
5 A plenary session of the co-operative members then receives each group's work and produces a short press-release indicating the format and direction of *Changes*.

The 'plenary session' ending of the simulation arose out of dissatisfaction with an earlier version which left participants feeling 'flat'. The revised ending, the authors concluded, created a rounded and satisfying structure, whilst at the same time allowing participants to keep a degree of open-endedness if they so wished.

Other versions of 'Sugar 'n' Spice' arising out of the type of vocational courses being pursued by participants included a fourth group called the finance team who were charged with the task of producing a breakdown of the likely expenditure incurred in launching the new magazine. Later triallings however, convinced Robson and Collier that the addition of the finance group was both unnecessary and irrelevant to the aims of the simulation, in that the designated work lacked creativity and did not address the central issue of gender stereotyping. In their account, the authors observe how painful it was for them to reach the decision to drop the finance group from the simulation, given the time and effort that had already been expended. 'Once more', they say,' we had learned from experience that simulation design has to be linked to the ability to deal effectively with issues in practice' (Robson and Collier, 1991).

The importance of trialling and evaluating sensitive simulations such as 'Sugar 'n' Spice' across a wide range of students is brought out in Robson and Collier's account. Some 16–18 year olds, they observe, tend to be a little insecure with their own sexual identities and may find discussing gender stereotyping somewhat difficult. Again, it should not be assumed that such students have been used to working independently or in groups. Simulation work can be unsettling and uncomfortable for some participants. There is a constant need to adapt the form and content of simulation to particular student groups. Thus, in the case of trainee teachers, Robson and Collier changed the focus from a teenage magazine to a woman's magazine. They found that 'Sugar 'n' Spice' was very successful with student teachers in raising gender stereotyping issues and in provoking stimulating debates in debriefing sessions.

ROLE-PLAYING IN AN EDUCATIONAL SETTING: A SECOND EXAMPLE

Our second example of role-play in an educational setting illustrates the fourth use of this approach that van Ments identifies (page 261), namely, simulating a situation from which others may learn. As part of a study of secondary school pupils' perceptions of teacher racism, Naylor[19] produced four 5-minute video presentations of actual classroom events reconstructed for the purposes of the research. The films were scripted and role-played by twenty-one comprehensive school pupils, each video focusing on the behaviour of a white, female teacher towards pupils of visible ethnic minority groups. A gifted teacher of drama elicited performances from the pupils and faithfully interpreted their directions in her portrayal of their devised teachers' roles. The four parts she

Box 12.8   Categorization of responses to the four video extracts

Level (Score)	Description
0	No response or nothing which is intelligibly about the 'ways in which people treat one another' in the extract. Alternatively this level of response may be wrong in terms of fact and/or in interpretation.
1	No reference to racism (i.e. unfairness towards visible ethnic minority pupils) either by the teacher or by pupils, either implicitly or explicitly.
2	Either some reference to pupils' racism (see level 1 above) but not to the teacher's, or, reference to racism is left unspecified as to its perpetrator. Such reference is likely to be implied and may relate to one or more examples drawn from the extract without any generalization or synthesizing statement(s). The account is at a superficial level of analysis, understanding and explanation.
3	There is some reference to the teacher's racist behaviour and actions. Such reference is, however, implied rather than openly stated. There may also be implied condemnation of the teacher's racist behaviour/actions. There will not be any generalized statement(s) about the teacher's racism supported with examples drawn from the extract.
4	At this level the account will explicitly discuss and illustrate the teacher's racism but the analysis will show a superficial knowledge and understanding of the deeper issues.
5	At this level the account will explicitly discuss the teacher's racism as a generalization and this will be well illustrated with examples drawn from the extract. One or more of these examples may well be of the less obvious and more subtle types of racist behaviour/ action portrayed in the extract.

Source: Naylor (unpublished)

played consisted of a supply teacher of Geography, a teacher of French, a teacher of English and a Mathematics teacher.

In an opportunity sample drawn throughout England, Naylor showed the videos to over 1000 adolescents differentiated by age, sex, ability and ethnicity. Pupils' written responses to the four videos were scored 0 to 5 on the Kohlberg-type scale set out in Box 12.8. The analysis of scripts from a stratified sample of some 480 pupils suggested that older, high-ability girls of visible ethnic minority group membership were most perceptive of teacher racism and younger, low-ability boys of indigenous white group membership, least perceptive.

EVALUATING ROLE-PLAYING AND OTHER SIMULATION EXERCISES

Because the use of simulation methods in classroom settings is growing, there is increasing need to evaluate claims concerning the advantages and effectiveness of these newer approaches against more traditional methods. Yet here lies a major problem. To date, as Megarry observes, a high proportion of evaluation effort has been directed towards the comparative experiment involving empirical comparisons between simulation-type exercises and more traditional teaching techniques in terms of specified learning pay-offs. One objection to this approach to evaluation has been detailed earlier (p. 256) but is worth reiterating here:

> the limitations [of the classical, experimental method] as applied to evaluating classroom simulation and games are obvious: not only are the inputs multiple, complex, and only partly known, but the outputs are disputed, difficult to isolate, detect or measure and the interaction among participants is considerable. Interacting forms, in some views, a major part of what simulation and gaming is about; it is *not* merely a source of 'noise' or experimental error.
>
> (Megarry, 1978)

What alternatives are there to the traditional type of evaluative effort? Megarry lists the following promising approaches to simulation evaluation:

1 using narrative reports
2 using checklists gathered from students' recollections of outstanding positive and negative learning experiences
3 encouraging players to relate ideas and concepts learned in games to other areas of their lives
4 using the instructional interview, a form of tutorial carried out earlier with an individual learner or a small group in which materials and methods are tested by an instructor who is versed not only in the use of the materials, but also in the ways in which pupils learn.

(See also Percival's discussion of observational and self-reporting techniques.)[20] Notice how each of the above evaluative techniques is primarily concerned with the process rather than the product of simulation.

By way of summary, simulation methods provide a means of alleviating a number of problems inherent in laboratory experiments. At the same time, they permit the retention of some of their virtues. Simulations, notes Palys,[21] share with the laboratory experiment the characteristic that the experimenter has complete manipulative control over every aspect of the situation. At the same time, the subjects' humanity is left intact in that they are given a realistic situation in which to act in whatever way they think appropriate. The inclusion of the time dimension is another important contribution of the simulation, allowing the subject to take an active role in interacting with the environment, and the experimenter the opportunity of observing a social system in action with its feedback loops, multidirectional causal connections and so forth. Finally, Palys observes, the high involvement normally associated with participation in simulations shows that the self-consciousness usually associated with the laboratory experiment is more easily dissipated.

REFERENCES AND NOTES

1 Ginsburg, G.P., 'Role playing and role performance in social psychological research', in Brenner, M., Marsh, P. and Brenner, M. (eds), *The Social Context of Method* (Croom Helm, London, 1978). For a recent account of a wide range of role play applications in psychotherapy, see Holmes, P. and Karp, M., *Psychodrama – Inspiration and Technique* (Routledge, London, 1991).

2 Hamilton, V.L., 'Role play and deception: a re-examination of the controversy', *Journal for the Theory of Social Behaviour*, 6 (1976) 233–50.

3 Rogers, V.M. and Atwood, R.K., 'Can we put ourselves in their place?', *Yearbook of the National Council for Social Studies*, 44 (1974) 80–111.

4 Haney, C., Banks, C. and Zimbardo, P., 'Interpersonal dynamics in a simulated prison', *International Journal of Criminology and Penology*, 1 (1973) 69–97.

5 Banuazizi, A. and Movahedi, A., 'Interpersonal dynamics in a simulated prison: a methodological analysis', *American Psychologist*, 30 (1975) 152–60.

6 However, this is not what advocates of role-play as an alternative to deception generally mean by role-play. See Hamilton (1976) and Forward, Canter and Kirsch (1976) for a fuller discussion.

7 Forward, J., Canter, R. and Kirsch, N., 'Role-enactment and deception methodologies', *American Psychologist*, 35 (1976) 595–604.

8 Milgram, S., *Obedience to Authority* (Harper & Row, New York, 1974).

9 Mixon, D., 'If you won't deceive, what can you do?', in Armistead, N. (ed.), *Reconstructing Social Psychology* (Penguin Books, London, 1974).

10 Mixon, D., 'Instead of deception', *Journal for the Theory of Social Behaviour*, 2 (1972) 146–77.

11 Brown, R. and Herrnstein, R.J., *Psychology* (Methuen, London, 1975).

12 Harré, R. and Secord, P.F., *The Explanation of Social Behaviour* (Basil Blackwell, Oxford, 1972).

13 Argyris, C., 'Dangers in applying results from experimental social psychology', *American Psychologist*, 30 (1975) 469–85.

14 Taylor, J.L. and Walford, R., *Simulation in the Classroom* (Penguin Books, London, 1972).

15 Megarry, J., 'Retrospect and prospect', in R. McAleese (ed.), *Perspectives on Academic Gaming and Simulation 3: Training and Professional Education* (Kogan Page, London, 1978).

16 van Ments, M., 'Role playing: playing a part or a mirror to meaning?', *Sagset Journal*, 8(3) (1978) 83–92.

17 van Ments, M., *The Effective Use of Role-Play: A Handbook for Teachers and Trainers* (Croom Helm, London, 1983).

18 Robson, J. and Collier, K., 'Designing "Sugar 'n' Spice" – An anti-sexist simulation', *Simulation/Games For Learning*, 21(3) (1991) 213–19.

19 Naylor, P., 'Pupils' perceptions of teacher racism', unpublished PhD dissertation, Loughborough University of Technology, 1995.

20 Percival, F., 'Evaluation procedures for simulating gaming exercises', in McAleese, R. (ed.), *Perspectives on Academic Gaming and Simulation 3: Training and Professional Education* (Kogan Page, London, 1978).

21 Palys, T.S., 'Simulation methods and social psychology', *Journal for the Theory of Social Behaviour*, 8 (1978) 341–68.

13

THE INTERVIEW

INTRODUCTION

Although the interview as a research technique is normally considered as one of a range of survey methods in social research, we treat it separately here chiefly to give us additional room to address ourselves more effectively to the details involved. The purposes of the interview in the wider context of life are many and varied. It may thus be used as a means of evaluating or assessing a person in some respect; for selecting or promoting an employee; for effecting therapeutic change, as in the psychiatric interview; for testing or developing hypotheses; for gathering data, as in surveys or experimental situations; or for sampling respondents' opinions, as in doorstep interviews. Although in each of these situations the respective roles of the interviewer and interviewee may vary and the motives for taking part may differ, a common denominator is the transaction that takes place between seeking information on the part of one and supplying information on the part of the other. As our interests lie primarily in reviewing research methods and techniques, we will subsequently limit ourselves to the use of the interview as a specific research tool. Interviews in this sense range from the formal interview in which set questions are asked and the answers recorded on a standardized schedule; through less formal interviews in which the interviewer is free to modify the sequence of questions, change the wording, explain them or add to them; to the completely informal interview where the interviewer may have a number of key issues which she raises in conversational style instead of having a set questionnaire. Beyond this point is located the non-directive interview in which the interviewer takes on a subordinate role.

The research interview has been defined as 'a two-person conversation initiated by the interviewer for the specific purpose of obtaining research-relevant information, and focused by him on content specified by research objectives of systematic description, prediction, or explanation' (Cannell and Kahn, 1968).[1] It is an unusual method in that it

271

Box 13.1   Summary of relative merits of interview versus questionnaire

Consideration	Interview	Questionnaire
1 Personal need to collect data	Requires interviewers	Requires a clerk
2 Major expense	Payment to interviewers	Postage and printing
3 Opportunities for response-keying (personalization)	Extensive	Limited
4 Opportunities for asking	Extensive	Limited
5 Opportunities for probing	Possible	Difficult
6 Relative magnitude of data reduction	Great (because of coding)	Mainly limited to rostering
7 Typically, the number of respondents who can be reached	Limited	Extensive
8 Rate of return	Good	Poor
9 Sources of error	Interviewer, instrument, coding, sample	Limited to instrument and sample
10 Overall reliability	Quite limited	Fair
11 Emphasis on writing skill	Limited	Extensive

Source: Tuckman, 1972

involves the gathering of data through direct verbal interaction between individuals. In this sense it differs from the questionnaire where the respondent is required to record in some way her responses to set questions. By way of interest, we illustrate the relative merits of the interview and the questionnaire in Box 13.1. It has been pointed out that the direct interaction of the interview is the source of both its advantages and disadvantages as a research technique (Borg, 1963).[2] One advantage, for example, is that it allows for greater depth than is the case with other methods of data collection. A disadvantage, on the other hand, is that it is prone to subjectivity and bias on the part of the interviewer.

As a distinctive research technique, the interview may serve three purposes. First, it may be used as the principal means of gathering information having direct bearing on the research objectives. As Tuckman describes it, 'By providing access to what is "inside a person's head", [it] makes it possible to measure what a person knows (knowledge or information), what a person likes or dislikes (values and preferences), and what a person thinks (attitudes and beliefs)' (Tuckman, 1972).[3] Second, it may be used to test hypotheses or to suggest new ones; or as an explanatory device to help identify variables and relationships. And third, the interview may be used in conjunction with other methods in a research undertaking. In this connection, Kerlinger[4] suggests that it might be used to follow up unexpected results, for example, or to validate other methods, or to go deeper into the motivations of respondents and their reasons for responding as they do.

There are four kinds of interview that may be used specifically as research tools: the structured interview; the unstructured interview; the non-directive interview; and the focused interview. The structured interview is one in which the content and procedures are organized in advance. This means that the sequence and wording of the questions are determined by means of a schedule and the interviewer is left little freedom to make modifications. Where some leeway is granted her, it too is specified in advance. It is therefore characterized by being a closed situation. In contrast to it in this respect, the unstructured interview is an open situation, having greater flexibility and freedom. As Kerlinger notes, although the research purposes govern the questions asked, their content, sequence and wording are entirely in the hands of the interviewer. This does not mean, however, that the unstructured interview is a more casual affair, for in its own way it also has to be carefully planned.

The non-directive interview as a research technique derives from the therapeutic or psychiatric interview. The principal features of it are the minimal direction or control exhibited by the interviewer and the freedom the respondent has to express her subjective feelings as fully and as spontaneously as she chooses or is able. As Moser and Kalton put it,

> The informant is encouraged to talk about the subject under investigation (usually himself) and the course of the interview is mainly guided by him. There are no set questions, and usually no predetermined framework for recorded answers. The interviewer confines himself to elucidating doubtful points, to rephrasing the respondent's answers and to probing generally. It is an approach especially to be recommended when complex attitudes are involved and when one's knowledge of them is still in a vague and unstructured form.
>
> (Moser and Kalton, 1977)[5]

The need to introduce rather more interviewer control into the non-directive situation led to the development of the focused interview. The distinctive feature of this type is that it focuses on a respondent's subjective responses to a known situation in which she has been involved and which has been analysed by the interviewer prior to the interview. She is thereby able to use the data from the interview to substantiate or reject previously formulated hypotheses. As Merton and Kendall explain,

> In the usual depth interview, one can urge informants to reminisce on their experiences. In the focused interview, however, the interviewer can, when expedient, play a more active role: he can introduce more explicit verbal cues to the stimulus pattern or even *represent* it. In either case this usually activates a concrete report of responses by informants.
>
> (Merton and Kendall, 1946)[6]

We shall be examining both the non-directive interview and the focused interview in more detail later in the chapter.

CONCEPTIONS OF THE INTERVIEW

In his examination of views of the interview held by those who write theoretically about it and those who actually use it as a research tool, Kitwood lucidly contrasts three conceptions of it. The first conception is that of a potential means of pure information transfer. He explains that:

> if the interviewer does his job well (establishes rapport, asks questions in an acceptable manner, etc.), and if the respondent is sincere and well-motivated, accurate data may be obtained. Of course all kinds of bias are liable to creep in, but with skill these can largely be eliminated. In its fullest expression, this view accords closely with that of the psychometricians, who apparently believe that there is a relatively permanent, consistent, 'core' to the personality, about which a person will give information under certain conditions. Such features as lying, or the tendency to give a socially desirable response, are to be eliminated where possible.
>
> (Kitwood, 1977)[8]

This conception of the interview appears to be widely held.

A second conception of the interview is that of a transaction which inevitably has bias, which is to be recognized and controlled. According to this viewpoint, Kitwood explains that 'each participant in an interview will define the situation in a particular way. This fact can be best handled by building controls into the research design, for example by having a range of interviewers with different biases.' The interview is best understood in terms of a theory of motivation which recognizes a range of non-rational factors governing human behaviour, like emotions, unconscious needs and interpersonal influences. Kitwood points out that both these views of the interview regard the inherent features of interpersonal transactions as if they were 'potential obstacles to sound

Box 13.2 Attributes of ethnographers as interviewers

Trust: There would have to be a relationship between the interviewer and interviewee that transcended the research, that promoted a bond of friendship, a feeling of togetherness and joint pursuit of a common mission rising above personal egos.
Curiosity: There would have to be a desire to know, to learn people's views and perceptions of the facts, to hear their stories, discover their feelings. This is the motive force, and it has to be a burning one, that drives researchers to tackle and overcome the many difficulties involved in setting up and conducting successful interviews.
Naturalness: As with observation one endeavours to be unobtrusive in order to witness events as they are, untainted by one's presence and actions, so in interviews the aim is to secure what is within the minds of interviewees, uncoloured and unaffected by the interviewer.

Source: Adapted from Woods, 1986

research, and therefore to be removed, controlled, or at least harnessed in some way'.

The third conception of the interview sees it as an encounter necessarily sharing many of the features of everyday life (see for example, Box 13.2). Kitwood suggests that what is required, according to this view, is not a technique for dealing with bias, but a theory of everyday life that takes account of the relevant features of interviews. These may include role-playing, stereotyping, perception and understanding. One of the strongest advocates of this viewpoint is Cicourel[9] who lists five of the unavoidable features of the interview situation that would normally be regarded as problems. Briefly, these state that:

1 There are many factors which inevitably differ from one interview to another, such as mutual trust, social distance and the interviewer's control.
2 The respondent may well feel uneasy and adopt avoidance tactics if the questioning is too deep.
3 Both interviewer and respondent are bound to hold back part of what it is in their power to state.
4 Many of the meanings which are clear to one will be relatively opaque to the other, even when the intention is genuine communication.
5 It is impossible, just as in everyday life, to bring every aspect of the encounter within rational control.

The message that proponents of this view would express is that no matter how hard an interviewer may try to be systematic and objective, the constraints of everyday life will be a part of whatever interpersonal transactions she initiates. Kitwood concludes:

The solution is to have as explicit a theory as possible to take the various factors into account. For those who hold this view, there are not good interviews and bad in the conventional sense. There are simply social encounters; goodness and badness are predicates applicable, rather, to the theories within which the phenomena are explained.

(Kitwood, 1977)

SOME FEATURES OF THE RESEARCH INTERVIEW

We turn our attention now to the structured interview since this is one of the most frequently used methods of eliciting information in social and educational research. From here onwards, we shall comply with convention and refer to it as the 'research interview'. After reviewing the types of schedule items used, we shall examine question format and the kinds of answers, or response modes, that may be elicited.

Construction of schedules

Three kinds of items are used in the construction of schedules used in research interviews (see Kerlinger, 1970). First, 'fixed-alternative' items allow the respondent to choose from two or more alternatives. The most frequently used is the dichotomous item which offers two alternatives only: 'yes–no' or 'agree–disagree', for instance. Sometimes a third alternative such as 'undecided' or 'don't know' is also offered.

Example:
Do you feel it is against the interests of a school to have to make public its examination results?
Yes...
No ....
Don't know...

Kerlinger has identified the chief advantages and disadvantages of fixed-alternative items. They have, for example, the advantage of achieving greater uniformity of measurement and therefore greater reliability; of making the respondents answer in a manner fitting the response category; and of being more easily coded. Disadvantages include their superficiality; the possibility of irritating respondents who find none of the alternatives suitable; and the possibility of forcing responses that are inappropriate, either because the alternative chosen conceals ignorance on the part of the respondent or because she may choose an alternative that does not accurately represent the true facts. These weaknesses can be overcome, however, if the items are written with care, mixed with open-ended ones, and used in conjunction with probes on the part of the interviewer.

Second, 'open-ended items' have been succinctly defined by Kerlinger as 'those that supply a frame of reference for respondents' answers, but put a minimum of restraint on the answers and their expression' (Kerlinger, 1970). Other than the subject of the question, which is determined by the nature of the problem under investigation, there are no other restrictions on either the content or the manner of the interviewee's reply.

Example:
What kind of television programmes do you most prefer to watch?

Open-ended questions have a number of advantages: they are flexible; they allow the interviewer to probe so that she may go into more depth if she chooses, or to clear up any misunderstandings; they enable the interviewer to test the limits of the respondent's knowledge; they encourage co-operation and help establish rapport; and they allow the interviewer to make a truer assessment of what the respondent really believes. Open-ended situations can also result in unexpected or unanticipated answers which may suggest hitherto unthought-of relationships or hypotheses. A particular kind of open-ended question is the 'funnel'. This starts with a broad question or statement and then narrows down to more specific ones. Kerlinger quotes an example from the study by Sears, Maccoby and Levin:

> All babies cry, of course. Some mothers feel that if you pick up a baby every time it cries, you will spoil it. Others think you should never let a baby cry for very long. How do you feel about this? What did you do about it? How about the middle of the night?
> (Sears, Maccoby and Levin, 1957)[10]

Third, the 'scale' is a set of verbal items to each of which the interviewee responds by indicating degrees of agreement or disagreement. The individual's response is thus located on a scale of fixed alternatives. The use of this technique along with open-ended questions is a comparatively recent development and means that scale scores can be checked against data elicited by the open-ended questions.

Example:
Attendance at school after the age of 14 should be voluntary:

Strongly agree   Agree   Undecided   Disagree   Strongly disagree

It is possible to use one of a number of scales in this context: attitude scales, rank-order scales, rating scales, and so on. We touch upon this subject again subsequently.

277

Question formats

We now look at the kinds of questions and modes of response associated with interviewing. First, the matter of question format: how is a question to be phrased or organized? Tuckman (1972) has listed four such formats that an interviewer may draw upon. Questions may, for example, take a direct or indirect form. Thus an interviewer could ask a teacher whether she likes teaching: this would be a direct question. Or else she could adopt an indirect approach by asking for the respondent's views on education in general and the ways schools function. From the answers proffered, the interviewer could make inferences about the teacher's opinions concerning her own job. Tuckman suggests that by making the purpose of questions less obvious, the indirect approach is more likely to produce frank and open responses.

There are also those kinds of questions which deal with either a general or specific issue. To ask a child what he thought of the teaching methods of the staff as a whole would be a general or non-specific question. To ask him what he thought of his teacher as a teacher would be a specific question. We have already made reference to that sequence of questions designated the funnel in which the movement is from the general and non-specific to the more specific. Tuckman comments, 'Specific questions, like direct ones, may cause a respondent to become cautious or guarded and give less-than-honest answers. Non-specific questions may lead circuitously to the desired information but with less alarm by the respondents' (Tuckman, 1972).

A further distinction is that between questions inviting factual answers and those inviting opinions. To ask a person what political party he supports would be a factual question. To ask her what she thinks of the current government's foreign policy would be an opinion question. Both fact and opinion questions can yield less than the truth, however: the former do not always produce factual answers; nor do the latter necessarily elicit honest opinions. In both instances, inaccuracy and bias may be minimized by careful structuring of the questions.

We may also note that an interviewee may be presented with either a question or a statement. In the case of the latter she will be asked for her response to it in one form or another.

Example question:
Do you think homework should be compulsory for all children between 11 and 16?

Example statement:
Homework should be compulsory for all children between 11 and 16 years old.

Agree   Disagree   Don't know

Response modes

If there are varied ways of asking questions, it follows there will be several ways in which they may be answered. It is to the different response modes that we now turn. In all, Tuckman (1972) lists seven such modes.

The first of these is the 'unstructured response'. This allows the respondent to give her answer in whatever way she chooses.

Example:
Why did you not go to university?

A 'structured response', by contrast, would limit her in some way.

Example:
Can you give me two reasons for not going to university?

Although the interviewer has little control over the unstructured response, it does insure that the respondent has the freedom to give her own answer as fully as she chooses rather than being constrained in some way by the nature of the question. The chief disadvantage of the unstructured response concerns the matter of quantification. Data yielded in the unstructured response is more difficult to code and quantify than data in the structured response.

A 'fill-in response' mode requires the respondent to supply rather than choose a response, though the response is often limited to a word or phrase.

Example:
What is your present occupation?
or
How long have you lived at your present address?

The differences between the fill-in response and the unstructured response is one of degree.

A 'tabular response' is similar to a fill-in response though more structured. It may demand words, figures or phrases.

Example:

University	Subject	Degree	Dates	
			From	*To*

It is thus a convenient and short-hand way of recording complex information.

A 'scaled response' is one structured by means of a series of gradations. The respondent is required to record her response to a given statement by selecting from a number of alternatives.

Example:

What are your chances of reaching a top managerial position within the next five years?

Excellent   Good   Fair   Poor   Very Poor

Tuckman draws our attention to the fact that, unlike an unstructured response which has to be coded to be useful as data, a scaled response is collected in the form of usable and analysable data.

A 'ranking response' is one in which a respondent is required to rank-order a series of words, phrases or statements according to a particular criterion.

Example:

Rank order the following people in terms of their usefulness to you as sources of advice and guidance on problems you have encountered in the classroom. Use numbers 1 to 5, with 1 representing the person most useful.

Education tutor
Subject tutor
Class teacher
Headteacher
Other student

Ranked data can be analysed by adding up the rank of each response across the respondents, thus resulting in an overall rank order of alternatives.

A 'checklist response' requires that the respondent selects one of the alternatives presented to her. In that they do not represent points on a continuum, they are nominal categories.

Example:

I get most satisfaction in college from:

the social life
studying on my own
attending lectures
college societies
giving a paper at a seminar

This kind of response tends to yield less information than the other kinds considered.

Finally, the 'categorical response' mode is similar to the checklist but simpler in that it offers respondents only two possibilities.

Example:

| Material progress results in greater happiness for people | True | False |

or

| In the event of another war, would you be prepared to fight for your country? | Yes | No |

Summing the numbers of respondents with the same responses yields a nominal measure.

SOME PROBLEMS SURROUNDING THE USE OF THE INTERVIEW IN RESEARCH

A number of problems appear to attend the use of the interview as a research technique. One of these is that of invalidity, at least as far as the first two conceptions of the interview that we spoke of earlier are concerned. Studies reported by Cannell and Kahn (1968), for instance, in which the interview was used, seemed to indicate that this was a persistent problem. In one such study, subjects interviewed on the existence and state of their bank accounts often presented a misleading picture: fewer accounts were reported than actually existed and the amounts declared frequently differed from bank records, often in the direction of understating assets. The reviewers suggest that inferences about validity are made too often on the basis of face validity, that is, whether the questions asked look as if they are measuring what they claim to measure. The cause of invalidity, they argue, is bias which they define as 'a systematic or persistent tendency to make errors in the same direction, that is, to overstate or understate the "true value" of an attribute' (Lansing, Ginsberg and Braaten, 1961).[11] The problem, it seems, is not limited to a narrow range of data but is widespread. One way of validating interview measures is to compare the interview measure with another measure that has already been shown to be valid. This kind of comparison is known as 'convergent validity'. If the two measures agree, it can be assumed that the validity of the interview is comparable with the proven validity of the other measure.

Perhaps the most practical way of achieving greater validity is to minimize the amount of bias as much as possible. The sources of bias are the characteristics of the interviewer, the characteristics of the respondent, and the substantive content of the questions. More particularly, these will include: the attitudes and opinions of the interviewer; a tendency for the interviewer to see the respondent in her own image; a tendency for the interviewer to seek answers that support her preconceived notions; misperceptions on the part of the interviewer of what the respondent is saying; and misunderstandings on the part of the respondent of what is being asked. Studies have also shown that race, religion, social class and age can in certain contexts be potent sources of bias. Various writers have suggested the following as means of reducing bias: careful formulation of questions so that the meaning is crystal clear; thorough training procedures so that an interviewer is more aware of the possible problems; probability sampling of respondents; and sometimes by matching interviewer characteristics with those of the sample being interviewed.

In his critique of the interview as a research tool, Kitwood draws attention to the conflict it generates between the traditional concepts of reliability and validity. Where increased reliability of the interview is brought about by greater control of its elements, this is achieved, he argues, at the cost of reduced validity. He explains,

> In proportion to the extent to which 'reliability' is enhanced by rationalization, 'validity' would decrease. For the main purpose of using an interview in research is that it is believed that in an interpersonal encounter people are more likely to disclose aspects of themselves, their thoughts, their feelings and values, than they would in a less human situation. At least for some purposes, it is necessary to generate a kind of conversation in which the 'respondent' feels at ease. In other words, the distinctively human element in the interview is necessary to its 'validity'. The more the interviewer becomes rational, calculating, and detached, the less likely the interview is to be perceived as a friendly transaction, and the more calculated the response also is likely to be.
>
> (Kitwood, 1977)

Where either of the first two conceptions of the interview outlined earlier is held, Kitwood suggests that a solution to the problem of reliability and validity might lie in the direction of a 'judicious compromise'; with the third conception, however, reliability and validity become 'redundant notions', for 'every interpersonal situation may be said to be valid, as such, whether or not it conforms to expectation, whether or not it involves a high degree of communication, and whether or not the participants emerge exhilarated or depressed' (Kitwood, 1977).

A cluster of problems surround the person being interviewed. Tuckman (1972), for example, has observed that when formulating her questions an interviewer has to consider the extent to which a question might influence the respondent to show herself in a good light; or the extent to which a question might influence the respondent to be unduly helpful by attempting to anticipate what the interviewer wants to hear; or the extent to which a question might be asking for information about a respondent that she is not certain or likely to know herself. Further, interviewing procedures are based on the assumption that the person interviewed has insight into the cause of her behaviour. It has now come to be realized that insight of this kind is rarely achieved and that when it is, it is after long and difficult effort, usually in the context of repeated clinical interviews.

As the interview has some things in common with the self-administered questionnaire, it is frequently compared with it. Each has advantages over the other in certain respects. The advantages of the questionnaire, for instance, are: it tends to be more reliable; because it is anonymous, it encourages greater honesty; it is more economical than the interview in terms of time and money; and there is the possibility that it may be mailed. Its disadvantages, on the other hand, are: there is often too low a percentage of returns; the interviewer is able to answer questions concerning both the purpose of the interview and any misunderstandings experienced by the interviewee, for it sometimes happens in the case of the latter that the same questions have different meanings for different people; if only closed items are used, the questionnaire will be subject to the weaknesses already discussed; if only open items are used, respondents may be unwilling to write their answers for one reason or another; questionnaires present problems to people of limited literacy; and an interview can be conducted at an appropriate speed whereas questionnaires are often filled in hurriedly.

One of the problems that has to be considered when open-ended questions are used in the interview is that of developing a satisfactory method of recording replies. One way is to summarize responses in the course of the interview. This has the disadvantage of breaking the continuity of the interview and may result in bias because the interviewer may unconsciously emphasize responses that agree with her expectations and fail to note those that do not. It is sometimes possible to summarize an individual's responses at the end of the interview. Although this preserves the continuity of the interview, it is likely to induce greater bias because the delay may lead to the interviewer forgetting some of the details. It is these forgotten details that are most likely to be the ones that disagree with her own expectations.

One final point concerns the analysis and interpretation of data derived from unstructured interviews, particularly where the data have been transcribed from tape-recordings. Hull, in an article on this topic, contrasts the historical perspective with his own preference for the traditions of criticism, and in particular literary criticism when analysing data. As he explains, 'From such traditions may be drawn frameworks for the interpretation and analysis of transcript data and the requirement that research be a public discourse' (Hull, 1985).[12] For further information, we refer to Hull's article.

PROCEDURES

As a guide for those using the interview as a research technique perhaps for the first time, we outline a possible sequence of stages for such an undertaking.

The preliminary stage of an interview study will be the point where the purpose of the research is decided. It may begin by outlining the theoretical basis of the study, its broad aims, its practical value and the reasons why the interview approach was chosen. There may then follow the translation of the general goals of the research into more detailed and specific objectives. This is the most important step, for only careful formulation of objectives at this point will eventually produce the right kind of data necessary for satisfactory answers to the research problem.

This stage having been accomplished, there follows the preparation of the interview schedule itself. This involves translating the research objectives into the questions that will make up the main body of the schedule. This needs to be done in such a way that the questions adequately reflect what it is the researcher is trying to find out. It is quite usual to begin this task by writing down the variables to be dealt with in the study. As one commentator says, 'The first step in constructing interview questions is to *specify your variables by name*. Your variables are what you are trying to measure. They tell you where to begin' (Tuckman, 1972).

Before the actual interview items are prepared, it is desirable to give some thought to the question format and the response mode. The choice of question format, for instance, depends on a consideration of one or more of the following factors: the objectives of the interview; the nature of the subject matter; whether the interviewer is dealing in facts, opinions or attitudes; whether specificity or depth is sought; the respondent's level of education; the kind of information she can be expected to have; whether or not her thought needs to be structured; some assessment of her motivational level; the extent of the interviewer's own insight into the respondent's situation; and the kind of relationship the interviewer can expect to develop with the respondent. Having given prior thought to these matters, the researcher is in a position to decide whether to use open and/or closed questions, direct and/or indirect questions, specific and/or non-specific questions, and so on.

As a general rule, the kind of information sought and the means of

Box 13.3   The selection of response mode

Response mode	Type of data	Chief advantages	Chief disadvantages
Fill-in	Nominal	Less biasing; greater response flexibility	More difficult to score
Scaled	Interval	Easy to score	Time consuming; can be biasing
Ranking	Ordinal	Easy to score; forces discrimination	Difficult to complete
Checklist or categorical	Nominal (may be interval when totalled)	Easy to score; easy to respond	Provides less data and fewer options

Source: Tuckman, 1972[3]

its acquisition will determine the choice of response mode. Data analysis, then, ought properly to be considered alongside the choice of response mode so that the interviewer can be confident that the data will serve her purposes and analysis of them can be duly prepared. Box 13.3 summarizes the relationship between response mode and type of data.

Once the variables to be measured or studied have been identified, questions can be constructed so as to reflect them. If, for example, one of the variables was to be a new social education project that had recently been attempted with 15-year-olds in a comprehensive school, one obvious question would be: 'How do you think the project has affected the pupils?' Or, less directly, 'Do you think the children have been given too much or too little responsibility?' It is important to bear in mind that more than one question format and more than one response mode may be employed when building up a schedule. The final mixture will depend on the kinds of factors mentioned earlier – the objectives of the research, and so on.

Where an interview schedule is to be used as part of a field survey in which a number of trained interviewers are to be used, it will of course be necessary to include in it appropriate instructions for both interviewer and interviewees.

Setting up and conducting the interview will make up the next stage in the procedure. Where the interviewer is initiating the research herself, she will clearly select her own respondents; where she is engaged by another agent, then she will probably be given a list of people to contact.

Tuckman has succinctly reviewed the procedures to adopt at the interview itself. He writes,

At the meeting, the interviewer should brief the respondent as to the nature or purpose of the interview (being as candid as possible without biasing responses) and attempt to make the respondent feel at ease. He should explain the manner in which he will be recording responses, and if he plans to tape record, he should get the respondent's assent. At all times, an interviewer must remember that he is a data collection instrument and try not to let his own biases, opinions, or curiosity affect his behaviour. It is important that the interviewer should not deviate from his format and interview schedule although many schedules will permit some flexibility in choice of questions. The respondent should be kept from rambling away from the essence of a question, but not at the sacrifice of courtesy.

(Tuckman, 1972)

Once data from the interview have been collected, the next stage involves coding and scoring them. Coding has been defined by Kerlinger as the translation of question responses and respondent information to specific categories for the purpose of analysis (see Kerlinger, 1970). As we have seen, many questions are precoded, that is, each response can be immediately and directly converted into a score in an objective way. Rating scales and checklists are examples of precoded questions.

Perhaps the biggest problem concerns the coding and scoring of open-ended questions. Two solutions are possible here. Even though a response is open-ended, the interviewer may precode her interview schedule so that while an interviewee is responding freely, the interviewer is assigning the content of her responses, or parts of it, to predetermined coding categories. Classifications of this kind may be developed during pilot studies.

Example:
Q. What is it that you like least about your job?
A. Mostly the way the place is run – and the long hours; and the prospects aren't too good.

Coding:	colleagues	....
	organization	....................................X..............................
	the work	....
	conditions	....................................X..............................
	other	......................future prospects..........................

Alternatively, data may be postcoded. Having recorded the interviewee's response, either by summarizing it during or after the interview itself, or verbatim by tape recorder, the researcher may subject it to

286

content analysis and submit it to one of the available scoring procedures – scaling, scoring, rank scoring, response counting, etc.

Finally, the data are analysed and interpreted in the light of the research objectives.

GROUP INTERVIEWING

One technique within the methodology of interviewing to have grown in popularity is that of group interviewing. Watts and Ebbutt, for example, have considered the advantages and disadvantages of group interviewing as a means of collecting data in educational research. The advantages the authors identify include the potential for discussions to develop, thus yielding a wide range of responses. They explain, 'such interviews are useful . . . where a group of people have been working together for some time or common purpose, or where it is seen as important that everyone concerned is aware of what others in the group are saying' (Watts and Ebbutt, 1987).[13] For example, Lewis (1992)[14] found that 10-year-olds' understanding of severe learning difficulties was enhanced in group interview situations, the children challenging and extending each other's ideas. There are practical and organizational advantages, too. Pre-arranged groups can be used for the purpose in question by teachers with minimum disruption. Alternatively, the group interview can bring together people with varied opinions, or as representatives of different collectivities.

As regards the disadvantages of group interviews, Watts and Ebbutt note that they are of little use in allowing personal matters to emerge, or in circumstances where the researcher has to aim a series of follow-up questions at one specific member of the group. As they explain, 'the dynamic of a group denies access to this sort of data' (Watts and Ebbutt, 1987). For further guidance on this topic and the procedures involved, we refer the reader to Watts and Ebbutt (1987), Hedges (1985),[15] Breakwell (1990),[16] Spencer and Flin (1990).[17]

THE NON-DIRECTIVE INTERVIEW AND THE FOCUSED INTERVIEW

Originating from psychiatric and therapeutic fields with which it is most readily associated, the non-directive interview is characterized by a situation in which the respondent is responsible for initiating and directing the course of the encounter and for the attitudes she expresses in it (in contrast to the structured or research interview we have already considered, where the dominating role assumed by the interviewer results in, to use Kitwood's phrase, 'an asymmetry of commitment' (Kitwood, 1977)). It has been shown to be a particularly valuable technique because it gets at the deeper attitudes and perceptions of the person being interviewed in such a way as to leave them free from interviewer bias. We shall examine briefly the characteristics of the therapeutic interview and then consider its usefulness as a research tool in the social and educational sciences.

The non-directive interview as it is currently understood grew out of the pioneering work of Freud and subsequent modifications to his approach by later analysts. His basic discovery was that if one can arrange a special set of conditions and have his patient talk about his difficulties in a certain way, behaviour changes of many kinds can be accomplished.[18] The technique developed was used to elicit highly personal data from patients in such a way as to increase their self-awareness and improve their skills in self-analysis. By these means they became better able to help themselves. As Madge observes, it is these techniques which have greatly influenced contemporary interviewing techniques, especially those of a more penetrating and less quantitative kind.[19]

The present-day therapeutic interview has its most persuasive advocate in Carl Rogers who has on different occasions testified to its efficacy. Basing his analysis on his own clinical studies, he has identified a sequence of characteristic stages in the therapeutic process, beginning with the client's decision to seek help.[20] He is met by a counsellor who is friendly and receptive, but not didactic. The next stage is signalled when the client begins to give vent to hostile, critical and destructive feelings, which the counsellor accepts, recognizes and clarifies. Subsequently, and invariably, these antagonistic impulses are used up and give way to the first expressions of positive feeling. The counsellor likewise accepts these until suddenly and spontaneously 'insight and self-understanding come bubbling through' (Rogers, 1942). With insight comes the realization of possible courses of action and also the power to make decisions. It is in translating these into practical terms that the client frees himself from dependence on the counsellor.

Rogers subsequently identified a number of qualities in the interviewer which he deemed essential: that she bases her work on attitudes of acceptance and permissiveness; that she respects the client's responsibility for his own situation; that she permits the client to explain his problem in his own way; and that she does nothing that would in any way arouse the client's defences.[21]

Such then are the principal characteristics of the non-directive interview technique in a therapeutic setting. But what of its usefulness as a purely research technique in societal and educational contexts? There are a number of features of the therapeutic interview which are peculiar to it and may well be inappropriate in other settings: for example, as we have seen, the interview is initiated by the respondent; his motivation is to obtain relief from a particular symptom; the interviewer is primarily a source of help, not a procurer of information; the actual interview is part of the therapeutic experience; the purpose of the interview is to change the behaviour and inner life of the person and its success is defined in these terms; and there is no restriction on the topics discussed.

A researcher has a different order of priorities, however, and what appear as advantages in a therapeutic context may be decided limitations when the technique is used for research purposes, even though she may be sympathetic to the spirit of the non-directive interview. As Madge explains, increasingly there are those 'who wish to retain the good qualities of the non-directive technique and at the same time are keen to evolve a method that is economical and precise enough to leave a residue of results rather than merely a posse of cured souls'.

One attempt to meet this need is to be found in a programme reported by Merton and Kendall (1946) in which the focused interview was developed. While seeking to follow closely the principle of non-direction, the method did introduce rather more interviewer control in the kinds of questions used and sought also to limit the discussion to certain parts of the respondent's experience.

The focused interview differs from other types of research interview in certain respects. These have been identified by Merton and Kendall as follows:

1 The persons interviewed are known to have been involved in a particular situation: they may, for example, have watched a TV programme; or seen a film; or read a book or article; or have been a participant in a social situation.

2 By means of the techniques of content analysis, elements in the situation which the researcher deems significant have previously been analysed by her. She has thus arrived at a set of hypotheses relating to the meaning and effects of the specified elements.

3 Using her analysis as a basis, the investigator constructs an interview guide. This identifies the major areas of enquiry and the hypotheses which determine the relevant data to be obtained in the interview.

4 The actual interview is focused on the subjective experiences of the people who have been exposed to the situation. Their responses enable the researcher both to test the validity of her hypotheses, and to ascertain unanticipated responses to the situation, thus giving rise to further hypotheses.

From this it can be seen that the distinctive feature of the focused interview is the prior analysis by the researcher of the situation in which subjects have been involved.

289

The advantages of this procedure have been cogently explained by Merton and Kendall:

> Fore-knowledge of the situation obviously reduces the task confronting the investigator, since the interview need not be devoted to discovering the objective nature of the situation. Equipped in advance with a content analysis, the interviewer can readily distinguish the objective facts of the case from the subjective definitions of the situation. He thus becomes alert to the entire field of 'selective response'. When the interviewer, through his familiarity with the objective situation, is able to recognize symbolic or functional silences, 'distortions', avoidances, or blockings, he is the more prepared to explore their implications.
>
> (Merton and Kendall, 1946)

In the quest for what Merton and Kendall term 'significant data', the interviewer must develop the ability to evaluate continuously the interview while it is in progress. To this end, they established a set of criteria by which productive and unproductive interview material can be distinguished. Briefly, these are:

1 *Non-direction*: interviewer guidance should be minimal.
2 *Specificity*: respondents' definitions of the situation should find full and specific expression.
3 *Range*: the interview should maximize the range of evocative stimuli and responses reported by the subject.

Box 13.4 Further education college principals and their views on training and enterprise councils (TECs)

Interviewee 14
'I'm afraid the TECs have started life with the arrogance of MSC (Manpower Service Commission), with the ignorance of MSC, with the almost blinding lack of knowledge . . .'
Interviewer's note: **an enigmatic grimace accompanied this remark.**
'. . . lack of vision, lack of leadership. I don't think any of them (directors of the TEC) have any interest or active involvement in Further Education . . .'
Interviewer's note: **further facial expression possibly indicating, 'what are people like this doing on the management of the TEC'.**
'I took a view about the TECs. You can either sit back on your hands and hope they will go away or you can work with them from day one and get a pole position on the starting grid. That's what I did!'

Interviewee 8
'They seem to have this dreadful image of college principals being a load of twisting no-gooders who are a load of rubbish.'
Interviewer's note: **spoken vociferously, fiercely castigating perceived attitudes of TEC officials.**

Source: Ashton, 1994

Box 13.5 Extract from a focused interview

Notes		Transcript
	147	Is there any special interest which you and Oliver share – something that the two of you follow together – would you say?
nothing yet	M	Mmmm . . . I don't *think* so.
	148	Is there anything which he and his Daddy are both specifically interested in?
may be pause to think – but definite negative	M	(pause) . . . *No*
	149	No special thing . . . would you say he's closer now to you or to his Daddy?
	M	He . . . is . . . closer . . .?
deliberately defuses by addition		Would you say Oliver is closer to you, or to his Daddy? . . . or is it about equal?
	M	About equal . . . might be a shade towards me.
	150	Does your husband like doing things with him?
ALERT quiet, but words quick and definite WAIT – nothing comes – probe probe is a challenge, retreat expected	M	(sigh) . . . Mmmm . . . not really – no.
	I	(pause) . . . How do you mean?
M retreats	M	Well – I suppose he *does* like doing things with him, but opportunity doesn't often present itself.
I accepts retreat	I	I see – yes . . . yes . . .
	M	He's . . . he's . . . well, he's home tonight, but some nights he's not home till 7 or 8, so he just sees them go to bed, really, and get up in the morning.
accepts, but probes from another angle, forcing issue	I	. . . yes . . . and does he give Oliver a lot of attention when he *is* there – would you say, um, about average, or more or less than most fathers?
M enabled to advance again	M	Well, I sometimes think he could give *more* . . . um . . . he could perhaps take them *off* more – the boys – and *play* with them more;
voice rises		if the boys play games, they play games with me! (. . . yes . . .) – this is what I *find*, you know? (I see yes . . . yes . . .) 'Cause he's always . . . *out*, or *busy*, (. . . yes . . .) or doing something (. . . yes . . .)

Box 13.5 (cont'd)

semi-retreat		I suppose it's circumstances not deliberate . . .
I accepts retreat	I	You're, sort of, more available . . .
M advances	M	Yes . . . yes. If we go to the cricket match – *he's playing* cricket – *I* play with the boys!
unbiased re-statement (giving time)	I	(laughter in which M joins) . . . And the boys sort of *feel* really that you're more available – that, er, you're the person they play with, I suppose?
M advances, voice rising	M	Yes! Now Oliver asks *me* to take him swimming – he doesn't ask his Daddy!
(Interview continues, but this is now recognized as a sensitive area and may be returned to if opportunity arises.)		

Source: Adapted from Shipman, 1976

4 *Depth and personal context*: The interview should bring out the affective and value-laden implications of the subjects' responses, to determine whether the experience had central or peripheral significance. It should elicit the relevant personal context, the idiosyncratic associations, beliefs and ideas.

By way of example of productive interview material, Ashton (1994)[22] used focused interviews to ascertain the strengths of beliefs and the personal reactions of principals of Further Education Colleges to various changes being pressed upon them by central government and local agencies (see Box 13.4).

Box 13.5 gives part of a transcript from the Newsons' longitudinal study of child-rearing practices.[23] It illustrates the skills involved in focused interviewing; notice particularly the subtle ways in which the interviewer (I) is able to get beneath the rather conventional initial response of the mother (M) to Question 147.

PHENOMENOLOGICAL ANALYSIS OF INTERVIEW DATA

Before giving examples of the use of the interview in educational research, we refer the reader to a study by Hycner in which he sets out procedures that can be followed when phenomenologically analysing interview data. We saw in Chapter 1 that the phenomenologist advocates the study of direct experience taken at face value and sees behaviour as determined by the phenomena of experience rather than by external, objective and physically described reality. Hycner points out that there is a reluctance on the part of phenomenologists to focus too much on specific steps in research methods for fear that they will become reified. The steps suggested by Hycner, however, offer a possible way of

[1]I was looking at Mary and [2]all of a sudden I knew [3]I was looking at her like I never looked at anybody in my whole life – and [4]my eyes were sort of just kind of staring at her and the reason that [5]I realized that it was tremendous was that she said to me – what are you doing – [6]and I just said I'm looking at you – [7]and so we just sat there and [8]she sort of watched me look at her – and [9]she was getting kind of uncomfortable [10]and yet also kept saying – what's going on [11]but not really wanting to hear – [12]just letting me – have enough sensitivity to let me experience it – [13] a lot was going on – [14]I didn't realize what – what it was – [15]I was just sort of sitting there – [16] *I couldn't move* – [17]I didn't want to move – [18]I just want to continue looking at her.	[1]Was looking at Mary [2]Suddenly he knew [3]He was looking at her like he never looked at anybody in his whole life [4]His eyes were just staring at her [5]Realized it was tremendous when she said 'What are you doing?' [6]He just said, 'I'm looking at you.' [7]Both just sat there [8]She sort of watched him look at her [9]She was getting kind of uncomfortable [10]She kept saying 'What's going on?' [11]She didn't seem to want a response [12]She had enough sensitivity to let him experience it [13]A lot was going on [14]He didn't realize what was going on [15]He continued to just sit there [16]He *couldn't move* [17]Didn't want to move [18]Just wanted to continue looking at her.

Source: Hycner, 1985

analysing data which allays such fears. As he himself explains, his guidelines 'have arisen out of a number of years of teaching pheno-menological research classes to graduate psychology students and trying to be true to the phenomenon of interview data while also providing concrete guidelines' (Hycner, 1985).[24] In summary, the guidelines are as follows:

1 *Transcription*: having the interview tape transcribed, noting not only the literal statements but also non-verbal and paralinguistic communication.
2 *Bracketing and phenomenological reduction*: for Hycner this means, 'sus-pending (bracketing) as much as possible the researcher's meaning and interpretations and entering into the world of the unique individual who was interviewed' (Hycner, 1985). The researcher thus sets out to understand what the interviewee is saying rather than what she expects that person to say.
3 *Listening to the interview for a sense of the whole*: this involves listening to the entire tape several times and reading the transcription a number of times in order to provide a context for the emergence of specific units of meaning and themes later on.

Box 13.7   Units of relevant meaning

---

¹Was looking at Mary
²Suddenly he knew
³He was looking at her like he never looked at anybody in his whole life
⁴His eyes were just staring at her
⁵Realized it was tremendous when she said 'What are you doing?'
⁶He just said, 'I'm looking at you.'
⁷Both just sat there
¹²She had enough sensitivity to let him experience it
¹³A lot was going on
¹⁴He didn't realize what was going on
¹⁵He continued to just sit there
¹⁶He *couldn't move* – ¹⁷Didn't want to move
¹⁸Just wanted to continue looking at her

Source: Hycner, 1985

4 *Delineating units of general meaning*: this entails a thorough scrutiny of both verbal and non-verbal gestures to elicit the participant's meaning. Hycner says, 'It is a crystallization and condensation of what the participant has said, still using as much as possible the literal words of the participant' (Hycner, 1985). (See Box 13.6 for Hycner's own example. This is the second page of transcription describing an experience of wonderment and awe. On the previous page, the participant discussed the background where he and his girlfriend were up in the mountains on vacation. The scene being described is the beginning of an experience of wonder.)

5 *Delineating units of meaning relevant to the research question*: once the units of general meaning have been noted, they are then reduced to units of meaning relevant to the research question. In the case of Hycner's study, the original eighteen general units (see Box 13.6) are reduced to thirteen units of meaning relevant to the research question (see Box 13.7).

6 *Training independent judges to verify the units of relevant meaning*: findings can be verified by using other researchers to carry out the above procedures. Hycner's own experience in working with graduate students well trained in this type of research is that there are rarely significant differences in the findings.

7 *Eliminating redundancies*: at this stage, the researcher checks the lists of relevant meaning and eliminates those clearly redundant to others previously listed.

8 *Clustering units of relevant meaning*: the researcher now tries to determine if any of the units of relevant meaning naturally cluster together; whether there seems to be some common theme or essence that unites several discrete units of relevant meaning. Box 13.8 gives an example of clustering units of relevant meaning.

Box 13.8 Clusters of relevant meaning

I   *The tremendousness of the looking at Mary*
   A Looking at Mary in a way totally different than he had ever looked at anyone in his life.[1,3]
   B His eyes were just staring.[4]
   C Realized it was tremendous when she said 'What are you doing?'[5]
   D Was (just) looking at her.[6]
   E A lot was going on.[13]
   F Just wanted to continue looking at her.[18]

II *Realization*
   A A sudden realization[2] (Almost like it breaks in).
   B Realized how tremendous it was (through her question).[5]
   C A lot was going on and he didn't realize what was going on[13,14] (rhythm of awareness).

III *Continuation of what was happening*
   A Both just (continued) to sit there.[7]
   B He continued to sit.[15]

IV *Inability to move*
   A *Couldn't move*[16] (issue of volition).
   B Didn't want to move[17] (didn't desire to move).

V   *Interpersonal dimension*
   A Was looking at Mary in a way he had never looked at anyone in his whole life.[1,3]
   B Her question elicited the realization of how tremendous it was.[5]
   C He just said 'I'm looking at you.'[6]
   D Both just sat there.[7]

Source: Hycner, 1985

9 *Determining themes from clusters of meaning*: the researcher examines all the clusters of meaning to determine if there is one (or more) central theme(s) which expresses the essence of these clusters.

10 *Writing a summary of each individual interview*: it is useful at this point, the author suggests, to go back to the interview transcription and write up a summary of the interview incorporating the themes that have been elicited from the data.

11 *Return to the participant with the summary and themes, conducting a second interview*: this is a check to see whether the essence of the first interview has been accurately and fully captured.

12 *Modifying themes and summary*: with the new data from the second interview, the researcher looks at all the data as a whole and modifies or adds themes as necessary.

13 *Identifying general and unique themes for all the interviews*: the researcher now looks for the themes common to most or all of the interviews as well as the individual variations. The first step is to note if there are themes common to all or most of the interviews. The second step is to note when there are themes that are unique to a single interview or a minority of the interviews.

14 *Contextualization of themes*: at this point it is helpful to place these themes back within the overall contexts or horizons from which these themes emerged.

15 *Composite summary*: the author considers it useful to write up a composite summary of all the interviews which would accurately capture the essence of the phenomenon being investigated. The author concludes, 'Such a composite summary describes the "world" in general, as experienced by the participants. At the end of such a summary the researcher might want to note significant individual differences' (Hycner, 1985).

Issues arising from this procedure are discussed in some detail in the second part of Hycner's article.

CONCLUSION: EXAMPLES OF THE USE OF INTERVIEWING IN RESEARCH

Many examples of interview studies and the use of interview techniques are to be found throughout the literature of social and educational research, the range varying from the comprehensiveness and sophistication of national polls at one extreme to small-scale investigations into educational issues at the other. We conclude this chapter with brief references to two educational studies. We choose them for their dependence on interview techniques and also their accessibility.

In his ethnographic study of a secondary school, Woods (1979)[25] uses interview techniques as part of his overall strategy of participant observation to describe and analyse the principal areas of experience and methods of adapting to school life for both pupils and teachers. Numerous extracts of interview material are given throughout the text.

Box 13.9 Reasons for subject choice

Linda:	I didn't want to do commerce.
Int:	Why have you chosen it then?
Linda:	Because my mother said so.
Int:	Why did she say that?
Linda:	Because she wants me to work in an office.
Int:	And what do you want to do?
Linda:	Be a hairdresser.
Int:	If it were left to you what to do, what would you have chosen?
Linda:	I haven't thought about it.
Int:	Will you be allowed to do commerce, do you think?
Linda:	I hope I'm knocked out.
Int:	What form will you go in?
Linda:	I'd go in 4L straight away.

Source: Adapted from Woods, 1979

One such example is given in Box 13.9. For a thorough account of the role of interviewing in ethnographic research, see the author's later work.[7]

Another ethnographic study, this time by MacPherson (1983)[26] working in an Australian school, directs its attention on pupils' accounts of relations and activities with classmates. The principal method of research was interviews with pupils. We give a sample of his questions in Box 13.10.

Finally, for further examples of the use of interviewing in educational research, see Powney and Watts;[27] and for instances of the use of the technique in educational and social research see Finch.[28]

Box 13.10   Sample questions used in ethnographic study in an Australian state high school

1   If you don't understand Mr . . . (teacher) what do you do?
2   When lessons get boring what do you do?
3   When people start to muck around what do you do?
4   Have you ever informed on any one for any reason?
5   How do you feel about others informing on people?
6   In what ways have you helped teachers?
How did other pupils feel about it?
7   What pupils often help teachers?
How do they help them?
8   Do you talk to teachers after class?
What do you talk to them about?

Source: Adapted from MacPherson, 1983

REFERENCES AND NOTES

1 Cannell, C.F. and Kahn, R.L., 'Interviewing', in Lindzey, G. and Aronson, E. (eds), *The Handbook of Social Psychology*, vol. 2, *Research Methods* (Addison-Wesley, New York, 1968).

2 Borg, W.R., *Educational Research: An Introduction* (Longman, London, 1963).

3 Tuckman, B.W., *Conducting Educational Research* (Harcourt Brace Jovanovich, New York, 1972).

4 Kerlinger, F.N., *Foundations of Behavioral Research* (Holt, Rinehart & Winston, New York, 1970).

5 Moser, C.A. and Kalton, G., *Survey Methods in Social Investigation* (Heinemann Educational Books, London, 1977). For another account of the use of questioning in interviews and surveys see Hargie, O., Saunders, C. and Dickson, D., *Social Skills in Interpersonal Communication* (Croom Helm, London, 1981).

6 Merton, R.K. and Kendall, P.L., 'The focused interview', *American Journal of Sociology*, 51 (1946) 541–57.

7 Woods, P., *Inside Schools: Ethnography in Educational Research* (Routledge & Kegan Paul, London, 1986).

8 Kitwood, T.M., 'Values in adolescent life: towards a critical description', unpublished PhD dissertation, School of Research in Education, University of Bradford, 1977.

9 Cicourel, A.V., *Method and Measurement in Sociology* (The Free Press, New York, 1964).

10 Sears, R., Maccoby, E. and Levin, H., *Patterns of Child Rearing* (Harper & Row, New York, 1957).

11 Lansing, J.B., Ginsberg, G.P. and Braaten, K., *An Investigation of Response Error* (Bureau of Economic and Business Research, University of Illinois, 1961). Reported in Cannell and Kahn (1968).

12 Hull, C., 'Between the lines: the analysis of interview data as an exact art', *British Educational Research Journal*, 11(1) (1985) 27–31.

13 Watts, M. and Ebbutt, D., 'More than the sum of the parts: research methods in group interviewing', *British Educational Research Journal*, 13(1) (1987) 25–34.

14 Lewis, A., 'Group child interviews as a research tool', *British Educational Research Journal*, 18(4) (1992) 413–21.

15 Hedges, A., 'Group interviewing', in Walker, R. (ed.), *Applied Qualitative Research* (Gower, Aldershot, 1985).

16 Breakwell, G., *Interviewing* (Routledge/BPS, London, 1990).

17 Spencer, J.R. and Flin, R., *The Evidence of Children* (Blackstone, London, 1990).

18 Ford, D.H. and Urban, H.B., *Systems of Psychotherapy: a Comparative Study* (John Wiley & Sons, New York, 1963).

19 Madge, J., *The Tools of Social Science* (Longman, London, 1965).

20 Rogers, C.R., *Counselling and Psychotherapy* (Houghton Mifflin, Boston, 1942).

21 Rogers, C.R., 'The non-directive method as a technique for social research', *American Journal of Sociology* 50 (1945) 279–83.

22 Ashton, E., 'Managing change in Further Education: some perspectives of college principals', unpublished PhD dissertation, Loughborough University of Technology, 1994.

23 Newson, J. and Newson, E., 'Parental roles and social contexts', in Shipman, M.D. (ed.), *The Organization and Impact of Social Research* (Routledge & Kegan Paul, London, 1976) 22–48.

24 Hycner, R.H., 'Some guidelines for the phenomenological analysis of interview data', *Human Studies*, 8 (1985) 279–303.

25 Woods, P., *The Divided School* (Routledge & Kegan Paul, London, 1979).

26 MacPherson, J., *The Feral Classroom* (Routledge & Kegan Paul, Melbourne, 1983).

27 Powney, J. and Watts, M., *Interviewing in Educational Research* (Routledge & Kegan Paul, London, 1987).

28 Finch, J., *Research and Policy: The Uses of Qualitative Methods in Social and Educational Research* (Falmer Press, Lewes, 1986).

14

PERSONAL CONSTRUCTS

INTRODUCTION

One of the most interesting theories of personality to have emerged this century and one that has had an increasing impact on educational research is 'personal construct theory'. Personal constructs are the basic units of analysis in a complete and formally stated theory of personality proposed by George Kelly in a book entitled *The Psychology of Personal Constructs* (1955). Because Kelly's own experiences were so intimately related to the development of his imaginative theory, we begin with some observations on Kelly, the man.

Kelly began his career as a school psychologist dealing with problem children referred to him by teachers. As his experiences widened, instead of merely corroborating a teacher's complaint about a pupil, Kelly tried to understand the complaint in the way the teacher construed it. This change of perspective constituted a significant reformulation of the problem. In practical terms it resulted in an analysis of the teacher making the complaint as well as the problem pupil. By viewing the problem from a wider perspective Kelly was able to envisage a wider range of solutions.

The insights George Kelly gained from his clinical work led him to the view that there is no objective, absolute truth and that events are only meaningful in relation to the ways that are construed by individuals. Kelly's primary focus is upon the way individuals perceive their environment, the way they interpret what they perceive in terms of their existing mental structure, and the way in which, as a consequence, they behave towards it. In *The Psychology of Personal Constructs*, Kelly proposes a view of people actively engaged in making sense of and extending their experience of the world. Personal constructs are the dimensions that we use to conceptualize aspects of our day-to-day world. The constructs that we create are used by us to forecast events and rehearse situations before their actual occurrence. According to Kelly, we take on the role of scientist seeking to predict and control the course of events in which we are caught up. For Kelly, the ultimate explanation of human behaviour 'lies in scanning man's undertakings, the questions he asks, the lines of inquiry he initiates and the strategies he employs' (Kelly, 1969).[1] Kelly's ideas have a good deal in common with current educational thought and practice. Education, in Kelly's view, is necessarily experimental. Its ultimate goal is individual fulfilment and the maximizing of individual potential. In emphasizing the need of each individual to question and explore, construct theory implies a view of education that capitalizes upon the child's natural motivation to engage in spontaneous learning activities. It follows that the teacher's task is to facilitate children's ongoing exploration of the world rather than impose adult perspectives upon them. Kelly's ideas have much in common with those to be found in Rousseau's *Emile*.

The central tenets of Kelly's theory are set out in terms of a fundamental postulate and a number of corollaries. It is not proposed here to undertake a detailed discussion of his theoretical propositions. Good commentaries are available in Bannister[2] and Ryle.[3] Instead, we look at the method suggested by Kelly of eliciting constructs and assessing the mathematical relationships between them, that is, repertory grid technique.

CHARACTERISTICS OF THE METHOD

Kelly proposes that each person has access to a limited number of 'constructs' by means of which she evaluates the phenomena that constitute her world. These phenomena – people, events, objects, ideas, institutions and so on – are known as 'elements'. He further suggests that the constructs that each of us employs may be thought of as bipolar, that is, capable of being defined in terms of polar adjectives (good–bad) or polar phrases (makes me feel happy–makes me feel sad).

A number of different forms of repertory grid technique have been developed since Kelly's first formulation. All have the two essential characteristics in common that we have already identified, that is, constructs – the dimensions used by a person in conceptualizing aspects of her world; and elements – the stimulus objects that a person evaluates in terms of the constructs she employs. In Box 14.1, we illustrate the empirical technique suggested by Kelly for eliciting constructs and identifying their relationship with elements in the form of a repertory grid.

Since Kelly's original account of what he called 'The Role Construct Repertory Grid Test', several variations of repertory grid have been developed and used in different areas of research. It is the flexibility and adaptability of repertory grid technique that has made it such an attractive tool to researchers in psychiatric, counselling, and more recently,

Box 14.1   Eliciting constructs and constructing a repertory grid

A person is asked to name a number of people who are significant to him. These might be, for example, mother, father, wife, friend, employer, priest. These constitute the *elements* in the repertory grid.

The subject is then asked to arrange the elements into groups of threes in such a manner that two are similar in some way but at the same time different from the third. The ways in which the elements may be alike or different are the *constructs*, generally expressed in bi-polar form (quiet – talkative; mean – generous; warm – cold). The way in which two of the elements are similar is called the *similarity pole* of the construct; and the way in which two of the elements are different from the third, the *contrast pole* of the construct.

A grid can now be constructed by asking the subject to place each element at either the *similarity* or the *contrast* pole of each construct. Let x = one pole of the construct, and blank = the other. The result can be set out as follows:

CONSTRUCTS   ELEMENTS

	A	B	C	D	E	F
1 quiet – talkative	x	x	x			x
2 mean – generous	x			x	x	
3 warm – cold		x			x	

It is now possible to derive different kinds of information from the grid. By studying each *row*, for example, we can get some idea of how a person defines each construct in terms of significant people in his life. From each *column*, we have a personality profile of each of the significant people in terms of the constructs selected by the subjects. More sophisticated treatments of grid data are discussed in examples presented in the text.

Source: Adapted from Kelly, 1969

educational settings. We now review a number of developments in the form and the use of the technique.

'ELICITED' VERSUS 'PROVIDED' CONSTRUCTS

A central assumption of this 'standard' form of repertory grid is that it enables the researcher to elicit constructs that subjects customarily use in interpreting and predicting the behaviour of those people who are important in their lives. Kelly's method of eliciting personal constructs required the subject to complete a number of cards, 'each showing the name of a person in [his/her] life'. Similarly, in identifying elements, the subject was asked, 'Is there an important way in which two of [the elements] – any two – differ from the third?' This insistence upon important persons and important ways that they are alike or differ, where both constructs and elements are nominated by the subjects themselves, is central to Personal Construct Theory. Kelly gives it precise expression in his Individuality Corollary – 'Persons differ from each other in their construction of events.'

Several forms of repertory grid technique now in common use represent a significant departure from Kelly's individuality corollary in that they provide constructs to subjects rather than elicit constructs from them.

One justification for the use of provided constructs is implicit in Ryle's commentary on the individuality corollary: 'Kelly paid rather little attention to developmental and social processes', Ryle observes, 'his own concern was with the personal and not the social'. Ryle believes that the individuality corollary would be strengthened by the additional statement that 'persons *resemble* each other in their construction of events' (Ryle, 1975).

Can the practice of providing constructs to subjects be reconciled with the individuality corollary assumptions? A review of a substantial body of research suggests a qualified 'yes':

> [While] it seems clear in the light of research that individuals prefer to use their own elicited constructs rather than provided dimensions to describe themselves and others . . . the results of several studies suggest that normal subjects, at least, exhibit approximately the same degree of differentiation in using carefully selected supplied lists of adjectives as when they employ their own elicited personal constructs.

> (Adams-Webber, 1970)[4]

However, see Fransella and Bannister[5] on elicited versus supplied constructs as a 'grid-generated' problem.

Bannister and Mair[6] support the use of supplied constructs in experiments where hypotheses have been formulated and in those involving group comparisons. The use of elicited constructs alongside supplied ones can serve as a useful check on the meaningfulness of those that are provided, substantially lower inter-correlations between elicited and supplied constructs suggesting, perhaps, the lack of relevance of those provided by the researcher. The danger with supplied constructs, Bannister and Mair argue, is that the researcher may assume that the polar adjectives or phrases she provides are the verbal equivalents of the psychological dimensions in which she is interested.

ALLOTTING ELEMENTS TO CONSTRUCTS

When a subject is allowed to classify as many or as few elements at the similarity or the contrast pole, the result is often a very lopsided

Box 14.2 Allotting elements to constructs: three methods

Example 1: Split-half form

				Elements						Constructs

1	2	3	4	5	6	7	8	9	10	
x		x	x		x		x			1 fast–slow
	x	x		x		x			x	2 late–early
		x	x		x			x	x	3 dangerous–safe

Since the subject is forced to allocate half of the elements to one pole, the chance expectancy of matchings occurring on 10 elements when two constructs are compared is 5. Deviation scores can be computed from chance level. Thus 5 matchings = 0; in constructs 1 and 2, matchings = −3; in constructs 1 and 3, matchings = +1; and in constructs 2 and 3, matchings = −1. The probability of particular matching scores being obtained can be had by reference to statistical tables.

Example 2: Rank-order form

				Elements						Constructs

1	2	3	4	5	6	7	8	9	10	
10	1	2	5	8	7	3	4	9	6	1 fast–slow
9	4	10	1	6	8	5	2	3	7	2 late–early
7	9	5	6	10	2	1	4	8	3	3 dangerous–safe

Spearman's rho (r_s)   Relationship scores

Constructs 1 and 2 = .15 $(0.15)^2 \times 100 = +23$
Constructs 1 and 3 = .24 $(0.24)^2 \times 100 = +58$
Constructs 2 and 3 = −.16 $(-0.16)^2 \times 100 = -26$

Example 3: Rating form

				Elements						Constructs

1	2	3	4	5	6	7	8	9	10	
4	4	2	1	4	3	5	1	5	2	1 fast
1	1	3	5	1	3	2	2	5	5	2 late
5	1	3	2	2	1	4	5	1	2	3 dangerous

A 5-point rating scale is shown in which, in this example, single poles of the constructs are rated as follows:

Not at all like				Very much like
		Average		

1	2	3	4	5

Bannister and Mair[6] suggest several methods for calculating relationships between constructs from the rating form (pp. 63–5). For a detailed discussion of measures of construct relationships, see Fransella and Bannister[5] (pp. 60–72).

Source: Adapted from Bannister and Mair, 1968

construct with consequent dangers of distortion in the estimation of construct relationships. Bannister and Mair (1968) suggest two methods for dealing with this problem which we illustrate in Box 14.2. The first, the 'split-half form', requires the subject to place half the elements at the similarity pole of each construct, by instructing her to decide which element most markedly shows the characteristics specified by each of the constructs. Those elements that are left are allocated to the contrast pole. As Bannister observes, this technique may result in the discarding of constructs (for example, male–female) which cannot be summarily allocated. A second method, the 'rank order form', as its name suggests, requires the subject to rank the elements from the one which most markedly exhibits the particular characteristic (shown by the similarity pole description) to the one which least exhibits it. As the second example in Box 14.2 shows, a rank order correlation coefficient can be used to estimate the extent to which there is similarity in the allotment of elements on any two constructs. Following Bannister, a 'construct relationship' score can be calculated by squaring the correlation coefficient and multiplying by 100. (Because correlations are not linearly related they cannot be used as scores.) The construct relationship score gives an estimate of the percentage variance that the two constructs share in common in terms of the rankings on the two grids.

A third method of allotting elements is the 'rating form'. Here, the subject is required to judge each element on a seven-point or a five-point scale, for example, absolutely beautiful (7) to absolutely ugly (1). Commenting on the advantages of the rating form, Bannister and Mair (1968) note that it offers the subject greater latitude in distinguishing between elements than that provided for in the original form proposed by Kelly. At the same time the degree of differentiation asked of the subject may not be as great as that demanded in the ranking method. As with the rank order method, the rating form approach also allows the use of most correlation techniques. The rating form is the third example illustrated in Box 14.2.

LADDERING

The technique known as laddering arises out of Hinkle's[7] important revision of the theory of personal constructs and the method employed in his research. Hinkle's concern was for the location of any construct within an individual's construct system, arguing that a construct has differential implications within a given hierarchical context. He went on to develop an Implication Grid or Impgrid, in which the subject is required to compare each of his constructs with every other to see which implies the other. The question 'why?' is asked over and over again to identify the position of any construct in an individual's hierarchical

Box 14.3 Laddering

Constructs	Elements teachers							
	A	B	C	D	E	F	G	H
masculine	2	1	5	4	3	6	8	7
serious	6	2	1	3	8	4	5	7
good teacher								
authoritarian								
sexy								
old								
gets on with others								
lonely								
like me in character								
like I hope to become								

A matrix of rankings for a repertory grid with teachers as elements

You may decide to stop when you have elicited seven or eight constructs from the teacher elements. But you could go on to 'ladder' two or three of them. This process of laddering is in effect asking yourself (or someone else) to abstract from one conceptual level to another. You could ladder from *man–woman*, but it might be easier to start off with *serious–light-hearted*. Ask yourself which you would prefer to be – *serious* or *light-hearted*. You might reply *light-hearted*. Now pose the question 'why'. Why would you rather be a *light-hearted* person than a *serious* person? Perhaps the answer would be that *light-hearted* people *get on better with others* than do *serious* people. Ask yourself 'why' again. Why do you want to be the sort of person who gets on better with others? Perhaps it transpires that you think that people who do not get on well with others are *lonely*. In this way you elicit more constructs but ones that stand on the shoulders of those previously elicited. Whatever constructs you have obtained can be put into the grid.

Source: Adapted from Fransella, 1975

construct system. Box 14.3 illustrates Hinkle's laddering technique with an example from educational research reported by Fransella.[8]

GRID ADMINISTRATION AND ANALYSIS

The example of grid administration and analysis outlined below employs the split-half method of allocating elements to constructs and a form of 'anchor analysis' devised by Bannister. We assume that 16 elements and 15 constructs have already been elicited by means of a technique such as the one illustrated in Box 14.1.

PROCEDURES IN GRID ADMINISTRATION

Draw up a grid measuring 16 (elements) by 15 (constructs) as in Figure 14.1, writing along the top the names of the elements, but first inserting the additional element, 'self'. Alongside the rows write in the construct poles.

You now have a grid in which each intersection or cell is defined by a particular column (element) and a particular row (construct). The administration takes the form of allocating every element on every construct. If, for example, your first construct is 'kind–cruel', allocate each element in turn on that dimension, putting a cross in the appropriate box if you consider that person (element) kind, or leaving it blank if you consider that person cruel. Make sure that half of the elements are designated kind and half cruel.

Proceed in this way for each construct in turn, always placing a cross where the construct pole to the left of the grid applies, and leaving it blank if the construct pole to the right is applicable. Every element must be allocated in this way, and half of the elements must always be allocated to the left-hand pole.

PROCEDURES IN GRID ANALYSIS

The grid may be regarded as a reflection of conceptual structure in which constructs are linked by virtue of their being applied to the same persons (elements). This linkage is measured by a process of matching construct rows.

To estimate the linkage between Constructs 1 and 2 in Box 14.4, for example, count the number of matches between corresponding boxes in each row. A match is counted where the same element has been designated with a cross (or a blank) on both constructs. So, for Constructs 1 and 2 in Box 14.4, we count 6 such matches. By chance we would expect 8 (out of 16) matches, and we may subtract this from the observed value to arrive at an estimate of such deviation from chance.

Constructs	Match	Difference score
1–2	6	6 − 8 = −2

By matching Construct 1 against all remaining constructs (3 . . . 15), we get a score for each comparison. Beginning then with Construct 2, and comparing this with every other construct (3 . . . 15), and so on, every construct on the grid is matched with every other one and a difference score for each obtained. This is recorded in matrix form, with the reflected half of the table also filled in (see difference score for Constructs 1–2 in Box 14.5). The sign of the difference score is retained. It indicates

Box 14.4 Elements

Construct	Self	1	2	3	4	5	6	7	8	9	10	11	12	13	14	15	Construct
KIND	x		x				x	x			x	x	x			x	CRUEL
CONFIDENT	x	x		x	x		x			x		x		x			UNSURE
‾‾‾																	‾‾‾
‾‾‾																	‾‾‾
‾‾‾																	‾‾‾

Box 14.5 Difference score for constructs

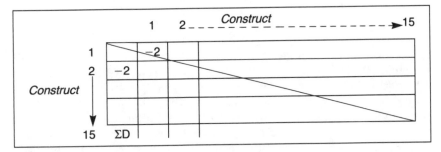

the direction of the linkage. A positive sign shows that the constructs are positively associated, a negative sign that they are negatively associated.

Now add up (without noting sign) the sum of the difference scores for each column (construct) in the matrix. The construct with the largest difference score is the one which, statistically, accounts for the greatest amount of variance in the grid. Note this down. Now look in the body of the matrix for that construct which has the largest non-significant association with the one which you have just noted (in the case of a 16-element grid as in Box 14.4, this will be a difference score of ± 3 or less). This second construct can be regarded as a dimension which is orthogonal to the first, and together they may form the axes for mapping the person's psychological space.

If we imagine the construct with the highest difference score to be 'kind–cruel' and the highest non-significant associated construct to be 'confident–unsure', then every other construct in the grid may be plotted with reference to these two axes. The coordinates for the map are provided by the difference scores relating to the matching of each construct with the two used to form the axes of the graph. In this way a pictorial representation of the individual's 'personal construct space' can be obtained, and inferences made from the spatial relationships between plotted constructs, (see Box 14.6).

Box 14.6   Grid matrix

	+8	Kind	
Confident			Unsure
−8		0	+8
	−8	Cruel	

By rotating the original grid 90 degrees and carrying out the same matching procedure on the columns (figures), a similar map may be obtained for the people (figures) included in the grid.

Grid matrices can be subjected to analyses of varying degrees of complexity. We have illustrated one of the simplest ways of calculating relationships between constructs in Box 14.5. For the statistically-minded researcher, a variety of programs exist in GAP, the Grid Analysis Package developed by Slater and described by Chetwynd.[9] GAP programs analyse the single grid, pairs of grids and grids in groups. Grids may be aligned either by construct, by element or both. A fuller discussion of metric factor analysis is given in Fransella and Bannister (1977: 73–81) and Pope and Keen (1981: 77–91).[10]

Non-metric methods of grid analysis make no assumptions about the linearity of relationships between the variables and the factors. Moreover, where the researcher is primarily interested in the relationships between elements, multi-dimensional scaling may prove a more useful approach to the data than principal components analysis.

The choice of one method rather than another must ultimately rest both upon what is statistically correct and what is psychologically desirable. The danger in the use of advanced computer programs, as Fransella and Bannister point out, is being caught up in the numbers game. Their plea is that grid users should have at least an intuitive grasp of the processes being so competently executed by their computers!

STRENGTHS OF REPERTORY GRID TECHNIQUE

It is in the application of interpretive perspectives in social research, where the investigator seeks to understand the meaning of events to those participating, that repertory grid technique offers exciting possibilities. It is particularly able to provide the researcher with an abundance and a richness of interpretable material. Repertory grid is, of course, especially suitable for the exploration of relationships between an individual's personal constructs as the studies of Foster[11] and Neimeyer,[12] for example, show. Foster employed a Grids Review and Organizing Workbook (GROW), a structured exercise based on personal construct theory, to help a 16-year-old boy articulate constructs relevant to his career goals. Neimeyer's career counselling used a Vocational Reptest with a 19-year-old female student who compared and contrasted various vocational elements (occupations), laddering techniques being employed to determine construct hierarchies. Repertory grid is equally adaptable to the problem of identifying changes in individuals that occur as a result of some educational experience. By way of example, Burke, Noller and Caird[13] identified changes in the constructs of a cohort of technical teacher trainees during the course of their two-year studies leading to qualified status.

In modified formats (the 'dyad' and the 'double dyad') repertory grid has employed relationships between people as elements, rather than people themselves, and demonstrated the increased sensitivity of this type of grid in identifying problems of adjustment in such diverse fields as family counselling (Alexander and Neimeyer[14]) and sports psychology (Feixas, Marti and Villegas[15]).

Finally, repertory grid can be used in studying the changing nature of construing and the patterning of relationships between constructs in groups of children from relatively young ages as the work of Epting,[16] Salmon[17] and Applebee[18] have shown.

DIFFICULTIES IN THE USE OF REPERTORY GRID TECHNIQUE

Fransella and Bannister (1977) point to a number of difficulties in the development and use of grid technique, the most important of which is, perhaps, the widening gulf between technical advances in grid forms and analyses and the theoretical basis from which these are derived. There is, it seems, a rapidly expanding grid industry. Small wonder, then, as Fransella and Bannister wryly observe, that studies such as a one-off analysis of the attitudes of a group of people to asparagus, which bears little or no relation to personal construct theory, are on the increase.

A second difficulty relates to the question of bi-polarity in those forms of the grid in which customarily only one pole of the construct is used. Researchers may make unwarranted inferences about constructs' polar opposites. Yorke's illustration of the possibility of the researcher obtaining 'bent' constructs suggests the usefulness of the opposite method (Epting et al.[19]) in ensuring the bi-polarity of elicited constructs.

A third caution is urged with respect to the elicitation and laddering of constructs. Laddering, note Fransella and Bannister, is an art, not a science. Great care must be taken not to impose constructs. Above all, the researcher must learn to listen to her subject(s).

A number of practical problems commonly experienced in rating grids are identified by Yorke.[20] These are:

1 Variable perception of elements of low personal relevance.
2 Varying the context in which the elements are perceived during the administration of the grid.
3 Halo effect intruding into the ratings where the subject sees the grid matrix building up.
4 Accidental reversal of the rating scale (mentally switching from 5 = high to 1 = high, perhaps because 'five points' and 'first' are both ways of describing high quality). This can happen both within and between constructs, and is particularly likely where a negative or implicitly negative property is ascribed to the pair during triadic elicitation.
5 Failure to follow the rules of the rating procedure. For example, where the pair has had to be rated at the high end of a five-point scale, triads have been found in a single grid rated as 5, 4, 4; 1, 1, 2; 1, 2, 4 which must call into question the constructs and their relationship with the elements.

More fundamental criticism of repertory grid, however, argues that it exhibits a nomothetic positivism that is discordant with the very theory on which it is based. Whatever the method of rating, ranking or dichotomous allocation of elements on constructs, is there not an implicit assumption, asks Yorke, that the construct is stable across all of the elements being rated? Similar to scales of measurement in the physical sciences, elements are assigned to positions on a fixed scale of meaning as though the researcher were dealing with length or weight. But meaning, Yorke reminds us, is 'anchored in the shifting sands of semantics'. This he ably demonstrates by means of a hypothetical problem of rating four people on the construct 'generous–mean'. Yorke shows that it would require a finely-wrought grid of enormous proportions to do justice to the nuances of meaning that could be elicited in respect of the chosen construct. The charge that the rating of elements on constructs and the subsequent statistical analyses retain a positivistic core in what purports to be a non-positivistic methodology is difficult to refute.

Finally, growing sophistication in computer-based analyses of repertory grid forms leads inevitably to a growing language of concepts by which to describe the complexity of what can be found within matrices. It would be ironic, would it not, Fransella and Bannister ask, if repertory grid technique were to become absorbed into the traditions of psychological testing and employed in terms of the assumptions which underpin such testing. From measures to traits is but a short step, they warn.

SOME EXAMPLES OF THE USE OF REPERTORY GRID IN EDUCATIONAL RESEARCH

Our first two examples of the use of personal constructs in education have to do with course evaluation, albeit one less directly than the other. The first study employs the triadic sorting procedure that Kelly originally suggested some forty years ago; the second illustrates the use of sophisticated interactive software in the elicitation and analysis of personal constructs.

Kremer-Hayon's[21] study sought to answer two questions: first, 'What are the personal constructs by which headteachers relate to their staff?' and second, 'To what extent can those constructs be made more "professional"?' The subjects of her research were thirty junior school headteachers participating in an in-service university programme to do with school organization and management, educational leadership and curriculum development. The broad aim of the course was to improve the professional functioning of its participants.

Headteachers' personal constructs were elicited through the triadic sorting procedure in the following way:

1 Participants were provided with ten cards which they numbered 1 to 10. On each card they wrote the name of a member of staff with whom they worked at school.
2 They were then required to arrange the cards in threes, according to arbitrarily-selected numbers provided by the researcher.
3 Finally, they were asked to suggest one way in which two of the three named teachers in any one triad were similar and one way in which the third member was different.

During the course of the two-year in-service programme, the triadic sorting procedure was undertaken on three occasions: Phase 1 at the beginning of the first year, Phase 2 at the beginning of the second year, and Phase 3 two months later, after participants had engaged in a workshop aimed at enriching and broadening their perspectives as a result of analysing personal constructs elicited during Phases 1 and 2. Specifically, the workshop involved the analysis of leadership situations, during which participants were encouraged to state their views and attitudes and to enlarge on the actual behaviour they would engage in were they to be involved in the educational incidents under exploration. Participants received continuous feedback from their colleagues during Phase 3, the course director's task at this point being to broaden the headteachers' perspectives by pointing out additional possible frames of reference in connection with the leadership situations under scrutiny.

The analysis of the personal construct data generated categories derived directly from the headteachers' sortings. Categories were counted separately for each and for all headteachers, thus yielding personal and group profiles. This part of the analysis was undertaken by two judges working independently, who had previously attained 85 per cent agreement on equivalent data. In classifying categories as 'professional' Kremer-Hayon drew on a research literature which included the following attributes of a profession: 'a specific body of knowledge and expertise, teaching skill, theory and research, accountability, commitment, code of ethics, solidarity and autonomy'. Descriptors were further differentiated as 'cognitive' and 'affective'. By way of example, the first three attributes of professionalism listed above, (specific body of knowledge, teaching skills and theory and research) were taken to connote cognitive aspects; the next four, affective. Various elicited descriptions from the headteacher group pertained to personality traits applicable to any occupational group, for example, loyal, friendly, intelligent and cheerful. Others referred to background information, and yet others, that defied a clear classification, were referred to as 'miscellaneous'.

Thus, the data were classified into the following categories:

professional features   (cognitive and affective)
general features   (cognitive and affective)
background data   (professional and non-professional)
miscellaneous

By way of example, we illustrate the above classification from the headteacher data:

professional cognitive   (knowledgeable, rational planners, mastery of teaching skills)
professional affective   (dedicated to teaching, accountable, good peer relationships)
general cognitive   (intelligent, bright)
general affective   (loyal, friendly, cheerful)
background data professional   (number of years of study, schooling, seniority, subject specialism)
background data non-professional   (age, sex, origin, family status)

Box 14.7 shows the *group categories* elicited at Phase 1, the beginning of the in-service programme; at Phase 2, after one year; and at Phase 3, following headteachers' participation in the workshop. Kremer-Hayon interprets her results as follows:

At the onset of the in-service programme, the group of headteachers related to their teaching staff by general rather than

Box 14.7   Teacher descriptor distribution (%)

| | Professional | | General | | Background | | |
Phase	Cognitive	Affective	Cognitive	Affective	Professional	General	Misc.
1	5	29	0	43	3	15	5
2	8	31	4	32	15	10	
3	20	30	5	25	15	5	

Source: Kremer-Hayon, 1991

professional descriptors, and by affective rather than cognitive descriptors. The overall group profile at Phase 1 appeared to be non-professional and affective. This patterning changed at the onset of the second year when, as far as professional descriptors were concerned, a more balanced picture emerged. Upon the completion of the workshop (Phase 3), there was a substantial change towards a professional direction.

(Kremer-Hayon, 1991)

Kremer-Hayon concludes that the growth in the number of descriptors pertaining to professional features bears some promise for professional staff development.

Fisher *et al.*'s[22] research report arose out of an evaluation of a two-year Diploma course in a College of Further and Higher Education. Repertory Grid was chosen as a particularly suitable means of helping students chart their way through the course of study and reveal to them aspects of their personal and professional growth. At the same time, it was felt that Repertory Grid would provide tutors and course directors with important feedback about teaching, examining and general management of the course as a whole.

'Flexigrid', the interactive software used in the study, was chosen to overcome what the authors identify as the major problem of grid production and subsequent exploration of emerging issues – the factor of time. 'Flexigrid', they opine, offers the following advantages:

1 A 'conversational' program, 'Pegasus', which allows respondents to insert their own elements and leads them through a number of triadic elicitations.
2 A variety of statistical programs which permit analysis of the relationships between different constructs on the one hand and elements on the other. Graphically, these 'clusters' are represented as 'trees' and stored as data files. The authors used a technique of analysis named 'Focus' to obtain trees of related elements and constructs.
3 The facility to produce print-outs of these relationship trees lending themselves to straightforward interpretation.

4 A program, 'Setgrid', which allows users to set up the grid elicitation in various ways, for example, using a bank of stored constructs, or writing one's own conversational introduction.
5 'Flexigrid' will run on any machine that is IBM compatible.

During the course of the Diploma, five three-hour sessions were set aside for training and the elicitation of grids. Students were issued with a booklet containing exact instructions on using the computer. They were asked to identify six items they felt important in connection with their Diploma course. These six elements, along with the constructs arising from the triads selected by the software were entered into the computer. Students worked singly using the software and then discussed their individual findings in pairs, having already been trained how to interpret

Box 14.8   Raw grids for Student H

First occasion

Constructs						Ratings					
Pole	Contrast	1	2	3	4	5	6	7	8	9	
heavy workload	light workload	1 1	5	1	3	2	2	1	1	3	
passing assignments	course content	2 2	5	1	5	1	1	3	3	5	
negative	positive	3 1	5	1	5	5	5	5	1	5	
long term	short term	4 4	5	3	5	1	1	3	1	3	

```
                           *  *  *  *  *  *  *  *    prof awareness
                           *  *  *  *  *  *  *   age
                           *  *  *  *  *  *   peer support
      Elements →           *  *  *  *  *   career development
                           *  *  *  *   passport
                           *  *  *   relevance
                           *  *   coping
                           *   enjoyment
                           interference
```

Second occasion

Constructs				Ratings		
Pole	Contrast	1	2	3	4	5 6
leisure time	none	1 1	1	5	5	3 5
short term	long term	2 2	2	4	5	1 1
encouraging	discouraging	3 3	5	5	4	1 5
satisfaction	dissonance	4 3	5	4	5	2 5

```
                      *  *  *  *  *   colleague support
                      *  *  *  *   peer support
                      *  *  *   credibility
      Elements →      *  *   relevance
                      *   time
                      assignments
```

Source: Adapted from Fisher *et al.*, 1991

314

the 'maps' that appeared on the printouts. Individuals' and partners' interpretations were then entered in the students' booklets. Tape-recorders were made available for recording conversations between pairs. The analysis of the data in the research report derives from a series of computer print-outs accompanied by detailed student commentaries, together with field notes made by the researchers and two sets of taped discussions. The student-generated data consist of first, a raw grid showing ratings for elements on two occasions, second, element trees on two occasions indicating clustering, and third, construct trees on two occasions, again showing clusters. By way of illustration, Box 14.8 shows raw grids for Student H taken some six months apart, the first occasion being at the commencement of the Diploma course.

From the raw grid data of Diploma course members, the researchers were able to obtain valuable insights of the impact of the curriculum and teaching on the student body; moreover, they were able to augment and extend the grid data with students' tape recordings and their own field notes. By way of example, Fisher, Russell and McSweeney deduced from the first grid elicitation of Student H that: 'Enjoyment' was linked strongly with the constructs 'short term', 'positive', 'course content' and 'light workload', and that 'Relevance' was also seen to be linked with 'positive', 'course content' and 'light workload'.

Student H's taped comments on the grid yielded the following comments:

Age/coping may prevent me from experiencing positive aspects of the course, e.g., relevance, enjoyment and professional awareness.

In the long term, passing assignments and the Diploma is my goal, but in the short term, course content is important.

Definite views about positive and negative aspects of the course. Crucial aspects seem to be career development and academic progression – tempered by the negative influences, e.g., age, interference, coping.

(Fisher, Russell and McSweeney, 1991)

From Student H's second grid elicitation, the researchers determined that 'peer support' was seen as being most positive, while 'time' and 'credibility' were viewed as negative. 'Colleague support' was also seen to be lacking. 'Enjoyment', 'passport', 'professional awareness' and 'career development' had also disappeared. Tape-recorded evidence again augmented the grid data.

My main preoccupation as far as the course is concerned seems to be the negative attitude of my work colleagues leading me to question the credibility of the course.

315

Positive peer support (with other Diploma students) does not help me with either of these things (i.e. relevance to practice and credibility of qualification).

Reflecting on his/her perceived changes between the first and the second grid elicitation, Student H observed:

My emphasis seems to have shifted from coping with the course in terms of time/managing assignments to questioning why I am doing it all!

(Fisher, Russell and McSweeney, 1991)

From a scrutiny of all Diploma student grids and commentaries, Fisher, Russell and McSweeney drew the following conclusions about students' changing reactions to their studies as the course progressed.

1 The over-riding student concerns were to do with anxiety and stress connected with the completion of assignments; such concerns, moreover, linked directly to the role of assessors.
2 Extrinsic factors took over from intrinsic ones, that is to say, finishing the course became more important than its intrinsic value.
3 Tutorial support was seen to provide a cushion against excessive stress and fear of failure. There was some evidence that tutors had not been particularly successful at defusing problems to do with external gradings.

The researchers were satisfied with the potential of 'Flexigrid' as a tool for course evaluation. Particularly pleasing was the high level of internal validity shown by the congruence of results from the focused grids and the content analysis of students' commentaries. 'Flexigrid', Fisher Russell and McSweeney contend, removed the tedium of analysis and the problem of drawing out 'trees' for visual interpretation. Encouraging students initially to note their views and discuss them with a partner avoided the problem of protracted one-to-one interviews with a consultant. The participants, the authors assert, showed that they were generally able to analyse and make meaning of the focused diagrams.

SOME APPLICATIONS OF REPERTORY GRID TO TEACHING AND LEARNING

The 'perception of trouble in school' technique

Harré and Rosser's account[23] of ethogenically-oriented research into the rules governing disorderly behaviour among secondary school leavers parallels both the spirit and the approach of an extension of Repertory Grid described by Ravenette.[24]

316

Ravenette's interest is in children's perception of troubles in school. His approach is to offer the participant eight pictures of ordinary situations in school that are purposely drawn with some ambiguity as to detail but otherwise are straightforward. The individual is then invited, by a series of questions, to isolate and describe the child who might be troubled or upset. 'What do you think is happening?', he is asked, and similarly, 'Who might be troubled and why?', 'How did this come about?', etc.

Ravenette goes on to describe a method of 'shaking out' the personal attributes' implications for the participant which shows how that individual actually perceives various school situations, how he understands some of the interactions occurring there, how willingly he identifies himself with these situations, and the extent of his grasp of various ways of coping with them. Ravenette then uses an implications grid procedure to reduce to manageable proportions the wealth of ideas generated by the 'perception of troubles in school' technique.

'Impoverishing' repertory grid data

In a study of student teachers' perceptions of the teaching practice situation, Osborne[25] employed 13×13 matrices to elicit elements (significant role incumbents) whose names remained secret from the researcher. Randomized triads were then identified and used to obtain constructs. Cluster analysis of the data provided a hierarchical picture of each students' grouping of constructs. Following a method devised by Smith and Leach,[26] she then quantified the hierarchical structure by impoverishing each subject's construct system, all constructs interrelating above the 0.05 level of significance being collapsed into one construct.

Osborne demonstrated the utility of her repertory grid data in illuminating case study reports of individual students compiled by teaching practice supervisors and headteachers over three teaching practice sessions.

GRID TECHNIQUE AND AUDIO/VIDEO LESSON RECORDING

Parsons et al.[27] show how grid technique and audio/video recordings of teachers' work in classrooms can be used to make explicit the 'implicit models' that teachers have of how children learn.

Fourteen children were randomly selected and, on the basis of individual photographs, triadic comparisons were made to elicit constructs concerning one teacher's ideas about the similarities and differences in the manner in which these children learned. In addition, extensive

317

Box 14.9   Mrs C's model of the manner in which children learn

Drawn largely from quantitative analysis		*Drawn largely from thematic analysis*

High achievers

Retain concepts		Tend to thrive on
Are intelligent		competition
Comprehend easily		Less anxious if wrong*
Appear able to order		Less easily satisfied
thoughts in written		Less likely to misbehave
work		Weaker emotional
Independent learners		attachment if
Good memories		motivated
Prefer discovery		Less likely to suffer
Can concretize alone		functional fixity
Cope better with	All learning	More likely to question*
uncertainty	needs to be	High work rate*
More able to transfer	meaningful	
concepts	(New material	
More able to follow	must be	
logical progression	related to old)	

Average achievers

Coping with uncertainty
depends on the
problem
Same rate learning
important* for all
Discovery learning not
helpful*

Low achievers

Do not retain concepts	All pupils to be	Tend not to worry
Less intelligent	taught as	about competition
Comprehend less easily	individuals	More anxious if wrong*
Less able to order		More easily satisfied
thoughts in written		More likely to misbehave
work		Stronger emotional
Dependent learners		attachment if
Poor memories		motivated
Prefer instruction		More likely to suffer
Need help to concretize		functional fixity
Cope less well with		Less likely to question*
uncertainty		Less likely to be
Less able to transfer		encouraged by
concepts		success
Less able to follow logical		Low work rate*
progression		

*Central themes for Mrs C.

Source: Parsons *et al.*, 1983

observations of the teacher's classroom behaviour were undertaken under naturalistic conditions and verbatim recordings (audio and video) were made for future review and discussion between the teacher and the researchers at the end of each recording session. The authors stress that the whole study was carried out in a spirit of mutual enquiry, the researchers and the teacher joining together in using the analysis of the repertory grid as a source of counter or confirmatory accounts in the gradual identification of her implicit view of children's learning.

What very soon became evident in these ongoing complementary analyses was the clear distinction that Mrs C (the teacher) held for high and low achievers. The analysis of the children in class as shown in the video tapes revealed that not only did high and low achievers sit in separate groups but the teacher's whole approach to these two groupings differed:

> With high achievers, Mrs C would often adopt a 'working with' approach, i.e. verbalising what children had done, with their help. When confronted with low achievers, Mrs C would more often ask 'why' they had tackled problems in a certain manner, and wait for an answer.
>
> (Parsons *et al.*, 1983)

The final picture of Mrs C's model of children as learners is shown in Box 14.9. The researchers point to the usefulness of their approach as a starting point for working with teachers on in-service education programmes.

Focused grids, non-verbal grids, exchange grids and sociogrids

A number of developments have been reported in the use of computer programs in repertory grid research.[28] We briefly identify these as follows:

1 Focusing a grid assists in the interpretation of raw grid data. Each element is compared with every other element and the ordering of elements in the grid is changed so that those most alike are clustered most closely together. A similar rearrangement is made in respect of each construct.
2 Physical objects can be used as elements and grid elicitation is then carried out in non-verbal terms. Thomas claims that this approach enhances the exploration of sensory and perceptual experiences.
3 Exchange grids are procedures developed to enhance the quality of conversational exchanges. Basically, one person's construing provides the format for an empty grid which is offered to another person for completion. The empty grid consists of the first person's verbal

descriptions from which his ratings have been deleted. The second person is then invited to test his comprehending of the first person's point of view by filling in the grid as he believes the other has already completed it. Various computer programs ('Pairs', 'Cores' and 'Difference') are available to assist analysis of the processes of negotiation elicited in exchange grids.

4 In the 'Pairs' analysis, all constructs in one grid are compared with all constructs in the other grid and a measure of commonality in construing is determined. 'Pairs' analysis leads on to 'Sociogrids' in which the pattern of relationships between the grids of one group can be identified. In turn, 'Sociogrids' can provide a mode grid for the whole group or a number of mode grids identifying cliques. 'Socionets' which reveal the pattern of shared construing can also be derived.

With these brief examples, the reader will catch something of the flavour of what can be achieved using the various manifestations of repertory grid techniques in the field of educational research.

REFERENCES AND NOTES

1 Kelly, G.A., *Clinical Psychology and Personality: the Selected Papers of George Kelly*, edited by B.A. Maher (Wiley, New York, 1969).
2 Bannister, D. (ed.), *Perspectives in Personal Construct Theory* (Academic Press, London, 1970).
3 Ryle, A., *Frames and Cages: The Repertory Grid Approach to Human Understanding* (Sussex University Press, Brighton, 1975).
4 Adams-Webber, J.R., 'Elicited versus provided constructs in repertory grid technique: a review', *Brit. J. Med. Psychol.*, 43 (1970) 349–54.
5 Fransella, F. and Bannister, D., *A Manual for Repertory Grid Technique* (Academic Press, London, 1977).
6 Bannister, D. and Mair, J.M.M., *The Evaluation of Personal Constructs* (Academic Press, London, 1968).
7 Hinkle, D.N., 'The change of personal constructs from the viewpoint of a theory of implications', unpublished PhD thesis (Ohio State University, 1965).
8 Fransella, F., *Need to Change?* (Methuen, London, 1975).
9 Chetwynd, S.J., 'Outline of the analyses available with G.A.P., the Grid Analysis Package' (St George's Hospital, London, SW17, 1974). See also UMRCC, *GAP: Grid Analysis Package* (University of Manchester Regional Computing Centre, Manchester, 1981).
10 Pope, M.L. and Keen, T.R., *Personal Construct Psychology and Education* (Academic Press, London, 1981).
11 Foster, J.R., 'Eliciting personal constructs and articulating goals', *Journal of Career Development*, 18 (3) (1992) 175–85. See also: Slater, P., *The Measurement of Interpersonal Space, Vol. 2* (Wiley, Chichester, 1977).
12 Neimeyer, G.J., 'Personal constructs in career counselling and development', *Journal of Career Development*, 18 (3) (1992) 163–73.
13 Burke, M., Noller, P. and Caird, D. 'Transition from probationer to educator: a repertory grid analysis', *International Journal of Personal Construct*

Psychology, 5 (2) (1992), 159–82. See also the following applications of personal construct theory to research on teachers and teacher groups: Lehrer, R. and Franke, M.L., 'Applying personal construct psychology to the study of teachers' knowledge of fractions', *Journal for Research in Mathematical Education*, 23 (3) (1992) 223–41; Shapiro, B.L., 'A collaborative approach to help novice science teachers reflect on changes in their construction of the role of the science teacher', *Alberta Journal of Educational Research*, 36(3) (1990) 203–22; Corporaal, A.H., 'Repertory grid research into cognitions of prospective primary school teachers', *Teaching and Teacher Education*, 36 (1991) 315–29; Shaw, E.L., 'The influence of methods instruction on the beliefs of preservice elementary and secondary science teachers: preliminary comparative analyses', *School Science and Mathematics*, 92 (1992) 14–22; Cole, A.L., 'Personal theories of teaching: development in the formative years', *Alberta Journal of Educational Research*, 37(2) (1991) 119–32.

14 Alexander, P.C. and Neimeyer, G.J., 'Constructivism and family therapy', *International Journal of Personal Construct Psychology*, 2(2) (1989) 111–21.

15 Feixas, G., Marti, J. and Villegas, M. 'Personal construct assessment of sports teams', *International Journal of Personal Construct Psychology*, 2(1) (1989) 49–54.

16 Epting, F.R., 'Journeying into the personal constructs of children', *International Journal of Personal Construct Psychology*, 1(1) (1988) 53–61.

17 Salmon, P., 'Differential conforming of the developmental process', *Brit. J. Soc. Clin. Psychol.*, 8 (1969) 22–31.

18 Applebee, A.N., 'The development of children's responses to repertory grids', *Brit. J. Soc. Clin. Psychol.*, 15 (1976) 101–2.

19 Epting, F.R., Suchman, D.I. and Nickeson, K.J., 'An evaluation of elicitation procedures for personal constructs', *Brit. J. Psychol.*, 62 (1971) 513–17.

20 Yorke, D.M., 'Repertory grids in educational research: some methodological considerations', *British Educational Research Journal*, 4(2) (1978) 63–74. See also Yorke, D.M. 'Indexes of stability in repertory grids: a small-scale comparison, *British Educational Research Journal*, 11(3) (1985) 221–5.

21 Kremer-Hayon, L., 'Personal constructs of elementary school principals in relation to teachers', *Research in Education*, 43 (1991) 15–21.

22 Fisher, B., Russell, T. and McSweeney, P., 'Using personal constructs for course evaluation', *Journal of Further and Higher Education*, 15(1) (1991) 44–57.

23 Harré, R. and Rosser, E., 'The rules of disorder', *The Times Educational Supplement*, 25 July 1975.

24 Ravenette, A.T., 'Psychological investigation of children and young people', in Bannister, D. (ed.), *New Perspectives in Personal Construct Theory* (Academic Press, London, 1977).

25 Osborne, J.I., 'College of education students' perceptions of the teaching situation', unpublished MEd dissertation (University of Liverpool, 1977).

26 Smith, S. and Leach, C., 'A hierarchical measure of cognitive complexity', *Brit. J. Psychol.*, 63(4) (1972) 561–8.

27 Parsons, J.M., Graham, N. and Honess, T., 'A teacher's implicit model of how children learn', *British Educational Research Journal*, 9(1) (1983) 91–101.

28 Thomas, L.F., 'A personal construct approach to learning in education, training and therapy', in Fransella, F. (ed.), *Personal Construct Psychology* (Academic Press, London, 1978). See also Pope, M.L. and Keen, T.R., *Personal Construct Psychology and Education* (Academic Press, London, 1981), especially chapters 8 and 9; Shaw, M.L.G. (ed.), *Recent Advances in Personal Construct Technology* (Academic Press, London, 1981); Thomas, L.F. and Harri-Augstein, E.S., *Self-organized Learning* (Routledge, London, 1992).

15

MULTI-DIMENSIONAL
MEASUREMENT

INTRODUCTION

However limited our knowledge of astronomy, most of us have learned to pick out certain clusterings of stars from the infinity of those that crowd the Northern skies and to name them as the familiar Plough, Orion, and the Great Bear. Few of us would identify constellations in the Southern Hemisphere that are instantly recognizable by our Australian friends. But we don't happen to live 'down under'.

Our predilection for reducing the complexity of elements that constitute our lives to a more simple order doesn't stop at star gazing. In numerous ways, each and every one of us attempts to discern patterns or shapes in seemingly unconnected events in order to better grasp their significance for us in the conduct of our daily lives. The educational researcher is no exception.

As research into a particular aspect of human activity progresses, the variables being explored frequently turn out to be more complex than was first realized. Investigation into the relationship between teaching styles and pupil achievement is a case in point. Global distinctions between behaviour identified as progressive or traditional, informal or formal, are vague and woolly and have led inevitably to research findings that are at worse inconsistent, at best, inconclusive. In reality, epithets such as informal or formal in the context of teaching and learning relate to 'multi-dimensional concepts', that is, concepts made up of a number of variables. 'Multi-dimensional scaling', on the other hand, is a way of analysing judgements of similarity between such variables in order that the dimensionality of those judgements can be assessed.[1] As regards research into teaching styles and pupil achievement, it has been suggested that multi-dimensional typologies of teacher behaviour should be developed. Such typologies, it is believed, would enable the researcher to group together similarities in teachers' judgements about specific aspects of their classroom organization and management, and their ways of motivating, assessing and instructing pupils.

Box 15.1   Rank ordering of ten children on seven constructs

	INTELLIGENT		SOCIABLE
(*favourable*)	1 Heather	(*favourable*)	1 Caroline
	2 Richard		2 Richard
	3 Caroline		3 Sharon
	4 Tim		4 Jane
	5 Patrick		5 Tim
	6 Sharon		6 Janice
	7 Janice		7 Heather
	8 Jane		8 Patrick
	9 Alex		9 Karen
(*unfavourable*)	10 Karen	(*unfavourable*)	10 Alex
	AGGRESSIVE		NOISY
(*unfavourable*)	10 Alex	(*unfavourable*)	10 Alex
	9 Patrick		9 Patrick
	8 Tim		8 Karen
	7 Karen		7 Tim
	6 Richard		6 Caroline
	5 Caroline		5 Richard
	4 Heather		4 Heather
	3 Jane		3 Janice
	2 Sharon		2 Sharon
(*favourable*)	1 Janice	(*favourable*)	1 Jane
	VERBALLY-GOOD		CLUMSY
(*favourable*)	1 Richard	(*unfavourable*)	10 Alex
	2 Caroline		9 Patrick
	3 Heather		8 Karen
	4 Janice		7 Tim
	5 Patrick		6 Richard
	6 Tim		5 Sharon
	7 Alex		4 Jane
	8 Sharon		3 Janice
	9 Jane		2 Caroline
(*unfavourable*)	10 Karen	(*favourable*)	1 Heather
	WELL-BEHAVED		
(*favourable*)	1 Janice		
	2 Jane		
	3 Sharon		
	4 Caroline		
	5 Heather		
	6 Richard		
	7 Tim		
	8 Karen		
	9 Patrick		
(*unfavourable*)	10 Alex		

Source: Cohen, 1977[3]

Techniques for grouping such judgements are many and various. What they all have in common is that they are methods for 'determining the number and nature of the underlying variables among a large number of measures', a definition which Kerlinger (1970)[2] uses to describe one of the best-known grouping techniques, 'factor analysis'. We begin the chapter by illustrating a number of methods of grouping or clustering variables ranging from elementary linkage analysis which can be undertaken by hand, to factor analysis, which is best left to the computer. We then outline one way of analysing data cast into multi-dimensional tables.

ELEMENTARY LINKAGE ANALYSIS: AN EXAMPLE

Seven constructs were elicited from an infant school teacher who was invited to discuss the ways in which she saw the children in her class (see Chapter 14). She identified favourable and unfavourable constructs as follows: 'intelligent' (+), 'sociable' (+), 'verbally-good' (+), 'well-behaved' (+), 'aggressive' (−), 'noisy' (−) and 'clumsy' (−).

Four boys and six girls were then selected at random from the class register and the teacher was asked to place each child in rank order under each of the seven constructs, using rank position 1 to indicate the child most like the particular construct, and rank position 10, the child least like the particular construct. The teacher's rank ordering is set out in Box 15.1.[3] Notice that on three constructs, the rankings have been reversed in order to maintain the consistency of Favourable = 1, Unfavourable = 10.

Elementary linkage analysis (McQuitty[4]) is one way of exploring the relationship between the teacher's personal constructs, that is, of assessing the dimensionality of the judgements that she makes about her pupils. It seeks to identify and define the clusterings of certain variables

Box 15.2   Intercorrelations between seven personal constructs

		(1)	(2)	(3)	(4)	(5)	(6)	(7)
Intelligent	(1)		53	−10	−16	83	−52	13
Sociable	(2)	53		−50	−59	44	−56	61
Aggressive	(3)	−10	−50		91	−07	79	−96
Noisy	(4)	−16	−59	91		−01	73	−93
Verbally-good	(5)	83	44	−07	−01		−43	12
Clumsy	(6)	−52	−56	79	73	−43		−81
Well-behaved	(7)	13	61	−96	−93	12	−81	
(decimal points omitted)								

Source: Cohen, 1977

Box 15.3   The structuring of relationships among the seven personal constructs

CLUSTER 1	badly behaved	⇌	aggressive
	noisy	clumsy	unsociable
CLUSTER 2	verbally-good	⇌	intelligent
⇌ denotes a reciprocal relationship between two variables			

Source: Cohen, 1977

within a set of variables. Like factor analysis which we shortly illustrate, elementary linkage analysis searches for interrelated groups of correlation coefficients. The objective of the search is to identify 'types'. By type, McQuitty refers to 'a category of people or other objects (personal constructs in our example) such that the members are internally self-contained in being like one another'. Box 15.2 sets out the intercorrelations between the seven personal construct ratings shown in Box 15.1 (Spearman's *rho* is the method of correlation used in this example).

STEPS IN ELEMENTARY LINKAGE ANALYSIS

1 In Box 15.2, underline the strongest, that is the highest, correlation coefficient in each column of the matrix. Ignore negative signs.
2 Identify the highest correlation coefficient in the entire matrix. The two variables having this correlation constitute the first two of Cluster 1.
3 Now identify all those variables which are most like the variables in Cluster 1. To do this, read along the rows of the variables which emerged in Step 2, selecting any of the coefficients which are underlined in the rows. Box 15.3 illustrates diagramatically the ways in which these new cluster members are related to the original pair which initially constituted Cluster 1.
4 Now identify any variables which are most like the variables elicited in Step 3. Repeat this procedure until no further variables are identified.
5 Excluding all those variables which belong within Cluster 1, repeat Steps 2 to 4 until all the variables have been accounted for.

CLUSTER ANALYSIS: AN EXAMPLE[5]

Elementary linkage analysis is one method of grouping or clustering together correlation coefficients which show similarities among a set of variables. We now illustrate another method of clustering which was used by Bennett[6] in his study of teaching styles and pupil progress. His

325

Box 15.4 Central profiles (percentage occurrence) at 12-cluster levels

Item		1	2	3	4	5	6	7	8	9	10	11	12
							Type						
1	Pupils have choice in where to sit	**63**	**66**	**17**	**46**	**50**	18	7	17	3	7	**77**	**00**
2	Pupils allocated to seating by ability	**14**	**16**	25	**0**	**12**	**45**	20	7	**81**	**58**	**3**	50
3	Pupils not allowed freedom of movement in the classroom	49	**38**	83	76	100	84	87	100	86	97	97	100
4	Teacher expects pupils to be quiet	31	**34**	92	61	**23**	55	56	90	81	74	**90**	**100**
5	Pupils taken out of school regularly as normal teaching activity	51	50	**83**	49	**81**	45	17	47	31	**19**	26	42
6	Pupils given homework regularly	9	22	**8**	27	**65**	3	**13**	**43**	36	29	21	**56**
	Teaching emphasis												
7	(i) Above average teacher talks to whole class	**29**	**16**	79	58	30	74	83	73	33	**94**	85	70
8	(ii) Above average pupils working in groups on teacher tasks	46	**13**	**83**	12	77	**92**	3	3	22	**68**	**10**	**8**
9	(iii) Above average pupils working in groups of own choice	**89**	3	29	**94**	19	32	13	3	**0**	23	0	0
10	(iv) Above average pupils working individually on teacher tasks	9	**97**	0	3	42	0	**73**	**83**	**100**	0	**72**	**92**
11	(v) Above average pupils working individually on work of own choice	**94**	9	42	**85**	42	**18**	57	57	8	3	8	28

	3	3	13	15	31	16	33	33	8	32	31	97
12 Pupils' work marked and graded	**3**	**3**	**13**	**15**	**31**	**16**	**33**	**33**	**8**	**32**	**31**	**97**
13 Stars given to pupils who produce best work	**9**	31	38	55	**8**	**18**	17	**73**	**17**	**87**	**69**	**75**
14 Arithmetic tests given at least once a week	**9**	9	71	88	**100**	8	10	70	50	**94**	**56**	**81**
15 Spelling tests given at least once a week	**23**	19	67	**94**	**92**	**18**	7	73	**92**	**94**	87	**92**
16 Teacher smacks for persistent disruptive behaviour	34	34	**96**	24	31	45	**80**	**93**	42	68	64	58
17 Teacher sends pupil out of room for persistent disruptive behaviour	11	25	13	6	8	3	7	10	**25**	0	**33**	11
18 Allocation of teaching time (i) Above average separate subject teaching	**20**	**31**	4	82	81	**100**	**100**	47	81	**100**	**100**	92
19 (ii) Above average integrated subject teaching	97	91	100	24	65	8	10	93	14	7	0	0
N in cluster	35	32	24	33	26	38	30	30	36	31	39	36

Source: Bennett.[5]

starting point was a disaffection for global descriptions such as 'progressive' and 'traditional' as applied to teaching styles in junior school classrooms. A more adequate theoretical and experimental conceptualization of the elements constituting teaching styles was attempted through the construction of a questionnaire containing 28 statements illustrating six major areas of teacher classroom behaviour: classroom management and control; teacher control and sanctions; curriculum content and planning; instructional strategies; motivational techniques; and assessment procedures.

Bennett constructed a typology of teaching styles from the responses of 468 top-junior-school classteachers to the questionnaire. His cluster analysis of their responses involved calculating coefficients of similarity between subjects across all the variables that constituted the final version of the questionnaire. This technique involves specifying the number of clusters of subjects to which the researcher wishes the data to be reduced. Examination of the central profiles of all solutions from twenty-two to three clusters, showed that at the twelve-cluster solution level, between-cluster differences were maximized in relation to within-cluster error (see Bennett, 1976). An essential prerequisite to the clustering technique employed in this study was the use of factor analysis to ensure that the variables were relatively independent of one another and that groups of variables were not overweighted in the analysis. Principal Components analysis followed by varimax rotation reduced the twenty-eight variables in Bennett's original questionnaire to the nineteen shown in Box 15.4. For purposes of exposition, Bennett ordered the types of teaching style shown in Box 15.4, from the most progressive cluster (Type 1) to the most traditional cluster (Type 12), noting however, that whilst the extreme types could be described in these terms, the remaining types all contained elements of both progressive and traditional teaching styles. The figures in heavy typeface show percentage response levels that were considered significantly different from the total population distribution.

Bennett described the twelve types of teacher styles as follows:

1 These teachers favour integration of subject matter, and, unlike most other groups, allow pupil choice of work, whether undertaken individually or in groups. Most allow pupils choice of seating. Less than half curb movement and talk. Assessment in all its forms, tests, grading and homework, appears to be discouraged. Intrinsic motivation is favoured.

2 These teachers also prefer integration of subject matter. Teacher control appears to be low, but less pupil choice of work is offered. However, most allow pupils choice of seating, and only one-third curb movement and talk. Few test or grade work.

3 The main teaching mode of this group is class teaching and group work. Integration of subject matter is preferred, associated with taking pupils out of school. They appear to be strict, most curbing movement and talk, and offenders are smacked. The amount of testing is average, but the amount of grading and homework is below average.

4 These teachers prefer separate subject teaching but a high proportion allow pupil choice both in group and individual work. None seat their pupils by ability. They test and grade more than average.

5 A mixture of separate subject and integrated subject teaching is characteristic of this group. The main teaching mode is pupils working in groups of their own choice on tasks set by the teacher. Teacher talk is lower than average. Control is high with regard to movement but not to talk. Most give tests every week and many give homework regularly. Stars are rarely used, and pupils are taken out of school regularly.

6 These teachers prefer to teach subjects separately with emphasis on groups working on teacher-specified tasks. The amount of individual work is small. These teachers appear to be fairly low on control, and are below average on assessment and the use of extrinsic motivation.

7 This group is separate subject oriented, with a high level of class teaching together with individual work. Teacher control appears to be tight, few allow movement or choice of seating, and offenders are smacked. Assessment, however, is low.

8 This group of teachers has very similar characteristics to those in Type 3, the difference being that these prefer to organize the work on an individual rather than group basis. Freedom of movement is restricted, and most expect pupils to be quiet.

9 These teachers favour separate subject teaching, the predominant teaching mode being individuals working on tasks set by the teacher. Teacher control appears to be high; most curb movement and talk, and seat by ability. Pupil choice is minimal. Regular spelling tests are given, but few mark or grade work or use stars.

10 All these teachers favour separate subject teaching. The teaching mode favoured is teacher talk to whole class, and pupils working in groups determined by the teacher, on tasks set by the teacher. Most curb movement and talk, and over two-thirds smack for disruptive behaviour. There is regular testing and most give stars for good work.

11 All members of this group stress separate subject teaching by way of class teaching and individual work. Pupil choice of work is minimal, although most teachers allow choice of seating. Movement and talk are curbed, and offenders smacked.

12 This is an extreme group in a number of respects. None favour an integrated approach. Subjects are taught separately by class teaching and individual work. None allow pupils' choice of seating, and every teacher curbs movement and talk. These teachers are above average on all assessment procedures, and extrinsic motivation predominates.

Bennett's typology of teacher styles and his analysis of pupil performance based on the typology aroused considerable debate. Readers may care to follow up critical comments on the cluster analysis procedures we have outlined here.[7]

FACTOR ANALYSIS: AN EXAMPLE

Factor analysis, we said earlier, is a way of determining the nature of underlying patterns among a large number of variables. It is particularly appropriate in research where investigators aim to impose an 'orderly simplification'[8] upon a number of interrelated measures. We illustrate the use of factor analysis in a study of occupational stress among teachers.[9]

Despite a decade or so of sustained research, the concept of occupational stress still causes difficulties for researchers intent upon obtaining objective measures in such fields as the physiological and the behavioural, because of the wide range of individual differences. Moreover, subjective measures such as self-reports, by their very nature, raise questions about the external validation of respondents' revelations. This latter difficulty notwithstanding, McCormick and Solman (1992) chose the methodology of self-report as the way into the problem, dichotomizing it into first, the teacher's view of self, and second, the external world as it is seen to impinge upon the occupation of teaching. Stress, according to the researchers, is considered as 'an unpleasant and unwelcome emotion' whose negative effect for many is 'associated with illness of varying degree' (McCormick and Solman, 1992). They began their study on the basis of the following premises:

1 Occupational stress is an undesirable and negative response to occupational experiences.
2 To be responsible for one's own occupational stress can indicate a personal failing.

Drawing on attribution theory, McCormick and Solman consider that the idea of blame is a key element in a framework for the exploration of occupational stress. The notion of blame for occupational stress, they assert, fits in well with tenets of attribution theory, particularly in terms of attribution of responsibility having a self-serving bias.[10] Taken in concert with organizational facets of schools, the researchers hypothesized that teachers would 'externalise responsibility for their stress increasingly to increasingly distant and identifiable domains' (McCormick and Solman, 1992). Their selection of dependent and independent variables in the research followed directly from this major hypothesis.

McCormick and Solman developed a questionnaire instrument that included thirty-two items to do with occupational satisfaction. These were scored on a continuum ranging from 'strongly disagree' to 'strongly agree'. Thirty-eight further items had to do with possible sources of occupational stress. Here, respondents rated the intensity of the stress they experienced when exposed to each source. Stress items were judged on a scale ranging from 'no stress' to 'extreme stress'. In yet another section of the questionnaire, respondents rated how responsible they felt certain nominated persons or institutions were for the occupational stress that they, the respondents, experienced. These entities included self, pupils, superiors, the Department of Education, the Government and society itself. Finally, the teacher-participants were asked to complete a fourteen-item Locus of Control scale, giving a measure of internality/externality. 'Internals' are people who see outcomes as a function of what they themselves do; 'externals' see outcomes as a result of forces beyond their control. The items included in this lengthy questionnaire arose partly from statements about teacher stress used in earlier investigations, but mainly as a result of hunches about blame for occupational stress that the researchers derived from attribution theory. As Child observes:

> In most instances, the factor analysis is preceded by a hunch as to the factors that might emerge. In fact, it would be difficult to conceive of a manageable analysis which started in an empty-headed fashion. . . . Even the 'let's see what happens' approach is pretty sure to have a hunch at the back of it somewhere. It is this testing and the generation of hypotheses which forms the principal concern of most factor analysts.
>
> (Child, 1970)

The 90-plus-item inventory was completed by 387 teachers. Separate correlation matrices composed of the inter-correlations of the thirty-two items on the satisfaction scale, the eight items in the persons/institutions responsibility measure and the thirty-eight items on the stress scale were factor analysed.

The technical details of factor analysis are beyond the scope of this book. Briefly, however, the procedures followed by McCormick and Solman involved a method called Principals Components, by means of which factors or groupings are extracted. These are rotated to produce a more meaningful interpretation of the underlying structure than that provided by the Principal Components method. (Readable

331

Box 15.5   Factor analysis of responsibility for stress items

Factor groupings of responsibility items with factor loadings and (rounded) percentages of teachers responding in the two most extreme categories of *much stress* and *extreme stress*.

	Loading	Percentage
Factor 1: School structure		
Superiors	0.85	29
School Organization	0.78	31
Peers	0.77	13
Factor 2: Bureaucratic authority		
Department of Education	0.89	70
Government	0.88	66
Factor 3: Teacher–student relationships		
Students	0.85	45
Society	0.60	60
Yourself	0.50	20

Source: McCormick and Solman, 1992

accounts of factor analysis may be found in Kerlinger (1970) and Child (1970).)

In the factor analysis of the eight-item responsibility for stress measure, the researchers identified three factors. Box 15.5 shows those three factors with what are called their 'factor loadings'. These are like correlation coefficients, ranging from −1.0 to +1.0 and are interpreted similarly. That is to say they indicate the correlation between the person/institution responsibility items shown in Box 15.5, and the factors. Looking at Factor 1, 'School structure', for example, it can be seen that in the three items loading there are, in descending order of weight, superiors (0.85), school organization (0.78) and peers (0.77). 'School structure' as a factor, the authors suggest, is easily-identified and readily-explained. But what of Factor 3, 'Teacher–student relationships', which includes the variables students, society and yourself? McCormick and Solman proffer the following tentative interpretation:

> An explanation for the inclusion of the variable 'yourself' in this factor is not readily at hand. Clearly, the difference between the variable 'yourself' and the 'students' and 'society' variables is that only 20% of these teachers rated themselves as very or extremely responsible for their own stress, compared to 45% and 60% respectively for the latter two. Possibly the degree of responsibility which teachers attribute to themselves for their occupational stress is associated with their perceptions of their part in controlling student behaviour. This would seem a reasonable explanation, but requiring further investigation.

(McCormick and Solman, 1992)

Box 15.6   Factor analysis of the occupational stress items

Factor groupings of stress items with factor loadings and (rounded) percentages of teachers responding to the two extremes of *much stress* and *extreme stress*

	Loading	Percentage
Factor 1: Student domain		
Poor work attitudes of students	0.79	49
Difficulty in motivating students	0.75	44
Having to deal with students who constantly misbehave	0.73	57
Inadequate discipline in the school	0.70	47
Maintaining discipline with difficult classes	0.64	55
Difficulty in setting and maintaining standards	0.63	26
Verbal abuse by students	0.62	39
Students coming to school without necessary equipment	0.56	23
Deterioration of society's control over children	0.49	55
Factor 2: External (to school) domain		
The Government's education policies	0.82	63
The relationship which the Department of Education has with its schools	0.80	55
Unrealistic demands from the Department of Education	0.78	63
The conviction that the education system is getting worse	0.66	49
Media criticism of teachers	0.64	52
Lack of respect in society for teachers	0.63	56
Having to implement Departmental policies	0.59	38
Feeling of powerlessness	0.55	44
Factor 3: Time demands		
Insufficient time for personal matters	0.74	43
Just not enough time in the school day	0.74	51
Difficulty of doing a good job in the classroom because of other delegated responsibilities	0.73	43
Insufficient time for lesson preparation and marking	0.69	50
Excessive curriculum demands	0.67	49
Difficulty in covering the syllabus in the time available	0.61	37
Demanding nature of the job	0.58	64
Factor 4: School domain		
Lack of support from the principal	0.83	21
Not being appreciated by the principal	0.83	14
Principal's reluctance to make tough decisions	0.77	30
Lack of opportunity to participate in school decision-making	0.74	16

Box 15.6   (cont'd)

Lack of support from other colleagues	0.57	11
Lack of a supportive and friendly atmosphere	0.55	17
Things happen at school over which you have no control	0.41	36
Factor 5: Personal domain		
Personal failings	0.76	13
Feeling of not being suited to teaching	0.72	10
Having to teach a subject for which you are not trained	0.64	23

Source: McCormick and Solman, 1992

Box 15.6 shows the factors derived from the analysis of the thirty-eight occupational stress items. Five factors were extracted. They were named: 'Student domain', 'External (to school) domain', 'Time demands', 'School domain' and 'Personal domain'. Whilst a detailed discussion of the factors and their loadings is inappropriate here, we draw readers' attention to one or two interesting findings. Notice, for example, how the second factor, 'External (to school) domain', is consistent with the factoring of the responsibility for stress items reported in Box 15.5. That is to say, the variables to do with the Government and the Department of Education have loaded on the same factor. The researchers venture this further elaboration of the point:

> when a teacher attributes occupational stress to the Department of Education, it is not as a member of the Department of Education, although such, in fact is the case. In this context, the Department of Education is outside 'the system to which the teacher belongs', namely the school. A similar argument can be posed for the nebulous concept of Society. The Government is clearly a discrete political structure.

(McCormick and Solman, 1992)

'School domain', Factor 4 in Box 15.6, consists of items concerned with support from the school principal and colleagues as well as the general nurturing atmosphere of the school. Of particular interest here is that teachers report relatively low levels of stress for these items.

Box 15.7 reports the factor analysis of the thirty-two items to do with occupational satisfaction. Five factors were extracted and named as 'Supervision', 'Income', 'External demands', 'Advancement' and 'School culture'. Again, space precludes a full outline of the results set out in Box 15.7. Notice, however, an apparent anomaly in the first factor, 'Supervision'. Responses to items to do with teachers' supervisors and recognition seem to indicate that in general, teachers are satisfied with their supervisors, but feel that they receive too little recognition. Box

Box 15.7   Factor analysis of the occupational satisfaction items

Factor groupings of satisfaction items with factor loadings and (rounded) percentages of teacher responses in the two positive extremes of 'strongly agree' and 'agree' for positive statements, or 'strongly disagree' and 'disagree' for statements of a negative nature; the latter items were reversed for analysis and are indicated by*

	Loading	*Percentage*
Factor 1: Supervision		
My immediate supervisor does not back me up*	0.83	70
I receive recognition from my immediate supervisor	0.80	52
My immediate supervisor is not willing to listen*	0.78	68
My immediate supervisor makes me feel uncomfortable*	0.78	68
My immediate supervisor treats everyone equitably	0.68	62
My superiors do not appreciate what a good job I do*	0.66	39
I receive too little recognition*	0.51	21
Factor 2: Income		
My income is less than I deserve*	0.80	10
I am well paid in proportion to my ability	0.78	8
My income from teaching is adequate	0.78	19
My pay compares well with other non-teaching jobs	0.66	6
Teachers' income is barely enough to live on*	0.56	24
Factor 3: External demands		
Teachers have an excessive workload*	0.72	5
Teachers are expected to do too many non-teaching tasks*	0.66	4
People expect too much of teachers*	0.56	4
There are too many changes in education*	0.53	10
I am satisfied with the Department of Education as an employer	0.44	12
People who aren't teachers do not understand the realities in schools*	0.34	1
Factor 4: Advancement		
Teaching provides me with an opportunity to advance professionally	0.76	37
I am not getting ahead in my present position*	0.67	16
The Government is striving for a better education system	0.54	22
The Department of Education is concerned for teachers' welfare	0.52	6
Factor 5: School culture		
I am happy to be working at this particular school	0.77	73
Working conditions in my school are good	0.64	46
Teaching is very interesting work	0.60	78

Source: McCormick and Solman, 1992

15.7 shows that 21 per cent of teacher-respondents agree or strongly agree that they receive too little recognition, yet 52 per cent agree or strongly agree that they do receive recognition from their immediate supervisors. McCormick and Solman offer the following explanation:

> The difference can be explained, in the first instance, by the degree or amount of recognition given. That is, immediate supervisors give recognition, but not enough. Another interpretation is that superiors other than the immediate supervisor do not give sufficient recognition for their work.
>
> (McCormick and Solman, 1992)

Here is a clear case for some form of respondent validation (see page 241).

Having identified the underlying structures of occupational stress and occupational satisfaction, the researchers then went on to explore the relationships between stress and satisfaction by using a technique called 'canonical correlation analysis'. The technical details of this procedure are beyond the scope of this book. Interested readers are referred to Levine, who suggests that 'the most acceptable approach to interpretation of canonical variates is the examination of the correlations of the original variables with the canonical variate' (Levine, 1984).[11] This is the procedure adopted by McCormick and Solman.

From Box 15.8 we see that factors having high correlations with Canonical Variate 1 are Stress: Student domain (−0.82) and Satisfaction: External demands (0.72). The researchers offer the following interpretation of this finding:

Box 15.8   Correlations between (dependent) stress and (independent) satisfaction factors and canonical variates

	Canonical variates		
	1	2	3
Stress factors			
Student domain	−0.82	−0.47	0.05
External (to school) domain	−0.15	−0.04	0.80
Time	−0.43	0.17	−0.52
School domain	−0.34	0.86	0.16
Personal domain	0.09	−0.05	−0.25
Satisfaction factors			
Supervision	0.23	−0.91	0.32
Income	0.45	0.13	0.12
External demands	0.72	0.33	0.28
Advancement	0.48	−0.04	−0.71
School culture	0.06	−0.28	−0.54

Source: Adapted from McCormick and Solman, 1992

(This) indicates that teachers perceive that 'non-teachers' or out-siders expect too much of them (*External demands*) and that stress results from poor student attitudes and behaviour (*Student domain*). One interpretation might be that for these teachers, high levels of stress attributable to the Student domain are associated with low levels of satisfaction in the context of demands from outside the school, and vice versa. It may well be that, for some teachers, high demand in one of these is perceived as affecting their capacity to cope or deal with the demands of the other. Certainly, the teacher who is experiencing the urgency of a struggle with student behaviour in the classroom, is unlikely to think of the requirements of persons and agencies outside the school as important.

(McCormick and Solman, 1992)

The outcomes of their factor analyses frequently puzzle researchers. Take, for example, one of the loadings on the third canonical variate. There, we see that the stress factor 'Time demands' correlates negatively (-0.52). One might have supposed, the authors say, that stress attri-butable to the external domain would have correlated with the variate in the same direction. But this is not so. It correlates positively at 0.80. One possible explanation, they suggest, is that an increase in stress experienced because of time demands coincides with a lowering of stress attributable to the external domain, as time is expended in meeting demands from the external domain. The researchers concede, however, that this explanation would need more close examination before it could be accepted.

McCormick and Solman's questionnaire also elicited biographical data from the teacher–respondents in respect of sex, number of years teaching, type and location of school and position held in school. By rescoring the stress items on a scale ranging from 'No stress' (1) to 'Extreme stress' (5) and using the means of the factor scores, the researchers were able to explore associations between the degree of perceived occupational stress and the biographical data supplied by participants. Space precludes a full account of McCormick and Solman's findings. We illustrate two or three significant results in Box 15.9. In the *School domain* more stress was reported by secondary school teachers than by their colleagues teaching younger pupils, not really a very surprising result, the researchers observe, given that infant/primary schools are generally much smaller than their secondary counterparts and that teachers are more likely to be part of a smaller, supportive group. In the domain of *Time demands*, females experienced more stress than males, a finding consistent with that of other research. In the *Personal domain*, a significant difference was found in respect of the school's location, the level of occupational stress increasing from the rural setting, through the country/city to the metropolitan area.

Box 15.9   Biographical data and stress factors

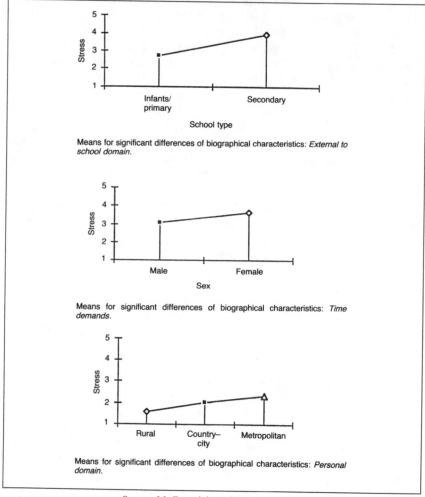

Means for significant differences of biographical characteristics: *External to school domain.*

Means for significant differences of biographical characteristics: *Time demands.*

Means for significant differences of biographical characteristics: *Personal domain.*

Source: McCormick and Solman, 1992

To conclude, factor analysis techniques are ideally suited to studies such as that of McCormick and Solman in which lengthy questionnaire-type data are elicited from a large number of participants and where researchers are concerned to explore underlying structures and relationships between dependent and independent variables.

Inevitably, such tentative explorations raise as many questions as they answer.

MULTI-DIMENSIONAL TABLES

Methods of analysing data cast into 2 × 2 contingency tables by means of the chi square test are generally well covered in research methods books. Increasingly however, educational data are classified in multiple rather than two-dimensional formats. Everitt[12] provides a useful account of methods for analysing multi-dimensional tables and has shown, incidentally, the erroneous conclusions that can result from the practice of analysing multi-dimensional data by summing over variables to reduce them to two-dimensional formats. In this section we too illustrate the misleading conclusions that can arise when the researcher employs bivariate rather than multivariate analysis (see p. 344). The outline that follows draws closely on an exposition by Whiteley.[13]

Box 15.10 Sex, voting preference and social class: a three-way classification table

| | Middle-class | | Working-class | |
	Conservative	Labour	Conservative	Labour
Men	80	30	40	130
Women	100	20	40	110

Source: Adapted from Whiteley, 1983

MULTI-DIMENSIONAL DATA: SOME WORDS ON NOTATION

The hypothetical data in Box 15.10 refer to a survey of voting behaviour in a sample of men and women in Britain:

the row variable (sex) is represented by i;
the column variable (voting preference) is represented by j;
the layer variable (social class) is represented by k.

The number in any one cell in Box 15.10 can be represented by the symbol n_{ijk} that is to say, the score in row category i, column category j, and layer category k, where:

$i = 1$ (men), 2 (women)
$j = 1$ (Conservative), 2 (Labour)
$k = 1$ (middle-class), 2 (working-class)

It follows therefore that the numbers in Box 15.10 can also be represented as in Box 15.11. Thus,

$n_{121} = 30$ (men, Labour, middle-class)

Box 15.11   Sex, voting preference and social class: a three-way notational classification

	Middle-class		Working-class	
	Conservative	*Labour*	*Conservative*	*Labour*
Men	n_{111}	n_{121}	n_{112}	n_{122}
Women	n_{211}	n_{221}	n_{212}	n_{222}

and

$n_{212} = 40$ (women, Conservative, working-class)

Three types of marginals can be obtained from Box 15.11 by:

1 Summing over two variables to give the marginal totals for the third. Thus:

n_{++k} = summing over sex and voting preference to give social class, for example:

$n_{111} + n_{121} + n_{211} + n_{221} = 230$ (middle-class)

$n_{112} + n_{122} + n_{212} + n_{222} = 320$ (working-class)

n_{+j+} = summing over sex and social class to give voting preference
n_{i++} = summing over voting preference and social class to give sex.

2 Summing over one variable to give the marginal totals for the second and third variables. Thus:

$n_{+11} = 180$ (middle-class Conservative)
$n_{+21} = 50$ (middle-class Labour)
$n_{+12} = 80$ (working-class Conservative)
$n_{+22} = 240$ (working-class Labour)

3 Summing over all three variables to give the grand total. Thus:

$n_{+++} = 550 = N$

Using the chi square test in a three-way classification table

Whiteley shows how easy it is to extent the 2×2 chi square test to the three-way case. The probability that an individual taken from the sample at random in Box 15.10 will be a woman is:

$$p_{2++} = \frac{n_{2++}}{n_{+++}} = \frac{270}{550} = 0.49$$

and the probability that a respondent's voting preference will be Labour is:

$$p_{+2+} = \frac{n_{+2+}}{n_{+++}} = \frac{290}{550} = 0.53$$

and the probability that a respondent will be working-class is:

$$p_{++2} = \frac{n_{++2}}{n_{+++}} = \frac{320}{550} = 0.58$$

To determine the expected probability of an individual being a woman, Labour supporter and working-class we assume that these variables are statistically independent (that is to say, there is no relationship between them) and simply apply the multiplication rule of probability theory:

$$P_{222} = (P_{2++}) (P_{+2+}) (P_{++2}) = (0.49)(0.53)(0.58) = 0.15$$

This can be expressed in terms of the expected frequency in cell n_{222} as:

$$N (P_{2++}) (P_{+2+}) (P_{++2}) = 550 (0.49)(0.53)(0.58) = 82.8$$

Similarly, the expected frequency in cell n_{112} is:

$N(p_{1++}) (p_{+1+})(p_{++2})$ where:

$$p_{1++} = \frac{n_{1++}}{n_{+++}} = \frac{280}{550} = 0.51$$

and

$$p_{+1+} = \frac{n_{+1+}}{n_{+++}} = \frac{260}{550} = 0.47$$

and

$$p_{++2} = \frac{n_{++2}}{n_{+++}} = \frac{320}{550} = 0.58$$

Thus $N (P_{1++}) (P_{+1+}) (P_{++2}) = 550 (0.51)(0.47)(0.58) = 77.0$

Box 15.12 gives the expected frequencies for the data shown in Box 15.10.

Box 15.12   Expected frequencies in sex, voting preference and social class

	Middle-class Conservative	Labour	Working-class Conservative	Labour
Men	55.4	61.7	77.0	85.9
Women	53.4	59.5	74.3	82.8

Source: Adapted from Whiteley, 1983

With the observed frequencies and the expected frequencies to hand, chi square is calculated in the usual way:

$$\chi^2 = \Sigma \frac{(O - E)^2}{E} = 159.41$$

DEGREES OF FREEDOM

As Whiteley observes, degrees of freedom in a three-way contingency table is more complex than in a 2×2 classification. Essentially, however, degrees of freedom refer to the freedom with which the researcher is able to assign values to the cells, given fixed marginal totals. This can be computed by first determining the degrees of freedom for the marginals.

Each of the variables in our example (sex, voting preference, and social class) contains two categories. It follows therefore that we have $(2 - 1)$ degrees of freedom for each of them, given that the marginal for each variable is fixed. Since the grand total of all the marginals (i.e. the sample size) is also fixed, it follows that one more degree of freedom is also lost. We subtract these fixed numbers from the total number of cells in our contingency table. In general therefore:

degrees of freedom (d.f.)   =   the number of cells in the table − 1 (for N) − the number of cells fixed by the hypothesis being tested.

Thus, where r = rows, c = columns and l = layers:

$$d.f. = rcl\,(r - 1) - (c - 1) - (l - 1) - 1$$
$$= rcl - r - c - l + 2$$

that is to say $d.f. = rcl - r - c - l + 2$ when we are testing the hypothesis of the mutual independence of the three variables.

In our example:

$$d.f. = (2)\,(2)\,(2) - 2 - 2 - 2 + 2 = 4$$

342

From chi square tables we see that the critical value of χ^2 with 4 degrees of freedom is 9.49 at $p = 0.05$. Our obtained value greatly exceeds that number. We reject the null hypothesis and conclude that sex, voting preference, and social class are significantly interrelated.

Having rejected the null hypothesis with respect to the mutual independence of the three variables, the researcher's task now is to identify which variables cause the null hypothesis to be rejected. We cannot simply assume that because our chi square test has given a significant result, it therefore follows that there are significant associations between all three variables. It may be the case, for example, that an association exists between two of the variables whilst the third is completely independent. What we need now is a test of 'partial independence'. Whiteley shows the following three such possible tests in respect of the data in Box 15.10. First, that sex is independent of social class and voting preference:

(1) $p_{ijk} = (p_i)(p_{jk})$

Second, that voting preference is independent of sex and social class

(2) $p_{ijk} = (p_j)(p_{ik})$

And third, that social class is independent of sex and voting preference

(3) $p_{ijk} = (p_k)(p_{ij})$

The following example shows how to construct the expected frequencies for the first hypothesis. We can determine the probability of an individual being, say, woman, Labour, and working-class, assuming hypothesis (1), as follows:

$$p_{222} = (p_{2++})(p_{+22}) = \frac{(n_{2++})}{(N)}\frac{(n_{+22})}{(N)}$$

$$p_{222} = \frac{(270)}{(550)}\frac{(240)}{(550)} = 0.214$$

$$E_{222} = N(p_{2++})(p_{+22}) = 550\frac{(270)}{(550)}\frac{(240)}{(550)} = \underline{117.8}$$

That is to say, assuming that sex is independent of social class and voting preference, the expected number of female, working class Labour supporters is 117.8.

343

Box 15.13   Expected frequencies assuming that sex is independent of social class and voting preference

| | Middle-class | | Working-class | |
	Conservative	Labour	Conservative	Labour
Men	91.6	25.5	40.7	122.2
Women	88.4	24.5	39.3	117.8

Source: Adapted from Whiteley (1983)

When we calculate the expected frequencies for each of the cells in our contingency table in respect of our first hypothesis $(p_{ijk}) = (p_i)(p_{jk})$, we obtain the results shown in Box 15.13.

$$\chi^2 = \Sigma \frac{(O - E)^2}{E} = \underline{5.71}$$

Degrees of freedom is given by:

$$d.f. = rcl - (cl - 1) - (r - 1) - 1$$
$$= rcl - cl - r + 1 = 8 - 4 - 2 + 1 = 3$$

Whiteley observes:

> Note that we are assuming c and l are interrelated so that once, say, p_{+11} is calculated, then p_{+12}, p_{+21} and p_{+22} are determined, so we have only 1 degree of freedom; that is to say, we lose $(cl - 1)$ degrees of freedom in calculating that relationship.
>
> (Whiteley, 1983)

From chi square tables we see that the critical value of χ^2 with 3 degrees of freedom is 7.81 at $p = 0.05$. Our obtained value is less than this. We therefore accept the null hypothesis and conclude that *there is no relationship between sex on the one hand and voting preference and social class on the other.*

Suppose now that instead of casting our data into a three-way classification as shown in Box 15.10, we had simply used a 2 × 2 contingency table and that we had sought to test the null hypothesis that *there is no relationship between sex and voting preference.* The data are shown in Box 15.14.

When we compute chi square from the above data our obtained value is $\chi^2 = 4.48$. Degrees of freedom are given by $(r - 1)(c - 1) = (2 - 1)(2 - 1) = 1$.

From chi square tables we see that the critical value of χ^2 with 1 degree of freedom is 3.84 at $p = 0.05$. Our obtained value exceeds this. We

Box 15.14 Sex and voting preference: a two-way classification table

	Conservative	Labour
Men	120	160
Women	140	130

Source: Adapted from Whiteley, 1983

reject the null hypothesis and conclude that *sex is significantly associated with voting preference.*

But how can we explain the differing conclusions that we have arrived at in respect of the data in Boxes 15.10 and 15.14? These examples illustrate an important and general point, Whiteley observes. In the bivariate analysis (Box 15.14) we concluded that there was a significant relationship between sex and voting preference. In the multivariate analysis (Box 15.10) that relationship was found to be non-significant when we controlled for social class. The lesson is plain; use a multivariate approach to the analysis of contingency tables wherever the data allow.

REFERENCES AND NOTES

1 Bennett, S. and Bowers, D., *An Introduction to Multivariate Techniques for Social and Behavioural Sciences* (Macmillan, London, 1977).

2 Kerlinger, F.N., *Foundations of Behavioral Research* (Holt, Rinehart & Winston, New York, 1970).

3 Cohen, L., *Education Research in Classrooms and Schools: A Manual of Materials and Methods* (Harper & Row, London, 1977).

4 McQuitty, L.L., 'Elementary linkage analysis for isolating orthogonal and oblique types and typal relevancies', *Educational and Psychological Measurement*, 17 (1957) 207–29.

5 For a fuller discussion of clustering methods, see B.S. Everitt, *Cluster Analysis* (Heinemann Educational Books, London 1974).

6 Bennett, N., *Teaching Styles and Pupil Progress* (Open Books, London, 1976); Bennett, N. and Jordan, J., 'A typology of teaching styles in primary schools', *British Journal of Educational Psychology*, 45 (1975) 20–8. Powerful cluster programs such as SAS, Version 5 Edition, (1985) SAS Institute Inc., Cary, NC, USA, can throw new light on data and reveal dimensions previously obscure. Using SAS in an analysis of the perceptions of some 686 teachers about their working lives, Poppleton and Riseborough (1990) identified four clusters of teachers with distinctively different orientations towards the pursuit of a career. See Poppleton, P. and Riseborough, G., 'Teaching in the mid-1980s: the centrality of work in secondary teachers' lives', *British Educational Research Journal*, 16(2) (1990) 105–24.

7 Gray, J. and Satterly, D., 'A chapter of errors: teaching styles and pupil progress in retrospect', *Educational Research*, 19 (1976) 45–56. Aitken, M., Bennett, N. and Hesketh, J., 'Teaching styles and pupil progress: a re-analysis', *British Journal of Educational Psychology*, 51(2) (1981) 170–86; Aitkin, M. Anderson, D. and Hinde, J., 'Statistical modelling of data on teaching styles', *Journal of the Royal Statistical Society*, 144(4) (1981) 419–61; Prais, S.J., 'Formal

and informal teaching: a further reconsideration of Professor Bennett's statistics', *Journal of the Royal Statistical Society*, 146(2) (1983) 163–9; Chatfield, C., 'The initial examination of data', *Journal of the Royal Statistical Society*, 148(3) (1985) 214–53.

8 Child, D., *The Essentials of Factor Analysis* (Holt, Rinehart & Winston, 1970).
9 McCormick, J. and Solman, R., 'Teachers' attributions of responsibility for occupational stress and satisfaction: an organisational perspective', *Educational Studies*, 18(2) (1992) 201–22.
10 Self-serving bias refers to our propensity to accept responsibility for our successes, but to deny responsibility for our failures.
11 Levine, M., *Canonical Analysis and Factor Comparisons* (Beverly Hills, Calif., Sage, 1984).
12 Everitt, B.S., *The Analysis of Contingency Tables* (Chapman & Hall, London, 1977).
13 Whiteley, P., 'The analysis of contingency tables', in McKay, D. Schofield, N. and Whiteley, P. (eds), *Data Analysis and the Social Sciences* (Frances Pinter, London, 1983); see also, Reid, S., *Working with Statistics: An Introduction to Quantitative Methods for Social Scientists* (Polity Press, Cambridge, 1987) 125–42, 'Working with three or more variables'.

16

THE ETHICS OF EDUCATIONAL AND SOCIAL RESEARCH

INTRODUCTION

Developments in the field of social science in recent years have been accompanied by a growing awareness of the attendant moral issues implicit in the work of social researchers and of their need to meet their obligations with respect to those involved in, or affected by, their investigations. This awareness, focusing chiefly, but by no means exclusively, on the subject matter and methods of research in so far as they affect the participants, is reflected in the growth of relevant literature and in the appearance of regulatory codes of research practice formulated by various agencies and professional bodies.[1] Ethical concerns encountered in educational research in particular can be extremely complex and subtle and can frequently place researchers in moral predicaments which may appear quite unresolvable. One such dilemma is that which requires researchers to strike a balance between the demands placed on them as professional scientists in pursuit of truth, and their subjects' rights and values potentially threatened by the research. This is known as the 'costs/benefits ratio', the essence of which is outlined in Box 16.1,[2] and is a concept we return to later in the chapter when we consider how ethical dilemmas arise from various sources of tension. It is a particularly thorny dilemma because, as Aronson and his colleagues note,[3] it cannot be shrugged off either by making pious statements about the inviolability of human dignity or by pledging glib allegiance to the cause of science. Most standard textbooks on ethics in social research would, in this case, advise researchers to proceed ethically without threatening the validity of the research endeavour in so far as it is possible to do so. Conventional wisdom of this kind is admirable in its way, but the problems for researchers can multiply surprisingly when the principle comes to be applied: when they move from the general to the particular, from the abstract to the concrete. Each research undertaking is different and investigators may find that on one occasion their work proceeds smoothly without the

Box 16.1   The costs–benefits ratio

The *costs/benefits ratio* is a fundamental concept expressing the primary ethical dilemma in social research. In planning their proposed research, social scientists have to consider the likely social benefits of their endeavours against the personal costs to the individuals taking part. Possible benefits accruing from the research may take the form of crucial findings leading to significant advances in theoretical and applied knowledge. Failure to do the research may cost society the advantages of the research findings and ultimately the opportunity to improve the human condition. The costs to participants may include affronts to dignity, embarrassment, loss of trust in social relations, loss of autonomy and self-determination, and lowered self-esteem. On the other hand, the benefits to participants could take the form of satisfaction in having made a contribution to science and a greater personal understanding of the research area under scrutiny. The process of balancing benefits against possible costs is chiefly a subjective one and not at all easy. There are few or no absolutes and researchers have to make decisions about research content and procedures in accordance with professional and personal values. This *costs/benefits ratio* is the basic dilemma residual in a great deal of social research.

Source: Adapted from Frankfort-Nachmias and Nachmias, 1992

Hydra-headed creature of ethical concern breaking surface. At another time, they may come to realize that, suddenly and without prior indication, they are in the middle of an ethical minefield, and that the residual problems of a technical and administrative nature that one expects as a matter of course when pursuing educational research are compounded by unforeseen moral questions.

Ethical issues may stem from the kinds of problems investigated by social scientists and the methods they use to obtain valid and reliable data. In theory at least, this means that each stage in the research sequence may be a potential source of ethical problems. Thus, they may arise from the nature of the research project itself (ethnic differences in intelligence, for example); the context for the research (a remand home); the procedures to be adopted (producing high levels of anxiety); methods of data collection (covert observation); the nature of the participants (emotionally disturbed adolescents); the type of data collected (highly personal information of a sensitive kind); and what is to be done with the data (publishing in a manner that causes the participants embarrassment).

Our initial observations would seem to indicate that the subject of ethics in social research is potentially a wide-ranging and challenging one. It is fitting, therefore, if in this chapter we present a conspectus of the main issues that may confront workers in the field. Although what follows offers advice and guidance in liberal amounts drawn from the work of seasoned researchers and from a range of empirical studies, we do not intend to be unduly prescriptive or proscriptive. As we suggested in our opening comments, each research undertaking is an event *sui generis*, and the conduct of researchers cannot be, indeed should not be, forced into a procrustean system of ethics. When it comes to the resolution of a specific moral problem, each situation frequently offers a spectrum of possibilities. In what follows, we have indulged in a certain amount of restatement of facts without, we hope, being repetitious. This has advantages since some of the ideas discussed are multi-faceted and their reappearance in different contexts may assist greater understanding.

We draw these prelusive remarks to a close with reference to the work of Hammersley and Atkinson.[4] Writing of the problem of gaining access to a situation for the purpose of conducting ethnographic research, they say that it involves drawing on the interpersonal resources and strategies that we all tend to develop in dealing with everyday life. So also across the whole field of educational research. John Dewey, the American philosopher and educator, once said that education is a social process, and so in its way is research into education. It too requires interpersonal skills of a high order, supported by humane personal and professional values rooted in a shared culture if investigators are to deal effectively with the ethical challenges of the research adventure. In this connection experience is a fine teacher (another Deweyan precept) and researchers will by the exercise of careful observation develop an intuitive ability to discern what works and what does not, what is appropriate and what is not. By these means they will be able to set the right *tone*, and unless they do so even the simplest of research procedures will cause subjects to feel uneasy or alienated.

From what we have said so far, we hope that we will be seen as informants rather than arbiters, and our counsels as markers and signposts in what for many readers will be a largely unexplored *terra incognita*. It is in this spirit that we review seriatim the problems of access to the research setting; the nature of ethics in social research generally; sources of tension in the ethical debate; problems and dilemmas confronting the researcher, including matters of privacy, anonymity, confidentiality, betrayal and deception; ethical problems endemic in particular research methods; ethics and teacher evaluation; regulations affecting research; and a final word on personal codes of practice. Before this, however, we examine another fundamental concept which, along with the *costs/benefits ratio*, contributes to the bedrock of ethical procedure – that of *informed consent*.

INFORMED CONSENT

Much social research necessitates obtaining the consent and co-operation of subjects who are to assist in investigations and of significant others in the institutions or organizations providing the research facilities. In some cultures, informed consent is absolutely essential whenever participants are exposed to substantial risks or asked to forfeit personal rights. Writing of the situation in the USA, for instance, Frankfort-Nachmias and Nachmias say:

> When research participants are to be exposed to pain, physical or emotional injury, invasions of privacy, or physical or psychological stress, or when they are asked to surrender their autonomy temporarily (as, for example, in drug research), informed consent must be fully guaranteed. Participants should know that their involvement is voluntary at all times, and they should receive a thorough explanation beforehand of the benefits, rights, risks, and dangers involved as a consequence of their participation in the research project.
>
> (Frankfort-Nachmias and Nachmias, 1992)

The principle of informed consent arises from the subject's right to freedom and self-determination. Being free is a condition of living in a democracy and when restrictions and limitations are placed on that freedom they must be justified and consented to, even in research proceedings. Consent thus protects and respects the right of self-determination and places some of the responsibility on the participant should anything go wrong in the research. Another aspect of the right to self-determination is that the subject has the right to refuse to take part, or to withdraw once the research has begun (see Frankfort-Nachmias and Nachmias, 1992). Thus informed consent implies informed refusal.

Informed consent has been defined by Diener and Crandall as 'the procedures in which individuals choose whether to participate in an investigation after being informed of facts that would be likely to influence their decisions' (Diener and Crandall, 1978).[5] This definition involves four elements: competence, voluntarism, full information, and comprehension. 'Competence' implies that responsible, mature individuals will make correct decisions if they are given the relevant information. It is incumbent on researchers to ensure they do not engage individuals incapable of making such decisions either because of immaturity or some form of psychological impairment. 'Voluntarism' entails applying the principle of informed consent and thus ensuring that participants freely choose to take part (or not) in the research and guarantees that exposure to risks is undertaken knowingly and voluntarily. This element can be problematical, especially in the field of medical research where unknowing patients are used as guinea-pigs. 'Full information' implies that consent is fully informed, though in practice it is often impossible for researchers to inform subjects on everything, e.g. on the statistical treatment of data; and, as we shall see

Box 16.2 Guidelines for reasonably informed consent

---

1 A fair explanation of the procedures to be followed and their purposes.
2 A description of the attendant discomforts and risks reasonably to be expected.
3 A description of the benefits reasonably to be expected.
4 A disclosure of appropriate alternative procedures that might be advantageous to the participants.
5 An offer to answer any inquiries concerning the procedures.
6 An instruction that the person is free to withdraw consent and to discontinue participation in the project at any time without prejudice to the participant.

Source: Institutional Guide to DHEW Policy, 1971

below, on those occasions when the researchers themselves do not know everything about the investigation. In such circumstances, the strategy of reasonably informed consent has to be applied. Box 16.2 illustrates a set of guidelines used in the USA that are based on the idea of *reasonably informed consent*.[6] 'Comprehension' refers to the fact that participants fully understand the nature of the research project, even when procedures are complicated and entail risks. Suggestions have been made to ensure that subjects fully comprehend the situation they are putting themselves into, e.g. by using highly-educated subjects, by engaging a consultant to explain difficulties, or by building into the research scheme a time lag between the request for participation and decision time.

If these four elements are present, researchers can be assured that subjects' rights will have been given appropriate consideration. As Frankfort-Nachmias and Nachmias note, however:

> The principle of informed consent should not . . . be made an absolute requirement of all social science research. Although usually desirable, it is not absolutely necessary to studies where no danger or risk is involved. The more serious the risk to research participants, the greater becomes the obligation to obtain informed consent.
>
> (Frankfort-Nachmias and Nachmias, 1992)

It must also be remembered that there are some research methods where it is impossible to seek informed consent. Covert observation, for example, as used in Patrick's study of a Glasgow gang (Chapter 5), or experimental techniques involving deception, as in Milgram's Obedience-to-authority experiments (Chapter 12), would, by their very nature, rule out the option. And, of course, there may be occasions when problems arise even though consent has been obtained. Burgess,[7] for example, cites his own research in which teachers had been informed that research was taking place but in which it was not possible to specify

351

exactly what data would be collected or how they would be used. It could be said, in this particular case, that individuals were not fully informed, that consent had not been obtained, and that privacy had been violated. As a general rule, however, informed consent is an important principle to abide by and the fact that moral philosophers have joined in the debate engendered by the concept is testimony to the seriousness with which it is viewed.[8] It is this principle that will form the basis, so to speak, of an implicit contractual relationship between the researcher and the researched and will serve as a foundation on which subsequent ethical considerations can be structured.

From our remarks and citations so far on this subject of informed consent, we may appear to be assuming relationships between peers — researcher and teachers, for example, or research professor and postgraduate students; and this assumption would seem to underpin many of the discussions of an ethical nature in the research literature generally. Readers will be aware, however, that much educational research involves children who cannot be regarded as being on equal terms with the researcher, and it is important to keep this in mind at all stages in the research process including the point where informed consent is sought. In this connection we refer to the important work of Fine and Sandstrom,[9] whose ethnographic and participant observational studies of children and young people focus, among other issues, on this asymmetry with respect to the problems of obtaining informed consent from their young subjects and explaining the research in a comprehensible fashion. As a guiding principle they advise that while it is desirable to lessen the power differential between children and adult researchers, the difference will remain and its elimination may be ethically inadvisable.

It may be of some help to readers if we refer briefly to other aspects of the problem of informed consent (or refusal) in relation to young, or very young, children. Seeking informed consent with regard to minors involves two stages. First, researchers consult and seek permission from those adults responsible for the prospective subjects; and second, they approach the young people themselves. The adults in question will be, for example, parents, teachers, tutors, or psychiatrists, youth leaders, or team coaches, depending on the research context. The point of the research will be explained, questions invited, and permission to proceed to the next stage sought. Objections, for whatever reason, will be duly respected. Obtaining approval from relevant adults may be more difficult than in the case of the children, but at a time of increasing sensitivity to children's welfare it is vital that researchers secure such approval. It may be useful if, in seeking the consent of children, researchers bear in mind the provisory comments below.

While seeking children's permission and co-operation is an automatic part of quantitative research (a child cannot unknowingly complete a simple questionnaire), the importance of informed consent in qualitative research is not always recognized. Speaking of participant observation, for example, Fine and Sandstrom say that researchers must provide a credible and meaningful explanation of their research intentions, especially in situations where they have little authority, and that children must be given a real and legitimate opportunity to say that they do not want to take part. The authors advise that where subjects do refuse, they should not be questioned, their actions should not be recorded, and they should not be included in any book or article (even under a pseudonym). Where they form part of a group, they may be included as part of a collectivity. Fine and Sandstrom consider that such rejections are sometimes a result of mistrust of the researcher. They suggest that at a later date, when the researcher has been able to establish greater rapport with the group, those who refused initially may be approached again, perhaps in private.

Two particular groups of children require special mention: very young children, and those not capable of making a decision. Researchers intending to work with pre-school or nursery children may dismiss the idea of seeking informed consent from their would-be subjects because of their age, but Fine and Sandstrom would recommend otherwise. Even though such children would not understand what research was, the authors advise that the children be given some explanation. For example, one to the effect that an adult will be watching and playing with them might be sufficient to provide a measure of informed consent consistent with the children's understanding. As Fine and Sandstrom comment:

> Our feeling is that children should be told as much as possible, even if some of them cannot understand the full explanation. Their age should not diminish their rights, although their level of understanding must be taken into account in the explanations that are shared with them.
>
> (Fine and Sandstrom, 1988)

The second group consists of those children who are to be used in a research project and who may not meet Diener and Crandall's (1978) criterion of 'competence' (a group of psychologically impaired children, for example). In such circumstances there may be LEA guidelines to follow. In the absence of these, the requirements of informed consent would be met by obtaining the permission of headteachers who will be acting *in loco parentis* or who have had delegated to them the responsibility for providing informed consent by the parents.

Two final cautions: first, where an extreme form of research is planned, parents would have to be fully informed in advance and their consent obtained; and second, whatever the nature of the research and whoever is involved, should a child show signs of discomfort or stress, the research should be terminated immediately.

ACCESS AND ACCEPTANCE

The relevance of the principle of informed consent becomes apparent at the initial stage of the research project – that of access to the institution or organization where the research is to be conducted, and acceptance by those whose permission one needs before embarking on the task. We highlight this stage of access and acceptance in particular at this point because it offers the best opportunity for researchers to present their credentials as serious investigators and establish their own ethical position with respect to their proposed research.

Investigators cannot expect access to a nursery, school, college, or factory as a matter of right. They have to demonstrate that they are worthy, as researchers and human beings, of being accorded the facilities needed to carry out their investigations. The advice of Bell is particularly apposite in this connection:

> Permission to carry out an investigation must always be sought at an early stage. As soon as you have an agreed project outline and have read enough to convince yourself that the topic is feasible, it is advisable to make a formal, written approach to the individuals and organisation concerned, outlining your plans. Be honest. If you are carrying out an investigation in connection with a diploma or degree course, say that is what you are doing. If you feel the study will probably yield useful and/or interesting information, make a particular point of that fact – but be careful not to claim more than the investigation merits.

(Bell, 1987)[10]

The first stage thus involves the gaining of official permission to undertake one's research in the target community. This will mean contacting, in person or in writing, an LEA official and/or the chairperson of the governors, if one is to work in a school, along with the headteacher or principal. At a later point, significant figures who will be responsible for, or assist in, the organization and administration of the research will also need to be contacted – the deputy head or senior teacher, for instance, and most certainly the classteacher if children are to be used in the research. Since the researcher's potential for intrusion and perhaps disruption is considerable, amicable relations with the classteacher in particular should be fostered as expeditiously as possible. If the investigation involves teachers as participants, propositions may have to be put to a full staff meeting and conditions negotiated. Where the research is to take place in another kind of institution – a youth club or

Box 16.3 Close encounters of a researcher kind

My first entry into a staffroom at the college was the occasion of some shuffling and shifting of books and chairs so that I could be given a comfortable seat whilst the tutor talked to me from a standing position. As time progressed my presence was almost taken for granted and later, when events threatened the security of the tutors, I was ignored. No one enquired as to whether they could assist me and my own enquiries were met with cursory answers and confused looks, followed by the immediate disappearance of the individuals concerned, bearing a pile of papers. I learned not to make too many enquiries. Unfortunately, when individuals feel insecure, when their world is threatened with change that is beyond their control, they are likely to respond in an unpredictable manner to persons within their midst whose role is unclear, and the role of the researcher is rarely understood by those not engaged in research.

Source: Foster, 1989

detention centre, for example – the principle of approach will be similar, although the organizational structure will be different.

Achieving goodwill and co-operation is especially important where the proposed research extends over a period of time: days, perhaps, in the case of an ethnographic study; months (or perhaps years!) where longitudinal research is involved. Access does not present quite such a problem when, for example, a one-off survey requires respondents to give up half-an-hour of their time; or when a researcher is normally a member of the organization where the research is taking place (an insider), though in the case of the latter, it is generally unwise to take co-operation for granted. Where research procedures are extensive and complicated, however, or where the design is developmental or longitudinal, or where researchers are not normally based in the target community, the problems of access are more involved and require greater preparation. Box 16.3 gives a flavour of the kinds of accessibility problems that can be experienced.[11]

Having identified the official and significant figures whose permission must be sought, and before actually meeting them, researchers will need to clarify in their own minds the precise nature and scope of their research. It is desirable that they have a total picture of what it all entails, even if the overall scheme is a provisional one (though we have to bear in mind that this may cause difficulties later). In this respect researchers could, for instance, identify the aims of the research; its practical applications, if any; the design, methods, and procedures to be used; the nature and size of samples or groups; what tests are to be administered and how; what activities are to be observed; what subjects are to be interviewed; observational needs; the time involved; the degree of disruption envisaged; arrangements to guarantee confidentiality with respect to data (if this is necessary); the role of feedback and how findings can best be disseminated; the overall timetable within which the research is to be encompassed; and finally, whether assistance will be required in the organization and administration of the research. Where the research arises from an in-service or degree/diploma course requirement, such matters can be discussed with one's supervisor in advance. By such planning and foresight, both researchers and institutions will have a good idea of the demands likely to be made on both subjects (be they children or teachers) and organizations. It is also a good opportunity to anticipate and resolve likely problems, especially those of a practical kind. A long, complicated questionnaire, for example, may place undue demands on the comprehension skills and attention spans of a particular class of 13-year-olds; or a relatively inexperienced teacher could feel threatened by sustained research scrutiny. Once this kind of information has been sorted out and clarified, researchers will be in a strong position to discuss their proposed plans in an informed, open and frank manner (though not necessarily too open, as we shall see) and will thereby more readily gain permission, acceptance, and support. It must be remembered that hosts will have perceptions of researchers and their intentions and that these need to be positive. Researchers can best influence such perceptions by presenting themselves as competent, trustworthy, and accommodating.

Once this preliminary information has been collected, researchers are duly prepared for the next stage: making actual contact in person, perhaps after an introductory letter, with appropriate people in the organization with a view to negotiating access. If the research is college-based, they will have the support of their college and course supervisors. Festinger and Katz[12] consider that there is real economy in going to the very top of the organization or system in question to obtain assent and co-operation. This is particularly so where the structure is clearly hierarchical and where lower levels are always dependent on their superiors. They consider that it is likely that the nature of the research will be referred to the top of the organization sooner or later, and that there is a much better chance for a favourable decision if leaders are consulted at the outset. It may also be the case that heads will be more open-minded than those lower down, who because of their insecurity, may be less co-operative. The authors also warn against using the easiest entrances into the organization when seeking permission. Researchers may perhaps seek to come in as allies of individuals or groups who have a special interest to exploit and who see research as a means to their ends. As Festinger and Katz put it, 'The researcher's aim should be to enter the situation in the common interests of all parties, and his findings should be equally available to all groups and individuals' (Festinger and Katz, 1966). Investigators should thus seek as broad a basis for their support as possible. Other potential problems may be circumvented by making use of accepted channels of communication in the institution or organization. In a school, for example, this may take the form of a staff forum. As Festinger and Katz say in this regard, 'If the information is limited to a single channel, the study may become identified with the interests associated with that channel' (Festinger and Katz, 1966).

Following contact, there will be a negotiation process. At this point researchers will give as much information about the aims, nature and procedures of the research as is appropriate. This is very important: information that may prejudice the results of the investigation should be withheld. Aronson and Carlsmith,[13] for instance, note that one cannot imagine researchers who are studying the effects of group pressure on conformity announcing their intentions in advance. On the other hand, researchers may find themselves on dangerous ground if they go to the extreme of maintaining a 'conspiracy of silence', because, as Festinger and Katz note, such a stance is hard to keep up if the research is extensive and lasts over several days or weeks. As they say in this respect, 'An attempt to preserve secrecy merely increases the spread and wildness of the rumours' (Festinger and Katz, 1966). If researchers do not want their potential hosts and/or subjects to know too much about specific hypotheses and objectives, then a simple way out is to present an explicit statement at a fairly general level with one or two examples of items that are not crucial to the study as a whole. As most research entails some risks, especially where field studies are concerned, and as the presence of an observer scrutinizing various aspects of community or school life may not be relished by all in the group, investigators must at all times manifest a sensitive appreciation of their hosts' and subjects' position and reassure anyone who feels threatened by the work. Such reassurance could take the form of a statement of conditions and guarantees given by researchers at this negotiation stage. By way of illustration, Box 16.4 contains conditions laid down by an Open University student for a school-based research project.

Box 16.4 Conditions and guarantees proffered for a school-based research project

---

1 All participants will be offered the opportunity to remain anonymous.
2 All information will be treated with the strictest confidentiality.
  3 Interviewees will have the opportunity to verify statements when the research is in draft form.
4 Participants will receive a copy of the final report.
5 The research is to be assessed by the Open University for examination purposes only, but should the question of publication arise at a later date, permission will be sought from the participants.
6 The research will attempt to explore educational management in practice. It is hoped the final report may be of benefit to the school and to those who take part.

Source: Bell, 1987

Box 16.5   Negotiating access checklist

---

1 Clear official channels by formally requesting permission to carry out your investigation as soon as you have an agreed project outline.
Some LEAs insist that requests to carry out research are channelled through the LEA office. Check what is required in your area.

2 Speak to the people who will be asked to co-operate.
Getting the LEA or head's permission is one thing, but you need to have the support of the people who will be asked to give interviews or complete questionnaires.

3 Submit the project outline to the head, if you are carrying out a study in your or another educational institution.
List people you would like to interview or to whom you wish to send questionnaires and state conditions under which the study will be conducted.

4 Decide what you mean by anonymity and confidentiality.
Remember that if you are writing about 'the head of English' and there is only one head of English in the school, the person concerned is immediately recognizable.

5 Decide whether participants will receive a copy of the report and/or see drafts or interview transcripts.
There are cost and time implications. Think carefully before you make promises.

6 Inform participants what is to be done with the information they provide.
Your eyes and those of the examiner only? Shown to the head, the LEA etc.?

7 Prepare an outline of intentions and conditions under which the study will be carried out to hand to the participants.
Even if you explain the purpose of the study the conditions and the guarantees, participants may forget.

8 Be honest about the purpose of the study and about the conditions of the research.
If you say an interview will last ten minutes, you will break faith if it lasts an hour. If you are conducting the investigation as part of a degree or diploma course, say so.

9 Remember that people who agree to help are doing you a favour.
Make sure you return papers and books in good order and on time. Letters of thanks should be sent, no matter how busy you are.

10 Never assume 'it will be all right'. Negotiating access is an important stage in your investigation.
If you are an inside researcher, you will have to live with your mistakes, so take care.

Source: Adapted from Bell, 1991

We might add that the teacher–researcher in particular must be aware that the aims and objectives of applied and action research are often to change practice in a particular direction (see Chapter 9). However well intentioned the researcher or team of researchers, such scrutiny may be perceived as subversive and threatening by some on the staff and a sweetener in such circumstances may take the form of giving members of staff opportunities to discuss professional issues which can arise from this kind of teacher-conducted school-based research.

We conclude this section by reminding beginning researchers in particular that there will be times when ethical considerations will pervade much of their work and that these will be no more so than at the stage of access and acceptance, where appropriateness of topic, design, methods, guarantees of confidentiality, analysis and dissemination of findings must be negotiated with relative openness, sensitivity, honesty, accuracy and scientific impartiality. As we have indicated earlier, there can be no rigid rules in this context. It will be a case of formulating and abiding by one's own situational ethics. These will determine what is acceptable and what is not acceptable. As Hitchcock and Hughes say in this regard:

> Individual circumstances must be the final arbiter. As far as possible it is better if the teacher can discuss the research with all parties involved. On other occasions it may be better for the teacher to develop a pilot study and uncover some of the problems in advance of the research proper. If it appears that the research is going to come into conflict with aspects of school policy, management styles, or individual personalities, it is better to confront the issues head on, consult relevant parties, and make rearrangements in the research design where possible or necessary.
>
> (Hitchcock and Hughes, 1988)[14]

Where a pilot study is not feasible it may be possible to arrange one or two scouting forays to assess possible problems and risks. By way of summary, we refer the reader to Box 16.5.

ETHICS OF SOCIAL RESEARCH

Social scientists generally have a responsibility not only to their profession in its search for knowledge and quest for truth, but also for the subjects they depend on for their work. Whatever the specific nature of their work, social researchers must take into account the effects of the research on participants, and act in such a way as to preserve their dignity as human beings. Such is ethical behaviour. Indeed, ethics has been defined as:

> a matter of principled sensitivity to the rights of others. Being ethical limits the choices we can make in the pursuit of truth. Ethics say that while truth is good, respect for human dignity is better, even if, in the extreme case, the respect of human nature leaves one ignorant of human nature.
>
> (Cavan, 1977)[15]

Kimmel[16] has pointed out that when attempting to describe ethical issues, it is important we remember to recognize that the distinction between ethical and unethical behaviour is not dichotomous, even though the normative code of prescribed ('ought') and proscribed ('ought not') behaviours, as represented by the ethical standards of a profession, seem to imply that it is. Judgements about whether behaviour conflicts with professional values lie on a continuum that ranges from the clearly ethical to the clearly unethical. The point to be borne in mind is that ethical principles are not absolute, generally speaking, though some maintain that they are as we shall see shortly, but must be interpreted in the light of the research context and of other values at stake.

It is perhaps worthwhile at this point to pause and remind ourselves that a considerable amount of research does not cause pain or indignity to the participants, that self-esteem is not necessarily undermined nor confidences betrayed, and that the social scientist may only infrequently be confronted with an unresolvable ethical dilemma. Where research is ethically sensitive, however, many factors may need to be taken into account and these may vary from situation to situation. By way of example, we identify a selection of such variables, the prior consideration of which will perhaps reduce the number of problems subsequently faced by the researcher. Thus, the age of those being researched; whether the subject matter of the research is a sensitive area; whether the aims of the research are in any way subversive (*vis-à-vis* subjects, teachers, or institution); the extent to which the researcher and researched can participate and collaborate in planning the research; how the data are to be processed, interpreted, and used; the dissemination of results; and guarantees of confidentiality are just some of the parameters that can form the basis of, to use Aronson and Carlsmith's phrase, 'a specification of democratic ethics'. Readers will no doubt be in a position to develop their own schema from the ideas and concepts expressed in this chapter as well as from their own widening experience as researchers.

SOURCES OF TENSION

We noted earlier that the question of ethics in research is a highly complex subject. This complexity stems from numerous sources of tension. We consider two of the most important. The first, as expressed by Aronson and Carlsmith (1969) is the tension that exists between two sets of related values held by society: a belief in the value of free scientific inquiry in pursuit of truth and knowledge; and a belief in the dignity of individuals and their right to those considerations that follow from it. It is this polarity that we referred to earlier as the costs/benefits ratio and by which 'greater consideration must be given to the risks to physical, psychological, humane, proprietary and cultural values than to the potential contribution of research to knowledge' (Social Sciences and

Humanities Research Council of Canada, 1981).[17] When researchers are confronted with this dilemma (and it is likely to occur much less in education than in social psychology or medicine), it is generally considered that they resolve it in a manner that avoids the extremes of, on the one hand, giving up the idea of research and, on the other, ignoring the rights of the subjects. At all times, the welfare of subjects should be kept in mind (though this has not always been the case, as we have seen), even if it involves compromising the impact of the research. Researchers should never lose sight of the obligations they owe to those who are helping, and should constantly be on the alert for alternative techniques should the ones they are employing at the time prove controversial. Indeed, this polarity between the research and the researched is reflected in the principles of the American Psychological Association who, as Zechmeister and Shaunghnessy show,[18] attempt to strike a balance between the rights of investigators to seek an understanding of human behaviour, and the rights and welfare of individuals who participate in the research. In the final reckoning, the decision to go ahead with a research project rests on a subjective evaluation of the costs both to the individual and society.

The second source of tension in this context is that generated by the competing absolutist and relativist positions. The absolutist view holds that clear, set principles should guide the researchers in their work and that these should determine what ought and what ought not to be done (see Box 16.6). To have taken a wholly absolutist stance, for example, in the case of the Stanford Prison Experiment (see Box 12.3, p. 255) where the researchers studied interpersonal dynamics in a simulated prison, would have meant that the experiment should not have taken place at all or that it should have been terminated well before the sixth day. Zimbardo has stated the ethical position:

> To search for those conditions which justify experiments that induce human suffering is not an appropriate enterprise to anyone who believes in the absolute ethical principle that human life is sacred and must not in any way be knowingly demeaned physically or mentally by experimental interventions. From such a position it is even reasonable to maintain that *no* research should be conducted in psychology or medicine which violates the biological or psychological integrity of any human being regardless of the benefits that might, or even would definitely, accrue to the society at large.
>
> (Zimbardo, 1984)[19]

By this absolute principle, the Stanford Prison Experiment must be regarded as unethical because the participants suffered considerably.

Those who hold a relativist position, by contrast to this, would argue that there can be no absolute guidelines and that the ethical considerations

Box 16.6   Absolute ethical principles in social research

Ethics embody individual and communal codes of conduct based upon adherence to a set of principles which may be explicit and codified or implicit and which may be abstract and impersonal or concrete and personal. For the sake of brevity, we may say that ethics can be dichotomized as 'absolute' and 'relative'. When behaviour is guided by absolute ethical standards, a higher-order moral principle can be postulated which is *invariant* with regard to the conditions of its applicability – across time, situations, persons and expediency. Such principled ethics allow no degree of freedom for ends to justify means or for any positive consequences to qualify instances where the principle is suspended or applied in an altered, watered-down form. In the extreme, there are no extenuating circumstances to be considered or weighed as justifying an abrogation of the ethical standard.

Source: Zimbardo, 1984

will arise from the very nature of the particular research being pursued at the time: situation determines behaviour. There are some contexts, however, where neither the absolutist nor the relativist position is clear cut. Writing of the application of the principle of informed consent with respect to life history studies, Plummer says:

> Both sides have a weakness. If, for instance, as the absolutists usually insist, there should be informed consent, it may leave relatively privileged groups under-researched (since they will say 'no') and underprivileged groups over-researched (they have nothing to lose and say 'yes' in hope). If the individual conscience is the guide, as the relativists insist, the door is wide open for the unscrupulous – even immoral – researcher.
>
> (Plummer, 1983)[20]

He suggests that broad guidelines laid down by professional bodies which offer the researcher room for personal ethical choice are a way out of the problem. Raffe and his colleagues[21] have identified other sources of tension which arose in their own research: that between different ethical principles, for instance, and between groups and other individuals or groups. Before we consider the problems set by ethical dilemmas, we touch upon one or two other trip-wires disclosed by empirical research.

VOICES OF EXPERIENCE

Whatever the ethical stance one assumes and no matter what forethought one brings to bear on one's work, there will always be unknown, unforeseen problems and difficulties lying in wait, (see Box 16.7). It may

Box 16.7   Some characteristics of ethical problems in social research

1 The complexity of a single research problem can give rise to multiple questions of proper behaviour.
2 Sensitivity to ethical issues is necessary but not sufficient for solving them.
3 Ethical problems are the result of conflicting values.
4 Ethical problems can relate to both the subject matter of the research and the conduct of the research.
5 An adequate understanding of an ethical problem sometimes requires a broad perspective based on the consequences of research.
6 Ethical problems involve both personal and professional elements.
7 Ethical problems can pertain to science (as a body of knowledge) and to research (conducted in such a way as to protect the rights of society and research participants).
8 Judgments about proper conduct lie on a continuum ranging from the clearly unethical to the clearly ethical.
9 An ethical problem can be encountered as a result of a decision to conduct a particular study or a decision not to conduct the study.

Source: Kimmel, 1988

therefore be of assistance to readers if we dip into the literature and identify some of these. Baumrind,[22] for example, warns of the possible failure on the researchers' part to perceive a positive indebtedness to their subjects for their services, perhaps, she suggests, because the detachment which investigators bring to their task prevents appreciation of subjects as individuals. This kind of omission can be averted if the experimenters are prepared to spend a few minutes with subjects afterwards in order to thank them for their participation, answer their questions, reassure them that they did well, and generally talk to them for a time. If the research involves subjects in a failure experience, isolation, or loss of self-esteem, for example, researchers must ensure that the subjects do not leave the situation more humiliated, insecure, and alienated than when they arrived. From the subject's point of view, procedures which involve loss of dignity, injury to self-esteem, or affect trust in rational authority are probably most harmful in the long run and may require the most carefully organized ways of recompensing the subject in some way if the researcher chooses to carry on with those methods. With particularly sensitive areas, participants need to be fully informed of the dangers of serious after-effects. There is reason to believe that at least some of the obedient subjects in Milgram's experiments[23] (see Chapter 12) came away from the experience with a lower self-esteem, having to live with the realization that they were willing to yield to destructive authority to the point of inflicting extreme pain on a fellow human being.[24] It follows that researchers need to reflect attitudes of compassion, respect, gratitude and common sense without being too effusive. Subjects clearly have a right to expect that the researchers with whom they are interacting have some concern for the welfare of participants. Further, the subject's sensibilities need also to be taken into account when the researcher comes to write up the research. There have been notorious instances in the research literature when even experienced researchers have shown scant regard for subjects' feelings at the report stage. A related and not insignificant issue concerns the formal recognition of those who have assisted in the investigation, if such be the case. This means that whatever form the written account takes, be it a report, article, chapter, or course thesis, and no matter the readership for which it is intended, its authors must acknowledge and thank all who helped in the research, even to the extent of identifying by name those whose contribution was significant. This can be done in a foreword, introduction or footnote. All this is really a question of common-sensical ethics, an approach that will go a long way in enabling researchers to overcome many of the challenges that beset them.

Ethical problems in educational research can often result from thoughtlessness, oversight, or taking matters for granted. For example, a researcher may be completely oblivious to attendant moral issues and perceive his/her work in an ethical void (not to be compared with the situation where a researcher knowingly treats moral issues as if they do not matter). Again, researchers engaged in sponsored research may feel they do not have to deal with ethical issues, believing their sponsors to have them in hand. Likewise, each researcher in a collaborative venture may take it for granted, wrongly, that colleagues have the relevant ethical questions in mind, consequently appropriate precautions go by default. A student whose research is part of a course requirement and who is motivated wholly by self-interest, or the academic researchers with professional advancement in mind, may overlook the 'oughts' and 'ought nots'. There is nothing wrong with either motivation providing that ethical issues are borne in mind. Finally, researchers should beware of adopting *modi operandi* in which correct ethical procedure unwittingly becomes a victim of convenience.

ETHICAL DILEMMAS

At the beginning of this chapter, we spoke of the costs/benefits ratio. This has been explained by Frankfort-Nachmias and Nachmias as a conflict between two rights which they express as:

> the right to research and acquire knowledge and the right of individual research participants to self-determination, privacy and dignity. A decision not to conduct a planned research project

because it interferes with the participants' welfare is a limit on the first of these rights. A decision to conduct research despite an ethically questionable practice . . . is a limit on the second right.

(Frankfort-Nachmias and Nachmias, 1992)

This constitutes the fundamental ethical dilemma of the social scientist for whom there are no absolute right or wrong answers. Which proposition is favoured, or how a balance between the two is struck will depend very much on the background, experience, and personal values of the individual researcher. With this issue in mind, we now examine other dilemmas that may confront investigators once they have come to some accommodation with this fundamental dilemma and decided to proceed with their research.

Privacy

For the most part, individual 'right to privacy' is usually contrasted with public 'right to know' and this has been defined in the *Ethical Guidelines for the Institutional Review Committee for Research with Human Subjects* as that which:

extends to all information relating to a person's physical and mental condition, personal circumstances and social relationships which is not already in the public domain. It gives to the individual or collectivity the freedom to decide for themselves when and where, in what circumstances and to what extent their personal attitudes, opinions, habits, eccentricities, doubts and fears are to be communicated to or withheld from others.

(Social Sciences and Humanities Research Council of Canada, 1981)

In the context of research, therefore, 'right to privacy' may easily be violated during the course of an investigation or denied after it has been completed. At either point the participant is vulnerable.

Privacy has been considered from three different perspectives by Diener and Crandall (1978). These are: the sensitivity of the information being given, the setting being observed, and dissemination of information. Sensitivity of information refers to how personal or potentially threatening the information is that is being collected by the researcher. Certain kinds of information are more personal than others and may be more threatening. According to a report by the American Psychological Association for example, 'Religious preferences, sexual practices, income, racial prejudices, and other personal attributes such as intelligence, honesty, and courage are more sensitive items than "name, rank and serial number"' (American Psychological Association,

1973).[25] Thus, the greater the sensitivity of the information, the more safeguards are called for to protect the privacy of the research participant. The setting being observed may vary from very private to completely public. The home, for example, is considered one of the most private settings and intrusions into people's homes without their consent are forbidden by law. Dissemination of information concerns the ability to match personal information with the identity of the research participants. Indeed, personal data are defined at law as those data which uniquely identify the individual providing them. When such information is publicized with names through the media, for example, privacy is seriously violated. The more people there are who can learn about the information, the more concern there must be about privacy (see Diener and Crandall, 1978).

As is the case with most rights, privacy can be voluntarily relinquished. Research participants may choose to give up their right to privacy by either allowing a researcher access to sensitive topics or settings or by agreeing that the research report may identify them by name. The latter case at least would be an occasion where informed consent would need to be sought.

Generally speaking, if researchers intend to probe into the private aspects of affairs of individuals, their intentions should be made clear and explicit and informed consent should be sought from those who are to be observed or scrutinized in private contexts. Other methods to protect participants are anonymity and confidentiality and our examination of these follows.

Anonymity

As Frankfort-Nachmias and Nachmias say, 'The obligation to protect the anonymity of research participants and to keep research data confidential is all-inclusive. It should be fulfilled at all costs unless arrangements to the contrary are made with the participants in advance.' (Frankfort-Nachmias and Nachmias, 1992).

The essence of anonymity is that information provided by participants should in no way reveal their identity. The obverse of this is, as we saw earlier, personal data that uniquely identify their supplier. A participant or subject is therefore considered anonymous when the researcher or another person cannot identify the participant or subject from the information provided. Where this situation holds, a participant's privacy is guaranteed, no matter how personal or sensitive the information is. Thus a respondent completing a questionnaire that bears absolutely no identifying marks – names, addresses, occupational details, or coding symbols – is ensured complete and total anonymity. A subject agreeing to a face-to-face interview, on the other hand, can in no way expect anonymity. At most, the interviewer can promise confidentiality.

The principal means of ensuring anonymity then, is not using the names of the participants or any other personal means of identification. Further ways of achieving anonymity have been listed by Frankfort-Nachmias and Nachmias as follows:

> participants may be asked to use an alias of their own creation or to transfer well-remembered personal data (birthdays or National Insurance number, for instance). Anonymity may be enhanced if names and other identifiers are linked to the information by a code number. Once the data have been prepared for analysis, anonymity can be maintained by separating identifying information from the research data. Further safeguards include the prevention of duplication of records and passwords to control access to data.
>
> (Frankfort-Nachmias and Nachmias, 1992)[26]

These directives may work satisfactorily in most situations, but as Raffe and his colleagues (1989) have shown, there is sometimes the difficulty of maintaining an assurance of anonymity when, for example, categorization of data may uniquely identify an individual or institution or when there is access to incoming returns by support staff. Plummer (1983), likewise, refers to life studies in which names have been changed, places shifted, and fictional events added to prevent acquaintances of subjects discovering their identity. Although one can go a long way down this path, there is no absolute guarantee of total anonymity as far as life studies are concerned. Fortunately, in experimental social psychological research the experimenter is interested in 'human' behaviour rather than in the behaviour of specific individuals, as Aronson and Carlsmith (1969) note. Consequently the researcher has absolutely no interest in linking the person as a unique, named individual to actual behaviour, and the research data can be transferred to coded, unnamed data sheets. As they comment, 'the very impersonality of the process is a great advantage ethically because it eliminates some of the negative consequences of the invasion of privacy' (Aronson and Carlsmith, 1969).

Confidentiality

The second way of protecting a participant's right to privacy is through the promise of confidentiality. This means that although researchers know who has provided the information or are able to identify participants from the information given, they will in no way make the connection known publicly; the boundaries surrounding the shared secret will be protected. The essence of the matter is the extent to which investigators keep faith with those who have helped them. It is generally at the access stage or at the point where researchers collect their data that they make their position clear to the hosts and/or subjects. They will thus be quite explicit in explaining to subjects what the meaning and limits of confidentiality are in relation to the particular research project. On the whole, the more sensitive, intimate, or discrediting the information, the greater is the obligation on the researcher's part to make sure that guarantees of confidentiality are carried out in spirit and letter. Promises must be taken seriously.

In his account of confidentiality and the right to privacy, Kimmel (1988) notes that one general finding that emerges from the empirical literature is that some potential respondents in research on sensitive topics will refuse to co-operate when an assurance of confidentiality is weak, vague, not understood, or thought likely to be breached. He concludes that the usefulness of data in sensitive research areas may be seriously affected by the researcher's inability to provide a credible promise of confidentiality. Assurances do not appear to affect co-operation rates in innocuous studies perhaps because, as Kimmel suggests, there is expectation on the part of most potential respondents that confidentiality will be protected.

A number of techniques have been developed to allow public access to data and information without confidentiality being betrayed. These have been listed by Frankfort-Nachmias and Nachmias (1992) as follows:

1 Deletion of identifiers (for example, deleting the names, addresses, or other means of identification from the data released on individuals)
2 Crude report categories (for example, releasing the year of birth rather than the specific date, profession but not the speciality within that profession, general information rather than specific)
3 Microaggregation (that is, the construction of 'average persons' from data on individuals and the release of these data, rather than data on individuals)
4 Error inoculation (deliberately introducing errors into individual records while leaving the aggregate data unchanged).

Betrayal

The term 'betrayal' is usually applied to those occasions where data disclosed in confidence are revealed publicly in such a way as to cause embarrassment, anxiety, or perhaps suffering to the subject or participant disclosing the information. It is a breach of trust, in contrast to confidentiality, and is often a consequence of selfish motives of either a personal or professional nature. Plummer comments, 'in sociology, there is something slightly awry when a sociologist can enter a group and a person's life for a lengthy period, learn their most closely guarded secrets, and then expose all in a critical light to the public' (Plummer, 1983). One of the research methods we have dealt with in this book that is perhaps most vulnerable to betrayal is action research. As Kelly notes, this can produce several ethical problems.[27] She says that if we treat teachers as collaborators in our day-to-day interactions, it may seem like betrayal of trust if these interactions are recorded and used as evidence. This is particularly the case where the evidence is negative. One way out, Kelly suggests, could be to submit reports and evaluations of teachers' reactions to the teachers involved for comment; to get them to assess their own changing attitudes. She warns, however, that this might work well with teachers who have become converts, but is more problematic where teachers remain indifferent or hostile to the aims of the research project. How does one write an honest but critical report of teachers' attitudes, she asks, if one hopes to continue to work with those involved? As she concludes, 'Our position lies uncomfortably between that of the internal evaluator whose main loyalty is to colleagues and the school, and the external researcher for whom informal comments and small incidents may provide the most revealing data' (Kelly, 1989).

Deception

The use of deception in social psychological and sociological research has attracted a certain amount of adverse publicity. In social psychological research, the term is applied to that kind of experimental situation where the researcher knowingly conceals the true purpose and conditions of the research, or else positively misinforms the subjects, or exposes them to unduly painful, stressful or embarrassing experiences, without the subjects having knowledge of what is going on. The deception lies in not telling the whole truth. Advocates of the method feel that if a deception experiment is the only way to discover something of real importance, the truth so discovered is worth the lies told in the process, so long as no harm comes to the subject (see Aronson *et al.*, 1990). Objections to the technique, on the other hand, have already been listed in Chapter 12, where the approach is contrasted with role playing. The problem from the researcher's point of view is: 'What is the proper balance between the interests of science and the thoughtful, humane treatment of people who, innocently, provide the data?' In other words, the problem again hinges on the costs/benefits ratio.

The pervasiveness of the problem of deception becomes even more apparent when we remember that it is even built into many of our measurement devices, since it is important to keep the respondent ignorant of the personality and attitude dimensions that we wish to investigate.

Box 16.8 An extreme case of deception

In an experiment designed to study the establishment of a conditioned response in a situation that is traumatic but not painful, Campbell, Sanderson, and Laverty[28] induced – through the use of a drug – a temporary interruption of respiration in their subjects. The subjects' reports confirmed that this was a 'horrific' experience for them. All the subjects thought they were dying. The subjects, male alcoholic patients who had volunteered for the experiment when they were told that it was connected with a possible therapy for alcoholism, were not warned in advance about the effect of the drug, since this information would have reduced the traumatic impact of the experience.

Source: Adapted from Kelman, 1967

There are many problems that cannot be investigated without deception and although there is some evidence that most subjects accept without resentment the fact of having been duped once they understand the necessity for it (see, for instance, Festinger and Katz, 1966), it is important to keep in the forefront of one's mind the question of whether the amount and type of deception is justified by the significance of the study and the unavailability of alternative procedures.

Ethical considerations loom particularly large when second order deception is involved; that is, letting persons believe they are acting as researchers or researchers' accomplices when they are in fact serving as the subjects (i.e., as unknowing participants). Such procedures can undermine the relationship between the researcher and subject even more than simply misinforming them. The use of deception resulting in particularly harmful consequences would be another occasion where ethical considerations would need to be given priority. An example here would be the study by Campbell, Sanderson, and Laverty[28] which created extremely stressful conditions by using drugs to induce temporary interruption of breathing (see Box 16.8).

Kelman (1967) has suggested three ways of dealing with the problem of deception. First, it is important that we increase our active awareness that it exists as a problem. It is crucial that we always ask ourselves the question whether deception is necessary and justified. We must be wary of the tendency to dismiss the question as irrelevant and to accept deception as a matter of course. Active awareness is thus in itself part of the solution, for it makes the use of deception a focus for discussion, deliberation, investigation, and choice.

The second way of approaching the problem concerns counteracting and minimizing the negative effects of deception. For example, subjects must be selected in a way that will exclude individuals who are especially vulnerable; any potentially harmful manipulation must be kept to a moderate level of intensity; researchers must be sensitive to danger signals in the reactions of subjects and be prepared to deal with crises

370

when they arise; and at the conclusion of the research, they must take time not only to reassure subjects, but also help them work through their feelings about the experience to whatever degree may be required. The principle that subjects ought not to leave the research situation with greater anxiety or lower levels of self-esteem than they came with is a good one to follow. Desirably, subjects should be enriched by the experience and should leave it with the feeling that they have learned something.

The primary way of counteracting negative effects of research employing deception is to ensure that adequate feedback is provided at the end of the research or research session. Feedback must be kept inviolable and in no circumstances should subjects be given false feedback or be misled into thinking they are receiving feedback when the researcher is in fact introducing another experimental manipulation.

Even here, however, there are dangers. As Aronson and Carlsmith say:

> debriefing a subject is not simply a matter of exposing him to the truth. There is nothing magically curative about the truth; indeed . . . if harshly presented, the truth can be more harmful than no explanation at all. There are vast differences in how this is accomplished, and it is precisely these differences that are of crucial importance in determining whether or not a subject is uncomfortable when he leaves the experimental room.
>
> (Aronson and Carlsmith, 1969)

They consider that the one essential aspect of the debriefing process is that researchers communicate their own sincerity as scientists seeking the truth and their own discomfort about the fact that they found it necessary to resort to deception in order to uncover the truth. As they say, 'No amount of postexperimental gentleness is as effective in relieving a subject's discomfort as an honest accounting of the experimenter's *own* discomfort in the situation' (Aronson and Carlsmith, 1969).

The third way of dealing with the problem of deception is to ensure that new procedures and novel techniques are developed. It is a question of tapping one's own creativity in the quest for alternative methods. It has been suggested that role-playing, or 'as-if' experiments, could prove a worthwhile avenue to explore – the 'role-playing versus deception' debate we raised in Chapter 12. By this method, as we saw then, the subject is asked to behave as if he/she were a particular person in a particular situation. Whatever form they take, however, new approaches will involve a radically different set of assumptions about the role of the subject in this type of research. They require us to use subjects' motivations rather than bypassing them. They may even call for increasing the sophistication of potential subjects, rather than maintaining their naivety.

371

Plummer (1983) informs us that even in an unlikely area like life history, deceptions of a lesser nature occur. Thus, for example, the general description given of research may leave out some key issues – indeed, to tell the subject what it is you are looking for may bias the outcome quite substantially. Further, different accounts of the research may have to be presented to different groups. He quotes an instance from his own research, a study of sexual minorities, which required various levels of release – for the subjects, for colleagues, for general enquiries, and for outside friends. None of these accounts actually lied, they merely emphasized a different aspect of the research.

In the social sciences, the dilemma of deception, as we have seen, has played an important part in experimental social psychology where subjects are not told the true nature of the experiment. Another area where it has been increasingly used in recent years is that of sociology, where researchers conceal their identities and 'con' their way into alien groups – the overt/covert debate. Covert, or secret participation, then, refers to that kind of research where researchers spend an extended period of time in particular research settings, concealing the fact that they are researchers and pretending to play some other role.

Bulmer[29] notes that such methods have produced an extremely lively on-going debate and that there are no simple and universally agreed answers to the ethical issues the method produces. Erikson,[30] for example, makes a number of points against covert research; among them, that sociologists have responsibilities to their subjects in general and that secret research can injure other people in ways that cannot be anticipated or compensated for afterwards; and that sociologists have responsibilities towards fellow-sociologists. Douglas,[31] by contrast, argues that covert observation is a necessary, useful, and revealing method. And Bulmer (1982) concludes that the most compelling argument in favour of covert observation is that it has produced good social science which would not have been possible without the method. It would be churlish, he adds, not to recognize that the use of covert methods has advanced our understanding of society.

The final word on the subject of deception in general goes to Kimmel (1988) who claims that few researchers feel that they can do without deception entirely, since the adoption of an overtly conservative approach could deem the study of important research hardly worth the effort. A study of racial prejudice, for example, accurately labelled as such would certainly affect the behaviour of the subjects taking part. Deception studies, he considers, differ so greatly that even the harshest critics would be hard pressed to state unequivocally that all deception has potentially harmful effects on participants or is otherwise wrong. We turn now to research methods used in educational settings and to some ethical issues associated with them.

ETHICS AND RESEARCH METHODS IN EDUCATION

Ethical problems arising from research methods used in educational contexts occur *passim* in Burgess's edited collection of papers, *The Ethics of Educational Research*[32] and the book is recommended to readers for their perusal. Every article reflects the reality of the day-to-day problems, issues and dilemmas that the educational researcher and beginning researchers are likely to encounter. In the first part of the book, chapters focus on different research strategies where authors highlight specific ethical problems associated with the use of such methods in educational inquiry. A chapter by Raffe, Bundell and Bibby, for example, discusses ethical problems arising from the use of survey designs. They examine matters to do with informed consent, the use of data-sets, and those legal and professional codes that have been established to protect subjects involved in survey research. Sammons, in her article, considers problems raised by the use of statistical methods and observes that whereas legislation has made it a requirement for schools to provide statistical evidence on examination results, there is no legislation about how to interpret or use the results. Burgess himself considers ethical issues emerging from ethnographic research. He illustrates the ethical implications involved in relationships between the researcher and researched when gaining access, and in the handling of field relations. A number of contextual problems are discussed. Similar themes characterize Riddell's paper in which she examines feminist research in two rural comprehensive schools. Her work illustrates how feminist investigations raise questions about honesty, power relations, the responsibility of the researcher to the researched, and collaboration. Corresponding topics are broached for action researchers by Kelly, who was co-director of the 'Girls into Science and Technology' project, a study focusing on girls' under-involvement in science and technology (see page 200). A range of questions are considered – researcher power and values, the problem of informed consent, and the manner in which research data are presented to the participants in the project. The ethical implications of case study research are under scrutiny in Simon's article. Again, fundamental issues such as confidentiality, informed consent, anonymity, and the right to privacy and knowledge are discussed. Further points of moral contention with respect to empirical research are considered in the second part of the book.

Reflection on the articles in Burgess will show that the issues thrown up by the complexities of research methods in educational institutions and their ethical consequences are probably among the least anticipated, particularly among the more inexperienced researchers. The latter need to be aware of those kinds of research which, by their nature, lead from one problem to another. Serial problems of this sort may arise in survey methods or ethnographic studies, for example, or in action research or the evaluation of developments. Indeed, the researcher will frequently find that methodological and ethical issues are inextricably interwoven in much of the research we have designated as qualitative or interpretative. As Hitchock and Hughes note:

> Doing participant observation or interviewing one's peers raises ethical problems that are directly related to the nature of the research technique employed. The degree of openness or closure of the nature of the research and its aims is one that directly faces the teacher researcher.
>
> (Hitchock and Hughes, 1988)

They go on to pose the kinds of question that may arise in such a situation. 'Where for the researcher does formal observation end and informal observation begin?' 'Is it justifiable to be open with some teachers and closed with others?' 'How much can the researcher tell the pupils about a particular piece of research?' 'When is a casual conversation part of the research data and when is it not?' 'Is gossip legitimate data and can the researcher ethically use material that has been passed on in confidence?' As Hitchock and Hughes conclude, the list of questions is endless yet they can be related to the nature of both the research technique involved and the social organization of the setting being investigated. The key to the successful resolution of such questions lies in establishing good relations. This will involve the development of a sense of rapport between researchers and their subjects that will lead to feelings of trust and confidence. Mention must be made once again in this particular context of the work of Fine and Sandstrom (1988) who discuss in some detail the ethical and practical aspects of doing field work with children. In particular they show how the ethical implications of participant observation research differ with the age of the children. Another feature of qualitative methods in this connection has been identified by Finch who observes that:

> there can be acute ethical and political dilemmas about how the material produced is *used*, both by the researcher her/himself, and by other people. Such questions are not absent in quantitative research, but greater distancing of the researcher from the research subjects may make them less personally agonizing. Further, in ethnographic work or depth interviewing, the researcher is very much in a position of trust in being accorded privileged access to information which is usually private or invisible. Working out how to ensure that such trust is not betrayed is no simple matter. . . . Where qualitative research is targeted upon social policy issues,

Box 16.9 Ethical principles for the guidance of action researchers

Observe protocol: Take care to ensure that the relevant persons, committees, and authorities have been consulted, informed and that the necessary permission and approval have been obtained.

Involve participants: Encourage others who have a stake in the improvement you envisage to shape and form the work.

Negotiate with those affected: Not everyone will want to be directly involved; your work should take account of the responsibilities and wishes of others.

Report progress: Keep the work visible and remain open to suggestions so that unforeseen and unseen ramifications can be taken account of; colleagues must have the opportunity to lodge a protest to you.

Obtain explicit authorizations: This applies where you wish to observe your professional colleagues; and where you wish to examine documentation.

Negotiate descriptions of people's work: Always allow those described to challenge your accounts on the grounds of fairness, relevance and accuracy.

Negotiate accounts of others' points of view: (e.g. in accounts of communication): Always allow those involved in interviews, meetings and written exchanges to require amendments which enhance fairness, relevance and accuracy.

Obtain explicit authorization before using quotations: Verbatim transcripts, attributed observations, excerpts of audio and video recordings, judgements, conclusions or recommendations in reports (written or to meetings).

Negotiate reports for various levels of release: Remember that different audiences require different kinds of reports; what is appropriate for an informal verbal report to a faculty meeting may not be appropriate for a staff meeting, a report to council, a journal article, a newspaper, a newsletter to parents; be conservative if you cannot control distribution.

Accept responsibility for maintaining confidentiality.

Retain the right to report your work: Provided that those involved are satisfied with the fairness, accuracy and relevance of accounts which pertain to them, and that the accounts do not unnecessarily expose or embarrass those involved, then accounts should not be subject to veto or be sheltered by prohibitions of confidentiality.

Make your principles of procedure binding and known: All of the people involved in your action research project must agree to the principles before the work begins; others must be aware of their rights in the process.

Source: Adapted from Kemmis and McTaggart (1981) and quoted in Hopkins (1985)

here is the special dilemma that findings could be used to worsen the situation of the target population in some way.

(Finch, 1985)[33]

Kelly's paper would seem to suggest, as we have noted elsewhere in this chapter, that the area in qualitative research where one's ethical antennae need to be especially sensitive is that of action research, and it is here that researchers, be they teachers or outsiders, must show particular awareness of the traps that lie in wait. These difficulties have been nowhere better summed up than in Hopkins when he says:

(The researchers') actions are deeply embedded in an existing social organisation and the failure to work within the general procedures of that organisation may not only jeopardise the process of improvement but existing valuable work. Principles of procedures for action research accordingly go beyond the usual concerns for confidentiality and respect for persons who are the subjects of enquiry and define in addition, appropriate ways of working with other participants in the social organisation.

(Hopkins, 1985)[34]

Box 16.9 presents a set of principles specially formulated for action researchers by Kemmis and McTaggart[35] and quoted by Hopkins (1985).

We conclude by reminding readers who may become involved in action research that the problem of access is not resolved once one has been given permission to use the school or organization. The advice given by Hammersley and Atkinson with respect to ethnographic research is equally applicable to action research. As they say:

(having) gained entry to a setting ... by no means guarantees access to all the data available within it. Not all parts of the setting will be equally open to observation, not everyone may be willing to talk, and even the most willing informant will not be prepared, or perhaps even able, to divulge all the information available to him or her. If the data required to develop and test the theory are to be acquired, negotiation of access is therefore likely to be a recurrent preoccupation for the ethnographer.

(Hammersley and Atkinson, 1983)

As the authors observe, different kinds of data will demand different roles, and these in turn result in varying ethical principles being applied to the various negotiating stances.

ETHICS AND TEACHER EVALUATION

After our brief excursus into the problems of ethics in relation to action research, an approach to classroom activities frequently concerned with the improvement of teacher performance and efficiency, it would seem logical to acknowledge the role and importance of ethics in teacher evaluation. The appraisal of teacher and headteacher performance is one that is going to play an increasingly important part as accountability, teacher needs, and management efficiency assume greater significance, as governments introduce pedagogic and curricular changes, and as market forces exert pressure on the educational system generally. By thus throwing teacher appraisal into greater relief, it becomes very important that training appraisal programmes are planned and designed in such a way as to give due recognition to the ethical implications at both school and LEA levels. With this in mind, we briefly review some basic principles and concepts formulated in the USA that may sensitize all those involved in appraisal procedures to the concomitant ethical factors.

Strike,[36] in his paper on the ethics of educational evaluation, offers two broad principles which may form the basis of further considerations in the field of evaluation. These are the principle of benefit maximization and the principle of equal respect. The former, the principle of benefit maximization, holds that the best decision is the one that results in the greatest benefit for most people. It is pragmatic in the sense that it judges the rightness of our actions by their consequences or, as Strike says, the best action is the one with the best results. In British philosophical circles it is known as utilitarianism and requires us to identify the particular benefits we wish to maximize, to identify a suitable population for maximization, specify what is to count as maximization, and fully understand the consequences of our actions. The second principle, that of equal respect, demands that we respect the equal worth of all people. This requires us to treat people as ends rather than means; to regard them as free and rational; and to accept that they are entitled to the same basic rights as others.

Strike then goes on to list the following ethical principles which he regards as particularly important to teacher evaluation and which may be seen in the light of the two broad principles outlined above:

1 *Due process* Evaluative procedures must ensure that judgements are reasonable: that known and accepted standards are consistently applied from case to case, that evidence is reasonable and that there are systematic and reasonable procedures for collecting and testing evidence.

2 *Privacy* This involves a right to control information about oneself, and protects people from unwarranted interference in their affairs. In evaluation, it requires that procedures are not overtly intrusive and that such evaluation pertains only to those aspects of a teacher's activity that are job related. It also protects the confidentiality of evaluation information.

3 *Equality* In the context of evaluation, this can best be understood as a prohibition against making decisions on irrelevant grounds, such as race, religion, gender, or ethnicity.

4 *Public perspicuity* This principle requires openness to the public concerning evaluative procedures, their purposes and their results.

5 *Humaneness* This principle requires that consideration is shown to the feelings and sensitivities of those in evaluative contexts.

Box 16.10 An extract from a bill of rights for teacher evaluation procedural rights

---

1 Teachers have the right to be evaluated according to general, public, and comprehensible standards.

2 Teachers have the right to notice concerning when they will be evaluated.

3 Teachers have the right to know the results of their evaluations.

4 Teachers have the right to express a reaction to the results of their evaluations in a meaningful way.

5 Teachers have the right to orderly and timely evaluation.

6 Teachers have the right to appeal against adverse decisions and to have their views considered by a competent and unbiased authority.

7 Teachers have the right to a statement of the reasons for any action taken in their cases.

Source: Adapted from Strike, 1990

6 *Client benefit* This principle requires that evaluative decisions are made in a way that respects the interests of students, parents, and the public, in preference to those of educational institutions and their staff.

7 *Academic freedom* This requires that an atmosphere of intellectual openness is maintained in the classroom for both teachers and students. Evaluation should not be conducted in a way that chills this environment.

8 *Respect for autonomy* Teachers are entitled to reasonable discretion in, and to exercise reasonable judgement about, their work. Evaluations should not be conducted so as to unreasonably restrict discretion and judgement.

Strike has developed these principles in a more extended and systematic form in his article (see the short extract in Box 16.10).

Finally, we note the three principles that Strike applies to the task of conflict resolution, to resolving the differences between teachers and the institutions in which they work as a result of the evaluation process. He recommends that where a conflict has to be resolved, remediation is to be preferred, where possible, to disciplinary action or termination; mediation is to be preferred, where possible, to more litigious forms and solutions; and that informal attempts to settle disputes should precede formal ones.

We have seen throughout this chapter and in this particular section how the codification and regulation of ethical principles is proceeding apace in the USA; and that this is occurring at both a formal and informal level. In this next, penultimate, section we look a little closer at these matters and their implications for the UK.

RESEARCH AND REGULATION

A glance at any current American textbook in the social sciences will reveal the extent to which professional researchers in the USA are governed by laws and regulations.[37] These exist at several levels: federal and state legal statutes, ethics review committees to oversee research in universities and other institutions, ethical codes of the professional bodies and associations as well as the personal ethics of individual researchers are all important regulatory mechanisms. All investigators, from undergraduates pursuing a course-based research project to professional researchers striving at the frontiers of knowledge, must take cognizance of the ethical codes and regulations governing their practice. Indeed, we have sampled some of the ethical research requirements of American investigators in this chapter. Failure to meet these responsibilities on the part of researchers is perceived as undermining the whole scientific process and may lead to legal and financial penalties for individuals and institutions.

If Britain has not yet gone as far as the USA down this path of regulation and litigation, it may only be a question of time. Even in the UK, however, professional societies have formulated working codes of practice which express the consensus of values within a particular group and which help individual researchers in indicating what is desirable and what is to be avoided. Of course, this does not solve all the problems, for there are few absolutes and in consequence ethical principles may be open to a wide range of interpretations. In addition, more informal codes of ethical principles have emerged as a result of individual initiative. The establishment of comprehensive regulatory mechanisms is thus well in hand in the UK, but it is perhaps in the field of information and data – how they are stored and the uses to which they are put, for example – that educational researchers are likely to find growing interest. This category would include, for instance, statistical data, data used as the basis for evaluation, curricular records, written records, transcripts, data sheets, personal documents, research data, computer files, and audio and video recordings.

As information technology establishes itself in a centre-stage position and as society becomes increasingly dependent on information economically and functionally, so we realize just how important the concept of information is to us. It is important not only for what it is, but for what it can do. Numerous writers have pointed out the connection between information and power. Harris, Pearce, and Johnstone, for instance, say:

> Information and power have a very close relationship. . . . Power over individuals . . . relies on the control of personal information. Power of professionalism involves both submission of the client to the professional's better judgment and a network of professional and inter-professional relationships, and probably rivalries, buttressed by exclusive sharing of information. It is well to recognise

that decisions about information-holding or access are, to an extent, always decisions about power.

(Harris, Pearce and Johnstone, 1992)[38]

When we reflect on the extent to which two key concepts in the world of contemporary education, namely 'evaluation' (or appraisal) and 'accountability', depend wholly on information in one form or another, that it is their very life blood, we realize just how powerful it is. Its misuse, therefore, or disclosure at the wrong time or to the wrong client or organ, can result in the most unfortunate consequences for an individual, group, or institution. And matters are greatly exacerbated if it is the wrong information, or incomplete, or deliberately misleading.

In a world awash with information, it is essential that safeguards be established to protect it from misuse or abuse. The Data Protection Act 1984[39] was designed to achieve such an end. This covered the principles of data protection, the responsibilities of data users, and the rights of data subjects, and its broad aims are embodied in eight principles. However, data held for 'historical and research' purposes are exempted from the principle which gives individuals the right of access to personal data about themselves, provided the data are not made available in a form which identifies individuals. Research data also have partial exemption from two further principles, with the effect that such data may be held indefinitely and the use of the data for research purposes need not be disclosed at the time of data collection.

Of the two most important principles which do concern research data, one states that personal data (i.e., data that uniquely identifies the person supplying it) shall be held only for specified and lawful purposes. The second principle states that appropriate security measures shall be taken against unauthorized access to, or alteration, disclosure, or destruction of personal data and against accidental loss or destruction of personal data. For a study of the effects of the Data Protection Act on the work of the Centre for Educational Sociology, see Raffe, Bundell and Bibby (1989).

CONCLUSION

This book has been concerned with the methods used in educational research and in our final chapter we have attempted to acquaint readers with some of the ethical difficulties they are likely to experience in the conduct of such research. To this end, we have drawn on key concepts and ideas from deliberations and investigations in the educational, psychological, social psychological, and sociological domains in order to elucidate some of the more important dilemmas and issues that are an inevitable part of social research. In doing this we are well aware that it is not possible to identify all potential ethical questions or adjudicate on what is correct researcher behaviour.[40] On the other hand, perhaps some of the things we have said will seem irrelevant to readers who are unlikely to be called upon to submit subjects to painful electric shocks, provoke aggression, embarrass them, have them tell lies, or eat grasshoppers, as Aronson and Carlsmith (1969) put it. Nevertheless, it is hoped that these few pages will have induced in readers a certain disposition that will enable them to approach their own more temperate projects with a greater awareness and fuller understanding of the ethical dilemmas and moral issues lurking in the interstices of the research process. However inexperienced in these matters researchers are, they will bring to the world of social research a sense of rightness[41] on which they can construct a set of rational principles appropriate to their own circumstances and based on personal, professional, and societal values (we stress the word 'rational' since reason is a prime ingredient of ethical thinking and it is the combination of reason and a sense of rightness that researchers must keep faith with if they are to bring a rich ethical quality to their work).

Although no code of practice can anticipate or resolve all problems, there is a six-fold advantage in fashioning a personal code of ethical practice.[42] First, such a code establishes one as a member of the wider scientific community having a shared interest in its values and concerns. Second, a code of ethical practice makes researchers aware of their obligations to their subjects and also to those problem areas where there is a general consensus about what is acceptable and what is not. In this sense it has a clarificatory value. Third, when one's professional behaviour is guided by a principled code of ethics, then it is possible to consider that there may be alternative ways of doing the same thing, ways that are more ethical or less unethical should one be confronted by a moral challenge. Fourth, a balanced code can be an important organizing factor in researchers' perceptions of the research situation, and as such may assist them in their need to anticipate and prepare. Fifth, a code of practice validated by their own sense of rightness will help researchers to develop an intuitive sensitivity that will be particularly helpful to them in dealing with the unknown and the unexpected, especially where the more fluidic methods such as ethnography and participant observation are concerned. And sixth, a code of practice will bring discipline to researchers' awareness. Indeed, it should be their aim to strike a balance between discipline and awareness. Discipline without awareness may result in largely mechanical behaviour; whereas awareness without discipline can produce inappropriate responses.

Finally, we live in a relative universe and it has been said that relativity seeks adjustment; that adjustment is art; and that the art of life lies in a constant readjustment to our surroundings.[43] What better precept for the art of the ethical researcher?

REFERENCES AND NOTES

1 For example, American Psychological Association (1982); American Sociological Association (1971); British Sociological Association (1982); Social Research Association (1986); and the British Educational Research Association (1989). Comparable developments may be found in other fields of endeavour. For an examination of key ethical issues in medicine, business, and journalism together with reviews of common ethical themes across these areas, see *Ethics and Social Concern*, ed. Anthony Serafini (Paragon House, New York, 1989). The book also contains an account of principal ethical theories from Socrates to R.M. Hare.

2 Frankfort-Nachmias, C. and Nachmias, D., *Research Methods in the Social Sciences* (Edward Arnold, London, 1992).

3 Aronson, E., Ellsworth, P.C., Carlsmith, J.M. and Gonzalez, M.H., *Methods of Research in Social Psychology* (McGraw-Hill, New York, 1990).

4 Hammersley, M. and Atkinson, P., *Ethnography: Principles and Practice* (Routledge, London, first published 1983, reprinted 1991).

5 Diener, E. and Crandall, R., *Ethics in Social and Behavioral Research* (University of Chicago Press, Chicago, 1978).

6 US Dept of Health, Education and Welfare, Public Health Service and National Institute of Health, *The Institutional Guide to D.H.E.W. Policy on Protecting Human Subjects*, DHEW Publication (NIH): December 2, 1971, 72–102.

7 Burgess, R.G., 'Grey areas: ethical dilemmas in educational ethnography', in Burgess, R.G. (ed.), *The Ethics of Educational Research* (Falmer Press, Lewes, 1989).

8 Soble, A., 'Deception in social science research: Is informed consent possible?', *Hastings Center Report*, 8 (1978) 40–6.

9 Fine, G.A. and Sandstrom, K.L., *Knowing Children: Participant Observation with Minors*, Qualitative Research Methods Series 15 (Sage, Calif., 1988).

10 Bell, J., *Doing Your Research Project* (Open University Press, Milton Keynes, first published 1987, reprinted 1991).

11 Foster, P., 'Change and adjustment in a Further Education College', in Burgess, R.G. (ed.), *The Ethics of Educational Research* (Falmer Press, Lewes, 1989).

12 Festinger, L. and Katz, D., *Research Methods in the Behavioral Sciences* (Holt, Rinehart & Winston, New York, 1966).

13 Aronson, E. and Carlsmith, J.M., 'Experimentation in social psychology', in Lindzey, G. and Aronson, E. (eds), *The Handbook of Social Psychology*, Vol. 2 (Addison-Wesley, Reading, Mass., 1969).

14 Hitchcock, G. and Hughes, D., *Research and the Teacher* (Routledge, London, 1988).

15 Cavan, S., *The American Journal of Sociology*, 83 (1977) 810.

16 Kimmel, A.J., *Ethics and Values in Applied Social Research* (Sage, Calif., 1988).

17 *Ethical Guidelines for the Institutional Review Committee for Research with Human Subjects* (Social Sciences and Humanities Research Council of Canada, 1981).

18 Zechmeister, E.B. and Shaunghnessy, J.J., *A Practical Introduction to Research Methods in Psychology* (McGraw-Hill, New York, 1992).

19 Zimbardo, P.C., 'On the ethics of intervention in human psychological research with specific reference to the "Stanford Prison Experiment"', in Murphy, J., John, M. and Brown, H. (eds), *Dialogues and Debates in Social Psychology* (Lawrence Erlbaum Associates in association with the Open University Press, first published 1984, reprinted 1992).

20 Plummer, K., *Documents of Life* (George Allen and Unwin, London, 1983).

21 Raffe, D., Bundell, I. and Bibby, J., 'Ethics and tactics: issues arising from an educational survey', in Burgess, R.G. (ed.), *The Ethics of Educational Research* (Falmer Press, Lewes, 1989).

22 Baumrind, D., 'Some thoughts on ethics of research', *American Psychologist*, 19 (1964) 421–3.

23 Milgram, S., 'Behavioral study of obedience', *Journal of Abnormal and Social Psychology*, 67 (1963) 371–8.

24 Kelman, H.C., 'Human use of human subjects', *Psychological Bulletin*, 67 (1) (1967) 1–11.

25 American Psychological Association, *Ethical Principles in the Conduct of Research with Human Subjects*, Ad Hoc Committee on Ethical Standards in Psychological Research, (Washington, D.C., 1973).

26 See also, Reynolds, P.D., *Ethical Dilemmas and Social Science Research* (San Francisco, Jossey-Bass, 1979).

27 Kelly, A., 'Education or indoctrination? The ethics of school-based action research', in Burgess, R.G. (ed.), *The Ethics of Educational Research* (Falmer Press, Lewes, 1989).

28 Campbell, D., Sanderson, R.E. and Laverty, S.G., 'Characteristics of a conditioned response in human subjects during extinction trials following a single traumatic conditioning trial', *Journal of Abnormal and Social Psychology* 68 (1964) 627–39.

29 Bulmer, M. (ed.), *Social Research Ethics* (Macmillan, London and Basingstoke, 1982).

30 Erikson, K.T., 'A comment on disguised observation in sociology', *Social Problems*, 14 (1967) 366–73.

31 Douglas, J.D., *Investigative Social Research* (Sage, Beverly Hills, 1976).

32 Burgess, R.G. (ed.), *The Ethics of Educational Research* (Falmer Press, Lewes, 1989).

33 Finch, J., 'Social policy and education: problems and possibilities of using qualitative research', in Burgess, R.G. (ed.), *Issues in Educational Research* (Falmer Press, Lewes, 1989).

34 Hopkins, D., *A Teacher's Guide to Classroom Research* (Open University Press, Milton Keynes, first published 1985, reprinted 1990).

35 Kemmis, S. and McTaggart, R., *Action Research Planner* (Deakins University Press, Victoria, Australia, 1981).

36 Strike, K.A., 'The ethics of educational evaluation', in *A New Handbook of Teacher Evaluation*, Millman, J. and Darling-Hammond, L. (eds), (Corwin Press, Sage, Calif., 1990).

37 For example, see Zechmeister, E.B. and Shaughnessy, J.J., *A Practical Introduction to Research Methods in Psychology* (McGraw-Hill, New York, 1992).

38 Harris, N., Pearce, P. and Johnstone, S., *The Legal Context of Teaching* (Longman, London, 1992).

39 *Data Protection Act*, HMSO, London, 1984.

40 As regards judging researchers' behaviour, perhaps the only area of educational research where the term ethical absolute can be unequivocally applied and where subsequent judgment is unquestionable is that concerning

the researcher's relationship with his data. Should they choose to abuse their data for whatever reason, the behaviour is categorically wrong; no place here for moral relativism. For once a clear dichotomy is relevant: if there is such a thing as clearly ethical behaviour, such abuse is clearly unethical. It can take the form of first, falsifying data to support a preconceived, often favoured, hypothesis; second, manipulating data, often statistically, for the same reason (or manipulating techniques used – deliberately including leading questions, for example); third, using data selectively, that is, ignoring or excluding the bits that don't fit one's hypothesis; and fourth, going beyond the data, in other words, arriving at conclusions not warranted by them (or over-interpreting them). But even malpractice as serious as these examples cannot be controlled by fiat: ethical injunctions would hardly be appropriate in this context, let alone enforceable. The only answer (in the absence of professional monitoring) is for the researcher to have a moral code that is 'rationally derived and intelligently applied', to use the words of the philosopher, R.S. Peters, and to be guided by it consistently. Moral competence, like other competencies, can be learned. One way of acquiring it is to bring interrogative reflection to bear on one's own code and practice. In sum, ethical behaviour depends on the concurrence of ethical thinking which in turn is based on fundamentally thought-out principles. Readers wishing to take the subject of data abuse further should read Peter Medawar's elegant and amusing essay, 'Scientific fraud', in *The Threat and the Glory: Reflections on Science and Scientists*, edited by David Pike, Oxford University Press, Oxford, 1991; and also W. Broad and N. Wade, *Betrayers of Truth: Fraud and Deceit in the Halls of Science*, Century, New York, 1983.

41 We would see the term 'a sense of rightness' as approximately equivalent to the word 'conscience' as used in the religious tradition, or to Carl Rogers' term 'internal locus of evaluation' as used in a humanistic context.

42 Readers seeking guidance on this matter are referred to Reynolds (1979), where the author has assembled a composite code of ethics based on statements appearing in twenty-four codes related to the conduct of social science research in the United States. The seventy-eight statements listed by him cover general issues related to the code of ethics: the decision to conduct the research; the actual conduct of the research; informed consent; protection of rights and welfare of participants; deception; confidentiality and anonymity; benefits to participants; effects on aggregates or communities; and the interpretation and reporting of the results of the research. The composite code is reprinted in Frankfort-Nachmias and Nachmias (1992). As we pointed out in the text, codes of practice are not a universal panacea, in spite of our advocacy, and their efficacy will vary with method and context. Some researchers, for example, have reported difficulties in working with codes of practice when doing field work. For the appropriate references to these cases, see R.G. Burgess, 'Grey areas: ethical dilemmas in educational ethnography' in Burgess, R.G. (ed.) *The Ethics of Educational Research* (Falmer Press, Lewes, 1989).

43 Okakura, Kakuzo, *The Book of Tea* (Kodansha International, Tokyo, 1991).

BIBLIOGRAPHY

Acker, S., *Teachers, Gender and Careers* (Falmer Press, Lewes, 1989).

Acker, S., 'Teachers' culture in an English primary school: continuity and change', *Brit. Journ. Sociol. Educat.*, 11, 3 (1990) 257–73.

Acton, H.B., 'Positivism', in J.O. Urmson (ed.), *The Concise Encyclopedia of Western Philosophy* (Hutchinson, London, 1975).

Adams-Webber, J.R., 'Elicited versus provided constructs in repertory grid technique: a review', *Brit. J. Med. Psychol.*, 43 (1970) 349–54.

Adelman, C., Jenkins, D. and Kemmis, S., 'Rethinking case study: notes from the Second Cambridge Conference', in H. Simons (ed.), *Towards a Science of the Singular* (Centre for Applied Research in Education, University of East Anglia, 1980).

Adeyemi, M.B., 'The effects of a social studies course on the philosophical orientations of history and geography graduate students in Botswana', *Educational Studies*, 18, 2 (1992) 235–44.

Aitkin, M., Bennett, N. and Hesketh, J., 'Teaching styles and pupil progress: a re-analysis', *British Journal of Educational Psychology*, 51, 2 (1981) 170–86.

Aitkin, M., Anderson, D. and Hinde, J., 'Statistical modelling of data on teaching styles, *Journal of the Royal Statistical Society*, 144, 4 (1981) 419–61.

Alexander, P.C. and Neimeyer, G.J., 'Constructivism and family therapy', *International Journal of Personal Construct Psychology*, 2, 2 (1989) 111–21.

American Psychological Association, *Ethical Principles in the Conduct of Research with Human Subjects*, Washington, DC: Ad Hoc Committee on Ethical Standards in Psychological Research, 1973.

Antonsen, E.A., 'Treatment of a boy of twelve: help with handwriting, play therapy and discussion of problems', *Journ. Educat. Therapy*, 2, 1 (1988) 25–32.

Applebee, A.M., 'The development of children's responses to repertory grids', *Brit. J. Soc. Clin. Psychol.*, 15 (1976) 101–2.

Argyle, M., 'Discussion chapter: an appraisal of the new approach to the study of social behaviour', in M. Brenner, P. Marsh and M. Brenner (eds), *The Social Context of Method* (Croom Helm, London, 1978).

Argyris, C., 'Dangers of applying results from experimental social psychology', *American Psychologist*, 30 (1975) 469–85.

Arnold, P. and Atkins, J., 'The social and emotional adjustment of hearing-impaired children integrated in primary schools', *Educational Research*, 33, 3 (1991) 223–8.

Armistead, N. (ed.), *Reconstructing Social Psychology* (Penguin Books, London, 1974).

Aronson, E. and Carlsmith, J.M., 'Experimentation in social psychology', in

G. Lindzey and E. Aronson (eds), *The Handbook of Social Psychology*, Vol. 2 (Addison-Wesley, Reading, Mass., 1969).

Aronson, E., Ellsworth, P.C., Carlsmith, J.M. and Gonzalez, M.H., *Methods of Research in Social Psychology* (McGraw-Hill, New York, 1990).

Aronson, E., *The Social Animal* (Freeman, San Francisco, 1976).

Ary, D., Jacobs, L.C. and Razavieh, A., *Introduction to Research in Education* (Holt, Rinehart & Winston, New York, 1972).

Ashton, E., 'Managing change in Further Education: some perspectives of college principals', unpublished PhD thesis, Loughborough University of Technology, 1994.

Backstrom, C.H. and Hursh, G.D., *Survey Research* (Northwestern University Press, Evanston, 1963).

Bailey, K.D., *Methods of Social Research* (Collier-Macmillan, London, 1978).

Ball, S.J., *Beachside Comprehensive: A Case Study of Secondary Schooling* (Cambridge University Press, Cambridge, 1981).

Ball, S.J., 'School politics, teachers' careers and educational change: a case study of becoming a comprehensive school', in L. Barton and S. Walker (eds), *Educational and Social Change* (Croom Helm, Beckenham, 1985).

Ball, S.J., *The Micro-Politics of the School* (Methuen, London, 1987).

Ball, S.J. and Goodson, I.F. (eds), *Teachers' Lives and Careers* (Falmer Press, Lewes, 1985).

Bannister, D. (ed.), *Perspectives in Personal Construct Theory* (Academic Press, London, 1970).

Bannister, D. (ed.), *New Perspectives in Personal Construct Theory* (Academic Press, London, 1977).

Bannister, D. and Mair, J.M.M., *The Evaluation of Personal Constructs* (Academic Press, London, 1968).

Banuazizi, A. and Movahedi, S., 'Interpersonal dynamics in a simulated prison: a methodological analysis', *American Psychologist*, 30 (1975) 152–60.

Barr Greenfield, T., 'Theory about organizations: a new perspective and its implications for schools', in M.G. Hughes (ed.), *Administrating Education: International Challenge* (Athlone Press, London, 1975).

Barratt, P.E.H., *Bases of Psychological Methods* (John Wiley and Sons, Queensland, 1971).

Baumrind, D., 'Some thoughts on ethics of research', *American Psychologist*, 19 (1964) 421–3.

Beck, R.N., *Handbook in Social Philosophy* (Macmillan, New York, 1979).

Belbin, R.M., *Management Teams: Why they Succeed or Fail* (Heinemann, London, 1981).

Bell, J., *Doing Your Research Project* (Open University Press, Milton Keynes, first published, 1987, reprinted 1991).

Belson, W.A., *Juvenile Theft: Causal Factors* (Harper and Row, London, 1975).

Belson, W.A., *Validity in Survey Research* (Gower Publishing Co., Aldershot, 1986).

Bennett, N., *Teaching Styles and Pupil Progress* (Open Books, London, 1975).

Bennett, N. and Jordan, J., 'A typology of teaching styles in primary schools', *British Journal of Educational Psychology*, 45 (1975) 20–8.

Bennett, S. and Bowers, D., *An Introduction to Multivariate Techniques for Social and Behavioural Sciences* (Macmillan, London, 1977).

Ben-Peretz, M. and Kremer-Hayon, L., 'The content and context of professional dilemmas encountered by novice and senior teachers', *Educational Review*, 42, 1 (1990) 31–40.

Berkowitz, L. (ed.), *Advances in Experimental Social Psychology*, vol. 10 (Academic Press, New York, 1977).

Bernstein, B., 'Sociology and the sociology of education: a brief account', in J. Rex (ed.), *Approaches to Sociology: an Introduction to Major Trends in British Sociology* (Routledge & Kegan Paul, London, 1974).

Best, J.W., *Research in Education* (Prentice-Hall, Englewood Cliffs, New Jersey, 1970).

Beynon, J., *Initial Encounters in the Secondary School* (Falmer Press, Lewes, 1985).

Beynon, J., 'Career histories in a comprehensive school', in S.J. Ball and I.F. Goodson (eds), *Teachers' Lives and Careers* (Falmer Press, Lewes, 1985).

Bhadwal, S.C. and Panda, P.K., 'The effects of a package of some curricular strategies on the study habits of rural primary school students: a year long study', *Educational Studies*, 17, 3 (1991) 261–72.

Billig, M., *Arguing and Thinking: A Rhetorical Approach to Social Psychology* (Cambridge University Press, Cambridge, 1987).

Blatchford, P., 'Children's attitudes to work at 11 years', *Educational Studies*, 18, 1 (1992) 107–18.

Blease, D., 'Broadwood School Update, 1991: Integration of I.T. into the curriculum three years on', unpublished document, Department of Education, Loughborough University of Technology.

Blease, D. and Cohen, L., *Coping with Computers: An Ethnographic Study in Primary Classrooms* (Paul Chapman Publishers, London, 1990).

Blease, D. and Lever, D., 'What do primary headteachers do?', *Educational Studies*, 18, 2 (1992) 185–99.

Bliss, J., Monk, M. and Ogborn, J., *Qualitative Data Analysis for Educational Research* (Croom Helm, Beckenham, 1983).

Bloor, M., 'On the analysis of observational data: a discussion of the worth and uses of induction techniques and respondent validation', *Sociology*, 12, 3 (1978) 545–52.

Borg, W.R., *Educational Research: An Introduction* (Longman, London, 1963).

Borg, W.R., *Applying Educational Research: A Practical Guide for Teachers* (Longman, New York, 1981) 218–19.

Boring, E.G., 'The role of theory in experimental psychology', *Amer. J. Psychol.*, 66 (1953) 169–84.

Borkowsky, F.T., 'The relationship of work quality in undergraduate music curricula to effectiveness in instrumental music teaching in the public schools', *J. Exp. Educ.*, 39 (1970) 14–19.

Boulton, M.J., 'Participation in playground activities at middle school', *Educational Research* 34, 3 (1992) 167–82.

Bracht, G.H. and Glass, G.V., 'The external validity of experiments', *Amer. Educ. Res. Journ.*, 4, 5 (1968) 437–74.

Bradburn, N.M. and Berlew, D.E., *Economic Development and Cultural Change* (University of Chicago Press, Chicago, 1961).

Breakwell, G., *Interviewing* (Routledge/BPS, London, 1990).

Briggs, J.P. and Peat, D.F., *Looking Glass Universe* (Fontana Paperbacks, London, 1984).

Broad, W. and Wade, N., *Betrayers of Truth: Fraud and Deceit in the Halls of Science* (Century, New York, 1983).

Bromley, D.B., *The Case Study Method in Psychology and Related Disciplines* (John Wiley, Chichester, 1986).

Brenner, M., Marsh, P. and Brenner, M. (eds), *The Social Context of Method* (Croom Helm, Beckenham, 1978).

Brown, J. and Sime, J.D., 'Accounts as a general methodology', paper presented to the British Psychological Society Conference, Exeter University, 1977.

Brown, J. and Sime, J.D., 'A methodology of accounts', in M. Brenner (ed.), *Social Method and Social Life* (Academic Press, London, 1981).

Brown, R. and Hernstein, P.J., *Psychology* (Methuen, London, 1975).

Buhler, C. and Allen, M., *Introduction to Humanistic Psychology* (Brooks/Cole, Monterey, California, 1972).

Bulmer, M. (ed.), *Social Research Ethics* (Macmillan, London and Basingstoke, 1982).

Burgess, R.G., *Experiencing Comprehensive Education* (Methuen, London, 1983).

Burgess, R.G., 'Conversations with a purpose? The ethnographic interview in educational research', paper presented at the *British Educational Research Association Annual Conference*, Sheffield, 1985.

Burgess, R.G. (ed.), *Issues in Educational Research* (Falmer Press, Lewes, 1985).

Burgess, R.G. (ed.), *The Ethics of Educational Research* (Falmer Press, Lewes, 1989).

Burgess, R.G., 'Grey areas: ethical dilemmas in educational ethnography', in R.G. Burgess (ed.), *The Ethics of Educational Research* (Falmer Press, Lewes, 1989).

Burke, M., Noller, P. and Caird, D., 'Transition from probationer to educator: a repertory grid analysis', *International Journal of Personal Construct Psychology*, 5, 2 (1992) 159–82.

Burrell, G. and Morgan, G., *Sociological Paradigms and Organisational Analysis* (Heinemann Educational Books, London, 1979).

Butler, N.R. and Golding, J., *From Birth to Five* (Pergamon Press, Oxford, 1986).

Campbell, D., Sanderson, R.E. and Laverty, S.G., 'Characteristics of a conditioned response in human subjects during extinction trials following a single traumatic conditioning trial', *Journal of Abnormal and Social Psychology*, 68 (1964) 627–39.

Campbell, D.T. and Fiske, D., 'Convergent and discriminant validation by the multi-trait multimethod matrix', *Psychological Bulletin*, 56 (1959) 81–105.

Campbell, D.T. and Stanley, J.C., 'Experimental and quasi-experimental designs for research on teaching', in N.L. Gage (ed.), *Handbook of Research on Teaching* (Rand McNally, Chicago, 1963).

Cannell, C.F. and Kahn, R.L., 'Interviewing', in G. Lindzey and A. Aronson (eds), *The Handbook of Social Psychology*, vol. 2, *Research Methods* (Addison Wesley, New York, 1968).

Carlsmith, J.M., Lepper, M.R. and Landauer, T.K., 'Children's obedience to adult requests: Interaction effects of anxiety arousal and apparent punitiveness of the adult', *Journal of Personality and Social Psychology*, 30 (1974) 822–8.

Cavan, S., *The American Journal of Sociology*, 83 (1977) 810.

Central Advisory Council for Education, *Children and their Primary Schools* (HMSO, London, 1967).

Chanan, G. and Delamont, S. (eds), *Frontiers of Classroom Research* (NFER, Windsor, 1975).

Chaplin, F.S., *Experimental Designs in Sociological Research* (Harper & Row, New York, 1947).

Chatfield, C., 'The initial examination of data', *Journal of the Royal Statistical Society*, 148, 3 (1985) 214–53.

Cicourel, A.V., *Method and Measurement in Sociology* (The Free Press, New York, 1964).

Chetwynd, S.J., 'Outline of the analyses available with G.A.P., the Grid Analysis Package' (St George's Hospital, London SW17, 1974).

Child, D., *The Essentials of Factor Analysis* (Holt, Rinehart & Winston, London, 1970).

Cohen, L., *Educational Research in Classrooms and Schools, a Manual of Materials and Methods* (Harper & Row, London, 1977).

Cohen, L. and Holliday, M., *Statistics for Education and Physical Education* (Harper & Row, London, 1979).

Cohen, L. and Holliday, M., *Statistics for Social Scientists: An Introductory Text with Computer Programs in BASIC* (Harper & Row, London, 1982).

Cohen, L. and Manion, L., *Perspectives on Classrooms and Schools* (Holt-Saunders, Eastbourne, 1981).

Cohen, L., *Racism Awareness Materials in Initial Teacher Training* (Report to the Leverhulme Trust, 15–19 New Fetter Lane, London EC4A 1NR. 1993).

Cohen, P.A., Kulik, J.A. and Kulik, C.C., 'Educational outcomes of tutoring: a meta-analysis of findings', *Amer. Educ. Research J.*, 19, 2 (1982) 237–48.

Cole, A.L., 'Personal theories of teaching: development in the formative years', *Alberta Journal of Educational Research*, 37, 2 (1991) 119–32.

Collins, H.M., *Changing Order: Replication and Induction in Scientific Practice* (Sage, London and Beverly Hills, 1985).

Collins, L., *The Use of Models in the Social Sciences* (Tavistock Publications, London, 1976).

Corey, S.M., *Action Research to Improve School Practices* (Bureau of Publications, Teachers College, Columbia University, New York, 1953).

Corporaal, A.H., 'Repertory grid research into cognitions of prospective primary school teachers, *Teaching and Teacher Education*, 36 (1991) 315–29.

Coulthard, M., *An Introduction to Discourse Analysis* (Longman, London, 1985).

Crocker, A.C. and Cheeseman, R.G., 'The ability of children to rank themselves for academic ability', *Educational Studies*, 14, 1 (1988) 105–10.

Croll, P., *Systematic Observation* (Falmer Press, Lewes, 1986).

Croll, P. and Moses, D., *One in Five: The Assessment and Incidence of Special Educational Needs* (Routledge & Kegan Paul, London, 1985).

Cuff, E.C. and Payne, G.C.F. (eds), *Perspectives in Sociology* (George Allen & Unwin, London, 1979).

Cunningham, D., McMahon, H. and O'Neill, B., *Bubble Dialogue: A New Tool for Instruction and Assessment*, (Language Development and Hypermedia Research Group, Faculty of Education, University of Ulster at Coleraine, 1991).

Curtis, B. and Mays, W. (eds.), *Phenomenology and Education* (Methuen, London, 1978).

Data Protection Act, HMSO, London, 1984.

Davidson, J., *Outdoor Recreation Surveys: The Design and Use of Questionnaires for Site Surveys* (Countryside Commission, London, 1970).

Davie, R., 'The longitudinal approach', *Trends in Education*, 2 (1972) 8–13.

Davies, B., *Life in the Classroom and Playground: The Accounts of Primary School Children* (Routledge & Kegan Paul, London, 1982).

Davies, L., *Pupil Power: Deviance and Gender in School* (Falmer Press, Lewes, 1984).

Delamont, S., *Interaction in the Classroom* (Methuen, London, 1976).

Denzin, N.K., *The Research Act in Sociology: A Theoretical Introduction to Sociological Methods* (The Butterworth Group, London, 1970).

Department of Education and Science, *A Study of School Buildings* (HMSO, London, 1977).

Department of Education and Science, *Primary Education in England* (HMSO, London, 1978).

Diener, E. and Crandall, R., *Ethics in Social and Behavioral Research* (University of Chicago Press, Chicago, 1978).

Diesing, P., *Patterns of Discovery in the Social Sciences* (Aldine, Chicago, 1971).

Dietz, S.M., 'An analysis of programming DRL schedules in educational settings', *Behaviour Research and Therapy*, 15 (1977) 103–11.

Dixon, K., *Sociological Theory: Pretence and Possibility* (Routledge & Kegan Paul, London, 1973).

Dobbert, M.L., *Ethnographic Research: Theory and Application For Modern Schools and Societies* (Praeger, New York, 1982).

Dollard, J., *Criteria for the Life History* (Yale University Press, New Haven, Conn., 1949).

Douglas, J.D., *Investigative Social Research* (Sage, Beverly Hills, 1976).

Douglas, J.D., *Understanding Everyday Life* (Routledge & Kegan Paul, London, 1973).

Douglas, J.W.B., 'The use and abuse of national cohorts', in M.D. Shipman, *The Organization and Impact of Social Research* (Routledge & Kegan Paul, London, 1976).

Duck, S. (ed.), *Theory and Practice in Interpersonal Attraction* (Academic Press, London, 1977).

Duncan Mitchell, G., *A Dictionary of Sociology* (Routledge & Kegan Paul, London, 1968).

Dunn, S. and Morgan, V., 'Nursery and infant school play patterns: sex-related differences', *British Educational Research Journal*, 13, 3 (1987) 271–81.

Eames, K., 'Growing your own: supporting the development of action researchers within an action-research approach to whole-school development', *British Journ. In-Service Education*, 16, 2 (1990) 122–7.

Edwards, D. and Mercer, N.M., 'Reconstructing context: the conventionalization of classroom knowledge', *Discourse Processes*, 12 (1989) 91–104.

Edwards, A.D. and Westgate, D.P.G., *Investigating Classroom Talk* (Falmer Press, Lewes, 1987).

Edwards, D. and Mercer, N.M., *Common Knowledge: The Development of Understanding in the Classroom* (Routledge & Kegan Paul, London, 1987).

Edwards, D., 'Discourse and the development of understanding in the classroom', in O. Boyd-Barrett and E. Scanlon (eds), *Computers and Learning*, (Addison-Wesley, Wokingham, 1991, 186–204).

Edwards, D. and Potter, J., 'Language and causation: a discursive action model of description and attribution', *Psychological Review*, 100, 1 (1993) 23–41.

Edwards, D., 'Concepts, memory and the organisation of pedagogic discourse: a case study', *International Journal of Educational Research*, 19, 3 (1993) 205–25.

Ekehammar, B. and Magnusson, D., 'A method to study stressful situations', *Journal of Personality and Social Psychology*, 27, 2 (1973) 176–9.

Elliott, J., 'Teachers as researchers', in J. Dunkin (ed.), *The International Encyclopedia of Teaching and Teacher Training* (Pergamon, Sydney, 1987, 162–4).

English, H.B. and English, A.C., *A Comprehensive Dictionary of Psychological and Psychoanalytic Terms* (Longman, London, 1958).

Entwistle, N.J. and Ramsden, P., *Understanding Student Learning* (Croom Helm, Beckenham, 1983).

Epting, F.R., Suchman, D.I. and Nickeson, K.J. 'An evaluation of elicitation procedures for personal constructs', *Brit. J. Psychol.*, 62 (1971) 513–17.

Epting, F.R., 'Journeying into the personal constructs of children', *International Journal of Personal Construct Psychology*, 1, 1 (1988) 53–61.

Erikson, K.T., 'A comment on disguised observation in sociology', *Social Problems*, 14 (1967) 366–73.

Ethical Guidelines for the Institutional Review Committee for Research with Human Subjects (Social Sciences and Humanities Research Council of Canada, 1981).

Evans, K.M., *Planning Small Scale Research* (NFER, Windsor, 1978).

Evans, L., 'Robbing Peter to pay Paul: teaching subtraction through role play', *Education 3–13*, March (1992) 48–53.

Everitt, B.S., *Cluster Analysis* (Heinemann Educational Books, London, 1974).

Everitt, B.S., *The Analysis of Contingency Tables* (Chapman & Hall, London, 1977).

Evetts, J., *Women in Primary Teaching* (Unwin Hyman, London, 1990).

Evetts, J., 'The experience of secondary headship selection: continuity and change', *Educational Studies*, 17, 3 (1991) 285–94.

Feixas, G., Marti, J. and Villegas, M., 'Personal construct assessment of sports teams', *International Journal of Personal Construct Psychology*, 2, 1 (1989) 49–54.

Festinger, L. and Katz, D., *Research Methods in the Behavioral Sciences* (Holt, Rinehart, & Winston, New York, 1966).

Fiedler, J., *Field Research: A Manual for Logistics and Management of Scientific Studies in Natural Settings* (Jossey-Bass, London, 1978).

Filstead, W.J. (ed.), *Qualitative Methodology: Firsthand Involvement with the Social World* (Markham, Chicago, 1970).

Finch, J., 'Social policy and education: problems and possibilities of using qualitative research', in R.G. Burgess (ed.), *Issues in Educational Research* (Falmer Press, Lewes, 1985).

Finch, J., *Research and Policy: The Uses of Qualitative Methods in Social and Educational Research* (Falmer Press, Lewes, 1986).

Fine, G.A. and Sandstrom, K.L., *Knowing Children: Participant Observation with Minors* (Sage, Calif., 1988).

Fisher, B., Russell, T. and McSweeney, P., 'Using personal constructs for course evaluation', *Journal of Further and Higher Education*, 15, 1 (1991) 44–57.

Fitz-Gibbon, C.T., 'Meta-analysis and educational research', *British Educational Research Journal*, 11, 1 (1985) 45–9.

Flanders, N., *Analyzing Teaching Behavior* (Addison-Wesley, Reading, Mass., 1970).

Floud, R., *An Introduction to Quantitative Methods for Historians*, 2nd edn, (Methuen, London, 1979).

Fogelman, K. (ed.), *Growing Up in Great Britain: Papers from the National Child Development Study* (Macmillan, London, 1983).

Ford, D.H. and Urban, H.B., *Systems of Psychotherapy: A Comparative Study* (John Wiley & Sons, New York, 1963).

Forgas, J.P., 'The perception of social episodes: categoric and dimensional representations in two different social milieu', *Journal of Personality and Social Psychology*, 34, 2 (1976) 199–209.

Forgas, J.P., 'Social episodes and social structure in an academic setting: the social environment of an integrated group', *Journal of Experimental Social Psychology*, 14 (1978) 434–48.

Forgas, J.P., *Social Episodes: The Study of Interaction Routines* (Academic Press, London, 1981).

Forward, J., Canter, R. and Kirsch, N., 'Role-enactment and deception methodologies', *American Psychologist*, 35 (1976) 595–604.

Fox, D.J., *The Research Process in Education* (Holt, Rinehart & Winston, New York, 1969).

Francis, H., 'Patterns of reading development in the first school', *British Journal of Educational Psychology*, 62 (1992) 225–32.

Frankfort-Nachmias, C. and Nachmias, D., *Research Methods in the Social Sciences* (Edward Arnold, London, 1992).

Fransella, F., *Need to Change?* (Methuen, London, 1975).

Fransella, F. and Bannister, D., *A Manual for Repertory Grid Technique* (Academic Press, London, 1977).

Fransella, F. (ed.), *Personal Construct Psychology* (Academic Press, London, 1978).

Foster, J.R., 'Eliciting personal constructs and articulating goals', *Journal of Career Development*, 18, 3 (1992) 175–85.

Foster, P., 'Change and adjustment in a further education college', in R.G. Burgess (ed.), *The Ethics of Educational Research* (Falmer Press, Lewes, 1989).

Gage, N.L. (ed.), *Handbook of Research on Teaching* (Rand McNally, Chicago, 1963).

Gardiner, P., *The Nature of Historical Explanation* (Oxford University Press, Oxford, first published 1961, reprinted 1978).

Garfinkel, H., *Studies in Ethnomethodology* (Prentice-Hall, Englewood Cliffs, New Jersey, 1968).

Gelwick, R., *The Way to Discovery: an Introduction to the Thought of Michael Polanyi* (Oxford University Press, New York, 1977).

Gersch, I., 'Behaviour modification and systems analysis in a secondary school: combining two approaches', *Behavioural Approaches With Children*, 8 (1984) 83–91.

Giddens, A. (ed.), *Positivism and Sociology* (Heinemann Educational Books, London, 1975).

Giddens, A., *New Rules of Sociological Method: A Positive Critique of Interpretive Sociologies* (Hutchinson, London, 1976).

Gilbert, G.N., 'Accounts and those accounts called actions', in G.N. Gilbert and P. Abell, *Accounts and Action* (Gower, Aldershot, 1983).

Ginsburg, G.P., 'Role playing and role performance in social psychological research', in M. Brenner, P. Marsh and M. Brenner (eds), *The Social Context of Method* (Croom Helm, Beckenham, 1978).

Glass, G.V., Cahen, L.S., Smith, M.L. and Filby, N.N., *School Class Size: Research and Policy* (Sage, Beverly Hills and London, 1982).

Glass, G.V., McGaw, B. and Smith, M.L., *Meta-analysis in Social Research* (Sage, London, 1981).

Glass, G.V. and Smith, M.L., 'Meta-analysis of research on the relationship of class-size and achievement' (Far West Laboratory, San Francisco, 1978).

Goffman, E., *The Presentation of Self in Everyday Life* (Penguin, London, 1969).

Good, C.V., *Introduction to Educational Research* (Appleton-Century-Crofts, New York, 1963).

Goodson, I., 'The use of life histories in the study of teaching', in M. Hammersley (ed.), *The Ethnography of Schooling* (Nafferton Books, Driffield, 1983).

Goodson, I. and Walker, R., 'Putting life into educational research', in R.R. Sherman and R.B. Webb (eds), *Qualitative Research in Education: Focus and Methods* (Falmer Press, Lewes, 1988).

Goodson, I., *The Making of Curriculum* (Falmer Press, Lewes, 1988).

Gottschalk, L., *Understanding History* (Alfred A. Knopf, New York, 1951).

Gray, J. and Satterly, D., 'A chapter of errors: teaching styles and pupil progress in retrospect', *Educational Research*, 19 (1976) 45–56.

Guildford, J.P. and Fruchter, B., *Fundamental Statistics in Psychology and Education* (McGraw-Hill, New York, 1973).

Hall, K., 'A case study of reading difficulty', *Education 3–13*, October (1992) 47–52.

Halpin, D., Croll, P. and Redman, K., 'Teachers' perceptions of the effects of inservice education', *British Educational Research Journal*, 16, 2 (1990) 163–77.

Halsey, A.H. (ed.), *Educational Priority: Volume 1: E.P.A. Problems and Policies* (HMSO, London, 1972).

Hamilton, D., 'Generalisation in the educational sciences: problems and purposes', in T.S. Popkewitz and R.S. Tabachnick (eds), *The Study of Schooling* (Praeger, New York, 1981).

Hamilton, V.L., 'Role play and deception: a re-examination of the controversy', *Journal for the Theory of Social Behaviour*, 6 (1976) 233–50.

Hammersley, M., 'From ethnograph to theory: a programme and a paradigm in the sociology of education', *Sociology*, 19 (1985) 244–59.

Hammersley, M., 'Some notes on the terms "validity" and "reliability"', *British Educational Research Journal*, 13, 1 (1987) 73–81.

Hammersley, M., 'Ethnograph and the cumulative development of theory', *British Educational Research Journal*, 13, 3 (1987) 283–96.

Hammersley, M. and Scarth, J., *The Impact of Examinations on Secondary School Teaching: A Research Report* (School of Education, The Open University, 1986).

Hammersley, M. and Atkinson, P., *Ethnography: Principles and Practice* (Routledge, London, first published 1983, reprinted 1991).

Hampden-Turner, C., *Radical Man* (Schenkman, Cambridge, Mass., 1970).

Haney, C., Banks, C. and Zimbardo, P., 'Interpersonal dynamics in a simulated prison', *International Journal of Criminology and Penology*, 1 (1973) 69–97.

Hannan, A. and Newby, M., 'Student teacher and headteacher views on current provision and proposals for the future of Initial Teacher Education for primary schools', Rolle Faculty of Education, University of Plymouth, July 1992, (mimeo.).

Hargie, O., Saunders, C. and Dickson, D., *Social Skills in Interpersonal Communication* (Croom Helm, Beckenham, 1981).

Hargreaves, D.H., *Social Relations in a Secondary School* (Routledge & Kegan Paul, London, 1967).

Hargreaves, D.H., Hester, S.K. and Mellor, F.J., *Deviance in Classrooms* (Routledge & Kegan Paul, London, 1975).

Harré, R., 'The ethnogenic approach: theory and practice', in L. Berkowitz (ed.), *Advances in Experimental Social Psychology*, vol. 10 (Academic Press, New York, 1971).

Harré, R., 'Some remarks on "rule" as a scientific concept', in T. Mischel (ed.), *On Understanding Persons* (Basil Blackwell, Oxford, 1974).

Harré, R., 'The constructive role of models', in L. Collins (ed.), *The Use of Models in the Social Sciences* (Tavistock Publications, London, 1976).

Harré, R., 'Friendship as an accomplishment', in S. Duck (ed.), *Theory and Practice in Interpersonal Attraction* (Academic Press, London, 1977).

Harré, R., 'Accounts, actions and meanings – the practice of participatory psychology', in M. Brenner, P. Marsh and M. Brenner (eds), *The Social Context of Method* (Croom Helm, Beckenham, 1978).

Harré, R. and Rosser, E., 'The rules of disorder', *The Times Educational Supplement*, 25 July 1975.

Harré, R. and Secord, P.F., *The Explanation of Social Behaviour* (Basil Blackwell, Oxford, 1972).

Harris, N., Pearce, P. and Johnstone, S., *The Legal Context of Teaching* (Longman, London, 1992).

Heath, S.B., 'Questioning at home and at school: a comparative study', in

G. Spindler (ed.), *Doing the Ethnography of Schooling* (Holt, Rinehart & Winston, New York, 1982).

Heather, N., *Radical Perspectives in Psychology* (Methuen, London, 1976).

Hedges, A., 'Group interviewing', in R. Walker (ed.), *Applied Qualitative Research* (Gower, Aldershot, 1985).

Hibbett, A., Fogelman, K. and Manor, O., 'Occupational outcomes of truancy', *British Journal of Educational Psychology*, 60 (1990) 23–36.

Hill, J.E. and Kerber, A., *Models, Methods, and Analytical Procedures in Educational Research* (Wayne State University Press, Detroit, 1967).

Hinkle, D.N., 'The change of personal constructs from the viewpoint of a theory of implications', unpublished PhD thesis, Ohio State University, 1965.

Hitchcock, G. and Hughes, D., *Research and the Teacher: A Qualitative Introduction to School-based Research* (Routledge, London, 1989).

Hockett, H.C., *The Critical Method in Historical Research and Writing* (Macmillan, London, 1955).

Hodgkinson, H.L., 'Action research – a critique', *J. Educ. Sociol.*, 31, 4 (1957) 137–53.

Hoinville, G. and Jowell, R., *Survey Research Practice* (Heinemann Educational Books, London, 1978).

Holbrook, D., *Education, Nihilism and Survival* (Darton, Longman & Todd, London, 1977).

Holland, J.L., *Making Vocational Choices: A Theory of Vocational Personalities and Work Environments* (Prentice-Hall, Englewood Cliffs, NJ, 1985).

Holly, P. and Whitehead, D., *Action Research in Schools: Getting it into Perspective* (Classroom Action Research Network, Bulletin Vol. 5., Cambridge Institute of Education, Cambridge, 1984).

Holly, P. and Whitehead, D., *Collaborative Action Research* (Classroom Action Research Network, Bulletin Vol. 7, Cambridge Institute of Education, Cambridge, 1986).

Holmes, P. and Karp, M., *Psychodrama – Inspiration and Technique* (Routledge, London, 1991).

Holsti, O.R., 'Content analysis', in G. Lindzey and E. Aronson, *The Handbook of Social Psychology*, vol. 2, *Research Methods* (Addison-Wesley, Reading, Mass., 1968).

Hopkins, D., *A Teacher's Guide to Classroom Research* (Open University Press, Milton Keynes, first published 1985, reprinted 1990).

Houghton, D., 'Mr Chong: a case study of a dependent learner of English for academic purposes', *System*, 19, 1/2 (1991) 75–90.

House, E.R., 'Technology versus craft: a ten-year perspective on innovation', *Journ. Curr. Studies*, 11, 1 (1979) 1–15.

Hughes, J.A., *Sociological Analysis: Methods of Discovery* (Nelson & Sons, Sunbury-on-Thames, 1978).

Hughes, M.G. (ed.), *Administering Education: International Challenge* (Athlone Press, London, 1975).

Hustler, D., Cassidy, A. and Cuff, E.C. (eds), *Action Research in Classrooms and Schools* (Allen & Unwin, London, 1986).

Hutchinson, B. and Whitehouse, P., 'Action research, professional competence and school organization', *British Educational Research Journal*, 12, 1 (1986) 85–94.

Hull, C., 'Between the lines: the analysis of interview data as an exact art', *British Educational Research Journal*, 11, 1 (1985) 27–31.

Hycner, R.H., 'Some guidelines for the phenomenological analysis of interview data', *Human Studies*, 8 (1985) 279–303.

Ions, E., *Against Behaviouralism: a Critique of Behavioural Science* (Basil Blackwell, Oxford, 1977).

Jackson, D. and Marsden, D., *Education and the Working Class* (Routledge & Kegan Paul, 1962).

Johnson, D. and Ransom, E., *Family and School* (Croom Helm, Beckenham, 1983).

Kaplan, A., *The Conduct of Inquiry* (Intertext Books, Aylesbury, 1973).

Kazdin, A.E., *Single Case Research Design* (Oxford University Press, New York, 1982).

Kelly, A. and Smail, B., 'Sex stereotypes and attitudes to science among eleven year old children.' *British Journal of Educational Psychology*, 56 (1986) 158–68.

Kelly, A., 'The development of children's attitudes to science: a longitudinal study', *European Journal of Science Education*, 8 (1986) 399–412.

Kelly, A. (ed.), *Science for Girls?* (Open University Press, Milton Keynes, 1987).

Kelly, A., *Getting the GIST: A Quantitative Study of the Effects of the Girls Into Science and Technology Project* (Manchester Sociology Occasional Papers, No. 22, 1989).

Kelly, A., 'Education or indoctrination? The ethics of school-based action research', in R.G. Burgess (ed.), *The Ethics of Educational Research* (Falmer Press, Lewes, 1989, 100–13).

Kelly, G.A., *The Psychology of Personal Constructs* (Norton, New York, 1955).

Kelly, G.A., *Clinical Psychology and Personality: the Selected Papers of George Kelly*, edited by B.A. Maher (John Wiley and Sons, New York, 1969).

Kelman, H.C., 'Human use of human subjects', *Psychological Bulletin*, 67, 1 (1967) 1–11.

Kemmis, S. and McTaggart, R., *The Action Research Planner* (Deakins University Press, Victoria, 1981).

Kerlinger, F.N., *Foundations of Behavioral Research* (Holt, Rinehart & Winston, New York, 1969).

Kierkegaard, S., *Conducting Unscientific Postscript* (Princeton University Press, Princeton, 1974).

Kimmel, A.J., *Ethics and Values in Applied Social Research* (Sage, Newbury Park, Calif., 1988).

King, R., *All Things Bright and Beautiful?* (John Wiley, Chichester, 1979).

Kitwood, T.M., 'Values in adolescent life: towards a critical description', unpublished PhD dissertation, School of Research in Education, University of Bradford, 1977.

Kremer-Hayon, L., 'Personal constructs of elementary school principals in relation to teachers', *Research in Education*, 43 (1991) 15–21.

Kuhn, T.S., *The Structure of Scientific Revolutions* (University of Chicago Press, Chicago, 1962).

Kumar, D.D., 'A meta-analysis of the relationship between science instruction and student engagement', *Educational Review*, 43, 1 (1991) 49–56.

Lansing, J.B., Ginsberg, G.P. and Braaten, K., *An Investigation of Response Error* (Bureau of Economic and Business Research, University of Illinois, 1961).

Lehrer, R., and Franke, M.L., 'Applying personal construct psychology to the study of teachers' knowledge of fractions', *Journal for Research in Mathematical Education*, 23, 3 (1992) 223–41.

Levine, M., *Canonical Analysis and Factor Comparisons* (Sage, Beverly Hills, 1984).

Levine, R.A., 'Towards a psychology of populations: the cross-cultural study of personality', *Human Development*, 3 (1966) 30–46.

Levine, R.H., 'Why the ethnogenic method and the dramaturgical perspective are incompatible', *Journal of the Theory of Social Behaviour*, 7, 2 (1977) 237–47.

Lewis, A., 'Group child interviews as a research tool', *British Educational Research Journal*, 18, 4 (1992) 413–21.

Lifshitz, M., 'Quality professionals: does training make a difference? A personal construct theory study of the issue', *Brit. J. Soc. Clin. Psychol.*, 13 (1974) 183–9.

Lin, N., *Foundations of Social Research* (McGraw-Hill, New York, 1976).

Lindzey, G. and Aronson, E., *The Handbook of Social Psychology*, vol. 2, *Research Methods* (Addison-Wesley, New York, 1968).

Lofland J., *Analysing Social Settings* (Wadsworth, Belmont, Calif., 1971).

McAleese, R. (ed.), *Perspectives on Academic Gaming and Simulation 3: Training and Professional Education* (Kogan Page, London, 1978).

McAleese, R. and Hamilton, D., *Understanding Classroom Life* (NFER, Windsor, 1978).

McClelland, D.C., Atkinson, J.W., Clark, R.A. and Lowell, E.L., *The Achievement Motive* (Appleton-Century-Crofts, New York, 1953).

McCormick, J. and Solman, R., 'Teachers' attributions of responsibility for occupational stress and satisfaction: an organisational perspective', *Educational Studies*, 18, 2 (1992) 201–22.

McCormick, R. and James, M., *Curriculum Evaluation in Schools* (Croom Helm, Beckenham, 1983).

McIntyre, D. and MacLeod, G., 'The characteristics and uses of systematic observation', in R. McAleese and D. Hamilton (eds), *Understanding Classroom Life* (NFER, Windsor, 1978) 102–31.

McLaughlin, J.F., Owen, S.L., Fors, S.W. and Levinson, R.M., 'The schoolchild as health educator: diffusion of hypertension information from sixth-grade children to their parents', *Qual. Studies in Education*, 5, 2 (1992) 147–65.

McNamara, E., 'The effectiveness of incentive and sanction systems used in secondary schools: a behavioural analysis', *Durham and Newcastle Research Review*, 10 (1986) 285–90.

MacPherson, J., *The Feral Classroom* (Routledge & Kegan Paul, Melbourne, 1983).

McQuitty, L.L., 'Elementary linkage analysis for isolating orthogonal and oblique types and typal relevancies', *Educational and Psychological Measurement*, 17 (1957) 207–9.

Madge, J., *The Origin of Scientific Sociology* (Tavistock Publications, London, 1963).

Madge, J., *The Tools of Social Science* (Longman, London, 1965).

Magnusson, D., 'An analysis of situational dimensions', *Perceptual and Motor Skills*, 32 (1971) 851–67.

Marris, P. and Rein, M., *Dilemmas of Social Reform: Poverty and Community Action in the United States* (Routledge & Kegan Paul, London, 1967).

Marsh, P., Rosser, E. and Harré, R., *The Rules of Disorder* (Routledge & Kegan Paul, London, 1978).

Maslow, A.H., *Motivation and Personality* (Harper & Row, New York, 1954).

Mason, M., Mason, B. and Quayle, T., 'Illuminating English: how explicit language teaching improved public examination results in a comprehensive school', *Educational Studies*, 18, 3 (1992) 341–54.

Mead, G.H., *Mind, Self and Society*, (ed.), Charles Morris (University of Chicago Press, Chicago, 1934).

Medawar, P.B., *The Hope of Progress* (Methuen, London, 1972).

Medawar, P.B., *Advice to a Young Scientist* (Pan Books, London, 1981).

Medawar, P.B., in D. Pike (ed.), *The Threat and the Glory: Reflections on Science and Scientists*, (ed.), (Oxford University Press, Oxford, 1991).

Megarry, J. (ed.), *Aspects of Simulation and Gaming* (Kogan Page, London, 1977).

Megarry, J., 'Retrospect and prospect', in R. McAleese (ed.), *Perspectives on Academic Gaming and Simulation 3: Training and Professional Education* (Kogan Page, London 1978).

Menzel, H., 'Meaning – who needs it?' in M. Brenner, P. Marsh and M. Brenner (eds), *The Social Context of Method* (Croom Helm, Beckenham, 1978).

Merrett, F., Wilkins, J., Houghton, S. and Wheldall, K., 'Rules, sanctions and rewards in secondary schools', *Educational Studies*, 14, 2 (1988) 139–49.

Merton, R.K. and Kendall, P.L., 'The focused interview', *American Journal of Sociology*, 51 (1946) 541–57.

Mevarech, Z., Shir, N. and Movshovitz-Hadar, N., 'Is more always better? The separate and combined effects of computer and video programme on mathematics learning', *British Journ. Educational Psychology* 62 (1992) 106–16.

Miles, M.B. and Huberman, A.M., *Qualitative Data Analysis* (Sage, Beverly Hills, 1984).

Milgram, S., 'Behavioral study of obedience', *Journal of Abnormal and Social Psychology*, 67 (1963) 371–78.

Milgram, S., *Obedience to Authority* (Harper and Row, New York, 1974).

Mischel, T. (ed.), *On Understanding Persons* (Basil Blackwell, Oxford, 1974).

Mishler, E.G., 'Validation in inquiry-guided research: the role of exemplars in narrative studies', *Harvard Educational Review*, 60, 4 (1990) 415–42.

Mitchell, S. and Wild, P., 'A task analysis of a computerised system to support administration in schools', *Educat. Mangt. and Administration*, 21, 1 (1993) 53–61.

Mixon, D., 'Instead of deception', *Journal for the Theory of Social Behaviour*, 2 (1972) 147–77.

Mixon, D., 'If you won't deceive, what can you do?', in N. Armistead (ed.), *Reconstructing Social Psychology* (Penguin Books, London, 1974).

Mortimore, P., Sammons, P., Stoll, L., Lewis, D. and Ecob, R., *School Matters: The Junior Years* (Open Books, London, 1988).

Moser, C.A. and Kalton, G., *Survey Methods in Social Investigation* (Heinemann Educational Books, London, 1977).

Mouly, G.J., *Educational Research: the Art and Science of Investigation* (Allyn and Bacon, Boston, 1978).

Munn, P., Johnstone, M. and Holligan, C., 'Pupils' perceptions of effective disciplinarians', *British Educational Research Journal*, 16, 2 (1990) 191–98.

Murphy, J., John, M. and Brown, H. (eds), *Dialogues and Debates in Social Psychology* (Lawrence Erlbaum Associates in association with the Open University Press, first published 1984, reprinted 1992).

National Educational Association of the United States: Association for Supervision and Curriculum Development, *Learning about Learning from Action Research* (Washington, DC, 1959).

Naylor, P., 'Pupils' perceptions of teacher racism', unpublished PhD dissertation, Loughborough University of Technology, 1995.

Neimeyer, G.J., 'Personal constructs in career counselling and development', *Journal of Career Development*, 18, 3 (1992) 163–73.

Nesfield-Cookson, B., *William Blake: Prophet of Universal Brotherhood* (Crucible, 1987).

Newson, J. and Newson, E., 'Parental roles and social contexts', in M.D. Shipman (ed.), *The Organisation and Impact of Social Research* (Routledge & Kegan Paul, London, 1976) 22–48.

Nias, J. and Groundwater-Smith, S., *The Enquiring Teacher: Supporting and Sustaining Teacher Research* (Falmer Press, Lewes, 1988).

Nias, J., *Primary Teachers Talking* (Routledge, London, 1989).

Nixon, J. (ed.), *A Teacher's Guide to Action Research* (Grant McIntyre, London, 1981).

Okakura, K., *The Book of Tea* (Kodansha International, Tokyo, 1991).

Osborne, J.I., 'College of Education students' perceptions of the teaching situation', unpublished M.Ed. dissertation, University of Liverpool, 1977.

O'Neill, B. and McMahon, H., *Opening New Windows with Bubble Dialogue* Language Development and Hypermedia Research Group, Faculty of Education, University of Ulster at Coleraine, 1990,

Palmer, M., 'An experimental study of the use of archive materials in the secondary school history curriculum', unpublished PhD dissertation, University of Leicester, 1976.

Palys, T.S., 'Simulation methods and social psychology', *Journal for the Theory of Social Behaviour*, 8 (1978) 341–68.

Parker, H.J., *View from the Boys* (David & Charles, Newton Abbott, 1974).

Parsons, J.M., Graham, N. and Honess, T., 'A teacher's implicit model of how children learn', *British Educational Research Journal*, 9, 1 (1983) 91–101.

Patrick, J., *A Glasgow Gang Observed* (Eyre Methuen, London, 1973).

Peevers, B.H. and Secord, P.F., 'Developmental changes in attribution of descriptive concepts of persons', *Journal of Personality and Social Psychology*, 27, 1 (1973) 120–8.

Percival, F., 'Evaluation procedures for simulation gaming exercises', in R. McAleese (ed.), *Perspectives on Academic Gaming and Simulation 3: Training and Professional Education* (Kogan Page, London, 1978).

Pierce, C.M.B. and Molloy, G.N., 'Psychological and biographical differences between secondary school teachers experiencing high and low levels of burnout', *British Journal of Educational Psychology*, 60 (1990) 37–51.

Pilliner, A., *Experiment in Educational Research*, (E341, Block 5) (The Open University Press, Bletchley, 1973).

Platt, J., 'Evidence and proof in documental research. 1. Some specific problems of documentary research; and 2. Some shared problems of documentary research', *Sociol. Review*, 29, 1 (1981) 31–52, 53–66.

Plewis, I., 'Pupils' progress in reading and maths during primary school: associations with ethnic group and sex', *Educational Research*, 33 (1991) 133–40.

Plummer, K., *Documents of Life: An Introduction to the Problems and Literature of a Humanistic Method* (George Allen & Unwin, London, 1983).

Pope, M.L. and Keen, T.R., *Personal Construct Psychology and Education* (Academic Press, London, 1981).

Potter, J. and Wetherell, M., *Discourse and Social Psychology* (Sage, London and Beverly Hills, 1987).

Powney, J. and Watts, M., *Interviewing in Educational Research*, (Routledge & Kegan Paul, London, 1987).

Prais, S.J., 'Formal and informal teaching: a further reconsideration of Professor Bennett's statistics', *Journal of the Royal Statistical Society*, 146, 2 (1983) 163–9.

Quicke, J.C., 'Personal and Social Education: a triangulated evaluation of an innovation?' *Educational Review*, 38, 3 (1986) 217–28.

Raffe, D., Bundell, I. and Bibby, J., 'Ethics and tactics: issues arising from an educational survey', in R.G. Burgess (ed.), *The Ethics of Educational Research* (Falmer Press, Lewes, 1989).

Ravenette, A.T., 'Psychological investigation of children and young people', in

D. Bannister (ed.), *New Perspectives in Personal Construct Theory* (Academic Press, London, 1977).

Reid, S., *Working with Statistics: An Introduction to Quantitative Methods for Social Scientists* (Polity Press, Cambridge, 1987).

Review Article, 'Why can't children do proportion sums?' *Education*, 18 May (1984) 403.

Rex, J. (ed.), *Approaches to Sociology: an Introduction to Major Trends in British Sociology* (Routledge & Kegan Paul, London, 1974).

Reynolds, P.D., *Ethical Dilemmas and Social Science Research* (Jossey-Bass, San Francisco, 1979).

Riley, M.W., *Sociological Research 1: A Case Approach* (Harcourt, Brace & World, New York, 1963).

Riseborough, G.F., 'The cream team: an ethnography of BTEC National Diploma (Catering and Hotel Management) students in a tertiary college', *Brit. Journ. Sociol. Educat.*, 13, 2 (1992) 215–45.

Robson, J. and Collier, K., 'Designing "Sugar 'n' Spice" – An anti-sexist simulation', *Simulation/Games for Learning*, 21, 3 (1991) 213–19.

Rogers, C.R., *Counselling and Psychotherapy* (Houghton Mifflin, Boston, 1942).

Rogers, C.R., 'The non-directive method as a technique for social research', *American Journal of Sociology*, 50 (1945) 279–83.

Rogers, C.R., *Freedom to Learn* (Merrill, Columbus, Ohio, 1969).

Rogers, C.R. and Stevens, B., *Person to Person: The Problems of Being Human* (Souvenir Press, London, 1967).

Rogers, V.M. and Atwood, R.K., 'Can we put ourselves in their place?' *Yearbook of the National Council for Social Studies*, 44 (1974) 80–111.

Rosen, C. and Rosen, H., *The Language of Primary School Children* (Penguin, London, 1973).

Roszak, T., *The Making of a Counter Culture* (Faber & Faber, London, 1970).

Roszak, T., *Where the Wasteland Ends* (Faber & Faber, London, 1972).

Salmon, P., 'Differential conforming of the developmental process', *Brit. J. Soc. Clin. Psychol.*, 8 (1969) 22–31.

Schonbach, P., *Account Episodes: The Management or Escalation of Conflict* (Cambridge University Press, Cambridge, 1990).

Schutz, A., *Collected Papers* (Nijhoff, The Hague, 1962).

Sears, R., Maccoby, E. and Levin, H., *Patterns of Child Rearing* (Harper & Row, New York, 1957).

Secord, P.F. and Peevers, B.H., 'The development and attribution of person concepts', in T. Mischel (ed.), *On Understanding Persons* (Basil Blackwell, Oxford, 1974).

Semin, G.R., and Manstead, A.S.R., *The Accountability of Conduct: A Social Psychological Analysis* (Academic Press, London, 1983).

Selltiz, C., Wrightsman, L.S. and Cook, S.W., *Research Methods in Social Relations* (Holt, Rinehart & Winston, New York, 1976).

Serafini, A., *Ethics and Social Concern* (Paragon House, New York, 1989).

Shapiro, B.L., 'A collaborative approach to help novice science teachers reflect on changes in their construction of the role of the science teacher', *Alberta Journal of Educational Research*, 36, 3 (1990) 203–22.

Sharp, R. and Green, A. (assisted by Lewis, J.), *Education and Social Control: A Study in Progressive Primary Education* (Routledge & Kegan Paul, London, 1975).

Sharpe, P., 'Behaviour modification in the secondary school: a survey of students' attitudes to rewards and praise', *Behavioural Approach With Children*, 9 (1985) 109–12.

Shaw, E.L., 'The influence of methods instruction on the beliefs of preservice elementary and secondary science teachers: preliminary comparative analyses', *School Science and Mathematics*, 92 (1992) 14–22.

Shaw, M.L.G. (ed.), *Recent Advances in Personal Construct Technology* (Academic Press, London, 1981).

Sikes, P., Measor, L. and Woods, P., *Teacher Careers* (Falmer Press, Lewes, 1985).

Sikes, P. and Troyna, B., 'True stories: a case study in the use of life histories in teacher education', *Educational Review*, 43, 1 (1991) 3–16.

Shipman, M.D., *The Limitations of Social Research* (Longman, London, 1972).

Shipman, M.D., *Inside a Curriculum Project* (Methuen, London, 1974).

Shipman, M.D. (ed.), *The Organization and Impact of Social Research* (Routledge & Kegan Paul, London, 1976).

Simon, J.L., *Basic Research Methods in Social Sciences* (Random House, New York, 1978).

Simons, H. (ed.), *Towards a Science of the Singular* (Centre for Applied Research in Education, University of East Anglia, 1980). C.A.R.E. Occasional Publications No. 10.

Slater, P., *The Measurement of Interpersonal Space. Vol. 2.* (Wiley, Chichester, 1977).

Sluckin, A., *Growing Up in the Playground: The Social Development of Children* (Routledge & Kegan Paul, London, 1981).

Smith, H.W., *Strategies of Social Research: The Methodological Imagination* (Prentice-Hall, London, 1975).

Smith, L.M., *Kensington Revisited* (Falmer Press, Lewes, 1987).

Smith, P.K., 'The reliability and validity of one-zero sampling: misconceived criticisms and unacknowledged assumptions', *British Educational Research Journal*, 11, 2 (1985) 215–20.

Smith, S. and Leach, C., 'A hierarchical measure of cognitive complexity', *Brit. J. Psychol.*, 63, 4 (1972) 561–8.

Soble, A., 'Deception in social science research: Is informed consent possible?' *Hastings Center Report*, 8 (1978) 40–6.

Social and Community Planning Research, *Questionnaire Design Manual No. 5* (16 Duncan Terrace, London N1 8BZ, 1972).

Social Science Research Council, *Research in Economic and Social History* (Heinemann, London 1971).

Solomon, R.L., 'An extension of control group design', *Psychological Bulletin*, 46 (1949) 137–50.

Spencer, J.R. and Flin, R., *The Evidence of Children* (Blackstone, London, 1990).

Spindler, G. (ed.), *Doing the Ethnography of Schooling* (Holt, Rinehart & Winston, New York, 1982).

Stables, A., 'Differences between pupils from mixed and single-sex schools in their enjoyment of school subjects and in their attitude to science in school', *Educational Review* 42, 3 (1990) 221–30.

Stake, R.E., 'The case study method in social inquiry', *Educational Researcher* (February 1978) 5–8.

Strauss, A.M., *Qualitative Analysis for Social Scientists* (Cambridge University Press, Cambridge, 1987).

Stenhouse, L., 'What is action-research', Norwich C.A.R.E., University of East Anglia, Norwich (mimeo.), 1979.

Strike, K.A., 'The ethics of educational evaluation', in J. Millman and L. Darling-Hammond (eds), *A New Handbook of Teacher Evaluation* (Sage, Newbury Park, Calif., 1990).

Sutherland, G., 'The study of the history of education', *History*, vol. LIV, no. 180 (February 1969).

Talbot, M., *The Holographic Universe* (Grafton Books, London, 1991).

Tanner, H., 'Managing perceptions through action research: introducing investigations and problem-solving – a case study', *School Organisation*, 9, 2 (1989) 261–9.

Taylor, J.L. and Walford, R., *Simulation in the Classroom* (Penguin Books, London, 1972).

Thomas, J.B., 'Birmingham University and teacher training: day training college to department of education', *History of Education*, 21, 3 (1992) 307–21.

Thomas, L.F., 'A personal construct approach to learning in education, training and therapy', in F. Fransella (ed.), *Personal Construct Psychology* (Academic Press, London, 1978).

Thomas, L.F. and Harri-Augstein, E.S., *Self Organised Learning* (Routledge, London, 1988).

Thomas, W.I. and Znaniecki, F., *The Polish Peasant in Europe and America* (University of Chicago Press, Chicago, 1918).

Travers, R.M.W., *An Introduction to Educational Research* (Collier-Macmillan, London, 1969).

Travers, R.M.W., extract quoted in A.H. Halsey (ed.), *Educational Priority: Volume 1: E.P.A. Problems and Policies* (HMSO, London, 1972).

Tripp, D.H., 'Case study generalisation: an agenda for action', *British Educational Research Journal*, 11, 1 (1985) 33–43.

Troyna, B. and Hatcher, R., *Racism in Children's Lives: A Study in Mainly-White Primary Schools* (Routledge, London, 1992).

Tuckman, B.W., *Conducting Educational Research* (Harcourt Brace Jovanovich, New York, 1972).

UMRCC, *GAP: Grid Analysis Package* (University of Manchester Regional Computing Centre, Manchester, 1981).

Urmston, J.O. (ed.), *The Concise Encyclopedia of Western Philosophy* (Hutchinson, London 1975).

US Dept of Health, Education and Welfare, Public Health Service and National Institutes of Health, *The Institutional Guide to D.H.E.W. Policy on Protecting Human Subjects*, DHEW Publication (NIH): December 2, 1971, 72–102.

van Dijk, T.A. (ed.), *Handbook of Discourse Analysis Vols 1–4* (Academic Press, London, 1985).

van Ments, M., 'Role-playing: playing a part or a mirror to meaning?', *Sagset Journal*, 8, 3 (1978) 83–92.

van Ments, M., *The Effective Use of Role-Play: a Handbook for Teachers and Trainers* (Croom Helm, Beckenham, 1983).

Vasta, R., *Studying Children: An Introduction to Research Methods* (W.H. Freeman, San Francisco, 1979).

Verma, G.K. and Beard, R.M., *What is Educational Research?* (Gower, Aldershot, 1981).

Walker, R., 'Making sense and losing meaning: Problems of selection in doing Case Study', in H. Simons (ed.), *Towards a Science of the Singular* (Centre for Applied Research in Education, University of East Anglia, 1980).

Walkerdine, V., *The Mastery of Reason: Cognitive Development and the Production of Rationality* (Routledge, London, 1988).

Warnock, M., *Existentialism* (Oxford University Press, London, 1970).

Watts, M. and Ebbutt, D., 'More than the sum of the parts: Research methods in group interviewing', *British Educational Research Journal*, 13, 1 (1987) 25–34.

Weber, M., *The Theory of Social and Economic Organization* (Free Press, Glencoe, 1964).

Wheldall, K, and Panagopoulou-Stamatelatou, A., 'The effects of pupil self-recording of on-task behaviour in primary school children', *British Educational Research Journal*, 17, 2 (1991) 113–27.

Whitley, P., 'The analysis of contingency tables', in D. McKay, N. Schofield and P. Whitley (eds), *Data Analysis and the Social Sciences* (Frances Pinter, London, 1983).

Whyte, J., *Girls into Science and Technology: the Story of a Project* (Routledge & Kegan Paul, London, 1986).

Wilbur, K. (ed.), *The Holographic Paradigm* (Shambhala, Boulder, Col., 1982).

Wild, P., Scivier, J.E. and Richardson, S.J., 'Evaluating information technology-supported local management of schools: the user acceptability audit', *Educat. Mangt. and Administration*, 20, 1 (1992) 40–8.

Willis, P.E., *Learning to Labour* (Saxon House, London, 1977).

Windisch, V., *Speech and Reasoning in Everyday Life* (Cambridge University Press, Cambridge, 1990).

Winkley, D., *Diplomats and Detectives: LEA Advisers and Work* (Robert Royce, London, 1985).

Winter, R., '"Dilemma Analysis": A contribution to methodology for action research', *Cambridge Journal of Education*, 12, 3 (1982) 161–74.

Wolcott, H.F., *The Man in the Principal's Office* (Holt, Rinehart & Winston, New York, 1973).

Woods, P., *The Divided School* (Routledge & Kegan Paul, London 1979).

Woods, P., 'Ethnography at the crossroads', *British Educational Research Journal*, 13, 3 (1987) 297–307.

Woods, P., *Working for Teacher Development* (Peter Francis, Dereham, 1989).

Woods, P. and Hammersley, M., *Gender and Ethnicity in Schools: Ethnographic Accounts* (Routledge, London, 1993).

Yorke, D.M., 'Repertory grids in educational research: Some methodological considerations', *British Educational Research Journal*, 4, 2 (1978) 63–74.

Yorke, D.M., 'Indexes of stability in repertory grids: a small-scale comparison', *British Educational Research Journal*, 11, 3 (1985) 221–5.

Yorke, D.M., 'Construing classrooms and curricula: a framework for research', *British Educational Research Journal*, 13, 1 (1987) 35–50.

Young, J., *The Drugtakers* (Paladin, London, 1971).

Young, M.F.D. (ed.), *Knowledge and Control: New Directions for the Sociology of Education* (Collier-Macmillan, London 1971).

Zechmeister, E.B. and Shaunghnessy, J.J., *A Practical Introduction to Research Methods in Psychology* (McGraw-Hill, New York, 1992).

Zimbardo, P.G., 'On the ethics of intervention in human psychological research with specific reference to the "Stanford Prison Experiment"', in J. Murphy, M. John and H. Brown (eds), *Dialogues and Debates in Social Psychology* (Lawrence Erlbaum Associates in association with the Open University Press, 1992).

INDEX

403